Using Systemic Integration to Interpret War Crimes at the International Criminal Court

International Humanitarian Law Series

VOLUME 74

The International Humanitarian Law Series is a series of monographs and edited volumes which aims to promote scholarly analysis and discussion of both the theory and practice of the international legal regulation of armed conflict.

The series explores substantive issues of International Humanitarian Law, including:

- Protection for victims of armed conflict and regulation of the means and method of warfare
- Questions of application of the various legal regimes for the conduct of armed conflict
- Issues relating to the implementation of International Humanitarian Law obligations
- National and international approaches to the enforcement of the law and
- The interactions between International Humanitarian Law and other related areas of international law such as Human Rights, Refugee Law, Arms Control and Disarmament Law, and International Criminal Law.

The titles published in this series are listed at *brill.com/ihul*

Using Systemic Integration to Interpret War Crimes at the International Criminal Court

From Vienna to Rome to Timbuktu

By

Matias Thomsen

BRILL | NIJHOFF

LEIDEN | BOSTON

Cover illustration: Children playing next to a sign in Timbuktu on January 31st 2013 which reads "The city of Timbuktu is founded on Islam and will only be judged by Islamic legislation (Sharia law)". The image depicts one of several signs promoting Sharia law in Timbuktu following the city's takeover by two rebel groups, Al-Qaeda in the Islamic Maghreb and Ansar Dine. These groups established 'Islamic Tribunals' to enforce their own interpretations of Sharia law, often to the detriment of the civilian population. In analysing Al Hassan's conviction by the International Criminal Court for his role in facilitating the work of the Islamic Tribunals, this book examines the circumstances under which the enforcement of rebel law by non-state courts can amount to the war crime of denying a fair trial. AFP Photo / Fred Dufour.

Library of Congress Cataloging-in-Publication Data

Names: Thomsen, Matias author
Title: Using systemic integration to interpret war crimes at the International Criminal Court : from Vienna to Rome to Timbuktu / by Matias Thomsen.
Description: Leiden ; Boston : Brill Academic Publishers, Inc, 2025. | Series: International humanitarian law series, 1389-6776 ; 74 | Includes bibliographical references and index.
Identifiers: LCCN 2025013539 (print) | LCCN 2025013540 (ebook) | ISBN 9789004690035 hardback | ISBN 9789004690042 pdf
Subjects: LCSH: International Criminal Court | War crimes (International law) | International criminal law | International criminal courts
Classification: LCC KZ7312 .T46 2025 (print) | LCC KZ7312 (ebook) | DDC 341.6/9--dc23/eng/20250331
LC record available at https://lccn.loc.gov/2025013539
LC ebook record available at https://lccn.loc.gov/2025013540

Typeface for the Latin, Greek, and Cyrillic scripts: "Brill". See and download: brill.com/brill-typeface.

ISSN 1389-6776
ISBN 978-90-04-69003-5 (hardback)
ISBN 978-90-04-69004-2 (e-book)
DOI 10.1163/9789004690042

This book is printed on acid-free paper and produced in a sustainable manner.

This book is dedicated to my mum, Erin, who has faced the most profound challenges over these last few years with inspiring courage and compassion; and my dad, Michael, who is always there for our ever-extending family with unwavering kindness and support

Contents

Acknowledgements

This book began as my doctoral thesis that I submitted to the University of Tasmania in July 2022. I express my sincere gratitude to Tim McCormack as my primary supervisor and mentor. I join a chorus of academics and legal professionals who have had the distinct privilege of Tim's guidance, which is matched only by his generous spirit and good sense of humour. I am indebted to Tim for the opportunities I have received in this profession and remain thankful for his ongoing collegiality and friendship. I extend my heartfelt thanks to my two co-supervisors, Anja Hilkemeijer and Matt Killingsworth. Anja has worked tirelessly with me to improve the quality of my research, analysis, and expression, while Matt is credited for always encouraging me to ask the 'so what?' question to ensure that my research achieves practical significance.

I extend a special thank you to the Hawkins family and the Tim Hawkins Memorial Scholarship that was established to commemorate the late Tim Hawkins, a University of Tasmania law graduate who was tragically killed in the 2002 Bali Bombings. The scholarship provides the recipient with the opportunity to work with the Office of the Prosecutor of the International Criminal Court in The Hague. I was humbled to have been awarded the Tim Hawkins Memorial Scholarship in 2016, and the experience of working with the Special Advisor on War Crimes, Professor Tim McCormack, paved the way for this book and the beginnings of my career in international humanitarian law.

This book was professionally copyedited by Jacqueline Fox in accordance with the Australian Standards for Editing Practice: Guidelines for Editing Research Theses.

CHAPTER 1

Introduction

1.1 The Paradox of International Criminal Law and the Quest for a Coherent Methodology

> International criminal law itself is built on a paradox. It reconciles at least three dimensions: the 'universalist' aspirations of public international law, the 'humanist' dimensions of human rights law and the legality and fairness-oriented foundations of criminal law.
>
> CARSTEN STAHN AND LARISSA VAN DEN HERIK[1]

The drafting of the *Rome Statute* of the International Criminal Court (ICC) brought the paradox of international criminal law (ICL) into sharp focus. Reflecting on the diversity of views at the Diplomatic Conference in Rome, Andrew Clapham identified three competing 'tribes' that hoped to influence how the Court's judges would come to interpret the applicable law.[2] The internationalists favoured cohesion within the international legal system. Those from the human rights tradition advocated for progressive, humanitarian interpretations of the law to protect human dignity. The criminal lawyers promoted strict positivism and domestic criminal law expectations of legal certainty. To reconcile these competing perspectives, Clapham suggested adorning '3D glasses' as a means of embracing the different values and dimensions of their respective legal traditions.[3]

---

1 Carsten Stahn and Larissa van den Herik, 'Fragmentation', Diversification and '3D' Legal Pluralism: International Criminal Law as the Jack-in-The-Box?' in van den Herik and Stahn (eds), *The Diversification and Fragmentation of International Criminal Law* (Martinus Nijhoff, 2012) 23.

2 Andrew Clapham, 'Concluding Remarks: Three Tribes Engage on the Future of International Criminal Law' (2011) 9(3) *Journal of International Criminal Justice* 689.

3 Ibid. The term '3D glasses' is used by Carsten Stahn and Larissa van den Herik (n 1) to describe a pluralist vision of international criminal law that incorporates criminal justice, human rights, and general international law. The term is adapted from a quote by William Schabas, who proposed minimising the risks of fragmentation by viewing the relationship between the European Court of Human Rights and international criminal law as one of synergy and opportunity, explaining that 'The international legal landscape increasingly appears in three dimensions, rich in contour, contrast and texture'. William Schabas,

 | DOI:10.1163/9789004690042_002

Associated with these approaches to interpretation are the three main sources of law that together comprise ICL, a legal discipline that has been described as the child of a 'tripartite' marriage between international humanitarian law (IHL), international human rights law (IHRL), and domestic criminal law.[4] Although a common purpose exists between these areas of law to protect human beings, combat impunity, and deter prohibited conduct, they are distinct in their origins, scope, and field of application. IHL seeks to mitigate the sufferings of war by striking a balance between the protection of civilians and military necessity. IHRL focuses on the fundamental rights of individuals *vis-à-vis* their governments. Domestic criminal law is characterised by procedural fairness, principles of individual criminal responsibility, and strict adherence to the prohibition on retroactive punishment (also known as the principle of legality). As a consequence, ICL is a 'paradox field that is torn apart by conflicting philosophies, aspirations, and methodologies'[5] that is suffering from an 'identity crisis'.[6] The complexity of ICL's origins and ambitions naturally complicates the quest for a coherent interpretive methodology.

Indeed, interpreting the *Rome Statute* requires balancing the divergent qualities of ICL generally, and the peculiarities ICC framework more specifically.[7] On the one hand, the *Rome Statute* and *Elements of Crimes* operate like a criminal code. The *Statute* exhaustively lists the crimes and modes of liability within the ICC's subject-matter jurisdiction and codifies the principle of strict construction in article 22(2), which requires giving the words of an offence their ordinary meaning, prohibits extending the definition of crimes by analogy, and dictates that ambiguity must be interpreted in favour of the accused. The *Elements of Crimes*, although not technically binding on judges,[8] provides the physical and mental elements of each offence

---

'Synergy or Fragmentation? International Criminal Law and the European Convention on Human Rights' (2011) 9 *Journal of International Criminal Justice* 609, 632.

4 Leena Grover, *Interpreting Crimes in the Rome Statute of the International Criminal Court* (Cambridge University Press, 2014) 550.

5 Vasiliev Sergey, 'The Making of International Criminal Law' in Catherine Brölmann and Yannick Radi (eds), *Research Handbook on the Theory and Practice of International Lawmaking* (Edward Elgar, 2016) 354, 363.

6 Darryl Robinson, 'The Identity Crisis of International Criminal Law' (2008) 21(4) *Leiden Journal of International Criminal Law* 925.

7 Mary Fan, 'Custom, General Principles and the Great Architect Cassese' (2012) 10(5) *Journal of International Criminal Justice* 1063.

8 *ICC Elements of Crimes*, 2 November 2000 sess, UN Doc PCNICC/2000/1/Add.2 (2 November 2000) ('*ICC Elements of Crimes*').

in plain language that is difficult for judges to disregard.[9] On the other hand, the *Statute* is a multilateral, constitutive treaty whose terms can only be understood by reference to their origins and scope in both treaty and customary law,[10] necessitating recourse to the *Vienna Convention on the Law of Treaties* (*VCLT*).[11] It is apparent that some form of interpretive synthesis is required.

So, how might these 3D glasses operate in practice? The best and most obvious approach is for the ICC to adopt a methodology that combines the rule of strict construction in article 22(2) of the *Statute* with the 'general rule of interpretation' in article 31 of the *VCLT*. Most significantly, article 31 (3)(c) of the *VCLT* requires relevant rules of international law to be taken 'into account', which has been construed as an obligation to interpret the definition of a term consistently with customary international law (CIL) unless there is a clear legislative intent to the contrary. Known as the 'principle of systemic integration', this provision, together with the other rules of the *VCLT* and the principle of strict construction, provides the best means to overcome the paradox of ICL and synthesise its complex origins and paradoxical aspirations within a single cohesive methodology.

At first glance, it might appear that the ICC has already adhered to this logic. In 2014, Trial Chamber II in *Prosecutor v Katanga* stated that, 'The chambers of the Court have unanimously and systematically based their interpretation of the Statute on the principles established by the Vienna Convention', adding that such an approach must 'always be consistent' with the restrictions imposed by the rule of strict construction.[12] The same approach was adopted by Trial Chamber III in *Prosecutor v Bemba* in 2016,[13] and both chambers affirmed the principle of systemic integration as part of this interpretive methodology.[14] While these decisions would appear to reflect a

---

9 David Hunt, 'The International Criminal Court: High Hopes, Creative Ambiguity and an Unfortunate Mistrust in International Judges' (2004) 2(1) *Journal of International Criminal Justice* 56, 59.

10 Fan (n 7) 1063.

11 *Vienna Convention on the Law of Treaties*, opened for signature 23 May 1969, 1155 UNTS 331, article 31(3)(c) (entered into force 27 January 1980) ('*VCLT*').

12 *Prosecutor v Germain Katanga and Mathieu Ngudjolo Chui* (*Judgment*) (International Criminal Court, Trial Chamber II, Case No ICC-01/04-01/07, 7 March 2014) [43], [51] ('*Katanga Trial Judgment*').

13 *Prosecutor v Jean-Pierre Bemba Gombo* (*Judgment*) (International Criminal Court, Trial Chamber III, Case No ICC-01/05-01/08, 21 March 2016) ('*Bemba Trial Judgment*') [75]–[86].

14 *Katanga Trial Judgment* (n 12) [47]; *Bemba Trial Judgment* (n 13) [78]–[79].

coherent approach, broader analysis reveals that they are the exception to the rule.[15] Most ICC decisions do not rely on the *VCLT*. Notably, the Court has shown a reluctance to adhere to the principle of systemic integration, often relying exclusively on the *Elements of Crimes* and making few references to external sources of law to support its interpretive conclusions. In short, there is no systematic cohesion between the *VCLT* and the rule of strict construction in the ICC's jurisprudence, as the former has largely been ignored.[16]

In this book, I argue that the ICC should combine the *VCLT* with the rule of strict construction to interpret the definition of crimes in the *Rome Statute*, focusing specifically on the obligation to interpret war crimes consistently with customary IHL,[17] as stipulated by the principle of systemic integration. There are three normative assumptions behind this argument. First, compliance with the principle of systemic integration will lead to greater consistency in judicial reasoning across ICC Chambers than is currently the case. Second, it will promote the ICC as a model international court whose decisions represent authoritative interpretations of CIL, thereby preventing unnecessary fragmentation between ICL and IHL. Third, interpreting war crimes consistently with CIL will facilitate the legitimate, incremental development of the law in accordance with the evolving practice and legal opinion of states.

While there is already strong academic support for using CIL as an obligatory interpretive aid,[18] there are significant gaps in the literature. To begin with, there is a lack empirical analyses of ICC jurisprudence to determine

15 See Chapter 4 of this thesis for an empirical analysis of the ICC's compliance with the principle of systemic integration.

16 Stewart Manley, Pardis Tehrani, Rajah Rasiah, 'Mapping interpretation by the International Criminal Court' (2023) 36(3) *Leiden Journal of International Law* 771, 780–1 (Stewart et al. analyse ten cases and conclude that 'the application of the VCLT across cases is markedly inconsistent and, in some instances, opaque and arguably unjustifiable', finding that the unsystematic use of the *VCLT* undermines the rule of strict construction).

17 *Rome Statute of the International Criminal Court*, opened for signature 17 July 1998, 2187 UNTS 38544, article 31(3)(c) (entered into force 1 July 2002) ('*Rome Statute of the International Criminal Court*').

18 Grover (n 4); Leila Sadat and Jarrod Jolly, 'Seven Canons of ICC Treaty Interpretation: Making Sense of Article 25's Rorschach Blot' (2014) 27(3) *Leiden Journal of International Law* 755; Robert Cryer, 'Royalism and the King: Article 21 of the Rome Statute and the Politics of Sources' (2009) 12(3) *New Criminal Law Review: An International and Interdisciplinary Journal* 390; Fausto Pocar, 'International Criminal Justice and the Unifying Role of Customary Law' (2016) 21(2–3) *Uniform Law Review* 171.

the extent of its compliance with the principle of systemic integration. Second, there remains debate over the methodology used to identify rules of CIL (particularly in the context of identifying prohibitive humanitarian rules) and there have been few attempts to apply the International Law Commission (ILC) *Draft Conclusions on Identification of Customary International Law* (Draft Conclusions) to the ICC context. Finally, there are no case studies examining what ICC compliance with the principle of systemic integration might look like in practice.

Through empirical research and qualitative case analysis, I show that the ICC has been reluctant to comply with the principle of systemic integration, and offer some reflections on why this might be the case. I provide an original contribution to the debate on how to identify customary rules in the international criminal context, and highlight the positive outcomes of those cases that have sought to ground their interpretations of war crimes within the established framework of international law.

Finally, to illustrate the pitfalls of failing to comply with the principle of systemic integration and to offer a better path forward, I provide a three-part case study on the war crime of denying a fair trial when applied to the courts of non-state armed groups (NSAGs). Focusing on the ICC's interpretation of the Islamic Tribunals established by rebel fighters in the Timbuktu province of Northern Mali, I aim to reveal the potential of a cohesive methodology for interpreting the definition of crimes in the *Rome Statute*. I use the principle of systemic integration in the *VCLT* to trace the origins and scope of the war crime of denying a fair trial, incorporate the interpretive peculiarities of the *Rome Statute*, and adapt this methodology to the administration of justice by NSAGs in Northern Mali: from Vienna to Rome to Timbuktu.

1.2 The Consequences of Failing to Apply Systemic Integration at the ICC

To understand the consequences of the ICC's reluctance to apply the principle of systemic integration on a consistent basis, we must first situate it within the 'general rule of interpretation' in article 31 of the *VCLT*, which reads as follows:

1. A treaty shall be interpreted in good faith in accordance with the ordinary meaning to be given to the terms of the treaty in their context and in the light of its object and purpose.
2. …

3. There shall be taken into account, together with the context:
   (a) any subsequent agreement between the parties regarding the interpretation of the treaty or the application of its provisions;
   (b) any subsequent practice in the application of the treaty which establishes the agreement of the parties regarding its interpretation;
   (c) any relevant rules of international law applicable between the parties.[19]

The reference to 'any relevant rules of international law' in article 31(3)(c) naturally includes CIL.[20] The obligation to take CIL 'into account' when interpreting a treaty suggests that it is a matter of discretion. However, the International Law Commission ('ILC') has concluded that article 31(3)(c) amounts to a presumption that, where a treaty covers the same subject matter as a rule of CIL, it should be interpreted consistently with that rule of CIL unless contradicted by express language in the treaty.[21] This presumption, known as the 'principle of systemic integration', finds support in international case law and academic literature.[22]

The principle of systemic integration is rebutted where there is a clear legislative intent to depart from CIL. Focusing on the ICC's war crimes jurisdiction under article 8 of the *Rome Statute*, there is no evidence of a legislative intent to deviate from customary international humanitarian law ('customary IHL'). On the contrary, the drafting history, text, and

---

19 *VCLT* (n 11) art 31.

20 Appellate Report, *European Communities and Certain Member States – Measures Affecting Trade in Large Civil Aircraft*, WT/DS316/AB/R (18 May 2011) 846 ('*European Communities and Certain Member States – Measures Affecting Trade in Large Civil Aircraft*'); Mark Villigier, *Customary International Law and Treaties* (Martinus Nijhoff, 1985) 268–9.

21 International Law Commission, *Fragmentation of International Law: Difficulties Arising from the Diversification and Expansion of International Law – Report of the Study Group of the International Law Commission, Finalized by Martti Koskenniemi*, UN Doc A/CN.4/L.682 (13 April 2006) para 419 ('*Fragmentation of International Law Study*').

22 For example, see *Legal Consequences for States of the Continued Presence of South Africa in Namibia (South West Africa) notwithstanding Security Council Resolution 276 (Advisory Opinion)* [1971] ICJ Rep 16, [53] ('*Legal Consequences for States of the Continued Presence of South Africa in Namibia (South West Africa) notwithstanding Security Council Resolution 276*'); *Interpretation of the Agreement of 25 March 1951 between the WHO and Egypt (Advisory Opinion)* [1980] ICJ Rep 73, [10] ('*Interpretation of the Agreement of 25 March 1951 between the WHO and Egypt*'); Campbell McLachlan, 'The Principle of Systemic Integration and Article 31(3)(C) of the Vienna Convention' (2005) 54(2) *International and Comparative Law Quarterly* 279.

jurisdictional reach of the *Rome Statute* and *Elements of Crimes* demonstrate a concerted effort on behalf of the drafters to ensure that the provisions reflected, and would be interpreted consistently with, customary IHL.[23]

At least with respect to the ICC's war crimes jurisdiction, the principle of systemic integration should be confirmed.[24] Yet, analysis of the ICC's war crimes jurisprudence reveals that the judges have been reluctant to apply the principle of systemic integration, often without explanation. Indeed, there are very few cases in which article 31(3)(c) is expressly mentioned or applied in practice. This failure to adhere to the principle of systemic integration raises several unwanted consequences.

1.2.1 *Methodological Inconsistency*

The ICC's inconsistent record with respect to the principle of systemic integration under article 31(3)(c) of the *VCLT* creates and perpetuates methodological inconsistency between the different Chambers of the Court. For example, in a case concerning the use of children under 15 to actively participate in hostilities contrary to article 8(2)(e)(VII) of the *Rome Statute*, the Appeals Chamber applied the principle of systemic integration in holding that all crimes falling under 'other violations of the laws and customs of war' in article 8(2)(e) 'must' be interpreted consistently with customary IHL.[25] In another case concerning the interpretation of the war crime of 'pillaging' under article 8(2)(e)(v), the Court ignored customary IHL without explanation.[26] Such methodological inconsistency in the interpretation of crimes leads to unpredictability in judicial reasoning and should be avoided.

When faithfully applied, the principle of systemic integration promotes consistency in the interpretation of the *Rome Statute*, as CIL operates as an objective benchmark against which to interpret the definition and scope of an offence. As stated by Andrea Carcano, 'Accurate and abundantly

23 Timothy McCormack and Sue Robertson, 'Jurisdictional Aspects of the Rome Statute for the New International Criminal Court' (1999) 23 *Melbourne University Law Review* 635; Hunt (n 9); Grover (n 4).

24 Sadat and Jolly (n 18) Cryer (n 18), Grover (n 4).

25 *Prosecutor v Thomas Lubanga Dyilo (Judgment)* (International Criminal Court, Appeals Chamber, Case No ICC-01/04-01/06 A5, 1 December 2014) [322] ('*Lubanga Appeals Judgement*').

26 *Prosecutor v Bosco Ntaganda (Judgment)* (International Criminal Court, Trial Chamber, Case No ICC-01/04-02/06, 8 July 2019) [1026]–[1030] ('*Ntagnada Trial Judgment*').

reasoned determinations of CIL, far from being judge-made law in disguise, help ensure a consistent and persuasive development of the applied law among different Chambers and across ICL'.[27]

1.2.2 *Fragmentation of International Law*

Failure to adhere to the principle of systemic integration contributes to the fragmentation of international law, with negative consequences both within the ICC regime and for the application of ICL generally.[28] In terms of the ICC's internal functioning, where the Court exercises jurisdiction by way of a United Nations Security Council ('UNSC') referral under article 13(b) of the *Statute* – as is the case with respect to the situations in Darfur and Libya – the nationals of non-member states will be subject to the retroactive application of the ICC's provisions in the territory of a non-member state.[29] In order to comply with the principle of legality in these situations, the substantive crimes must reflect CIL.

This conclusion was confirmed by the Appeals Chamber in 2021 in *Prosecutor v Ali Kushayb*, a case which challenged the ICC's jurisdiction over the situation in Darfur pursuant to a UNSC referral.[30] The Appeals Chamber held that the ICC's exercise of jurisdiction does not violate the principle of legality precisely because 'the crimes under the Statute were intended to be generally representative of the state of customary international law when the Statute was drafted'.[31] Naturally, this justification only remains valid to the extent that the crimes are interpreted and applied consistently with CIL. If, over the course of its jurisprudence, the ICC's interpretation of its subject-matter jurisdiction were to deviate from CIL, it would not be able to apply its past decisions as precedent in cases involving a UNSC referral. This scenario should be avoided as it would create two sets of laws: ICC law (which deviates from CIL and is therefore only applicable to member

27 Andrea Carcano, 'Of Fragmentation and Precedents in International Criminal Law' (2016) 14(4) *Journal of International Criminal Justice* 771, 789.

28 Sadat and Jolly (n 18).

29 Kenneth Gallant, 'Jurisdiction to Adjudicate and Jurisdiction to Prescribe in International Criminal Courts' (2003) 48 *Villanova Law Review* 763.

30 *Prosecutor v Ali Muhammad Ali Abd-Alrahman ('Ali Kushayb') (Appeal of Mr Abd-Al-Rahman against the Pre-Trial Chamber II's 'Decision on the Defence "Exception d'incompétence" (ICC-02/05-01/20-302)')* (International Criminal Court, Appeals Chamber, Case No ICC-02/05-01/20 OA8, 1 November 2021) [2]–[3] (*'Ali Kushayb Jurisdictional Appeal'*).

31 Ibid [88]–[90].

states); and CIL (which is applicable to non-member states under a UNSC referral).

The fragmentation of ICL also weakens the ICC's precedential authority. In situations where individual states or regional courts adjudicate international crimes, their jurisdiction is usually limited to crimes existing under CIL. For example, states exercising universal jurisdiction or future tribunals established in the wake of the UN Independent Mechanisms in Syria and Myanmar would each derive authority to prosecute individuals because the alleged crimes violate CIL. ICC jurisprudence that deviates from CIL is therefore of little precedential value and belies the hope that the ICC would serve as a model court with the 'promise of universal justice'.[32]

1.2.3 *Fragmentation of International Criminal and Humanitarian Law*

Fragmentation has real-world consequences for the application of IHL on the ground. For ICL to effectively adjudicate violations of IHL, the interpretation of war crimes must preserve the balance between humanity and military necessity, circumscribing miliary action in the name of humanity without frustrating the feasibility of lawful operations. This balance can be upset in either direction.

Overly progressive or 'utopian' interpretations of IHL that expand the definition of crimes can make military action unworkable and damage the legitimacy of ICL in the eyes of those whose conduct it seeks to regulate.[33] The outcome of such unrealistic standards can, paradoxically, lead to less humanity in war. For example, there might be a temptation for the prosecution to classify a situation as an armed conflict to afford the relevant court jurisdiction over war crimes. However, lowering the threshold for the applicability of IHL in the courtroom may come to influence how a situation of violence is classified on the ground. The premature determination of an armed conflict, while invoking IHL's protective regime, also enlivens its permissive aspects, legalising the use of lethal force and the collateral destruction of civilian infrastructure in the pursuit of legitimate military aims.[34] The application of this body of law may have significantly worse

32 Kofi Annan, *Press Release of the United Nations Secretary General*, UN Doc SG/SM/6257 (12 June 1997) ('*Press Release of the United Nations Secretary General*').

33 Payam Akhavan, 'Reconciling Crimes against Humanities with the Laws of War – Human Rights, Armed Conflict, and the Limits of Progressive Jurisprudence' (2008) 6 Journal of International Criminal Justice 37, 37.

34 Rogier Bartels, 'A Fine Line Between Protection and Humanisation: The Interplay Between the Scope of Application of International Humanitarian Law and Jurisdiction

consequences for the civilian population than if the domestic law and human rights paradigm were to remain in force.

Similarly, Trial Chamber II in *Lubanga* took an expansive interpretation of the term 'active participation in hostilities' to broaden the criminal responsibility of those who would use children in armed conflict. In doing so, the Chamber inadvertently risked expanding the lawful targetability of such children, as IHL also permits the use of lethal force against those who 'actively participate' in hostilities.[35] Importantly, this consequence appears to have been avoided by the *Lubanga* Appeals Chamber.[36]

In the other direction, overly conservative interpretations of IHL in the courtroom risk loosening its regulatory function to the detriment of victims. The drafting of the *Elements of Crimes* has, in many cases, sought to narrow the definitions of war crimes and modes of liability, setting the threshold for violations of IHL beyond that which is required under CIL.[37] This can be seen in the elements of the war crime of launching a disproportionate attack, which change the anticipated civilian harm from 'excessive' under customary IHL to 'clearly excessive', and which appear to replace the objective standard of the 'reasonable commander' with a purely subjective test in which the offender must have 'known' the attack would be clearly excessive.[38] Similarly, the war crime of pillage is limited under the *Elements of Crimes* to appropriations of property 'for private and personal use', despite the Trial Chamber in *Bemba* acknowledging that 'this requirement is not explicitly expressed in customary or conventional international humanitarian law'.[39] The Appeals Chambers in the same case ultimately acquitted the

over Alleged War Crimes Under International Criminal Law', in Terry Gill et al (eds) *Yearbook of International Humanitarian Law*, Vol 20, 2017.

35 *Prosecutor v Thomas Lubanga Dyilo (Judgment)* (International Criminal Court, Trial Chamber I, Case No ICC-01/04-01/06, 14 March 2012) ('*Lubanga Trial Judgment*'); Mark Drumbl, 'The Effects of the Lubanga Case on Understanding and Preventing Child Soldiering' (2012) 15 *Yearbook of International Humanitarian Law* 87, 121; Chris Jenks, 'Law as Shield, Law as Sword: The ICC's Lubanga Decision, Child Soldiers and the Perverse Mutualism of Direct Participation in Hostilities' (2013) 3 *University of Miami National Security and Armed Conflict Law Review* 106.

36 *Lubanga Appeals Judgement* (n 25) [324].

37 Otto Triffterer, 'Can The "Elements of Crimes" Narrow or Broaden Responsibility for Criminal Behaviour Defined in the Rome Statute?', *The Emerging Practice of the International Criminal Court* (Brill Nijhoff, 2009) 381, 394.

38 International Criminal Court, *Elements of Crimes*, 2 November 2000 sess, UN Doc PCNICC/2000/1/Add.2 (2 November 2000), article 8(2)(b)(iv) ('*Elements of Crimes*').

39 *Bemba Trial Judgment* (n 13) [120].

accused by imposing a significantly higher threshold of command responsibility than its customary equivalent.[40]

What do these judicial departures from CIL mean for the conduct of military operations? As a matter of law, customary IHL continues to apply. But there is a risk that regressive interpretations will lower the protection to victims and foster impunity, while utopian interpretations may lose the support of member states. ICL and IHL have a symbiotic relationship in which one can legitimately influence the other. Developments in customary IHL can update ICL, as seen most notably in the jurisprudence of the International Criminal Tribunal for the former Yugoslavia (ICTY).[41] By the same token, the judicial process of identifying and articulating rules of customary IHL can influence the content of such rules, helping states to inform their position and shape their practice in response to a judicial decision on a complex issue of international law.[42]

The problem, therefore, is not the mutual influence or cross-fertilisation of IHL and ICL, but rather the risk that lurching too far in one direction will upset the balance and fragment the law. Part of the solution is to interpret war crimes in the *Rome Statute* consistently with customary IHL to the greatest possible extent. The value of custom is that it offers stability through the requirement of consistent practice and is at the same time responsive to change. Interpretations consistent with CIL will help maintain the delicate balance between IHL (the body of regulatory rules) and ICL (the means of enforcement).

1.2.4 *Stagnation of International Criminal Law*

Failure to apply the principle of systemic integration also limits opportunities for the legitimate, incremental development of the law. CIL is, by

40 *Prosecutor v Jean-Pierre Bemba Gombo (Judgment)* (International Criminal Court, Appeals Chamber, Case No ICC-01/05-01/08 A, 8 June 2018); Matteo Colorio, 'A Commander's Motivations and Geographical Remoteness under Command Responsibility: An Analysis of Controversial Issues of the Bemba Appeal Judgment' (2021) 21(3) *International Criminal Law Review* 445. For an alternative view, see Robinson (n 6). Robinson argues that the different standards in ICL are justified because principles of criminal responsibility should impose a higher threshold.

41 Fan (n 7); Shane Darcy, 'The Reinvention of War Crimes by the International Criminal Tribunals' in Shane Darcy and Joseph Powderly (eds) *Judicial Creativity at the International Criminal Tribunals* (OUP 2010) 106, 111.

42 Roozbeh Baker, 'Legal Recursivity and International Law: Rethinking the Customary Element' (2016) 14(1) *Dartmouth Law Journal* 41. Allison Danner, 'When Courts Make Law: How the International Criminal Tribunals Recast the Laws of War' (2006) 59 *Vanderbilt Law Review* 1.

definition, a dynamic body of law that reflects the contemporary practice and opinions of states. While the ICC's subject-matter jurisdiction is limited to those crimes enumerated in the *Rome Statute* – meaning that any substantive amendments must be undertaken by the Assembly of States Parties – CIL allows judges to interpret those provisions in accordance with the expectations of the international community.

Failure to adhere to the principle of systemic integration will lead to one of two possible scenarios: (I) ICC law will develop without reference to state practice and *opinio juris*, leading to unpredictable judicial reasoning; or (II) ICC law will stagnate while CIL develops in a different direction.[43] To some degree, such divergence is inevitable, as the ordinary meaning of an offence in the *Rome Statute* may be unable to accommodate development in CIL, leading to a difference in the substantive law that can only be rectified by amending the *Statute*. However, to the extent that developments in CIL can be accommodated by the ordinary meaning of the words, the definition of crimes in the *Rome Statute* should be interpreted consistently with CIL to avoid both unnecessary stagnation and fragmentation of ICC law.

1.2.5 *Lowering the Protection of Victims of Armed Conflict*

Finally, although it cannot be claimed that an interpretation consistent with customary IHL will categorically provide greater protection to the victims of armed conflict, it is difficult to justify situations where the ICC regime offers less protection to victims than customary IHL. Since the *Elements of Crimes* tends to narrow the customary definition of crimes in favour of the accused,[44] several decisions in which the ICC has deviated from customary IHL have resulted in a lower standard of protection against international crimes and increased the likelihood of impunity.[45]

---

43 Hunt (n 9).

44 Triffterer (n 37) 394.

45 *Bemba Trial Judgment* (n 13) [120] (noting that the 'private or personal use' element in the *Elements of Crimes* is not required under CIL); *Prosecutor v Omar Hassan Al Bashir* (*Decision on the Prosecution's Application for a Warrant of Arrest against Omar Hassan Ahmad Al Bashir*) (International Criminal Court, Pre-Trial Chamber I, Case No ICC-02/05–01/09, 4 March 2009) [121] ('*Al Bashir Arrest Warrant*') (noting that the definition of genocide in article 6 of the *Rome Statute* is more onerous due to the *Elements of Crimes* adding a contextual element that is not required under CIL); *The Prosecutor v Al Hassan Ag Abdoul Aziz Ag Mohamed Ag Mahmoud* (Corrected version of *Décision relative à la Confirmation des Charges Portées contre Al Hassan Ag Abdoul Aziz Ag Mohamed Ag Mahmoud*) (International Criminal Court, Pre-Trial Chamber I, Case No ICC-01/12-01/18, 13 November 2019) [375]–[378] (English Translation) (*Al Hassan Pre-Trial Judgment*) (noting that the *Elements of Crimes* defines a 'regularly constituted

In sum, the ICC's reluctance to seek interpretive consistency with CIL in accordance with the principle of systemic integration in article 31(3)(c) of the *VCLT* is not only incorrect from a legal standpoint, it also detracts from consistent judicial reasoning, contributes to the fragmentation of international law, limits opportunities for the development of ICL, and risks lowering the protection of victims of armed conflict. In this book, I highlight the many ways in which compliance with the principle of systemic integration can address these problems by facilitating methodological consistency, promoting unity in the international system, and contributing to the incremental development of the law.

1.3 Convoluted Custom as a Possible Reason for Noncompliance with Systemic Integration

Conceptual and methodological uncertainty in the identification of CIL, particularly in the context of identifying prohibitive humanitarian rules, is likely part of the reason behind the ICC's reluctance to apply the principle of systemic integration to the interpretation crimes in the *Rome Statute*. To help facilitate reliance on CIL, we must resolve some of the theoretical and practical debates about what CIL *is* and how it is to be identified by courts and tribunals.

The International Court of Justice (ICJ) has routinely espoused that CIL is the widespread, consistent, and observable practice of states (state practice), seemingly performed under a sense of legal obligation (*opinio juris*). The requisite level of state practice has variously been described as 'extensive and virtually uniform' (*North-Sea Continental Shelf Cases*),[46] 'constant and uniform' (*Asylum Case*),[47] or 'in general ... consistent' (*Nicaragua*).[48] It is distinguished from mere normative patterns of behaviour by the notion that the states 'felt' legally obliged to act in the manner they did. In theory, then, CIL is a quantitative analysis of state behaviour, the

court' by exclusive reference to independence and impartiality, thereby ignoring its additional components under CIL).

46 *North Sea Continental Shelf (Federal Public of Germany v Denmark) (Merits)* [1969] ICJ Rep 3, [74] (*'North Sea Continental Shelf'*).

47 *Asylum Case (Colombia v Peru) (Judgment)* [1950] ICJ Rep 266, 276 (*'Asylum Case'*).

48 *Military and Paramilitary Activities in and against Nicaragua (Nicaragua v United States of America) (Merits)* [1986] 14, [186] (*'Military and Paramilitary Activities in and against Nicaragua'*).

motivation for which is derived from the obligation to act in conformity with international law.

Empirical studies of the ICJ's jurisprudence demonstrate that it has never successfully applied this definition in practice when positively identifying rules of CIL.[49] Instead, the ICJ is shown to rely on 'representative' (rather than individual) state practice, as evidenced in the content of multilateral treaties and UN Resolutions.[50] The content of these international agreements is taken to represent how states behave in substitution of a quantitative analysis of their actual behaviour, challenging the theoretical foundation of CIL. Moreover, where the ICJ encounters a rule contained in a widely ratified treaty that has been subject to contrary state practice, particularly where the rule is of a prohibitive humanitarian nature (such as those found in IHL treaties), the Court has tended to 'deduce' the existence of the customary norm based on its humanitarian importance, without referencing state practice or *opinio juris* at all.[51]

Studies on the ICTY's approach to custom identification equally demonstrate a strong preference for representative state practice as contained in relevant international instruments. Birgit Schlütter calculates that the ICTY used the 'international instrument approach' (representative state practice) on 27 occasions, the 'deductive' approach on 14 occasions, and engaged in a quantitative analysis of individual state practice and *opinio juris* on only two occasions.[52] Where the ICTY has been faced with a proposed rule of CIL that is subject to widespread noncompliance (such as the prohibition on torture),[53] the Court has occasionally attempted to reformulate the

---

49 Niels Petersen, 'The International Court of Justice and the Judicial Politics of Identifying Customary International Law' (2017) 17(2) *European Journal of International Law* 357, 366; Stephen J Choi and Mitu Gulati, 'Customary International Law: How Do Courts Do It?' in Curtis A Bradley (ed), *Custom's Future: Customary International Law in a Changing World* (2016) 117.

50 Petersen (n 49) 369–72.

51 Birgit Schlütter, *Developments in Customary International Law: Theory and the Practice of the International Court of Justice and the International Ad Hoc Criminal Tribunals for Rwanda and Yugoslavia* (Martinus Nijhoff, 2010) 140–170; Stefan Talmon, 'Determining Customary International Law: The ICJ's Methodology between Induction, Deduction and Assertion' (2015) 26(2) *European Journal of International Law* 417.

52 Schlütter (n 51) 280 nn 544–7.

53 Amnesty International, 'Human Rights Facts and Figures for 2016: 160 Countries' (Web Page, 23 February 2016) <https://www.amnesty.org/en/documents/pol10/3320/2016/en/> (Amnesty International Reports that over three-quartes of states have practised torture over the past five years); Pieter Kooijmans, Special Rapporteur, *Report on Torture and other Cruel, Inhuman or Degrading Treatment or Punishment*, UN Doc E/

constituent elements of CIL such that *opinio juris* could be considered the 'decisive element' under the 'pressure of the demands of humanity or the dictates of public conscience'.[54]

This reliance on *opinio juris* to overcome inconsistent state practice, although in practice comparable to the ICJ's use of the deductive approach, has attracted considerable criticism for betraying the conceptual basis of CIL. Building on the ILC Draft Conclusions and existing theories of CIL, I hope to make a tangible contribution to this debate by proposing a hierarchy of evidence in which, depending on the context, certain forms of practice could be considered more probative than other forms of (non-conforming) practice when identifying CIL rules.

1.4 Methodology, Premise, and Structure

I have adopted the doctrinal methodologies of hermeneutic reasoning and legal argumentation to argue that ICC judges should prefer one interpretation of the *Rome Statute* over another. Hermeneutics presupposes that proper textual analysis can arrive at a superior conclusion on the correct meaning of words in a particular context. Amid competing interpretations, legal argumentation is the method used to arrive at this conclusion. Given that 'most arguments in legal reasoning are not true or false, but rather more or less convincing',[55] this process does not always lend itself to empirical verification. Rather, the strength of the argument and the value of the evidence are usually the determinative factors.[56] Nonetheless, my analysis of judicial reasoning at the ICC can be viewed as relatively objective providing one accepts the underlying premise that interpreting war crimes in the *Rome Statute* consistently with their counterparts under

CN.4/1988/17 (12 January 1988) 23 para 76 ('*Report on Torture and other Cruel, Inhuman or Degrading Treatment or Punishment*') ('How can this remarkable discrepancy between legal opinion (opinio Juris) and practice be explained, a discrepancy which is not unknown in the field of human rights in general but is all the more remarkable with respect to torture.').

54 *Prosecutor v Kupreškić et al.* (*Judgment*) (International Criminal Tribunal for the former Yugoslavia, Trial Chamber, Case No IT-95-16-T, 14 January 2000) [227] ('*Kupreškić Trial Judgment*').

55 Mark van Hoecke, *Methodologies of Legal Research: Which Kind of Method for What Kind of Discipline?* (Hart, 2011) 7.

56 Terry Hutchinson and Nigel Duncan, 'Defining and Describing What We Do: Doctrinal Legal Research' (2012) 17 *Deakin Law Review* 83.

CIL is preferable to treating the *Statute* as a self-contained regime that is divorced from general international law.

Earlier I highlighted several justifications for this underlying premise, advancing the position that interpretations consistent with CIL promote consistency in judicial reasoning, prevent unnecessary fragmentation, and allow for the legitimate, incremental development of the law. While I endeavour to substantiate this position throughout the book, it is largely assumed that the coherence of international law generally, and the synergy between IHL and ICL more specifically, are preferable to fragmentation and disunity. While there are those who argue that the ICC should be treated as a self-contained regime in which interpretations of the *Statute* are not bound by CIL or the *VCLT*,[57] this position reflects a minority view that does not feature heavily in my analysis. Similarly, while it is feasible that some may argue in favour of unfettered judicial flexibility, I proceed under the assumption that a more transparent and theoretically consistent methodology for the identification of CIL and its use in the interpretation of the *Rome Statute* is preferable to 'methodological mayhem'.[58]

Others have certainly advanced this position before me. Most notable for its influence on this book is Leena Grover's 2014 publication 'Interpreting Crimes in the Rome Statute of the International Criminal Court', in which she outlines a methodology for the interpretation of the *Rome Statute* that combines the peculiarities of the ICC system with the general rule of interpretation in article 31 of the *VCLT*. Grover argues that adherence to an interpretive methodology promotes consistency both within and across ICC judgments by creating a shared language and a 'measure of accountability' against which ICC decisions can be objectively evaluated.[59] Speaking on the *VCLT* rules more generally, Panos Merkouris argues that creating this common lexicon 'gently forces courts and tribunals (both international and domestic) to give more substantiated and clearly argued judgments', which in turn 'helps to hold these courts and their judgments

57 For example, see Dov Jacobs 'International Criminal Law' in Jörg Kammerhofer and Jean D'Aspremont (eds) *International Legal Positivism in a Post-Modern World* (CUP 2014) 451, 468–70.

58 Harlen Cohen, 'Methodology and Misdirection: Custom and the ICJ', *EJIL: Talk! Blog-post of the European Journal of International Law* (Blog Post, 1 December 2015) <https://www.ejiltalk.org/methodology-and-misdirection-a-response-to-stefan-talmon-on-custom-and-the-icj/> (Cohen uses the term to describe the practice of identifying CIL at the ICJ.)

59 Grover (n 4) 34.

accountable to a higher standard of reasoning and to a methodological coherence that is necessary for our discipline'.[60] Creating this shared language and adhering to interpretive standards is especially important when one considers that the ICC is incorporating multiple sources of international law, accommodating judges come from different legal traditions, and adjudicating the imposition of individual criminal responsibility. Such high stakes demand methodological consistency.[61]

Returning to the principle of systemic integration, interpreting the *Rome Statute* consistently with CIL will promote this shared language and help to ensure consistency in judicial reasoning, both between ICC judgments and in relation to the general framework of international law. Grover argues that, as the crimes in the *Statute* were intended to reflect CIL, there is a presumption of interpretive consistency with CIL that is only rebutted by clear legislative intent.[62] In setting the scene for future research on this topic, Grover suggests that recognising this presumption could 'lend momentum' to the to the ongoing debates over the formation and interpretation of CIL,[63] and proposes that it would be worth testing her methodology against a representative sample of ICC jurisprudence.[64] Among the other research objectives of this book, I have endeavoured to respond to both challenges.

My own experience working at the ICC led me query the extent to which the principle of systemic integration (or interpretive consistency with CIL) is reflected in practice. ICC judges appeared to demonstrate considerable deference to the *Elements of Crimes,* and, for certain decisions, there seemed to be a reluctance to ground interpretive conclusions within the international legal framework, with some decisions making very few references to the *VCLT* or relevant rules of CIL. To determine whether this initial perception was empirically true and, if so, to understand the possible

60 Panos Merkouris 'Debating interpretation: On the road to Ithaca' (2022) 35 *Leiden Journal of International Law* 461, 463.

61 Manley, Tehrani, and Rasiah (n 16) 796.

62 Grover (n 4) 246–344.

63 Ibid 356 ('If the interpretive presumption proposed were recognized, this would, of course, lend momentum to the revived interest in custom's interpretation as well as the 'existential' issues of its formation and aids to its interpretation.')

64 Ibid 419 ('In the future, it might be worthwhile to test the functionality of the method of interpretation developed in this study on a representative sample of the jurisprudence emerging from the Court. Such an exercise would help to unearth its shortcomings and rectify them.')

reasons behind the ICC's approach, I developed five questions to guide my analysis:

1. Does the ICC adhere to the *VCLT* generally, or the principle of systemic integration more specifically, when interpreting the definition of war crimes?
2. If not, is part of the reason for the reluctance to apply the principle of systemic integration based on an interpretive deference to the *Elements of Crimes*?
3. If there is an interpretive deference to the *Elements of Crimes*, to what extent is it informed by the ICC's codification of the principle of legality and the concomitant rules of strict construction?
4. Can the reluctance to identify and use CIL in the interpretation of the *Rome Statute* also be explained by the lack of clarity surrounding the constituent elements of CIL and the evidence necessary to establish their existence in a court of law?
5. What lessons can be drawn from a comparative analysis of those decisions that adhere to the principle of systemic integration and those that do not?

The following chapters of this book have been developed in response to these questions. I provide an empirical analysis of the extent to which the ICC has applied the *VCLT* and the principle of systemic integration in its war crimes jurisprudence, propose a refinement of the methodology for identifying customary rules in the ICL context, and engage in a three part case-study on using the principle of systemic integration to interpret the war crime of denying a fair trial in the context of a non-international armed conflict (NIAC).

1.4.1 *Harmonising Rule of Strict Construction with the Vienna Convention on the Law of Treaties*

Chapter 2 outlines a methodology for the interpretation of the *Rome Statute* that harmonises the rules of strict construction and the principles of criminal responsibility with the interpretive rules of the *VCLT*. Particular attention is paid to the obligation to interpret the definition of war crimes consistently with CIL, in accordance with the principle of systemic integration. The methodology consists of three applicable sets of rules: (I) the principle of legality and its concomitant rules of strict construction in article 22(2) of the *Statute*; (II) the 'general rule of interpretation' in article 31 of the *VCLT*; and (III) the nonbinding interpretive guidance in the *Elements of Crimes*.

Chapter 2 develops two hypotheses that will be tested throughout the book. The first is that ICC judges tend to view the *Elements of Crimes* as circumventing the need to ascertain the definition of an offence under CIL. The second hypothesis is that ICC judges tend to justify this interpretive approach by referring to the principle of legality. I argue that neither of these reasons, if substantiated, would justify non-compliance with the principle of systemic integration.

1.4.2 *The Judicial Identification of Customary International Law*

Chapter 3 aims to provide a more accurate reflection of what courts are already doing in practice when they identify rules of CIL. The purpose of Chapter 3 is to provide greater clarity on the evidence needed to prove the elements of CIL, particularly in the context of identifying prohibitive humanitarian rules, as a means of facilitating greater compliance with the principle of systemic integration at the ICC.

Empirical studies reveal that courts predominantly rely on the representative practice of states, as expressed in the text of multilateral treaties and UN Resolutions, rather than evidence of individual state conduct performed under a sense of legal obligation. While this approach appears at odds with the traditional methodology for identifying CIL, the ILC *Draft Conclusions on Identification of Customary International Law* (Draft Conclusions) have taken considerable steps in bridging the gap between the theory and practice of CIL identification. Most notably, the proposal to revert to the language of 'a general practice accepted as law' (rather than the oft-cited 'state practice and *opinio juris*) appears to accommodate representative forms of state practice. Furthermore, the acknowledgment that the same conduct can provide evidence of both elements, irrespective of which comes first, appears to overcome the '*opinio juris* paradox' (in which a state would otherwise have to act as if it were legally bound by a not-yet-existent rule).

Chapter 3 also addresses a significant gap in the ILC's Draft Conclusions: the phenomenon of courts identifying a rule of CIL despite evidence of widespread noncompliance. Several authors have attempted to resolve this issue by arguing that certain rules of custom can be 'deduced' on account of their humanitarian significance or by elevating the importance of *opinio juris* to compensate for the lack of consistent state practice.[65] In a novel

65 Frederic Kirgis, 'Custom on a Sliding Scale' (1987) 81(1) *American Journal of International Law* 146; Anthea Roberts, 'Traditional and Modern Approaches to Customary International Law: A Reconciliation' (2001) 95(4) *American Journal of International Law*

contribution to this debate, Chapter 3 advocates for a contextually dependent hierarchy of evidence in which, for prohibitive humanitarian rules, evidence of what states do in the international diplomatic arena is afforded more weight than examples of noncompliance on the ground. Courts are already adopting a similar approach in practice, but this would allow for a more transparent methodology that better conforms with the theoretical underpinnings of CIL. Importantly, the ILC Draft Conclusions recognise that certain forms of evidence may be given more weight in particular contexts.[66]

1.4.3 *Quantitative and Qualitative Analysis of the ICC's Compliance with the Principle of Systemic Integration*

Chapter 4 uses quantitative and qualitative analyses of the ICC's war crimes jurisprudence to test Hypothesis 1, that judges tend to view the *Elements of Crimes* as obviating the need to ascertain the definition and scope of an offence under CIL; and Hypothesis 2, that judges tend to view the codification of the principle of legality and its concomitant rules of strict construction in article 22(2) of the *Statute* as limiting or precluding interpretive reliance on CIL. The quantitative data reveals that the ICC's compliance with the principle of systemic integration is poor. Qualitative analysis of select cases suggests that the ICC tends to limit the interpretive value of CIL to situations where the *Elements of Crimes* have not provided definition (confirming Hypothesis 1). Furthermore, this approach is usually justified by reference to the principle of legality (confirming Hypothesis 2).

Further qualitative analysis of two important cases, *Lubanga* and *Ntaganda* – in which the ICC held that war crimes in article 8(2)(e) and, by extension, 8(2)(b) 'must' be interpreted consistently with customary IHL[67] – demonstrates how compliance with the principle of systemic integration can provide greater clarity on the scope of an offence, prevent

757; John Tasioulas, 'Customary International Law and the Quest for Global Justice' in Amanda Perreau-Saussine and James Murphy (eds), *The Nature of Customary International Law* (CUP 2007) 307.

66 *Report of the International Law Commission, Chapter V: Identification of Customary International Law*, UN GAOR, 73rd sess, Supp No 10, UN Doc A/73/10 (2018), Conclusion 6(3), 134 para 8.

67 *Lubanga Appeals Judgement* (n 25) [322]; *Prosecutor v Bosco Ntaganda (Judgement on the appeal of Mr Ntaganda against the "Second decision on the Defence's challenge to the jurisdiction of the Court in respect of Counts 6 and 9)* (International Criminal Court, Appeals Chamber, Case No ICC-01/04-02/06 OA5, 15 June 2017) (*'Appeals Chamber's Second Decision on Mr Ntaganda's Jurisdictional Appeal'*).

unnecessary fragmentation, and contribute to incremental development of the law.

1.4.4 *Case Study on the War Crime of Denying a Fair Trial*

Chapters 5 to 7 provide a three-part case study on the role of CIL in interpreting the crime of 'the passing of sentences or the carrying out of executions without previous judgment pronounced by a *regularly constituted court*, affording all judicial guarantees *generally recognized as indispensable*' under article 8(2)(c)(iv) of the *Statute* – in other words, the crime of denying a fair trial.

Chapter 5 offers a critique of Pre-Trial Chamber I and Trial Chamber X's decisions in *Al Hassan*, both of which defined a 'regularly constituted court' as an independent and impartial court, pursuant to the definition provided in the *Elements of Crimes*, but ignored both the ordinary meaning of this term and its definition and scope under customary IHL. Consistent with the principle of systemic integration, I argue that future ICC Chambers should interpret the term 'regularly constituted court' consistently with its definition under customary IHL. Not only is this approach correct from a legal standpoint and an important means of promoting consistency in judicial reasoning, it also better reflects the specific purpose of this provision in prohibiting special courts with irregular jurisdiction.

Chapter 6 focuses on the definition of a 'regularly constituted court' under CIL when applied to the courts of NSAGs. It is generally accepted that NSAGs exercising territorial control to the exclusion of the state incur the responsibility to maintain the civilian population, which requires the use of courts. There is disagreement, however, on how such courts can satisfy the 'regularly constituted' requirement, as NSAGs possess no constitutional authority to establish courts or enact law. While some argue that NSAGs can provide their own legal basis to establish courts and therefore set their own jurisdictional competence, others suggest that NSAG courts are limited to enforcing the pre-existing laws of the state in a manner analogous to the law of occupation. By examining states' attitudes towards NSAG courts, from the drafting of *Additional Protocol II* to the funding of Kurdish tribunals in modern day Syria, I argue that IHL provides the necessary legal basis for such courts and delimits their jurisdictional competence. There is a consistent trend of states recognising the legality of NSAG courts only to the extent that they are necessary to give effect the rules of IHL and maintain the safety of the civilian population under their territorial control. This trend suggests that IHL authorises the establishment of such courts and provides an outer limit on their jurisdictional scope.

Chapter 7 is the final instalment of the case study on the war crime of denying a fair trial. It focuses on the requirement that regularly constituted courts afford 'all judicial guarantees which are generally recognized as indispensable'. This process will require the ICC to ascertain such guarantees in the practice and legal opinion of states. I provide a list of those guarantees that are likely to be accepted as indispensable under customary IHL and, using a version of the doctrine of 'common but differentiated responsibilities', I examine how NSAGs can comply with such guarantees in practice. As there is no explicit legal basis for incorporating this doctrine into the interpretation of the *Rome Statute*, I argue that the ICC should account for the divergent means with which NSAGs can apply judicial guarantees by exercising both prosecutorial and judicial discretion in the application of article 8 (2)(c)(iv), a point which has been acknowledged by Trial Chamber X in *Al Hassan*.[68]

The Conclusion offers some reflections on the importance of adhering to the principle of systemic integration in the interpretation of the *Rome Statute*. I return to my central argument that interpretive consistency with CIL promotes consistency in judicial reasoning, prevents unnecessary fragmentation, and contributes to the incremental development of the law. For these reasons, I argue that ICC Chambers should adopt a unified methodology for interpreting the definition of crimes that harmonises the principle of systemic integration with the *Elements of Crimes* and the rule of strict construction in article 22(2) of the *Rome Statute*.

68 *Prosecutor v Al Hassan* (International Criminal Court, ICC-01/12-01/18, Trial Judgment, 26 June 2024) [1173].

CHAPTER 2

A Methodology for the Interpretation of the *Rome Statute*

2.1 Introduction

In *Prosecutor v Katanga,* Trial Chamber II of the International Criminal Court (ICC) exclaimed that, 'The chambers of the Court have unanimously and systematically based their interpretation of the Statute on the principles established by the Vienna Convention'.[1] However, quantitative analysis of ICC jurisprudence reveals that this is not the case. Only 36 out of the 190 decisions analysed referred directly to the *Vienna Convention on the Law of Treaties* (*VCLT*),[2] which is fewer than 19 per cent.[3] Obligatory rules of interpretation in the *VCLT* have largely been overlooked, with approximately 24 per cent of decisions referring to the 'object and purpose' of the *Rome Statute* (the *Statute*), 21 per cent to the principle of 'good faith', 16 per cent to the 'ordinary meaning' of the text, seven per cent to the obligation to interpret the treaty 'in its context', and only one per cent to the obligation to take international law 'into account' in accordance with the principle of systemic integration.[4] The numbers are significantly lower when the data is limited to the use of the *VCLT* to interpret definition of crimes or modes of liability. Several significant decisions, including those in which an accused was acquitted or convicted at trial or on appeal, made no reference these customary rules of interpretation when construing the definition of crimes.[5]

1 *Prosecutor v Germain Katanga and Mathieu Ngudjolo Chui* (*Judgment*) (International Criminal Court, Trial Chamber II, Case No ICC-01/04-01/07, 7 March 2014) [43] (*Katanga Trial Judgment*).

2 *Vienna Convention on the Law of Treaties*, opened for signature 23 May 1969, 1155 UNTS 331 (entered into force 27 January 1980) (*VCLT*).

3 See Figure 4.1 in Chapter 4 of this book and accompanying discussion.

4 Ibid; *Rome Statute of the International Criminal Court,* opened for signature 17 July 1998 (2187 UNTS 38544, entered into force 1 July 2002) (*Rome Statute of the International Criminal Court*).

5 *Prosecutor v Ahmad Al Faqi Al Mahdi* (*Judgment and Sentence*) (International Criminal Court, Trial Chamber VIII, Case No ICC-01/12-01/15, 27 September 2016) (*Al Mahdi Trial Judgment*); *Prosecutor v Jean-Pierre Bemba Gombo* (*Judgment*) (International Criminal Court, Appeals Chamber, Case No ICC-01/05-01/08 A, 8 June 2018) (*Bemba Appeals*

 | DOI:10.1163/9789004690042_003

The failure to implement the *VCLT* generally, and the principle of systemic integration more specifically, has led to an inconsistent application of international law rules in the interpretation of the *Rome Statute*. Some decisions incorporate external sources of law where it is convenient, while others ignore them completely and rely exclusively on the *Elements of Crimes*.[6] With no agreed approach to interpreting the definition of crimes in the *Rome Statute*, the jurisprudence of the ICC is replete with inconsistencies and contradictions, leading to a kind of 'methodological mayhem'[7] that detracts from the Court's predictability and institutional legitimacy.

In response, I draw on existing scholarship in this area to outline a methodology that harmonises the general rule of interpretation in article 31 of the *VCLT* with the rules of strict construction in article 22(2) of the *Statute* and the interpretive guidance in the *Elements of Crimes*.[8] The overarching argument is that, while the rule of strict construction and the *Elements of Crimes* may necessitate a more conservative approach to interpretation, they can and should be reconciled with the *VCLT*, an approach that has been endorsed by the Court itself on a couple of occasions.[9] In advocating for greater compliance with the *VCLT*, I pay special attention to the obligation to interpret the definition of war crimes consistently with customary international humanitarian law (customary IHL) pursuant to the principle of systemic integration in article 31(3)(c) of the *VCLT*.

To this end, section 2.2 outlines the inconsistent methodological approaches to interpreting the definition of crimes at the ICC. Section 2.3 argues that the ICC should interpret war crimes consistently with customary

---

Judgment); *Prosecutor v Bosco Ntaganda* (*Judgment*) (International Criminal Court, Trial Chamber, Case No ICC-01/04-02/06, 8 July 2019) (*Ntagnada Trial Judgment*); *Prosecutor v Bosco Ntaganda* (*Judgment*) (International Criminal Court, Appeals Chamber, Case No ICC-01/04-02/06 A A2, 30 March 2021) [564] (*Ntagnanda Appeals Judgment*); *Prosecutor v Dominic Ongwen* (*Judgment*) (International Criminal Court, Trial Chamber IX, Case No ICC-02/04-01/15, 4 February 2021) (*Prosecutor v Dominic Ongwen*).

6 International Criminal Court, *Elements of Crimes*, 2 November 2000 sess, UN Doc PCNICC/2000/1/Add.2 (2 November 2000) (*Elements of Crimes*).

7 Harlen Cohen, 'Methodology and Misdirection: Custom and the ICJ', *EJIL: Talk! Blogpost of the European Journal of International Law* (Blog Post, 1 December 2015) <https://www.ejiltalk.org/methodology-and-misdirection-a-response-to-stefan-talmon-on-custom-and-the-icj/> (Cohen uses the term to describe the practice of the ICJ, but it is also apt in the present context).

8 Leena Grover, *Interpreting Crimes in the Rome Statute of the International Criminal Court* (Cambridge University Press, 2014); Andrea Carcano, 'Of Fragmentation and Precedents in International Criminal Law' (2016) 14(4) *Journal of International Criminal Justice* 771, 789.

9 *Katanga Trial Judgment* (n 1) [43]–[51]; *Prosecutor v Jean-Pierre Bemba Gombo* (*Judgment*) (International Criminal Court, Trial Chamber III, Case No ICC-01/05-01/08, 21 March 2016) (*Bemba Trial Judgment*) [75]–[86].

IHL, as dictated by the principle of systemic integration. Section 2.4 examines whether the principle of systemic integration can be reconciled with the *Elements of Crimes* and what happens in cases of interpretive conflict between the two sources of law. Section 2.5 argues that the *VCLT* more generally can be harmonised with the rules of strict construction, which operate to protect the rights of the accused in criminal trials.

The proposed methodology recognises the unique situation of the ICC as an institution that is bound both by the principles of strict construction and the customary rules of treaty interpretation. I argue that adopting a single cohesive methodology will achieve multiple benefits. It will promote consistency in judicial reasoning, which in turn fosters predictability, legal certainty, and fairness to the accused. It will also ground the Court's decisions in applicable rules of international law, thereby preventing unnecessary fragmentation and enhancing the legitimacy and influence of the ICC as a truly international court.

2.2 Methodological Mayhem at the ICC and the Need for a Cohesive Approach

The ICC's failure to consistently adhere to the *VCLT* prompts the question: what interpretive methodology does the Court employ on a reliable basis? With respect to the interpretation of war crimes, the answer appears to be that the ICC relies almost exclusively on the definitions provided in the *Elements of Crimes*, even though the *Elements of Crimes* is a non-binding interpretive guidance[10] that 'shall be interpreted within the established framework of the international law of armed conflict'.[11] The ICC tends to buttress the *Elements of Crimes* with the rule of strict construction in article 22(2) of the *Statute,* which provides that the definition of crimes must be strictly construed, must not be extended by analogy, and that any ambiguity must be interpreted in favour of the accused. The interpretive value of customary international law (CIL) is largely relegated to situations where the *Elements of Crimes* are silent,[12] treating the *Rome Statute* as a criminal code that only permits reliance on external sources of law in cases of ambiguity.

10 *Elements of Crimes* (n 6) article 9(1).

11 Ibid article 8 'Introduction'.

12 David Hunt, 'The International Criminal Court: High Hopes, Creative Ambiguity and an Unfortunate Mistrust in International Judges' (2004) 2(1) *Journal of International Criminal Justice* 56.

Indeed, most ICC cases seem to reject the obligation in article 31(3)(c) of the *VCLT* to take international law 'into account'. Only 2 out of the 203 decisions analysed made explicit reference to article 31(3)(c) and only 15 percent referred to the terms 'customary' or 'international humanitarian law'. While external sources of international law are cited in ICC jurisprudence with some regularity, interpretive reliance on international law is inconsistent, subservient to the *Elements of Crimes*, and generally not in compliance with the principle of systemic integration.

The uncertainty regarding the interpretive value of international law leads to inconsistency between ICC Chambers. For example, although three Appeals Chamber decisions confirmed that war crimes under article 8(2)(b) and article 8(2)(e) 'must' be interpreted consistently with customary IHL,[13] no other chamber has applied this ruling, including a Trial Chamber that was supposed to be applying one of the above Appeals Chamber decisions on subject-matter jurisdiction.[14] Meanwhile, two other Trial Chamber decisions have interpreted the principle of systemic integration under article 31(3)(c) as providing them with a 'right' to refer to external sources of law,[15] whereas one Pre-Trial Chamber determined that external sources of law may only be referred to in cases of ambiguity.[16] The inconsistency across different ICC Chambers and the reluctance to incorporate accepted rules of treaty interpretation has led to 'methodological mayhem' in the interpretation of the *Rome Statute*.[17]

The inconsistency in judicial reasoning may be explained in part by the divergent origins and goals the *Rome Statute*,[18] complicating efforts to

---

13 *Prosecutor v Thomas Lubanga Dyilo* (*Judgment*) (International Criminal Court, Appeals Chamber, Case No ICC-01/04-01/06 A5, 1 December 2014) [322] (*Lubanga Appeals Judgement*); *Prosecutor v Bosco Ntaganda* (*Judgement on the appeal of Mr Ntaganda against the Second decision on the Defence's challenge to the jurisdiction of the Court in respect of Counts 6 and 9*) (International Criminal Court, Appeals Chamber, Case No ICC-01/04-02/06 OA5, 15 June 2017) [52]–[53] (*Appeals Chamber's Second Decision on Mr Ntaganda's Jurisdictional Appeal*); *Ntagnanda Appeals Judgment* [564] (n 5).

14 *Ntagnada Trial Judgment* (n 5).

15 *Katanga Trial Judgment* (n 1) [47], [1100], [1395] nn 1394; *Bemba Trial Judgment* (n 9) [78]–[79].

16 *Prosecutor v Omar Hassan Al Bashir* (*Decision on the Prosecution's Application for a Warrant of Arrest against Omar Hassan Ahmad Al Bashir*) (International Criminal Court, Pre-Trial Chamber I, Case No ICC-02/05-01/09, 4 March 2009) [132]–[133] (*Al Bashir Arrest Warrant*).

17 Cohen (n 7).

18 Antonio Cassese, *International Criminal Law* (2nd ed, OUP 2008) 6–7; Mary Fan, 'Custom, General Principles and the Great Architect Cassese' (2012) 10(5) *Journal of International Criminal Justice* 1063.

establish a unified interpretive approach. The *Rome Statute* and *Elements of Crimes* resemble a criminal code, exhaustively codifying the Court's subject-matter jurisdiction, principles of criminal responsibility, and modes of liability. Meanwhile, the *Statute* is also a multilateral treaty whose terms must be understood by reference to their origins in both treaty and CIL,[19] necessitating recourse to the *VCLT*. This duality has led to the characterisation of ICL as a paradoxical field, marked by conflicting philosophies, goals, and interpretive methods.[20]

To resolve these issues, ICC judges need to adopt a cohesive methodology that incorporates the distinctive features of the *Rome Statute*. Beginning with the principle of systemic integration in article 31(3)(c), the following section examines whether the crimes in the *Rome Statute* create a presumption of interpretive consistency with CIL, focusing on the Court's war crimes jurisdiction. I then look at whether the definitions provided in the *Elements of Crimes* can be harmonised with those under CIL, and consider which source of law would prevail in situations of interpretive conflict. Finally, I explore the extent to which the rules of strict construction in article 22(2) of the *Statute* limit the applicability of the *VCLT* when interpreting the definition of crimes. While there are several important nuances and caveats to address, I ultimately conclude that the ICC can adopt a cohesive methodology that combines the *VCLT* with the rule of strict construction in article 22(2) of the *Statute* and the interpretive guidance in the *Elements of Crimes*.

2.3 Systemic Integration and the Interpretation of Crimes in the *Rome Statute*

It is generally accepted that the *VCLT* applies to the interpretation of the *Rome Statute*.[21] Entitled the 'general rule of interpretation', article 31 of the *VCLT* provides the following rules.

---

19 Cassese (n 18) 6–7.

20 Vasiliev Sergey, 'The Making of International Criminal Law' in Catherine Brölmann and Yannick Radi (eds), *Research Handbook on the Theory and Practice of International Lawmaking* (Edward Elgar, 2016) 354, 363.

21 Despite the limited substantive reliance on the *VCLT* in the ICC's jurisprudence, a number of cases have confirmed its application, and no cases have asserted that the *VCLT* is inapplicable. Further, the *VCLT* was considered applicable to the ICTY Statute, even though it was not technically the product of an international treaty. See William

1. A treaty shall be interpreted in good faith in accordance with the ordinary meaning to be given to the terms of the treaty in their context and in the light of its object and purpose.
2. [...]
3. There shall be taken into account, together with the context:
   (d) any subsequent agreement between the parties regarding the interpretation of the treaty or the application of its provisions;
   (e) any subsequent practice in the application of the treaty which establishes the agreement of the parties regarding its interpretation;
   (f) any relevant rules of international law applicable between the parties.[22]

The reference to 'any relevant rules of international law' in article 31(3)(c) naturally includes CIL.[23] The obligation to take CIL 'into account' when interpreting a treaty suggests that it is a matter of discretion. However, the International Law Commission (ILC) has concluded that article 31(3)(c) amounts to a presumption that, where a treaty covers the same subject matter as a rule of CIL, the treaty should be interpreted consistently with that customary rule unless contradicted by express language in the treaty.[24] This presumption is known as the 'principle of systemic integration' and ensures the enduring relevance of CIL in the interpretation of the *Rome Statute*.

This section examines the interpretation of article 31(3)(c) by international courts and argues that the principle of systemic integration should be confirmed in the context of the ICC's war crimes jurisdiction, as there is no evidence in the *Rome Statute* (nor in the negotiating history of the

---

Schabas, 'Interpreting the Statutes of the Ad Hoc Tribunals' in Lal Chand Vohrah (ed), *Man's Inhumanity to Man: Essays in International Law in Honour of Antonio Cassese* (Kluwer Law International 2003) 847, 849–52. For an opposing view, see Dov Jacobs 'International Criminal Law' in Jörg Kammerhofer and Jean D'Aspremont (eds) *International Legal Positivism in a Post-Modern World* (CUP 2014) 451, 468–70.

22 *VCLT* (n 2).

23 Appellate Report, *European Communities and Certain Member States – Measures Affecting Trade in Large Civil Aircraft*, WT/DS316/AB/R (18 May 2011) 846 ('*European Communities and Certain Member States – Measures Affecting Trade in Large Civil Aircraft*'); Mark Villigier, *Customary International Law and Treaties* (Martinus Nijhoff 1985) 268–69.

24 International Law Commission, Martti Koskenniemi, *Report on Fragmentation of International Law: Difficulties Arising from the Diversification and Expansion of International Law*, UN Doc A/CN.4/L.682 (13 April 2006) para 465 (*Fragmentation of International Law Study*).

Statute) of a general intent to deviate from customary IHL. On the contrary, while the *Rome Statute*'s war crimes provisions are under-inclusive of custom, those offences that were included were specifically intended to reflect customary IHL.

2.3.1 *The Principle of Systemic Integration*

In 2006, the ILC Study Group, led by Martti Koskenniemi, published a report entitled *Fragmentation of International Law: Difficulties Arising from the Diversification and Expansion of International Law*.[25] The report defines article 31(3)(c) as a codification of the 'principle of systemic integration',[26] according to which 'international obligations are interpreted by reference to their normative environment' in order to ensure 'coherence and meaningfulness' in the interpretation of international law.[27] The report makes it clear that article 31(3)(c) does not elevate 'relevant rules of international law' to the status of *jus cogens* such that the impugned treaty provision *must* be interpreted consistently with such rules;[28] treaties, by their very nature, are capable of modifying general rules of international law. Rather, article 31(3)(c) creates a presumption of interpretive consistency with CIL that is only displaced by clear legislative intent.[29] The presumption ensures that the interpretive outcome is 'linked to the legal environment', which means that any deviation from the standards applicable under general international law must be acknowledged by the judge and justified by reference to the treaty.[30]

---

25 Ibid.

26 The principle of systemic integration is broader than article 31(3)(c), as the latter applies relevant rules of international law 'applicable in the relations between the parties', whereas the former applies to the interpretation of instruments without disputing parties (such as human rights or criminal law). However, it is common to use the terms interchangeably, which is the approach adopted here.

27 International Law Commission, *Fragmentation of International Law Study* (n 24) para 413.

28 Ibid para 473.

29 Ibid para 465.

30 Ibid para 480; Philippe Sands, 'Treaty, Custom and the Cross-fertilization of International Law' (1998) 1 *Yale Human Rights and Development Law Journal* 85, 102–3 ('[I]n interpreting the customary norm an adjudicatory body is not entitled to exercise discretion. It must "take account" of the customary norm. Ordinary usage suggests that th[is] formulation is stronger than "take into consideration" but weaker than "apply"'.) cf Alexander Orakhelashvili, *The Interpretation of Acts and Rules in Public International Law* (OUP 2008) 367.

The International Court of Justice (ICJ) notably affirmed the principle of systemic integration in the 2003 *Oil Platforms Case*,[31] in which the Court held that a bilateral treaty between the United States (US) and Iran could not be read independently of the CIL rules on the use of force, as the application of such rules 'forms an integral part of the task of interpretation entrusted to the Court'.[32] In the 1971 *Namibia Advisory Opinion*, the ICJ similarly held that 'an international instrument has to be interpreted and applied within the framework of the entire legal system prevailing at the time of the interpretation'.[33] The European Court of Human Rights (ECtHR), meanwhile, 'has made it clear on many occasions that the Convention must be interpreted in harmony with other rules of international law of which it forms part',[34] emphasising that 'the principles underlying the Convention cannot be interpreted and applied in a vacuum'.[35] The principle of systemic integration has also been affirmed in the jurisprudence of the Inter-American Court of Human Rights,[36] the Inter-American Commission of

31 *Case Concerning Oil Platforms (Islamic Republic of Iran v United States of America) (Merits)* [2003] ICJ Reports 161 (*Case Concerning Oil Platforms*).

32 Ibid [78].

33 *Legal Consequences for States of the Continued Presence of South Africa in Namibia (South West Africa) notwithstanding Security Council Resolution 276 (Advisory Opinion)* [1971] ICJ Rep 16 (*Legal Consequences for States of the Continued Presence of South Africa in Namibia (South West Africa) notwithstanding Security Council Resolution 276*), [53]; *Interpretation of the Agreement of 25 March 1951 between the WHO and Egypt (Advisory Opinion)* [1980] ICJ Rep 73, [10] (*Interpretation of the Agreement of 25 March 1951 between the WHO and Egypt*).

34 *Hassan v the United Kingdom* [2014] Application No 29750/09, Eur Court HR (Grand Chamber), [102] (*Hassan v the United Kingdom*).

35 *Bankovic v Belgium and others (Admissibility)* [2001] Application No 52207/99, Eur Court HR, [57] (*Bankovic v Belgium and others (Admissibility)*); *Al-Adsani v the United Kingdom* [2001] Application No 35763/97, XI Eur Court HR, [55] (*Al-Adsani v the United Kingdom*); *Bosphorus Hava Yolları Turizm ve Ticaret Anonim Şirketi v Ireland* [2005] Application No 45036/98, VI Eur Court HR, [150] (*Bosphorus Hava Yolları Turizm ve Ticaret Anonim Şirketi v Ireland*); *Magyar Helsinki Bizottság v Hungary* [2011] Application No 18030/11, Eur Court HR (Grand Chamber), [123] (*Magyar Helsinki Bizottság v Hungary*).

36 *The Right to Information on Consular Assistance in the Framework of the Guarantees of the Due Process of Law* (Advisory Opinion, IACtHR Series A no 16 No OC- 16/99, 1 October 1999) [113] (*The Right to Information on Consular Assistance in the Framework of the Guarantees of the Due Process of Law*); *Serrano-Cruz Sisters v El Salvador (Preliminary Objections)* (Inter-American Court of Human Rights, Series C No 118, 23 November 2004) [119] (*Serrano-Cruz Sisters v El Salvador*).

Human Rights,[37] and the African Commission on Human and Peoples' Rights.[38]

Turning to the jurisprudence of the ICC, only one case has explicitly endorsed the principle of systemic integration, despite the apparent consensus on the applicability of the *VCLT* to the interpretation of the *Rome Statute*. In *Prosecutor v Ruto*, ICC Trial Chamber V(A) stated that article 31(3)(c) of the *VCLT* 'require[s] the interpreter to keep broader international law in view, in order to determine … whether the drafter of the particular treaty has truly indicated an intention to displace applicable broader international law'.[39] The Chamber held that, absent such an intention, the treaty is to be interpreted consistently with applicable international law. As will be discussed in Chapter 4, while two other ICC decisions have acknowledged the relevance of general international law pursuant to article 31(3)(c), they have not gone so far as to adopt a presumption of interpretive consistency.[40] Other cases have simply ignored the *VCLT* and the principle of systemic integration altogether.[41]

---

37 *Coard v United States (Merits)* (Inter-American Commission on Human Rights, Report No 109/99, 29 September 1999) [40] (*Coard v United States*); *Las Palmeras v Colombia (Preliminary Objections)* (Inter-American Court of Human Rights, Series C No 67, 4 February 2000) [33] (*Las Palmeras v Colombia*); *Bámaca-Velásquez v Guatemala (Merits)* (Inter-American Court of Human Rights, Series C No 70, 25 November 2000) (*Bámaca-Velásquez v Guatemala*); *Mapiripán Massacre v Colombia (Merits, Reparations, and Costs)* (Inter-American Court of Human Rights, Series C No 134, 15 September 2005) [114]–[115] ('*Mapiripán Massacre v Colombia*'); *Ituango Massacres v Colombia* (Inter-American Court of Human Rights, Series C No 148, 1 July 2006) [180]–[183] (*Ituango Massacres v Colombia*); *Massacres of El Mozote and Nearby Places v El Salvador (Merits, Reparations and Costs)* (Inter-American Court of Human Rights, Series C No 252, 25 October 2012) [148], [153], [155]–[156] (*Massacres of El Mozote and Nearby Places v El Salvador*).

38 *Mohammed Abdullah Saleh Al-Asad v Djibout* (Judgment, ACHPR 55th Ordinary Session, Communication 383/110, 14 October 2014) [127] (*Mohammed Abdullah Saleh Al-Asad v Djibout*); *Democratic Republic of Congo v Burundi, Rwanda and Uganda* (African Commission on Human and Peoples Rights, Communication 227/1999 33rd Ordinary Session, May 2003) [64], [69] (*Democratic Republic of Congo v Burundi, Rwanda and Uganda*).

39 *Prosecutor v William Samoei Ruto (Decision on Mr Ruto's Request for Excusal from Continuous Presence at Trial)* (International Criminal Court, Trial Chamber V(A), Case No ICC-01/09-01/11, 18 June 2013) [101]–[102] (*Decision on Mr Ruto's Request for Excusal*).

40 *Katanga Trial Judgment* (n 1) [47]; *Bemba Trial Judgment* (n 9) [78]–[79].

41 *Prosecutor v Thomas Lubanga Dyilo (Judgment)* (International Criminal Court, Trial Chamber I, Case No ICC-01/04-01/06, 14 March 2012) (*Lubanga Trial Judgment*); *Lubanga Appeals Judgement* (n 13); *Ntagnanda Appeals Judgment* (n 5).

2.3.2 *Does the Principle of Systemic Integration Apply to the Interpretation of War Crimes in the* Rome Statute?

The drafting history, text, and jurisdictional reach of the *Rome Statute* and *Elements of Crimes* support the conclusion that the principle of systemic integration applies to the interpretation of crimes in the *Rome Statute*, and to war crimes in particular. Rather than demonstrate any legislative intent to deviate from CIL, there was a clear intention for the definition of crimes to reflect and be interpreted consistently with CIL.

Starting with the drafting history, Phillipe Kirsch, Chair of the Committee of the Whole at the Rome Diplomatic Conference, stated that the *Statute* 'clearly reflects the *opinio juris* of the international community, further supporting the customary nature of crimes within the Court's jurisdiction'.[42] Specific to war crimes, Michael Cottier notes that the two cumulative criteria used to justify inclusion in the Draft Statute were that the conduct must amount to a violation of IHL and must be specifically criminalised under CIL,[43] while Kirsch emphasised that, 'It was generally agreed that the crimes should reflect customary international law, but there were substantial disagreements about the current content of that law'.[44] Former International Criminal Tribunal for the former Yugoslavia (ICTY) judge David Hunt notes that the crimes in the *Statute* were limited to those under CIL to avoid law-making and to garner consensus.[45] Far from evincing a legislative intent to deviate from CIL, the drafting history of the *Rome Statute* demonstrates a concerted effort for the definition of crimes to reflect CIL, supporting recognition of the principle of systemic integration. As Stated by James Crawford, 'The customary status of each of the particular non-treaty-based heads of criminal responsibility eventually included in the 1994 Draft Statute was considered incontestable and uncontroversial, even if questions of definition remained'.[46]

---

42 Philip Kirsch, 'Customary International Humanitarian Law, its Enforcement, and the Role of the International Criminal Court' in Larry Maybee and Benarji Chakka (eds), *Custom as a Source of International Humanitarian Law* (ICRC 2006) 79–83.

43 Michael Cottier, 'Article 8' in Otto Triffterer (ed), *Commentary on the Rome Statute of the International Criminal Court* (2nd edn, Beck-Hart 2008) 275, 283, 287–88.

44 Adriaan Bos, 'From the International Law Commission to the Rome Conference (1994–1998)' in Antonio Cassese, Paola Gaeta and John RWD Jones (eds), *The Rome Statute of the International Criminal Court: A Commentary* (OUP 2002) 69

45 Hunt (n 12) 67.

46 James Crawford, 'The Work of the International Law Commission' in Antionio Cassese et al (eds) *The Rome Statute of the International Criminal Court: A Commentary* (vol 1) (OUP 2002).

The treaty provisions themselves also support this conclusion. It has been noted that the principle of systemic integration is strongest where the treaty adopts established terminology or 'words of art' that have obtained a specialised legal meaning under international law.[47] Indeed, article 31(4) of the *VCLT* states that 'special meaning shall be given to a term if it is established that the parties so intended'. The ILC has stated that using terms with a recognised meaning under CIL presupposes that the parties intended to refer to that meaning,[48] and this approach is also reflected in international jurisprudence.[49] The majority of crimes in the *Rome Statute* are drafted using terms with recognised meaning under CIL. As demonstrated below, this is especially the case with respect to the ICC's war crimes jurisdiction under article 8 of the *Statute*, which is the focus of this book.

Articles 8(2)(a) and 8(2)(c) replicate almost *verbatim* grave breaches of the *Geneva Conventions* applicable in international armed conflict (IAC) and common article 3 of the *Geneva Conventions* applicable in non-international armed conflict (NIAC), respectively. The customary status of these treaty provisions giving rise to individual criminal responsibility was not disputed at the Rome Conference.[50] Articles 8(2)(b) and 8(2)(e), meanwhile, derive from a 'patchwork' of legal sources, but are preceded by the qualification that the enumerated crimes constitute 'other serious violations of the laws and customs applicable in armed conflicts ... within the established framework of international law'. As stated by Antonio Cassese, '[B]y the use of that expression the draughtsmen aimed at making it clear that these two provisions were declaratory of customary international law'.[51] Indeed, two ICC Appeals Chamber decisions have confirmed that the reference to 'the

47 Grover (n 8) 223, 381.

48 International Law Commission, *Fragmentation of International Law Study* (n 24) para 467 ('[T]he terms used in the treaty have a recognized meaning in CIL, to which the parties can therefore be taken to have intended to refer.').

49 Panel Report – Action by the Dispute Settlement Body, *Korea – Measures Affecting Government Procurement*, WT/DS163/R (1 May 2000) 183 [7.96] (*Korea – Measures Affecting Government Procurement*); *Pope & Talbot Inc v Canada* (Damages, NAFTA Arbitral Tribunal, 41 ILM 1347, 31 May 2002) 1347 (*Pope & Talbot Inc v Canada*).

50 Timothy McCormack and Sue Robertson, 'Jurisdictional Aspects of the Rome Statute for the New International Criminal Court' (1999) 23 *Melbourne University Law Review* 635; Knut Dörmann, 'Article 8' in Otto Triffterer (ed), *Commentary on the Rome Statute of the International Criminal Court* (2nd edn, Beck-Hart 2008) 275.

51 Antonio Cassese, 'The Statute of the International Criminal Court: Some Preliminary Reflections' (1999) 10 *European Journal of International Law* 144, 152.

established framework of international law' requires interpretive consistency with customary IHL. By replicating provisions of the *Geneva Conventions* with established meanings under customary IHL and making explicit reference to the 'laws and customs applicable in armed conflict', the text of the *Rome Statute*'s war crimes provisions clearly supports the default position that its terms should be interpreted consistently with customary IHL in accordance with the principle of systemic integration.

The *Elements of Crimes* provides further evidence in recognition of the principle of systemic integration. Specific to the interpretation of war crimes, the 'Introduction' to the *Elements of Crimes* explicitly states that, '[T]he Elements here shall be interpreted consistently with the established framework of the international law of armed conflict'. More generally, the *Elements* were designed to function as a 'decoder' of the sometimes-archaic language in the *Statute* and to assist judges in navigating the patchwork of sources that inform its provisions.[52] As stated by Knut Dörmann, the purpose behind the *Elements of Crimes* was 'properly reflecting the state of existing law without prejudicing its future development'.[53]

The ICC's jurisdictional reach also presupposes the customary status of its substantive provisions and indicates that the drafters intended for the *Rome Statute* to be interpreted consistently with CIL. Pursuant to article 13(b) of the *Statute*, the United Nations (UN) Security Council can refer a situation to the ICC, irrespective of whether it concerns the conduct of nationals of a non-member state on the territory of a non-member state. As a rule, treaties do not bind third states[54] and the Security Council has no general legislative competence to prescribe non-customary criminal offences.[55] However, it is well understood that, 'The Security Council, in the exercise of its enforcement power to maintain or restore international peace and security, has the authority to give an international tribunal jurisdiction over what are already customary international crimes'.[56] UN Security Council

52 Grover (n 8) 291.

53 Knut Dörmann, 'Contributions by the Ad Hoc Tribunals for the Former Yugoslavia and Rwanda to the Ongoing Work on Elements of Crimes in the Context of the ICC' (2000) 94 *American Society of International Law Proceedings* 284, 284.

54 *VCLT* (n 2) art 34.

55 Kenneth Gallant, 'Jurisdiction to Adjudicate and Jurisdiction to Prescribe in International Criminal Courts' (2003) 48 *Villanova Law Review* 763, 826 (some contend that the UN Security Council may have a limited capacity to prescribe substantive law to fulfill its mandate of restoring international peace and security, but this is contested.)

56 Ibid 825.

referrals, as a matter of law, are therefore limited to the prosecution of *Rome Statute* offences with a CIL equivalent. This limitation was also reflected in the establishment of the ICTY, wherein the UN Secretary-General stated that the Tribunal's jurisdiction must be limited to crimes that were 'beyond doubt' part of CIL due to concerns over incomplete ratification of the *Geneva Conventions* for those states involved in an armed conflict at the relevant time.[57]

The fact that article 13(b) permits the UN Security Council to refer a situation to the ICC, with no apparent limit on the Court's subject-matter jurisdiction, suggests that the drafters considered the crimes in the *Rome Statute* as constitutive of CIL. By the same token, one can also infer an expectation that the definition of crimes would be interpreted consistently with CIL to ensure that *Rome Statute* law continues to align with CIL.

Moreover, if the relevant provision of the *Rome Statute* lacks customary status, the prosecution of nationals of a non-member state for alleged conduct on the territory of a non-member would violate the principle of legality. Article 22(1) of the *Statute* states that, 'A person shall not be criminally responsible under this Statute unless the conduct in question constitutes, at the time it takes place, a crime within the jurisdiction of the Court'. If the provision is non-customary, it is not a 'crime' at the time it takes place, as there is no applicable law criminalising it.[58] Once again, the ICC's jurisdictional reach by way of UN Security Council referral thus presupposes the customary status of the crimes in the *Rome Statute*, as the drafters would not have intended to violate the principle of legality.[59] The ICC Appeals Chamber reached the same conclusion in the 2021 jurisdictional appeal in *Prosecutor v Ali Kushayb*, wherein the Court held that the customary status of the crimes in the *Rome Statute* was sufficient to respect the principle of legality, contrary to the submission of the defence.[60]

---

57 United Nations, *Report of the Secretary-General Pursuant to Paragraph 2 of Security Council Resolution 808 (1993)*, UN Doc S/25704 (3 May 1993) 9 para 34 (*Secretary-General Report on Establishing the ICTY*).

58 Gallant (n 55) 839.

59 Bruce Broomhall, 'Article 22' in Otto Triffterer (ed), *Commentary on the Rome Statute of the International Criminal Court – Observers' Notes* (2nd edn, Beck-Hart 2008) 713, 720.

60 *Prosecutor v Ali Muhammad Ali Abd-Alrahman (Ali Kushayb) (Appeal of Mr Abd-Al-Rahman against the Pre-Trial Chamber II's 'Decision on the Defence "Exception d'incompétence" (ICC-02/05-01/20-302)')* (International Criminal Court, Appeals Chamber, Case No ICC-02/05-01/20 OA8, 1 November 2021) [88]–[90] (*Ali Kushayb Jurisdictional Appeal*).

The ICC's jurisdictional reach under article 13(b) therefore mandates that the ICC interpret the definition of crimes consistently with CIL to avoid creating two sets of laws: (I) ICC law that has deviated from CIL and is therefore only applicable to member states; and (II) general ICL that is consistent with CIL and can be applied to non-member states by way of UN Security Council referral.[61]

The drafting history, text, and jurisdictional reach of the *Rome Statute* support the conclusion that the principle of systemic integration applies to its interpretation. There is no evidence of a legislative intent to deviate from CIL. On the contrary, the drafters intended for the definition of crimes – and for war crimes, in particular – to reflect and be interpreted consistently with CIL.

Applying the principle of systemic integration to the interpretation of the *Rome Statute* has several important consequences. First, it promotes consistency in judicial reasoning, as CIL provides an objective benchmark against which the Court can ground its interpretation of the scope of an offence. Second, it promotes unity in ICL and prevents unnecessary fragmentation, as the standards applicable under CIL will apply equally to the definition of crimes in the *Rome Statute*. As stated by Leila Sadat and Jarrod Jolly:

> The ICC should see itself as the permanent embodiment of the CIL principles established in and by the ad hoc international tribunals except insofar as the Statute clearly directs it in a different direction. This will ensure the universality of the ICC Statute [...] enhance its legitimacy, and help to strengthen and consolidate rather than fragment the application of international criminal law.[62]

Third, interpretations consistent with CIL allow for the incremental development of the law. CIL is an inherently evolutive concept that adapts to

61 Leila Sadat and Jarrod Jolly, 'Seven Canons of ICC Treaty Interpretation: Making Sense of Article 25's Rorschach Blot' (2014) 27(3) *Leiden Journal of International Law* 755, 770; Talita de Souza Dias, 'The Retroactive Application of the Rome Statute in Cases of Security Council Referrals and Ad hoc Declarations: An Appraisal of the Existing Solutions to an Under-discussed Problem' (2018) 16(1) *Journal of International Criminal Justice* 65; Alexandre Galand, 'The Nature of the Rome Statute of the International Criminal Court (and its Amended Jurisdictional Scheme)' (2019) 17(5) *Journal of International Criminal Justice* 933.

62 Sadat and Jolly (n 61) 770. See also Fausto Pocar, 'International Criminal Justice and the Unifying Role of Customary Law' (2016) 21(2–3) *Uniform Law Review* 171.

reflect the contemporary practice and legal opinions of states. Providing that the interpretation remains consistent with the ordinary meaning of the terms, seeking consistency with contemporary CIL will equally allow the *Rome Statute* to adapt to changing circumstances. This approach is consistent with the default position in international law that legal concepts continue to evolve, and treaty terms must be interpreted accordingly.[63] The following two sections examine the possible reasons behind the ICC's reluctance to apply the principle of systemic integration and offer solutions for incorporating the principle alongside the other applicable rules of interpretation.

2.4 Harmonising the *Elements of Crimes* with Article 31(3)(c) of the *VCLT*

The primary reason for the ICC's reluctance to apply the principle of systemic integration under article 31(3)(c) of the *VCLT* appears to arise from an interpretive deference to the *Elements of Crimes*, ostensibly circumventing the need to ascertain the definition and scope of an offence under CIL (see Chapter 4). This trend is likely to be motivated, at least in part, by efficiency, as the *Element of Crimes* were designed to assist judges in navigating the tangled web of CIL sources by providing a 'shortcut' to the core content of the relevant rule. However, in many cases, this interpretive deference to the *Elements of Crimes* appears to derive from the misconception that the *Elements* are legally binding or, in any case, carry greater authority than CIL when interpreting the definition of crimes.

---

63 Rosalyn Higgins, 'Some Observations on the Inter-Temporal Rule in International Law' in Jerzy Makarczyk (ed), *Theory of International Law at the Threshold of the 21st Century – Essays in Honour of Krysztof Skubiszewski* (Brill 1997) 173; Rosalyn Higgins, 'Time and the Law: International Perspectives on an Old Problem' (1997) 46 *International and Comparative Law Quarterly* 501, 515–9; Joost Pauwelyn, *Conflict of Norms in Public International Law: How WTO Law Relates to Other Rules of International Law* (CUP 2003) 264–65; Phillip Jessup, 'The Palmas Island Arbitration' (1928) 22 *American Journal of International Law* 739; Hugh Thirlway, 'The Law and Procedure of the International Court of Justice, 1960–1989, Part Two' (1990) 61 *British Yearbook of International Law* 10, 135; Institut de Droit International, 'The Intertemporal Problem in Public International Law' (1975) 56(1) *Annuaire de l'Institut de Droit International* 536; Nancy Kontou, *The Termination and Revision of Treaties in the Light of New CIL* (OUP 1994); International Law Commission, *Fragmentation of International Law Study* (n 24) para 22.

The source of this misconception is the 'applicable law' section in article 21(1) of the *Rome Statute*, which is 'notorious for giving rise to some ambiguity on the non-binding nature of the Elements of Crimes'.[64] Article 21(1) reads as follows:

1. The Court shall apply:
   (a) In the first place, this Statute, Elements of Crimes and its Rules of Procedure and Evidence;
   (b) In the second place, where appropriate, applicable treaties and the principles and rules of international law, including the established principles of the international law of armed conflict;
   (c) Failing that, general principles of law derived by the Court from national laws of legal systems of the world including, as appropriate, the national laws of States that would normally exercise jurisdiction over the crime, provided that those principles are not inconsistent with this Statute and with international law and internationally recognized norms and standards.[65]

The direction that the Court 'shall apply' the *Elements of Crimes* 'in the first place' would appear to render them both binding on the judges and superior to CIL in the interpretation of the *Rome Statute*, thereby rebutting the principle of systemic integration. However, to understand why this is not the case, it is necessary to look to other provisions of the *Rome Statute* that confirm the non-binding nature of the *Elements of Crimes* and to distinguish between the concepts of 'application' of the applicable law (to which article 21 applies) and 'interpretation' of the applicable law (to which the *VCLT* and the principle of systemic integration apply).

---

64 Grover (n 8) 288.

65 It should be noted that article 21(3) of the *Rome Statute* states: 'The application and interpretation of law pursuant to this article must be consistent with internationally recognized human rights'. At first glance, this would appear to superimpose interpretive consistency with IHRL when interpreting the definition of crimes. However, such an approach would contradict the *lex specialis* of IHL in the interpretation of war crimes and likely broaden criminal responsibility of certain crimes to the detriment of the accused. This book adopts the position (consistent with the writings of Grover (n 8) 132 and others) that article 21(3) relates to *procedural* consistency with IHRL not *substantive* consistency. This also appears to be the approach adopted in the ICC's case law: *Prosecutor v Thomas Lubanga Dyilo* (*Appeal of the Prosecutor against the decision of Trial Chamber I entitled 'Decision on the release of Thomas Lubanga Dyilo'*) (International Criminal Court, Appeals Chamber, Case No ICC-01/04-01/06 OA 12, 21 October 2008) [12] (*Prosecutor v Thomas Lubanga Dyilo*); *Bemba Trial Judgment* (n 9) [36].

2.4.1 *The Non-binding Nature of the Elements of Crimes*

The *Elements of Crimes* provides the *actus reus* (physical elements) and *mens rea* (mental elements) for each crime in the *Rome Statute*. Article 21(1)(a) of the *Statute* states that 'the Court *shall apply*, in the first place, the Statute and Elements of Crimes'.[66] In contrast, article 9(3) of the *Statute* provides that the *Elements of Crimes* is a non-binding document that '*shall assist*' judges in the interpretation and application of the *Statute*.[67] The *Elements of Crimes* was never intended to legislate and, as a subsequent and non-binding agreement between the parties adopted on a two-thirds majority, it does not have the authority to legislate. Its role is therefore limited to that of interpretive guidance. As stated by Otto Triffterer, 'This wording "shall apply" means no more than "has to consider", because the norm to be applied [i.e., the *Elements of Crimes*] does not express more, and does not want to be more, than a guideline'.[68]

The drafting history confirms that the *Elements of Crimes* are non-binding and that they were not intended to replace reliance on CIL in the interpretation of the *Rome Statute*. Some feared at the time that the internal structure of the *Statute* and *Elements* had restricted judges to a 'mechanical application of the law' that would stifle future development at a time when ICL as a body of law had only recently evolved from 'infancy' to 'adolescence'.[69] Others expressed concern that the *Statute* had 'frozen customary definitions in a process of rapid evolution'.[70] However, the drafting history clearly demonstrates that the *Elements* were designed to assist judges in 'decoding' CIL without overriding the ordinary interpretive process in accordance with the *VCLT*.[71]

The United States had proposed that the elements of each crime be included in the *Statute*, which would have given them binding force. This proposal was rejected. As stated by Grover:

---

66 *Rome Statute of the International Criminal Court* (n 4) (emphasis added).

67 *Elements of Crimes* (n 6) (emphasis added).

68 Otto Triffterer, 'Can The "Elements of Crimes" Narrow or Broaden Responsibility for Criminal Behaviour Defined in the Rome Statute?', *The Emerging Practice of the International Criminal Court* (Brill Nijhoff, 2009) 381, 388.

69 Hunt (n 12); Cassese (n 18) 17.

70 Alain Pellet, 'Applicable Law' in Antonio Cassese (ed), *The Rome Statute of the International Criminal Court: A Commentary* (OUP 2002) 1056.

71 Herman von Hebel and Darryl Robinson, 'Reflections on the Elements of Crimes' in Roy S Lee (ed), *The International Criminal Court: The Making of the Rome Statute* (Kluwer Law International 1999) 219, 224–5.

> The majority argued inter alia that drafting such elements was not necessary because the definitions in the Draft Statute were sufficiently precise to respect the principle of legality, the general principles of criminal law adequately covered the subject matter and such a text would unduly bind the judges, who are best situated to discern such elements.[72]

While states subsequently agreed to draft what became the *Elements of Crimes*, it was conditional upon the inclusion of article 9 in the *Statute*, which states that they 'shall assist judges in the interpretation and application of article 6, 7, 8 and 8*bis*' (that is, the Court's subject-matter jurisdiction). States insisted that the *Elements of Crimes* were to be non-binding so as not to interfere with the ordinary process of interpreting international criminal statutes, which includes reliance on applicable sources of international law.

In a similar vein, France proposed including an official commentary to the *Elements* that would have included references to the relevant case law identified by the International Committee of the Red Cross (ICRC).[73] While this idea received some support, it was ultimately rejected due to, *inter alia,* 'concern that such commentaries would inadvertently freeze interpretations and principles of law in time'.[74] States were aware that the *Elements* would provide a snapshot of CIL as it existed in 1998 and were keen to emphasise that it should not unduly hinder the ability of the Court to make reference to developments in CIL. As stated by Dörmann, who led the ICRC in assisting the Preparatory Commission's drafting of the *Elements* by conducting a study of the relevant case law, the drafters' objective was 'properly reflecting the state of existing law without prejudicing its future development'.[75] That the *Elements* were designed to assist judges in ascertaining CIL without replacing it is explicitly confirmed with respect to war crimes. The 'Introduction' to article 8 states that 'the elements for war crimes shall be interpreted … within the established framework of the international law of armed conflict'.[76] It is therefore incorrect to interpret the *Elements of Crimes*

72 Grover (n 8) 312.

73 Valerie Oosterveld, 'The Elements of Genocide' in Roy S Lee (ed), *The International Criminal Court: Elements of Crimes and Rules of Procedure and Evidence* (Transnational 2001) 41, 43.

74 Ibid.

75 Dörmann, 'Contributions by the Ad Hoc Tribunals' (n 53) 284.

76 *Elements of Crimes* (n 6) 13 (emphasis added).

as foreclosing the need to rely on CIL in the interpretation of the *Rome Statute*.

The decisions to make the *Elements* non-binding and to avoid including an official commentary were significant. At the time of drafting, much of the case law relied upon in the *Elements* was subject to appeal. Daryl Mundis notes that only four out of the 10 ICTY Trial Chamber Judgements listed in the table of cases informing the *Elements of Crimes* had the benefit of an appellate decision.[77] There are several examples where the definition of crimes in the *Elements of Crimes* has misrepresented, or been overtaken by developments in, CIL, both of which lead to the critical question of whether the *Elements of Crimes* or an interpretation consistent with CIL should take precedence in cases of conflict.

2.4.2 *Article 21(1) of the* Rome Statute: *Distinguishing between the 'Application' and 'Interpretation' of the Applicable Law*

The direction in article 21(1) to apply the *Rome Statute* and *Elements of Crimes* 'in the first place' and to apply applicable treaties and CIL 'in the second place' might appear to relegate the interpretive authority of CIL behind that of the *Elements of Crimes*. While this appears to have been the approach taken in a 2009 decision by Pre-Trial Chamber I,[78] subsequent decisions have confirmed that this is not the case.

The 2013 decision of Trial Chamber V(A) in *Ruto* stated that there is 'no conflict' between the principle of systemic integration in article 31(3)(c) of the *VCLT* and article 21(1) of the *Rome Statute*, and noted that rules governing the interpretation of the *Statute* are separate to those governing the applicable law.[79] In 2014, Trial Chamber II in *Katanga* held that the Court is permitted, wherever necessary, 'to draw on customary law in the course of systemic interpretation'.[80] Similarly, the 2016 decision of Trial Chamber III in *Bemba* emphasised that CIL can be used both as a secondary source of law to fill gaps in the *Statute* (i.e., a direct 'application' regulated by article 21(1)) *or* in the interpretation of the *Statute* in accordance with the principle of systemic integration. The hierarchy of laws in article 21(1) of the *Rome*

---

77 Daryl Mundis, 'Elements of War Crimes under the Rome Statute of the International Criminal Court, Sources and Commentary' (2004) 2(3) *Journal of International Criminal Justice* 929, 931.

78 *Al Bashir Arrest Warrant* (n 16).

79 *Decision on Mr Ruto's Request for Excusal* (n 39) [101]–[102].

80 *Katanga Trial Judgment* (n 1) [1395] n 1394.

Statute does not equate to a hierarchy of interpretive aids and does not, therefore, rebut the principle of systemic integration.

However, closer analysis of the ICC's jurisprudence reveals a tendency for the Court to resort to CIL (or to external sources of law more generally) only where the *Elements of Crimes* has not provided its own definition (see Chapter 4). Where the *Elements of Crimes* has provided a definition, irrespective of whether it is consistent or wholly representative of CIL, the Court has tended to take it at face value. This approach is contrary to the drafting history of the *Elements of Crimes*, the 'Introduction' to the war crimes section of the *Elements of Crimes*, and the principle of systemic integration, all of which stipulate that the *Elements* should be given an interpretation that is consistent with CIL.

2.4.3 *Custom versus the* Elements of Crimes *in Cases of Interpretive Conflict*

The conclusion that the *Elements of Crimes* should be interpreted consistently with CIL does not resolve the issue of which interpretive aid should take precedence where there is an irreconcilable conflict between the two. There are legitimate arguments on both sides of this issue.

Pursuant to her conclusion that the *Rome Statute* was intended to reflect CIL, Grover argues that interpretive consistency with CIL should take precedence over consistency with the *Elements of Crimes* in cases of conflict.[81] The thrust of Grover's argument relies on the fact that article 9(3) of the *Statute* requires that 'The Elements of Crimes and amendments thereto shall be consistent with this Statute'. Accordingly, if the *Statute* is intended to reflect custom but the *Elements of Crimes* contradicts custom, then the *Elements* are not consistent with the *Statute* and must be overruled.[82] This interpretation reflects the intention of the drafters for the *Elements of Crimes* to guide the judges without prejudicing the progressive development of the law and their decision not to include an official commentary or make the *Elements* legally binding. It also reflects the intention to limit the crimes in the *Statute* to those existing under CIL and not to legislate new crimes,[83] which would be the indirect consequence of preferencing the *Elements* over custom in cases of conflict.

It is, therefore, reasonable to argue that an interpretation consistent with CIL should take precedence over the *Elements of Crimes* in cases of

81 Grover (n 8) 363.

82 Ibid.

83 Ibid 288, 291, 312.

irreconcilable conflict. Because the *Elements of Crimes* are non-binding, it has been argued that overruling them in favour of an alternative interpretation does not violate the principle of legality. As stated by Triffterer:

> The Court is independent and may, therefore, freely select Elements to be accepted or refused. The application or non-application of Elements does therefore not fall under the guarantees of the rule of law and can only in limited circumstances be the object of an appeal.[84]

Practically speaking, however, it is difficult to envision a judge overruling an element of an offence contained within the *Elements of Crimes* where it would broaden the criminal responsibility of the accused.[85] While it could be argued that the discretionary status of the *Elements* in article 9(1) puts potential defendants 'on notice' that the elements of the offences in the *Rome Statute* may be substituted for those under CIL, this does not sit well with the *Statute*'s overriding objective to embody domestic criminal law standards of legality and legal certainty, including the principle of *lex scripta* (written law).[86] The *Elements of Crimes* represents the will of the majority of the Assembly of States Parties and is clearly documented for the benefit of judges, lawyers, and potential defendants. When compared with the inherently vague and indeterminate nature of CIL, a judge is unlikely to favour CIL over the *Elements* where an individual's liberty is at stake, even though they may be legally entitled to do so.

However, the fact that the *Elements of Crimes* is non-binding, and that its observance is not strictly required by the principle of legality, lends further

84 Triffterer (n 68) 388. See also Robert Cryer, 'Royalism and the King: Article 21 of the Rome Statute and the Politics of Sources' (2009) 12(3) *New Criminal Law Review: An International and Interdisciplinary Journal* 390, 403 ('With respect, the nullum crimen quite clearly does not bear the weight the majority [of Pre-Trial Chamber I in Al-Bashir] seek to put on it. That principle requires that a court not hold someone responsible for conduct that was not criminal at the time of its commission. It does not require that the chamber take the Elements as being more than they are.'); *Al Bashir Arrest Warrant* (n 16) Separate and Partly Dissenting Opinion of Judge Ušacka [17].

85 Margaret DeGuzman, 'Article 21, Applicable Law' in Otto Triffterer and Kai Ambros (eds), *The Rome Statute of the International Criminal Court: A Commentary* (3rd edn, Beck 2016) 933, 938–39.

86 This is not to say that the principle of legality *requires* consistency with the *Elements of Crimes*, as previously pointed out: see Grover (n 8) 289. Rather, practically speaking, judges are more likely to preference the *Elements* over custom in cases of conflict when interpreting the *Statute* and cite the principle of legality in support, as was the approach of the *Bemba* Trial Chamber: *Bemba Trial Judgment* (n 9) [68].

weight to the argument that the *Elements* should be interpreted consistently with CIL, even where this involves additional elements that are not explicitly included in the text. In other words, interpreting the *Elements* consistently with CIL (unlike the interpretation of the *Statute*) is not bound by the principle of strict construction and can therefore be approached more liberally by the Court. This approach is consistent with the suggestion of one ICC judge who, when asked whether they would preference CIL or the *Elements of Crimes* in cases of interpretive conflict, stated that the best course of action would be to interpret the *Elements* consistently with CIL to the greatest possible extent.[87]

Notwithstanding the conclusion that the *Elements* will likely prevail in cases of direct interpretive conflict with CIL, the situation may be different for the interpretation of war crimes in articles 8(2)(b) and 8(2)(e). The *chapeaux* to these provisions define the crimes contained therein as 'other serious violations of the laws and customs applicable in [...] armed conflict, within the established framework of international law'. The Appeals Chamber in *Ntaganda* and *Lubanga* construed this explicit reference to customary IHL in the *Statute* as an obligation to interpret the relevant provisions consistently with customary IHL, even if this means imposing additional elements.[88] Given that this interpretive consistency with custom is obligatory, whereas the *Elements* are discretionary, it would seem reasonable to conclude that customary IHL takes precedence over the *Elements* when interpreting war crimes in articles 8(2)(b) and (e) of the *Statute*. This conclusion is strengthened by the fact that, in such circumstances, the *Elements* would be inconsistent with the *Statute* itself and must therefore be overruled in accordance with article 9(3).[89]

---

87 Interviews conducted with ICC judges in November 2018.

88 *Prosecutor v Thomas Lubanga Dyilo (Judgment)* (International Criminal Court, Appeals Chamber, Case No ICC-01/04-01/06 A5, 1 December 2014) [322] (*Lubanga Appeals Judgement*); *Prosecutor v Bosco Ntaganda (Judgement on the appeal of Mr Ntaganda against the Second decision on the Defence's challenge to the jurisdiction of the Court in respect of Counts 6 and 9)* (International Criminal Court, Appeals Chamber, Case No ICC-01/04-02/06 OA5, 15 June 2017) [52]–[53] (*Appeals Chamber's Second Decision on Mr Ntaganda's Jurisdictional Appeal*); *Prosecutor v Bosco Ntaganda (Judgment)* (International Criminal Court, Appeals Chamber, Case No ICC-01/04-02/06 A A2, 30 March 2021) [564] (*Ntagnanda Appeals Judgment*).

89 Triffterer (n 68) 388. Triffterer warns that 'special care' should be taken when preferring the *Elements of Crimes* over CIL: 'Such "narrowing elements" may be desirable in the interest of the rule of law to limit unjustified investigation, prosecution and

So far, however, this approach has not been adopted. Indeed, in one notable case where the Court identified a direct inconsistency between the *Elements* and the corresponding definition under customary IHL, the *Elements* took precedence.[90] No mention was made of the direction in article 8 of the *Elements* to interpret war crimes consistently with customary IHL, nor the explicit obligation in the *chapeaux* to interpret the offences in article 8(2)(b) and (e) in accordance with the established framework of the international law of armed conflict.

In sum, the definition of an offence in the *Elements of Crimes* should be harmonised with the definition provided under CIL. Where there is an irreconcilable conflict between the two, it may be that the *Elements* must prevail to ensure fairness to the accused, which will result in a fragmentation of ICL. In this scenario, it is still incumbent upon the Court to articulate the definition and scope of the offence under CIL so that it may highlight the discrepancy and give the Assembly of States Parties the opportunity to update the *Elements of Crimes*, should they choose to do so. For war crimes under article 8(2)(b) and 8(2)(e), the *Elements* may ultimately yield to customary IHL due to the explicit reference to the 'laws and customs of war [...] within the established framework of international law', but this is not yet reflected in ICC jurisprudence.

2.5 Harmonising the Rules of Strict Construction in Article 22(2) of the *Rome Statute* with Article 31 of the *Vienna Convention*

Another likely reason the ICC has resisted the principle of systemic integration under article 31(3)(c), along with other obligatory rules in the *VCLT*, is the codification of strict construction in article 22(2) of the *Rome Statute*. Article 22(2) provides a 'robust' codification of the principle of legality and divides its concomitant rules of strict construction into three discernible obligations: (I) the definitions of crimes must be strictly construed; (II) the definitions of crimes cannot be extended by analogy; and (III) ambiguity must be interpreted in favour of the accused. While these rules of strict construction warrant a more conservative approach and may limit the application of the *VCLT* in certain contexts, they do not detract from the obligation

sentencing. But they may, at the same time, support impunity for crimes within the jurisdiction of the Court. This is not (always) "in the interest of justice".'

90 *Bemba Trial Judgment* (n 9) [120].

to interpret the definitions of crimes in the *Rome Statute* consistently with CIL under the principle of systemic integration or preclude the general applicability of the *VCLT*.

It should be noted at the outset that the principle of strict construction is not an exact science. Due to the inherently indeterminate nature of language, 'No set of words, devised by either legislators or judges, will place a clearly and completely defined set of possible acts within the definition of a crime while clearly defining all other acts to be outside the definition'.[91] Accordingly, while ICC judges must comply with the obligation to give words their ordinary meaning and are precluded from extending the definition of crimes by analogy, the principle of strict construction does not prevent judges from using ordinary tools of interpretation to determine whether the conduct reasonably falls within the meaning of a provision.

2.5.1 *Textualism*

The preeminent rule of strict construction is that the words of the relevant statute or treaty must be interpreted in accordance with their literal meaning. Often referred to as textualism or literalism, this principle ensures that the use of judicial interpretive devices does not arrive at a conclusion unsupported by the language of the text itself.[92] Textualism is consistent with article 31(1) of the *VCLT*, which states that, 'A treaty shall be interpreted in good faith in accordance with the ordinary meaning to be given to the terms of the treaty'.[93] In the context of interpreting criminal statutes, textualism serves as a corollary of the principle of fair warning in the sense that an individual knows that they will only be found liable for conduct that falls reasonably within the ordinary meaning of the words of the relevant prohibition.[94] The obligation to strictly construe the *Rome Statute* has been recognised by ICC Chambers to 'give the relevant terms their plain meaning'[95] and 'to apply the language in the Statute in as natural a manner as possible'.[96]

91 Kenneth Gallant, 'Legality in Criminal Law, Its Purposes, and Its Competitors' in Kenneth Gallant (ed), *The Principle of Legality in International and Comparative Criminal Law* (CUP 2008) 11, 31–32.

92 *Bemba Trial Judgment* (n 9) [79].

93 *VCLT* (n 2).

94 Grover (n 8) 104; Cassese, *International Criminal Law* (n 18) 48.

95 *Lubanga Trial Judgment* (n 41) Separate Opinion of Judge Fulford [6]–[18].

96 *Prosecutor v Mathieu Ngudjolo Chui (Judgement)* (International Criminal Court, Trial Chamber II, Case No ICC-01/04-02/12, 18 December 2012) [70] (*Ngudjolo Chui Trial Chamber Judgement*).

It is conceivable that some would view textualism as precluding reliance on CIL in the interpretation of treaties, particularly where the definition and scope of a term under CIL has evolved over time and provides greater detail than the ordinary meaning of the relevant words. However, it is important to note that textualism does not replace the other rules of interpretation; it simply prohibits any interpretation that would contradict the ordinary meaning of the text.[97] Furthermore, treaties may also defer to the technical meaning of words under CIL by using terms with a pre-existing meaning under CIL. In these situations, the CIL meaning trumps the ordinary meaning. In other situations, the drafters may defer to the bench to resolve disputes regarding the precise meaning and scope of a treaty's terms. This judicial deference is usually achieved by adopting deliberately open-textured language,[98] non-exhaustive lists,[99] express reference to CIL, or the existence of gaps, intentional or otherwise, that must be filled to avoid situations of *non liquet* (no applicable law).[100] As stated by Tom Ginsburg, this process 'serves an interest of the parties in reducing transaction costs of negotiation the details of a treaty … [w]hen states are unsure about the precise type of issues that will arise … they will implicitly empower the tribunal to resolve disputes and clarify conventions'.[101] Commenting specifically on the ICC context, Caroline Davidson argues that:

> Where states agreed to a compromise definition in the Rome Statute that was intentionally ambiguous, as in the case of gender, they were on notice that the court might land on an interpretation that differed from their own by consulting other sources of law and using standard tools of interpretation, such as those set out in the Vienna Convention.[102]

Jared Wessel has similarly noted that 'some delegates to the ICC's Preparatory Commission argued that problems arising from ambiguity in the treaty

97 *Katanga Trial Judgment* (n 1) [56].

98 Grover (n 8) 129.

99 *Rome Statute of the International Criminal Court* (n 4).

100 Allison Marston Danner, 'When Court Make Law: How the International Criminal Tribunals Recast the Laws of War' (2006) 59(1) *Vanderbilt Law Review* 1, 4–5.

101 Tom Ginsburg, 'Bounded Discretion in International Judicial Lawmaking' (2005) 45 *Virginia Journal of International Law* 631, 644.

102 Caroline Davidson, 'How to Read International Criminal Law: Strict Construction and the Rome Statute of the International Criminal Court' (2017) 91(1) *St John's Law Review* 37, 89.

would be naturally addressed by the bench',[103] while William Lietzau has observed that 'many delegations sought open-ended elements in order to expand the discretion of the Court ... these states envisioned a Court that would not only adjudicate criminal cases, but also could define the law and thus foster its evolution'.[104]

There are several instances where it is not possible to rely solely on textualism because the *Rome Statute* expresses an intention import CIL to fill gaps or determine the content of an offence. For example, article 7 prohibits as a crime against humanity the deprivation of liberty 'in violation of fundamental rules of international law',[105] which defers to judges to determine what constitutes 'fundamental rules of international law'. The same is true for persecution as a crime against humanity that is committed on 'other grounds that are universally recognised as impermissible under international law',[106] and the codification of '[o]ther inhumane acts of a similar character' as a standalone crime against humanity.[107] Specific to war crimes, article 8(2)(c)(iv) prohibits the passing a criminal sentence without affording all judicial guarantees 'generally recognized as indispensable',[108] and article 8(2)(e)(VI) criminalises 'other forms of sexual violence'.[109]

Each of these examples not only leaves it to judges to refer to CIL for the *interpretation* of an offence in accordance with article 31(3)(c), but also directs judges to identify the actual offence under CIL. In short, the examples amount to a gap in the *Rome Statute* that must be addressed using CIL in accordance with article 21(1)(b) of the *Statute*, which states that the Court shall apply '[i]n the second place, where appropriate, applicable treaties and the principles and rules of international law'. The rule of textualism will not help the judge in determining what constitutes 'judicial guarantees generally recognized as indispensable'; rather, it must be determined by direct reliance on CIL.

The approach is slightly different where the *Rome Statute* uses terms with a distinct but evolving meaning under CIL. For example, in the context of

103 Jared Wessel, 'Judicial Policy-Making at the International Criminal Court: An Institutional Guide to Analyzing International Adjudication' (2006) 44 *Columbia Journal of Transnational Law* 377, 386, 413–4.

104 William Lietzau, 'Checks and Balances and Elements of Proof: Structural Pillars for the International Criminal Court' (1999) 32 *Cornell International Law Journal* 477, 482.

105 *Rome Statute of the International Criminal Court* (n 4) art 7(e).

106 Ibid art 7(h).

107 Ibid art 7(k).

108 Ibid art 8(2)(c)(iv).

109 Ibid art 8(2)(e)(vi).

the ICC's war crimes jurisdiction, terms such as 'armed conflict', 'protected persons', 'attack', and 'military necessity' will benefit only marginally from an analysis of their ordinary meaning, as it is their technical definition and scope under CIL that is instructive.[110] The ICC has confirmed that 'the Statute itself, in many of its provisions, entrusts the judges with the judicial task of identifying, in other primary or even secondary sources of law, the required elements for the definition of a specific conduct'.[111]

In short, the rule of textualism in article 22(2) of the *Rome Statute* operates in harmony with the principle of systemic integration under article 31(3)(c) of the *VCLT*. Although textualism will ordinarily limit interpretations gleaned from CIL in accordance with the literal meaning of the words, there are certain situations where the drafters have expressed an intent for the judges to apply CIL directly.

2.5.2 *The Prohibition on Analogy*

Another possible reason for the ICC's reluctance to apply the principle of systemic integration in article 31(3)(c) is the prohibition on analogy in article 22(2) of the *Rome Statute*, which states that the definition of crimes 'shall not be extended by analogy'. Interpreting the meaning of an offence by reference to its definition and scope under CIL and determining whether the impugned conduct falls within that definition, especially where CIL has evolved, will invariably involve some degree of analogous reasoning. Given that analogy is an ordinary and essential tool of judicial reasoning, it is necessary to distinguish between the type of analogy prohibited under article 22(2) and that which is permitted.

Susan Lamb convincingly argues that 'the use of analogy as a tool of law-making is prohibited by Article 22(2) but analogy as a tool of interpretation is not prohibited',[112] meaning that judges are only precluded from using analogy to create a 'substantially new crime'.[113] As stated by ICC Trial Chamber III in *Prosecutor v Bemba*:

---

110 Lietzau (n 104) 483–4.

111 *Bemba Trial Judgment* (n 9) 85. See also *Katanga Trial Judgment* (n 1) [48] ('This is the case, for example, for war crimes under articles 8(2)(a) and 8(2)(b) of the Statute, which refer verbatim to the Geneva Conventions and "the established framework of international law".').

112 Susan Lamb, 'Nullum crimen, nulla poena sine lege in International Criminal Law' in Antonio Cassese (ed), *The Rome Statute of the International Criminal Court: A Commentary* (OUP 2002), 752–53.

113 *Okçuoglu v Turkey* [1999] Application Nos 24246/94 and 24408/94, Eur Court HR (Grand Chamber), [39] (*Okçuoglu v Turkey*).

> [I]t needs to be stressed that the bar on the use of analogy does not prevent the Chamber from resorting to other sources of law whenever necessary to determine the precise content of the definition of a specific criminal conduct.[114]

The types of interpretive analogy that are *not* prohibited by article 22(2) include logical analogy (i.e., 'to bring the facts of a case within the scope of a treaty or unwritten criminal prohibition by reasoning that they are sufficiently similar to the facts of a case previously held to be covered by the relevant law');[115] interpreting judicial precedent by analogy ('so as to build consistency, certainty and predictability in the Court's interpretation of crimes');[116] and contextual reasoning (interpreting provisions in light of their specific context, which includes relevant rules of general international law).[117] Accordingly, interpretive analogy is a 'valid and . . . necessary tool . . . [that] does not extend to law-making, but is restricted to interpretation. It can thus be used to fill gaps in legislated definitions'.[118]

The point at which analogy and other judicial interpretive techniques cross the line into judicial law-making is not always clear,[119] especially where a judge interprets an offence by reference to developments in the law. When applied, the principle of systemic integration mandates that the definition of crimes be interpreted consistently with contemporary CIL. Be that as it may, it is necessary for judges to determine the limits of an interpretive method so that 'the process of treaty interpretation does not replace the applicable law'.[120] One approach to determining whether the judicial development of the law amounts to law creation in violation of the principle of legality is the 'essence of the offence' test, developed by the ECtHR.

The 'essence of the offence' test has been used by the ECtHR in relation to domestic criminal law cases to demonstrate that judicial developments of the law do not violate the principle of legality, provided those developments fall within the scope of the original offence and are foreseeable to the defendant. The ICTY has used a very similar test. While the general lines of inquiry within the 'essence of the offence' test apply to the interpretation

114 *Bemba Trial Judgment* (n 9) [83].

115 Grover (n 8) 219.

116 Ibid.

117 Ibid; Davidson (n 102) 68.

118 Broomhall (n 59) 725. See also *Bemba Trial Judgment* (n 9) 83.

119 Damiano Canale and Giovanni Tuzet, 'Analogical Reasoning and Extensive Interpretation' (2017) 103(1) *Archives for Philosophy of Law and Social Philosophy* 117, 124–6.

120 *Bemba Trial Judgment* (n 9) 79.

of the *Rome Statute*, the way the test has been formulated by the ECtHR has been argued to be 'too malleable' for the ICC context and inconsistent with the prohibition on analogy, thus necessitating a more restrictive approach.

In a landmark case before the ECtHR in 1995, an English man appealed his conviction for rape on the basis that, at the time of the alleged conduct, English common law recognised an implied consent to sex within marriage and the defence of marital immunity from allegations of rape.[121] The United Kingdom Court of Criminal Appeal had held that 'the time has now arrived when the law should declare that a rapist remains a rapist subject to the criminal law, irrespective of his relationship with his victim'.[122] At the time, no statutory amendment had been undertaken to formally remove the defence of marital immunity.[123] Accordingly, the applicant claimed that his conviction by the House of Lords violated the principle of legality and appealed to the ECtHR.

The ECtHR held that the principle of legality is not offended 'provided that the resultant development is consistent with the essence of the offence and could reasonably be foreseen', noting that, 'However clearly drafted a legal provision may be in any system of law including criminal law, there is an inevitable element of judicial interpretation. There will always be a need for elucidation of doubtful points and for adaptation to changing circumstances'.[124] The ECtHR reaffirmed the test more recently in *K.-H.W. v Germany*, this time concerning alleged violations of IHL and crimes against humanity.[125]

The ICTY has adopted a similar test,[126] stating that, 'The emphasis on conduct, rather than on the specific description of the offence in substantive criminal law, is of primary relevance'.[127] In *Prosecutor v Ojdanić*, the

---

121 *CR v United Kingdom* [1995] Application Nos 20190/92 and A/355-C, Eur Court of HR ('*CR v United Kingdom*').

122 Ibid [119].

123 Mohamed Shahabuddeen, 'Does the Principle of Legality Stand in the Way of Progressive Development of Law?' (2004) 2(4) *Journal of International Criminal Justice* 1007, 1013–17.

124 *CR v United Kingdom* (n 121) [36].

125 *K.-H.W. v Germany* [2001] Application Nos 34044/96, 35532/97, and 44801/98, Eur Court HR (Grand Chamber), [85] (*K.-H.W. v Germany*). See also *Jorgić v Germany* [2007] Application No 74613/01, III Eur Court HR 583, [114] (*Jorgić v Germany*).

126 *Prosecutor v Stakić* (*Judgment*) (International Criminal Tribunal for the former Yugoslavia, Appeals Chamber, Case No ICTY97-24-A, 22 March 2006) [23] (*Prosecutor v Stakić*).

127 *Prosecutor v Hadžihasanović et al.* (*Decision on Joint Challenge to Jurisdiction*) (International Criminal Tribunal for the former former Yugoslavia, Appeals Chamber, Case No IT-04-84-A, 12 November 2002) [62] (*Prosecutor v Hadžihasanović et al.*).

ICTY stated that, while the principle of legality 'does not prevent a court from interpreting and clarifying the elements of a particular crime' or 'preclude the progressive development of the law', it 'does prevent a court from creating new law or from interpreting existing law beyond the reasonable limits of acceptable clarification'.[128] The ICTY held that it must be 'satisfied that the crime or the form of liability with which an accused is charged was sufficiently foreseeable and that the law providing for such liability must be sufficiently accessible', while also accounting for 'the specificity of international law'.[129]

In the ICC context, the prosecution could argue that reasonably foreseeable developments in CIL which remain within the essence of an offence under the *Rome Statute* are prosecutable without violating the principle of legality. While some scholars have advocated for its adoption,[130] others have argued that it is 'insufficiently rigorous' for the ICC's institutional context,[131] noting that the ECtHR provides a margin of appreciation to domestic courts in the interpretation of their own criminal laws that is not applicable at the ICC.[132] So far, the ICC appears to have adopted a more cautious approach. Trial Chamber II in *Katanga* reasoned that, 'The primary task of the bench in criminal cases is the application and interpretation of the law but, under no circumstances, creation of the law, since the sole purpose of the bench's interpretative activity is to impart meaning to existing law'.[133] Although the purpose of the 'essence of the offence' test is to determine what constitutes 'creation of the law', this passage suggests that the ICC will adopt a more restrictive approach to incorporating developments in the law. As stated by Grover, 'the "essence" of the offence is a concept that may well be invoked for noble reasons but is perhaps too malleable for criminal law and

128 *Prosecutor v Milutinović et al.* (*Decision on Dragoljub Ojdanić's Motion Challenging Jurisdiction - Joint Criminal Enterprise*) (International Criminal Tribunal for the former Yugoslavia, Appeals Chamber, Case No IT-99-37-AR72, 21 May 2003) [38] (*Prosecutor v Milutinović et al.*). See also *Prosecutor v Norman* (*Decision on Preliminary Motion Based on Lack of Jurisdiction*) (Special Court for Sierra Leone, Appeals Chamber, Case No SCSL-2004-14-AR72(E), 31 May 2004) [25] (*Prosecutor v Norman*).

129 *Prosecutor v Milutinović et al.* (n 128) [37].

130 Sadat and Jolly (n 61) 763; Mohamed Shahabuddeen, 'Policy-Oriented Law in the International Criminal Tribunal for the Former Yugoslavia' in Lal Chand Vohrah et al (eds), *Man's Inhumanity to Man: Essays in International Law in Honour of Antonio Cassese* (Brill 2003) 889.

131 Davidson (n 102) 84.

132 Ibid 83.

133 *Katanga Trial Judgment* (n 1) [52].

therefore at risk of being abused' and 'may also not sit well with the ban on analogous reasoning in article 22(2)'.[134]

2.5.3 *Interpreting Ambiguity in Favour of the Accused*

The final component in article 22(2)'s codification of strict construction that may have contributed to the ICC's reluctance to apply the principle of systemic integration under article 31(3)(c) – and article 31 of the *VCLT* more generally – is the obligation to interpret ambiguity in favour of the accused. Article 22(2) states: 'In case of ambiguity, the definition [of a crime] shall be interpreted in favour of the person being investigated, prosecuted or convicted'. In the criminal context, this concept is usually referred to as *in dubio pro reo* (in doubt, for the accused).[135]

Applying *in dubio pro reo* early in the interpretive sequence would be 'nonsensical',[136] as that would mean that all contentious points of law would have to be resolved in favour of the accused.[137] Accordingly, it has been confirmed in the jurisprudence of both the ICC and the ICTY that *in dubio pro reo* applies last, once the other applicable rules of interpretation in the *VCLT* have been exhausted.[138] On the other hand, it has also been argued that placing *in dubio pro reo* last makes it irrelevant due to the breadth of interpretive possibilities under the *VCLT*.[139] This has led some to claim that *in dubio pro reo* overrides the *VCLT* in the interpretation of the *Rome Statute*. Rather than excluding the operation of the *VCLT*, however, *in dubio pro reo* is better understood as imposing a limit on the application of the *VCLT* in certain contexts so as not to prejudice the accused.

Reflecting on the jurisprudence of the ICTY, Benjamin Perrin states that:

> Due to the relative exhaustiveness of international interpretive doctrines, the maxim [*in dubio pro reo*] which is a fundamental interpretive principle in many national systems was essentially eviscerated,

134 Grover (n 8) 173.

135 Robert Jennings and Arthur Watts, *Oppenheim's International Law* (9th edn, Longman Harlow 1992) 1276–81.

136 Anna Ashworth, 'Interpreting Criminal Statutes: A Crisis of Legality?' (1991) 107 *Law Quarterly Review* 419, 432, cited in Grover (n 8) 195.

137 Grover (n 8) 147.

138 *Katanga Trial Judgment* (n 1) [53].

139 Grover (n 8) 60.

demonstrating the repercussions of relying on public international law interpretive canons to resolve international criminal law issues.[140]

The ICTY's reliance on object and purpose or 'teleological' interpretations has attracted the most scholarly criticism on the basis that they can be used to justify almost any result where the object and purpose is to promote substantive justice.[141] As stated by Darryl Robinson, 'Applying, at a prior stage, a teleological approach that maximizes victim protection means that there is never an ambiguity left for strict construction to resolve, because all ambiguities have already been resolved against the accused'.[142]

In *Prosecutor v Ngudjolo*, Judge Van den Wyngaert held that object and purpose interpretations under article 31(1) of the *VCLT* are inconsistent with *in dubio pro reo* and therefore inapplicable in the ICC context. She stated that article 22(2) of the *Statute* 'overrides the conventional methods of treaty interpretation, as defined in the Vienna Convention on the Law of Treaties, particularly the teleological method' and noted that article 22(2) was included because 'the drafters wanted to make sure that the Court could not engage in the kind of "judicial creativity" of which other jurisdictions may at times have been suspected'.[143]

Judge Van de Wyngaert's rejection of object and purpose interpretations in favour of *in dubio pro reo* highlights the tension between the rules governing the interpretation of treaties and those peculiar to the construction of criminal statutes. However, as stated by ICC Trial Chamber II in *Katanga* and confirmed by Trial Chamber III in *Bemba*, the rules of interpretation in article 31 'must be applied together and simultaneously, rather than individually and in a hierarchical or chronological order'.[144] Accordingly, it is

140 Benjamin Perrin, 'Searching for Law While Seeking Justice: The Difficulties of Enforcing International Humanitarian Law in International Criminal Trials' (2007) 39 *Ottawa Law Review* 367, 385.

141 *Prosecutor v Hadžihasanović et al* (n 127) [25] (Reproducing the Defence Brief: 'The lack of a clear basis in international law for the present prosecution cannot be side-stepped by drawing upon the object and purpose of IHL, in general, and the Statute of the ICTY [....] The protection of humanity and preservation of world order as the overriding aims of IHL cannot serve as a basis to criminalise behaviour beyond the "existing law".')

142 Darryl Robinson, 'The Identity Crisis of International Criminal Law' (2008) 21(4) *Leiden Journal of International Criminal Law* 925, 934.

143 *Ngudjolo Chui Trial Chamber Judgement* (n 96) Concurring Opinion of Judge Christine Van den Wyngaert [18].

144 *Bemba Trial Judgment* (n 9) [77].

difficult to justify 'overriding' the object and purpose approach in its entirety. Instead, it is preferable to view *in dubio pro reo* as limiting the scope of object and purpose interpretations, which was the approach subsequently taken in *Katanga*.

In *Katanga*, Trial Chamber II stated that reliance on a teleological interpretation of the *Statute* to end impunity 'could be considered antithetical to the principle of legality and, more specifically, to the rule of strict construction and the principle of *in dubio pro reo*'.[145] It went on to say that it is 'self-evident' that the goal of ending impunity 'can under no circumstances be used to create a body of law extraneous to the terms of the treaty or incompatible with a purely literal reading of its text',[146] effectively reaffirming the principle of textualism. However, the *Katanga* Trial Chamber (which also included Judge Van den Wyngaert) did not reject the object and purpose of the *Statute*, but instead stated that it 'must always be borne in mind and fully considered during the interpretation of its provisions as they are one of the components which make it possible to establish its definitive meaning'.[147] The Chamber held that textualism is sufficient to prevent expansive or results-orientated judicial reasoning, concluding that, 'The Vienna Convention therefore provides for a method of interpretation which is both circumscribed and rigorous and which leaves little scope for any risk of misinterpretation of the Statute'.[148]

Academic literature has also sought to reconcile *in dubio pro reo* with object and purpose in the interpretation of the *Rome Statute*. Davidson argues that the broad aim of 'ending impunity' as a justification for expansive interpretations of ICL 'has rightly been criticised'.[149] Instead, she argues, a more accurate understanding of the *Statute*'s object and purpose is to condemn and punish persons found guilty 'through fair trials conducted in accordance with international human rights and the rule of law'.[150] Rather than rely on the often-circular logic of ending impunity, this interpretation recognises that the goal of States Parties was to ensure that alleged violations of ICL would be prosecuted fairly. Davidson argues that the references to 'justice' and 'effective prosecution' in the *Statute*'s

145 *Katanga Trial Judgment* (n 1) [54].
146 Ibid [55].
147 Ibid.
148 Ibid.
149 Davidson (n 102) 92.
150 Ibid.

preamble are properly understood as creating an institution whose primary goal is to ensure fair trials for persons accused of committing international crimes.

Grover states that the principle of strict construction operates in harmony with the other interpretive principles in the VCLT as part of the 'proper balance of the distribution of rights within a treaty system'.[151] She posits that any reference to object and purpose must be limited to that of the specific provision in light of its factual and legal context, rather than the object and purpose of the *Statute* as a whole.[152] This approach appears to have been adopted by the ICC Appeals Chamber in *Lubanga*. In that case, the Court differentiated the concept of active/direct participation in hostilities under the law of targeting from the prohibition on using children to actively participate in hostilities under article 8(2)(e)(VII) by adopting 'an interpretation that bears in mind *that provision's purpose*'.[153] Rather than the indeterminate goal of ending impunity, article 8(2)(e)(VII) was interpreted in light of its specific purpose to protect individuals under the age of 15 from the risks of armed conflict.

The decisions in *Katanga, Lubanga,* and the scholarly writings of Davidson and Grover, demonstrate that *in dubio pro reo* is not inconsistent with article 31 of the VCLT, but it may serve to restrict the application of article 31 in certain circumstances where it would unduly prejudice the accused. Another possible application of *in dubio pro reo* may be to help determine the issue of whether an interpretation consistent with CIL or the *Elements of Crimes* should take precedence in cases of irreconcilable conflict. Since there are cogent reasons for preferring either option, it could be argued that the residual ambiguity must be interpreted in favour of the accused, meaning that whichever interpretive mechanism is more favourable to the accused should take precedence.

In any event, it is clear that *in dubio pro reo* does not justify the ICC's reluctance to apply the principle of systemic integration under article 31(3)(c) of the VCLT, as the Court must apply the ordinary rules of interpretation before determining whether there is any residual ambiguity that must be interpreted in favour of the accused.

---

151 Grover (n 8) 202.

152 Ibid 199–202.

153 *Lubanga Appeals Judgement* (n 13) [324] (emphasis added).

2.6 Conclusion: a Proposed Methodology for Interpreting the *Rome Statute*

The principle of systemic integration applies to the interpretation of war crimes in the *Rome Statute*. Rather than demonstrating an intention to deviate from the standards applicable under customary IHL, the drafting history, text, and jurisdictional reach of the ICC's war crimes provisions evince a clear intention for the definition of crimes to reflect and be interpreted consistently with customary IHL. Moreover, neither the *Elements of Crimes* nor the rules of strict construction in article 22(2) of the *Statute* justifies the ICC's reluctance to apply the principle of systemic integration. Instead, each of these rules can and should operate in harmony with the general rule of interpretation in article 31 of the *VCLT*.

Based on this analysis and building on the interpretive methodology proposed by Grover, I argue that the ICC should apply the following six-part methodology to the interpretation of war crimes the *Rome Statute*.

1. The definition of crimes must be strictly construed in accordance with article 22(2) of the *Rome Statute* and article 31(1) of the *VCLT*; however, open-textured language, terms with specialised meaning under CIL, and directions to fill gaps in the *Statute* each require judges to identify and apply CIL directly.
2. The definition of crimes shall not be extended by analogy in accordance with article 22(2) of the *Rome Statute*; however, judges are not prevented from using analogous reasoning to determine whether developments in CIL are incorporated within the limits of the original offence or whether the impugned conduct reasonably falls within the definition of the offence.
3. Ambiguity that persists after the ordinary rules of treaty interpretation have been exhausted must be interpreted in favour of the accused in accordance with article 22(2) of the *Rome Statute*; however, this rule (also known as *in dubio pro reo*) precludes judges from relying on broad object and purpose interpretations that would negate the possibility of any residual ambiguity.
4. The definition of crimes must be interpreted in accordance with the object and purpose of the *Rome Statute* in accordance with article 31(1) of the *VCLT*; however, consistent with the above application of *in dubio pro reo*, object and purpose interpretations should be limited in the following way: (I) the object and purpose of the *Rome Statute* includes ensuring a fair trial in accordance with the principle of legality;

and (II) it is necessary to refer to the object and purpose of the specific provision to understand its meaning.
5. The definition of war crimes must be interpreted consistently with customary IHL unless there is a clear legislative intent to the contrary in accordance with article 31(3)(c) of the *VCLT* (also known as the principle of systemic integration).
6. Consideration must be given to the *Elements of Crimes* as an obligatory but non-binding interpretive guidance, pursuant to articles 21(1) and 9(3) of the *Rome Statute*. The *Elements of Crimes* must be interpreted consistently with customary IHL to prevent the unnecessary fragmentation of the law. Where such conflict cannot be reconciled, the *Elements of Crimes* is likely to prevail, but the deviation from custom should be noted in the judgment.

The ICC has failed to adhere consistently to Steps 5 and 6; namely the obligation the obligation to interpret the definition of war crimes in both the *Statute* and *Elements of Crimes* consistently with customary IHL. This failure, verified by reference to both quantitative and qualitative analysis in Chapter 4, has significant consequences. It risks unpredictability in judicial reasoning and unnecessarily fragmenting ICL to the detriment of the ICC's internal operation and its claim to be a model international court.

The following chapter considers another potential reason for the ICC's reluctance to apply the principle of systemic integration; namely, that there remains considerable doubt over the theoretical boundaries of CIL and how it is to be identified by courts and tribunals in the international criminal context. It is hoped that resolving these issues will help to facilitate the ICC's compliance with the principle of systemic integration.

CHAPTER 3

The Identification of Customary International Law

3.1 Introduction

> Professor Antonio Cassese, a former President of the Yugoslav Tribunal, put it mildly when he said that the ICC's Statute 'seems to evince a certain mistrust in the Judges'. It would be more accurate to say that the Statute evinces a deep suspicion of the Court's judges.
>
> The HON DAVID HUNT, AO, former Judge of the International Criminal Tribunal for the former-Yugoslavia[1]

The drafters of the *Rome Statute* are said to have feared the 'Cassese approach', which is a reference to the late president of the International Criminal Tribunal for the former Yugoslavia ('ICTY') Antonio Cassese's 'creative' use of customary international law ('CIL') to progressively develop the law.[2] This mistrust or 'deep suspicion' of how judges of the International Criminal Court ('ICC') might use CIL to expand the Court's subject matter jurisdiction has had a lasting impact on custom's role within the ICC framework and the extent to which judges have used it as an interpretative aid.

The ICTY is largely credited for using CIL to update field of international criminal law ('ICL'),[3] paving the way for the establishment of the ICC and the 'promise of universal justice'.[4] While few scholars deny the positive legacy of these tribunals, it is equally routine in academic circles to criticise

---

1 David Hunt, 'The International Criminal Court – High Hopes, 'Creative Ambiguity' and an Unfortunate Mistrust in International Judges' (2004) 2(1) *Journal of International Criminal Justice* 56, 61.

2 Heikelien Stuart and Marlise Simons, *The Prosecutor and the Judge: Benjamin Ferencz and Antonio Cassese* (Amsterdam University Press, 2009) 52–3.

3 Shane Darcy, 'The Reinvention of War Crimes by the International Criminal Tribunals' in Shane Darcy and Joseph Powderly (eds) *Judicial Creativity at the International Criminal Tribunals* (OUP 2010) 106, 111. Darcy notes that by relying on customary international law, the ICTY had a greater impact in developing war crimes law than the International Criminal Tribunal for Rwanda.

4 Kofi Annan, *Press Release of the United Nations Secretary General*, UN Doc SG/SM/6257 (12 June 1997) ('*Press Release of the United Nations Secretary General*').

 | DOI:10.1163/9789004690042_004

their approach to CIL as 'a dramatic expression of judicial activism',[5] in which CIL 'mainly seems to provide a convenient licence for judicial law-making'.[6] Irrespective of whether such criticisms are justified, concern over the ad-hoc tribunals' approach to custom identification led to an 'overwhelming exercise in legal positivism' in the drafting of the *Rome Statute* and *Elements of Crimes*,[7] which has cast doubt on the use of CIL in the international criminal context and caused it to be treated as 'something of a taboo'.[8]

The substance behind these criticisms is that the ad-hoc tribunals deviated from the 'traditional' methodology for identifying CIL in favour of the 'modern' approach.[9] The traditional approach asserts that CIL is found in the widespread, consistent, and observable practice of individual states (state practice), performed under a sense of legal obligation (*opinio juris*). Modern approaches to CIL tend to place greater emphasis on *opinio juris* and at times 'deduce' the existence of a rule on account of its moral character, rather than inductively quantifying state behaviour. This deviation is usually explained by reference to the fact that prohibitive humanitarian rules of the type adjudicated in international criminal law are marred by evidence of contrary state practice and therefore ill-suited to a process of induction.[10] The problem with deviating from the accepted definition of CIL is that it has an adverse effect on legal and evidentiary certainty, and is therefore inappropriate in a criminal context. These concerns explain the perception at the Diplomatic Conference in Rome that, while CIL identification at the ad-hoc tribunals proved useful in developing the law, it should not be replicated by ICC judges.[11]

---

5 William Schabas, 'Prosecutorial Discretion v. Judicial Activism at the International Criminal Court' (2008) 6 *Journal of International Criminal Justice* 731, 755.

6 William Schabas, 'Customary Law or "Judge-Made" Law? Judicial Creativity at the UN Criminal Tribunals', in Jose Doria et al (eds) *The Legal Regime of the International Criminal Court: Essays in Honour of Professor Igor Blishchenko* (Martinus Nijhoff, 2009) 77, 100.

7 Hunt (n 1) 59.

8 Alain Pellet, 'Applicable Law', in Antonio Cassese et al (eds) *The Rome Statute of the International Criminal Court: A Commentary*, Vol. II (OUP 2002) 1051, 1059.

9 For a description of these terms, see: Anthea Roberts, 'Traditional and Modern Approaches to Customary International Law: A Reconciliation' (2001) 95(4) *American Journal of International Law* 757.

10 Ibid; Oscar Schachter, 'New Custom: Power, *Opinio Juris* and Contrary State Practice' in Krzysztof Skubiszewski (ed), *Theory of International Law at the Threshold of the 21st Century* (Springer 1996) 531.

11 Schabas, 'Prosecutorial Discretion v. Judicial Activism at the International Criminal Court' (n 5) 755.

The ICTY is often singled out for deviating from the traditional approach to CIL, but several empirical studies have concluded that the International Court of Justice ('ICJ') also fails to apply this approach in practice.[12] Instead, the ICJ relies primarily on 'representative' state practice, usually in the form of multilateral treaties and United Nations (UN) Resolutions, as evidence of both elements.[13] For its part, the ICTY, despite some notable attempts to explain its divergence from the traditional methodology,[14] similarly demonstrates far greater reliance on the representative state practice in the diplomatic arena than on the individual conduct of states on the ground.[15] These studies reveal that there is a discrepancy between the conventional definition of CIL and its application in practice. Such inconsistencies may help to explain the reluctance of ICC judges to rely on CIL when interpreting the *Rome Statute*.

Building on the International Law Commission (ILC) *Draft Conclusions on Identification of Customary International Law* (Draft Conclusions),[16] this chapter proposes a refined methodology for identifying CIL that accounts for the phenomenon of contrary state practice, but without deviating from the accepted definition of CIL. It is hoped that by bringing greater clarity to the evidence and conceptual boundaries of CIL, ICC judges will feel empowered to use CIL when interpreting the definition of crimes in the *Rome Statute*, leading to greater compliance with the principle of systemic integration.

---

12 Niels Petersen, 'The International Court of Justice and the Judicial Politics of Identifying Customary International Law' (2017) 17(2) *European Journal of International Law* 357, 366; Stephen J Choi and Mitu Gulati, 'Customary International Law: How Do Courts Do It?' in Curtis A Bradley (ed), *Custom's Future: Customary International Law in a Changing World* (CUP 2016) 117.

13 Ibid.

14 *Prosecutor v Tadić (Decision on the Defence Motion for Interlocutory Appeal)* (International Criminal Tribunal for the former Yugoslavia, Appeals Chamber, Case No IT-94-1, 2 October 1995) [99] ('*Tadić Jurisdictional Appeal*').

15 Birgit Schlütter, *Developments in Customary International Law: Theory and the Practice of the International Court of Justice and the International ad hoc Criminal Tribunals for Rwanda and Yugoslavia* (Martinus Nijhoff 2010).

16 *Report of the International Law Commission, Chapter V: Identification of Customary International Law*, UN GAOR, 73rd sess, Supp No 10, UN Doc A/73/10 (2018) 127–8 [2]–[5], 133 Conclusion 6(3), 134 [8] ('*Report of the International Law Commission, Chapter V: Identification of Customary International Law*'). Michael Wood, Special Rapporteur, *Fifth Report on Identification of Customary International Law*, UN Doc A/CN.4/717 (14 March 2018) 25–6 paras 56–8 ('*Fifth Report on Identification of Customary International Law*').

3.2 Suspicion of Customary International Law and the Drafting of the *Rome Statute*

The ICTY's approach to identifying CIL has attracted considerable criticism. Alexander Zahar contends that 'an aspiration to fill gaps in the law – to legislate from the bench – is often the only method discernible in the tribunal's efforts to prove the existence of a rule of customary law'.[17] Hoffman argues that 'the Tribunal provided remarkably few instances of state practice, and instead invoked humanitarian ideals as a form of opinion juris'[18], while Shane Darcy concluded that 'There is little doubt that the judicial creativity demonstrated at the international criminal tribunals in the area of war crimes has amounted to judicial lawmaking'.[19]

The line between the identification and formation of CIL – or between judicial interpretation and lawmaking – is not always clear. It is often observed, including by those critical of the ICTY's approach to custom, that the Tribunal existed in somewhat of a legal vacuum and was required to use the concept of CIL to make up for the distinct lack of definitions and modes of liability in the field of ICL. As stated by former ICTY Judge Patricia Wald:

> It was a shock to me to judge in a system that basically had no precedent or statutory base to rely upon as to what the law was. There were some fairly pithy definitions of war crimes and crimes against humanity in the ICTY charter based on the Geneva Conventions and Nuremberg principles, but beyond that judges were left pretty much on their own to discern what international customary humanitarian law required.[20]

Irrespective of the extent to which judicial creativity at the ICTY veered into activism or lawmaking, the results have generally been welcomed by the international community of states, judicial bodies, and academics.

---

17 Alexander Zahar 'Civilizing Civil War: Writing Morality as Law at the ICTY' in Bert Swart et al (eds) *The Legacy of the International Criminal Tribunal for the Former Yugoslavia* (OUP 2011) 469, 483.

18 Tamás Hoffmann, 'Freezing or Consolidating the Development of War Crimes Law? The International Criminal Court and the Role of Judicial Innovation', in Martin Faix, and Ondřej Svaček (eds) *ICC Jurisprudence and the Development of International Humanitarian Law* (Springer, 2024) 13, 23.

19 Darcy (n 3) 127.

20 Patricia Wald, 'International Criminal Courts: Some Kudos and Concerns', 150(2) *Proceedings of the American Philosophical Society* (2006) 241, 244.

From dispensing with the armed conflict nexus requirement for crimes against humanity to recognising individual criminal responsibility of perpetrators and commanders in non-international armed conflicts (NIACS), the ICTY filled a 50-year hiatus in the development of ICL and paved the way for the establishment of the ICC. The classification of armed conflicts, definition of crimes, and modes of liability that appear in the *Rome Statute* derive in large part from the ICTY's approach to CIL identification. It is no exaggeration to say that modern international criminal law owes much of its form and substance to the ad hoc international criminal tribunals of the 1990s, and to the ICTY in particular.[21]

Despite this legacy, suspicion over the ICTY's so-called 'creative' approach to custom led to a concerted effort at the Diplomatic Conference in Rome to limit the role of CIL in the ICC framework. Under the *Rome Statute*, CIL is excluded as an independent source of law on which to base individual criminal responsibility. Accused persons can only be found guilty of violating crimes enumerated in the *Statute* itself pursuant to article 22(1). Custom's role in interpreting the *Statute* is limited by the 'robust' codification of legality in article 22(2), according to which the definition of crimes must be strictly construed, cannot be expanded by analogy, and residual ambiguity must be interpreted in favour of the accused. Schabas suggests that 'while [the drafters] appreciated the results of judicial activism in the past, they were not anxious for it to be repeated',[22] while ICC Judge Van den Wyngaert held in *Ngudjolo Chui* Trial Judgment that 'the drafters wanted to make sure that the Court could not engage in the kind of 'judicial creativity' of which other jurisdictions may at times have been suspected'.[23]

The positivist drafting of the *Rome Statute* and *Elements of Crimes* has equally attracted criticism. Former ICTY judge David Hunt bemoans the *Statute* for 'reducing the role of judges to a mere mechanical function' and, in doing so, 'preventing them from fulfilling their mandate'.[24] He contends that the drafters 'have sought to codify the law, even the Elements

21 Darcy (n 3) 111 ('It is the ICTY that has made the greater and perhaps most lasting impact on the law of war crimes, by way of judicial creativity towards both its Statute and customary international law.').

22 Schabas, 'Prosecutorial Discretion v. Judicial Activism at the International Criminal Court' (n 5) 755.

23 *Prosecutor v Mathieu Ngudjolo Chui* (*Concurring Opinion of Judge Christine Van den Wyngaert*) (International Criminal Court, Trial Chamber II, Case No ICC-01/04-02/12-4, 18 December 2012) [19] (*Ngudjolo Concurring Opinion of Judge Christine Van den Wyngaert*).

24 Hunt (n 1) 56.

of Crimes, in a wealth of minute detail which may well have the effect of stultifying further growth in the law.'[25] Described as an 'overwhelming exercise in legal positivism',[26] the drafting of the *Rome Statute* has been argued to reflect a 'veritable obsession' with the principle of legality[27] and a 'deep suspicion'[28] that ICC judges would use CIL to radically expand the definition of crimes. Those critical of the restrictions imposed on CIL lament that the *Rome Statute* and *Elements of Crimes* have 'frozen customary definitions in a process of rapid evolution'.[29]

As an antidote to the positivist drafting of the *Rome Statute*, several scholars predicted that the interpretation of the law would assume an elevated role in ensuring that the ICC is able to reflect developments in CIL. Alain Pellet forecasted that judges will use judicial interpretation 'to recover the powers inherent in all courts, of which the drafters of the Statute clearly wanted to deprive them',[30] while Joseph Powderly has reassured that 'Textual clarity does not transform adjudication into a simple and entirely predictable mechanical process; however much states may wish this to be the case'.[31] Claus Kress opined that 'this unprecedented emphasis on the legality principle should not detract from the fact that the ICC definitions of crimes are nevertheless vague in many respects', concluding that 'Judges interpreting these definitions will therefore need to flesh out and concretize the precise scope of these crimes.'[32] So far, the results have been mixed. While there are several ICC decisions that have embraced the opportunity to use CIL in the interpretation of the *Statute*, there remains a distinct trend to ignore CIL in favour of the *Elements of Crimes*, treating the ICC as a self-contained regime.[33]

---

25 Ibid

26 Ibid 59.

27 Claus Kress, 'The International Criminal Court as a Turning Point in the History of International Criminal Justice', in A Cassese (ed), *The Oxford Companion to International Criminal Justice* (OUP 2009) 143, 146.

28 Hunt (n 1) 61.

29 Pellet (n 8) 1056.

30 Ibid 1053.

31 Joseph Powderly, *Judges and the Making of International Criminal Law* (Brill Nijhoff, 2020) 456.

32 Kress (n 27) 146.

33 For an empirical analysis of the ICC's use of custom in its jurisprudence, see Chapter 4 'Assessing the International Criminal Court's Compliance with the Principle of Systemic Integration'.

The central argument of this book is that ICC judges should interpret war crimes in the *Rome Statute* consistently with customary international humanitarian law (customary IHL), pursuant to the principle of systemic integration in article 31(3)(c) of the *Vienna Convention on the Law of Treaties* ('*VCLT*'). Empirical analysis of the Court's jurisprudence reveals that the ICC is not complying with this principle on a consistent basis, which risks fragmenting international law and weakening the ICC's institutional influence. The conceptual confusion surrounding what CIL *is* and the inconsistent approaches to the judicial identification of CIL have rendered it 'something of a taboo',[34] dissuading ICC judges from relying on CIL in the interpretation of the *Statute*.

Empirical studies of both the ICJ and the ICTY reveal that neither is adopting the so-called 'traditional' approach to CIL by quantitatively identifying widespread state practice performed under a sense of legal obligation. Instead, both tend to rely on 'representative' forms of practice contained in treaties and other international instruments.[35] To retain integrity in CIL as a source of law and promote compliance with the principle of systemic integration, the constituent elements of CIL and the evidence necessary to prove their existence must be articulated with greater precision. After reviewing the practice of the ICJ and ICTY in more detail, it will be shown that the ILC *Draft Conclusions on Identification of Customary International Law* have made significant progress in fulfilling this objective.

3.3 The Identification of Custom at the ICJ: Theory vs Practice

Analysis of the ICJ's jurisprudence reveals a disparity between its stated methodology for identifying CIL and the application of this methodology practice. A more transparent and methodologically consistent approach is needed if the ICC is going fulfil its obligations under article 31(3)(c) of the *VCLT* and interpret the definition of war crimes consistently with customary IHL.

3.3.1 *The Orthodox Definition of Customary International Law*

The concept of CIL arose, in part, as a response to the naturalist conceptions espoused by some of the founding theorists of international law, such

34 Pellet (n 8) 1059.

35 Petersen (n 12); Schlütter (n 15).

as Hugo Grotius and Emer de Vattel, in order to align international law with the more positivist tendencies of the late- eighteenth and early nineteenth centuries.[36] Early Roman jurists grappled with the concept of transforming customary practice into obligatory rules and determined that what gave these rules their legally binding character was the notion that the relevant conduct was performed under a sense of legal obligation or *opinio juris sive necessitatis* (an opinion of law or necessity) and not simply convenience or habit.[37] This conception would come to represent the twin elements of CIL as propounded by the ICJ and repeated in textbooks of international law; namely, the widespread practice of states performed under a sense of pre-existing legal duty (also known as state practice and *opinio juris*). As famously stated in the *North Sea Continental Shelf Cases*, an 'indispensable requirement' in the formation of custom is that:

> State practice, including that of States whose interests are specially affected, should have been both extensive and virtually uniform in the sense of the provision invoked; and should moreover have occurred in such a way as to show a general recognition that a rule of law or legal obligation is involved.[38]

The requisite level of state practice has oscillated from 'uniformity' to the more relaxed approach taken by the ICJ in *Nicaragua*,[39] in which the Court held that there need not be 'absolute rigorous conformity' but that the 'conduct of States, should, in general, be consistent' and that contrary state practice should be treated as a breach of the rule where it is denied or qualified by the offending state. The ICJ has almost exclusively formulated this test as an inductive exercise based on a quantitative analysis of individual state practice. Regarding *opinio juris*, the Court has stated that:

---

36 Ignacio De La Rasilla, 'The Shifting Origins of International Law' (2015) 28(3) *Leiden Journal of International Law* 419 (challenging the Eurocentrism of the origins of international law).

37 David J Bederman, *Custom as a Source of Law* (CUP 2010) 19–21.

38 *North Sea Continental Shelf* (*Federal Public of Germany v Denmark*) (*Merits*) [1969] ICJ Rep 3, [74] ('*North Sea Continental Shelf*').

39 *Military and Paramilitary Activities in and against Nicaragua* (*Nicaragua v United States of America*) (*Merits*) [1986] 14, [186] ('*Military and Paramilitary Activities in and against Nicaragua*'). The ICJ had previously described the state practice requirement as 'virtually uniform' in *North Sea Continental Shelf* (*Federal Public of Germany v Denmark*) (*Merits*) [1969] ICJ Rep 3, [74] ('*North Sea Continental Shelf*'); and 'constant and uniform' in *Asylum Case* (*Colombia v Peru*) (*Judgment*) [1950] ICJ Rep 266, 276 ('*Asylum Case*').

> Not only must the acts concerned amount to a settled practice, but they also must ... be evidence of a belief that this practice is rendered obligatory by the existence of a rule of law requiring it. The need for such a belief, i.e., the existence of a subjective element, is implicit in the very notion of the *opinio juris sive necessitatis*. The States concerned must therefore feel that they are conforming to what amounts to a legal obligation.[40]

The ICJ has therefore maintained that the evidence necessary to prove the existence of a rule of CIL derives from the quantifiable practice of states, objectively motivated by belief in a pre-existing legal duty. As stated by the Court, 'It is of course axiomatic that the material of [CIL] is to be looked for primarily in the actual practice and *opinio juris* of States'.[41] However, the ICJ's claimed methodology for the identification of CIL is not reflected in its judicial practice.

3.3.2 *The Discrepancy between the Theory and Practice in the Identification of Customary International Law at the ICJ*

Notwithstanding the frequency with which the ICJ has referred to the above conception of state practice and *opinio juris* as the prevailing (or, indeed, the only) test for the formation and identification of CIL,[42] an analysis of the Court's own jurisprudence paints a different picture.[43] In an article published in 2017, Niels Petersen undertook an analysis of all ICJ judgments and advisory opinions for the purposes of uncovering the Court's approach to the identification of CIL.[44] The data comprises 48 ICJ decisions, from the *Corfu Channel Case* of 1949[45] to its 2015 judgement in *Costa*

40 *North Sea Continental Shelf* (n 38) [77].

41 *Continental Shelf (Libyan Arab Jamahiriya/Malta) (Judgment)* [1985] ICJ Rep 13, 29 [27] ('*Continental Shelf*').

42 *Jurisdictional Immunities of the State (Germany v Italy) (Judgment)* [2012] ICJ Rep 99, 143 [101] ('*Jurisdictional Immunities of the State*'); *Barcelona Traction, Light and Power Company, Limited (Belgium v Spain) (Judgment)* [1970] ICJ Rep 3, 261 (Judge Padilla Nervo) ('*Barcelona Traction, Light and Power Company, Limited*'); *Fisheries Jurisdiction (United Kingdom v Iceland) (Merits)* [1974] ICJ Rep 3, 83 (Judge De Castro) ('*Fisheries Jurisdiction*'); *Arrest Warrant of 11 April 2000 (Democratic Republic of the Congo v Belgium) (Judgment)* [2002] ICJ Rep 3, 75–76 (Judges Higgins, Kooijmans and Buergenthal) ('*Arrest Warrant of 11 April 2000*'); *Questions relating to the Obligation to Prosecute or Extradite (Belgium v Senegal) (Judgment)* ICJ Rep 422, 457 ('*Questions relating to the Obligation to Prosecute or Extradite*').

43 Petersen (n 12) 366.

44 Ibid.

45 *Corfu Channel (UK v Albania) (Judgment)* [1949] ICJ Rep 4 ('*Corfu Channel*').

Rica v Nicaragua,[46] and yields a total of 95 separate instances in which the ICJ positively identified a rule of CIL.[47] On the basis of this empirical analysis, Petersen concludes that, 'There is not one case in which the positive identification of a customary norm was based on a detailed analysis of individual state practice'.[48] Where the ICJ did identify the existence of a rule of CIL, Peterson found, state practice played a 'mere auxiliary' role: it was referred to in the abstract rather than in detail, and used in most cases only to confirm 'a result that had already been found through other means'.[49] This general, abstract and/or auxiliary reference to state practice is identified only 13 times in eleven separate cases before the Court.[50]

There are two important caveats on the scope of Petersen's study. The first is that Petersen excludes instances in which the ICJ *rejected* a proposed rule of CIL on the basis that 'the burden of justification for confirming a customary rule is higher than for rejecting a customary norm'.[51] It should be noted, however, that the ICJ's approach in rejecting a proposed rule of CIL provides a useful insight into its methodology. For example, Mario Alvarez-Jiménez's qualitative analysis of four ICJ decisions between 2000 to 2009 in which the ICJ undertook a detailed appraisal of individual state practice in accordance with the orthodox definition of CIL[52] concludes that the inductive approach 'was applied with more relevant consequences for the development of international law' in the first decade of the twenty-first century than any other approach the Court might use.[53] In each of Alvarez-Jiménez's examples, the Court *rejected* the existence of the proposed customary rule; thus, these decisions did not feature in Petersen's empirical analysis.

When the Alvarez-Jiménez and Peterson studies are considered together, it appears that the ICJ only applies a quantitative analysis of individual

46 *Construction of a Road in Costa Rica along the San Juan River (Nicaragua v Costa Rica) (Judgment)* [2015] ICJ Rep 665 ('*Construction of a Road in Costa Rica along the San Juan River*').

47 Petersen (n 12) 367.

48 Ibid 369.

49 Ibid 377.

50 Ibid 376.

51 Ibid.

52 Alberto Alvarez-Jiménez, 'Methods for the Identification for the Identification of Customary International Law in the International Court of Justice's Jurisprudence: 2000–2009' (2011) 60(3) *International and Comparative Law Quarterly* 681, 689.

53 Ibid.

state conduct when rejecting a proposed rule of custom. Fernando Lusa Bordin agrees, arguing that the Court tends to apply a strict inductive method to reject claims of CIL because, were it to attempt to apply it in the positive identification of rules, 'its reasoning would be more exposed to criticism'.[54] Other scholars have reached a similar conclusion.[55]

The second caveat is that Petersen defines state practice as a quantitative analysis of individual state conduct (in accordance with the orthodox definition of CIL) and excludes what might be termed 'representative' or 'aspirational' state practice; namely, the content of United Nations General Assembly (UNGA) Resolutions and other UN materials involving state participation, multilateral treaties, and consultative publications of expert bodies, such as those prepared by the ILC or International Human Rights Committee.[56] Petersen's findings therefore need to be understood in terms of the Court's unwillingness to provide a quantitative analysis of individual state practice when identifying positive rules. Instead, the ICJ defers to the text of international treaties to which states are signatory and the content of UN Resolutions in which states participated (i.e., representative state practice), rather than a quantitative analysis of individual state conduct.

According to Petersen, the combination of multilateral treaties, UNGA Resolutions and, to a lesser extent, the ILC *Draft Articles on State Responsibility* appear in 63.2 per cent of all positive identifications of customary rules of international law by the ICJ, with treaties providing the main source

54 Fernando Bordin, 'Induction, Assertion and the Limits of the Existing Methodologies to Identify Customary International Law', *EJIL: Talk! Blog of the European Journal of International Law* (Blog Post, 2 December 2015) <https://www.ejiltalk.org/induction-assertion-and-the-limits-of-the-existing-methodologies-to-identify-customary-international-law/> accessed 15 July 2024.

55 Rudolf Geiger, 'Customary International Law in the Jurisprudence of the International Court of Justice: A Critical Appraisal' in Ulrich Fastenrath and others (eds), *From Bilateralism to Community Interest: Essays in Honour of Bruno Simma* (OUP 2011) 673, 694 ('In all these rare examples, where the Court was at least initially looking for specific State practice and opinio juris, the answer was given in constant view of treaties and resolutions and, based on very short arguments, it was negative.').

56 On the significance of the decisions and General Comments of the Human Rights Committee Comments as evidence of custom. See Yutaka Arai, *The Law of Occupation: Continuity and Change of International Humanitarian Law, and Its Interaction with International Human Rights Law* (Martinus Nijhoff 2009) 518–19 (noting the similarities between Committee decisions and judicial decisions and General Comments as a "subsequent practice in the application of the treaty" under article 31(3)(b) of the *VCLT*).

of evidence at 47.4 per cent.[57] In 30.5 per cent of cases, the ICJ relied on the consent of the parties concerned as to the existence of a customary rule, thereby circumventing the need for any empirical analysis, in the interests of judicial expediency, by deferring only to the *opinio juris* of those states involved in the dispute.[58] In 17.9 per cent of cases, the ICJ relied on its own precedent, while in 10.5 per cent of cases, Petersen concludes, the ICJ simply 'asserts' the existence of a rule of CIL. In stark contrast to its professed methodology, there were no examples in which the ICJ positively identified a rule of custom through a quantitative analysis of individual state practice and *opinio juris*.

In a 2016 empirical study, Stephen Choi and Mitu Gulati arrived at the same conclusion as Petersen: that the ICJ's stated methodology is not reflected in practice.[59] Choi and Gulati analysed all judgments from the ICJ and Permanent Court of International Justice (PCIJ) in which a determination of custom was made, whether positive or negative. This data was supplemented with a subset of all decisions from other international courts and tribunals cited in the ILC's 2013 Report on CIL.[60] Notably, the results are substantially the same when the data is limited to the decisions of the ICJ and PCIJ. Choi and Gulati concluded that:

> [I]nternational courts do not come anywhere close to engaging in the type of analysis the officially stated two-part rule for the evolution of CIL sets up. Instead, as best we can tell, courts analyzing CIL – whether they find it or not – are generally engaged in a forward-looking or aspirational exercise. We draw this inference from the fact that, by far, the dominant form of evidence used in determinations of CIL is that gleaned from international treaties.[61]

A qualitative analysis of the ICJ's jurisprudence yields comparable results. Mark Weisburd analysed 27 ICJ cases decided between 1984 and 2007 and concluded that the ICJ routinely substitutes a quantitative evaluation of individual state practice for the content of treaties and UN Resolutions, even

57 Petersen (n 12) 368, 372–75.
58 Ibid 368–72.
59 Choi and Gulati (n 12).
60 Ibid 126.
61 Ibid 146–7.

where the treaties in question have limited reach.[62] Several other academic commentators have echoed this sentiment.[63]

Notable examples in which the ICJ ignored individual state practice in favour of representative practice include: the *Nuclear Weapons Advisory Opinion*, in which the Court relied on a non-binding declaration made at a United Nations Conference, one UNGA Resolution, and articles 35(3) and 55 of *Additional Protocol I* (*AP I*) to conclude that, 'States must take environmental considerations into account when assessing what is necessary and proportionate in the pursuit of legitimate military objectives';[64] the *Israeli Wall Advisory Opinion*, in which the Court made repeated reference to UNGA Resolutions, the work of the ILC and Human Rights Committee, and on one occasion a determination by the International Committee of the Red Cross (ICRC) regarding the applicability of *Geneva Convention IV* under CIL;[65] and *Congo v Uganda*, in which the Court relied exclusively on UNGA Resolutions to conclude that a state enjoys permanent sovereignty over its natural resources.[66] In several other cases, the Court substituted an analysis of individual state practice for the work of the ILC as a form of delegation, or otherwise relied on its previous decisions.[67] Weisburd concludes that:

> It is clear then that what the Court has *not* been doing in CIL cases is basing its judgments on carefully described state practice. What is has

62 Mark Weisburd, 'The International Court of Justice and the Concept of State Practice' (2009) 31 *University of Pennsylvania Journal of International Law* 295, 301–40.

63 Theodor Meron, 'Customary Humanitarian Law Today: From the Academy to the Courtroom' in Andrew Clapham and Paola Gaeta (eds), *The Oxford Handbook of International Law in Armed Conflict* (OUP 2014) 37, 39; Geiger (n 55) 692; Stefan Talmon, 'Determining Customary International Law: The ICJ's Methodology between Induction, Deduction and Assertion' (2015) 26(2) *European Journal of International Law* 417, 441.

64 *Legality of the Threat or Use of Nuclear Weapons* (*Advisory Opinion*) [1996] ICJ Rep 226, 242 [30] ('*Legality of the Threat or Use of Nuclear Weapons*'); Weisburd (n 62) 323.

65 *Legal Consequences of the Construction of a Wall in the Occupied Palestinian Territory* (*Advisory Opinion*) [2004] ICJ Rep 136, 171–77 [86]–[101] ('*Legal Consequences of the Construction of a Wall in the Occupied Palestinian Territory*'); Weisburd (n 62) 328–29.

66 *Armed Activities on the Territory of the Congo* (*Democratic Republic of the Congo v Uganda*) (*Judgment*) [2005] ICJ Rep 168, 251–2 [244] ('*Armed Activities on the Territory of the Congo*').

67 Weisburd (n 62) 310–20 (for example, Weisburd notes at 313 that, in the *Gulf of Maine Case*, the Court relied on the *Convention on the Continental Shelf* and the drafting history of the *United Nations Convention on the Law of the Sea* ('*UNCLOS*') to reject the argument that the equidistant line used as the first stage of delimitation cannot be modified, despite the fact that only 19 states had ratified *UNCLOS* at the time).

> been doing instead is also significant: … the Court has relied, 1) on actions by the General Assembly and by states meeting in international conferences; 2) on determinations by bodies composed of individual experts; and 3) on its own precedents and policy determinations.[68]

It is apparent that what the ICJ does and what it says it does are two different things. The relevance of this finding is simple: disparity between the theory and practice of CIL in the ICJ's jurisprudence makes it difficult for other courts and tribunals to replicate, particularly in the international criminal context where there is greater scrutiny and expectations of evidentiary certainty. It is therefore essential that all courts and tribunals, including the ICJ, adopt a transparent and consistent methodology for the identification of CIL that reflects their judicial practice. Empirical analysis makes it clear that such a methodology must acknowledge the predominant role of representative state practice and the comparatively minor role of individual state conduct.

3.3.3 *The* 'opinio juris *paradox'*

The discrepancy between the ICJ's stated methodology and the methodology it applies in practice when identifying CIL also creates an internal inconsistency regarding the true meaning of *opinio juris*. Representative forms of state practice, such as the signing of multilateral treaties and voting in UN Resolutions, are not necessarily performed under a sense of legal obligation because (apart from treaties or Resolutions that codify existing CIL) the obligation contained in the relevant instrument is not yet, or may never be, legally binding. This conundrum is known as the '*opinio juris* paradox'.[69]

The ICJ's decisions in the 1971 *South West Africa/Namibia Advisory Opinion* and the 1975 *Western Sahara Advisory Opinion* provide suitable examples of the *opinio juris* paradox. These cases concerned, *inter alia*, the legal status of the principle of self-determination. In *South West Africa/Namibia*, the ICJ traced the development of the principle from article 22 of the League of Nations Covenant, which held that former colonies and territories that are 'not yet able to stand by themselves' are entitled to the 'well-being and

---

68 Ibid 352 (emphasis added).

69 John Tasioulas, 'Opinio Juris and the Genesis of Custom: A Solution to the "Paradox"' (2007) 26 *Australian Yearbook of International Law* 199; David Lefkowitz, '(Dis)solving the Chronological Paradox in CIL: A Hartian Approach' (2008) 21 *Canadian Journal of Law and Jurisprudence* 129.

development of such peoples from a sacred trust of civilisation' until such a time that they are 'able to stand alone'.[70] The Court made further reference to UNGA Resolution 1514 (XV) of 1960 on the *Granting of Independence to Colonial Countries and Peoples* as evidence that the 'objective of the sacred trust was self-determination and independence of the people concerned'.[71] In the subsequent *Western Sahara Advisory Opinion*, the Court buttressed this conclusion by reference to UNGA Resolution 2625 of 1970, the so-called *Friendly Relations Declaration*, thereby affirming the customary status of the principle of self-determination.[72]

However, these UNGA Resolutions did not provide a codification of CIL based on the consistent practice of states acting under a sense of legal obligation, but indicated only what states wanted the law to be (*lex ferenda*). Accordingly, the 'practice' inferred from these Resolutions, that of states voting in favour of their specific content, cannot have been formed under a sense of legal obligation, as no such obligation existed. Rather, it was hoped that the content of the Resolutions themselves would develop into a legally binding obligation and thus influence future state practice. As then-President of the UN General Assembly, Edvard Hambro of Norway, stated after the adoption of UNGA Resolution 2625: 'In a sense ... the work has just begun. We have proclaimed the principles; from now on we must strive to make them a living reality in the life of states, because these principles lie at the very heart of peace, justice and progress'.[73] To find that the content of UNGA Resolutions is customary based on the participation of states in forming the Resolution is akin to making a specifically intended instrument of soft law legally binding on all states. At the very least, it does not comport with the supposed customary pre-requisite of consistent state practice performed under a sense of legal obligation.

---

70 *Legal Consequences for States of the Contitiued Presence of South Africa in Namibia (South West Africa) notwithstanding Security Council Resolution 276 (1970) (Advisory Opinion)* [1971] ICJ Rep 16, 28–32 [44]–[54] ('*Legal Consequences for States of the Contitiued Presence of South Africa in Namibia (South West Africa) notwithstanding Security Council Resolution 276 (1970)*').

71 Ibid 30–31 [53]–[54]; Geiger (n 55) 682–83.

72 *Western Sahara (Advisory Opinion)* [1975] ICJ Rep 12, 31–3 [54]–[59] ('*Western Sahara*').

73 United Nations, 'Declaration on Principles of International Law concerning Friendly Relations and Cooperation among States in accordance with the Charter of the United Nations. 24 October 1970' *Audiovisual Library of International Law* (Web Page, 2023) <http://legal.un.org/avl/ha/dpilfrcscun/dpilfrcscun.html> accessed 15 July 2024.

The *opinio juris* paradox is not unique to representative state practice. The orthodox definition of CIL is consistent state practice performed under a sense of legal obligation, which means that those states would need to have been initially acting under the *mistaken* belief that the rule was legally binding, as its customary status had not yet been realised.[74] As stated by Curtis Bradley, 'While it might be tempting to dismiss this paradox as a mere pet concern of legal philosophers, it may provide further reason to doubt that the standard account of CIL accurately describes how this body of law operates in practice'.[75]

3.3.4 *The Failure to Distinguish between the Two Elements of Custom*

The ICJ's unexplained reliance on representative state practice also means that it has failed to appropriately delineate between the two elements of CIL. The Court in the *Nuclear Weapons Advisory Opinion* limited the utility of UNGA Resolutions in the formation of *opinio juris* and did not consider those sources as evidence of state practice.[76] Similarly, some scholars argue that, while the signing of a treaty may be relevant *opinio juris*, it can only be considered state practice if the content of that treaty is incorporated into domestic law or can otherwise be shown to have influenced the actual behaviour of the relevant state.[77] The basis for these critiques is that the twin elements of state practice and *opinio juris* must be distinguishable, with the former comprising quantifiable conduct performed under the pre-existing belief in the latter. If the content of treaties and UN Resolutions is to be accepted as a form of representative state practice in lieu of individual state practice, the Court must acknowledge that the same conduct can be used as evidence of both elements simultaneously.

In sum, the ICJ's approach to the identification of CIL demonstrates a clear reliance on forward-looking international instruments that reflect an intention to create law, rather than a quantifiable analysis of the individual practice of states acting under a sense of a pre-existing legal obligation.

3.3.5 *Consequences of the ICJ's Approach to Identifying Custom*

There are several negative consequences arising from the discrepancy between the ICJ's stated methodology and that which it applies in practice.

74 Michael Byers, *Custom, Power and the Power of Rules: International Relations and Customary International Law* (CUP 1999) 130–31.

75 Curtis A Bradley, 'Introduction: Custom's Future' in Curtis A Bradley (ed), *Custom's Future: International Law in a Changing World* (CUP 2016) 1, 2.

76 *Legality of the Threat or Use of Nuclear Weapons* (n 64) 32–33 [70]–[73]

77 Hiram Chodosh, 'Neither Treaty nor Custom: The Emergence of Declarative International Law' (1991) 26(1) *Texas International Law Journal* 87, 95.

Most significantly, this discrepancy has the potential to undermine the Court's authority and lose the support of UN member states due to a lack of transparency, clarity, and consistency in judicial reasoning. According to some commentators, this consequence is already reflected in the limited number of states which accept the ICJ's compulsory jurisdiction, as well as in scholarly critiques of the Court's jurisprudence.[78] Another consequence is that the discrepancy does not stand up to the level of evidentiary certainty expected in criminal trials. For this reason, ICTY judges have at times felt compelled to depart from the ICJ's stated methodology and, in some cases, reject its substantive rulings.[79]

To promote the use of CIL in the interpretation of the *Rome Statute*, greater evidentiary certainty regarding the identification of CIL is required.

3.4 The Identification of Custom at the ICTY: Embracing 'Representative' State Practice

The ICTY's approach to the identification of CIL is comparable to that of the ICJ, at least to the extent that it relies primarily on treaties, judicial decisions, and the work of the ILC as evidence of both state practice and *opinio juris*. Despite some notable attempts to explain its methodology and justify its reliance on 'representative' rather than individual state practice, the critique of the ICTY's jurisprudence is essentially the same as that of the ICJ: there should be greater transparency in acknowledging that representative forms of state practice comprise the principal evidence of both elements of CIL simultaneously, which will lead to greater clarity and consistency in judicial reasoning.

Faced with a jurisdictional appeal that challenged, among other things, the ICTY's subject-matter jurisdiction over customary IHL applicable in NIACs, the ICTY Appeals Chamber in *Tadić* provided the caveat that, in the theatre of war, reliable examples of state practice on the ground were extremely difficult, if not impossible, to ascertain.[80] It held that:

> In appraising the formation of customary rules or general principles one should therefore be aware that, on account of the inherent nature

78 Weisburd (n 62) 361–2, 370–1.

79 *Prosecutor v Tadić (Judgment)* (International Criminal Tribunal for the former Yugoslavia, Appeals Chamber, Case No IT-94-1-A, 15 July 1999) [115]–[145] (*Tadić Appeals Judgment*).

80 *Tadić Jurisdictional Appeal* (n 14) 99.

> of this subject-matter, reliance must primarily be placed on such elements as official pronouncements of States, military manuals and judicial decisions.[81]

Over the course of its tenure, the ICTY would come to place greater emphasis on treaties and the work of the ILC when identifying rules of CIL than on the 'official pronouncements' of individual states. Notwithstanding, this statement can be viewed as a candid attempt by the *Tadić* Appeals Chamber to explain a methodological preference for representative forms of state practice on account of the inadequacies of the 'traditional' approach. Empirical analysis confirms that the ICTY tended to rely on representative state practice, often with limited attention paid to whether the rules in such documents were complied with by the physical conduct of state agents 'on the ground'.[82]

Birgit Schlütter's empirical analysis of the ICTY's jurisprudence reveals that the Tribunal mainly relies on the following three sources of evidence in what she refers to as the 'international instrument approach': (I) the Charter and jurisprudence of the International Military Tribunals (IMTS) for Nuremberg and the Far East; (II) *Additional Protocols I and II* (*APS I and II*); and (III) the 1992 *ILC Draft Code of Crimes Against the Peace and Security of Mankind* (*Draft Code of Crimes*).[83] Other important, though usually secondary, sources include military manuals and the *Customary IHL Study* prepared by the ICRC.[84]

By way of example, the Trial Chamber in *Prosecutor v Kupreškić* stated that, while judicial decisions are a subsidiary source of international law and thus cannot be automatically equated with rules of CIL, 'great value' must be afforded to the Charter and jurisprudence of the IMTS on the basis that they represent CIL.[85] It has been noted that, when relying on judicial decisions, the ICTY usually did not attempt ascertain whether such rules were reflected in the physical practice of states.[86]

81 Ibid.

82 Others have used the term 'paper practice'. See, for example, Niels Petersen, 'Customary Law without Custom? Rules, Principles, and the Role of State Practice in International Norm Creation' (2007) 23(2) *American University International Law Review* 275, 278.

83 Ibid 187–220.

84 Schlütter (n 15).

85 *Prosecutor v Kupreškić et al.* (*Judgment*) (International Criminal Tribunal for the former Yugoslavia, Trial Chamber, Case No IT-95-16-T, 14 January 2000) [540]–[541] (*Kupreškić Trial Judgment*).

86 Noora Arajarvi, *The Changing Nature of Customary International Law: Methods of Interpreting the Concept of Custom in International Criminal Tribunals* (Routledge 2014) 40.

Regarding the ILC's *Draft Code of Crimes*, the Trial Chamber in *Prosecutor v Furundžija* held that:

> [T]he Draft Code is an authoritative international instrument which, depending upon the specific question at issue, may (I) constitute evidence of customary law, or (II) shed light on customary rules which are of uncertain contents or are in the process of formation, or, at the very least, (III) be indicative of the legal views of eminently qualified publicists representing the major legal systems of the world.[87]

Similar statements concerning the authoritative value of the ILC *Draft Code of Crimes* were made in *Prosecutor v Kunarac et al.*[88] Several other cases have used the ILC's work as further evidence of a rule of CIL otherwise contained in the IMT Charters, treaties, or other relevant international instruments.[89] Finally, the inclusion of a rule in *AP I* also tended to provide sufficient proof of its customary status, without attempting to ascertain whether such rules were reflected in the individual practice of states on the ground.[90]

There are certainly a few examples where the ICTY went beyond an inductive analysis of international instruments and attempted to deduce the existence of a customary rule. In determining the customary status of the

87 *Prosecutor v Furundžija (Judgment)* (International Criminal Tribunal for the former Yugoslavia, Trial Chamber, Case No IT-95-17/1-T, 10 December 1998) [227] (*Furundžiija Trial Judgment*).

88 *Prosecutor v Kunarac et al. (Judgment)* (International Criminal Tribunal for the former Yugoslavia, Trial Chamber, Case No IT-96-23-T and IT-96-23/1-T, 22 February 2001) [537] (*Kunarac Trial Judgment*) ('As a body consisting of experts in international law, including government legal advisers, elected by the UN General Assembly, the work of the ILC, at least in relation to this issue, may be considered as evidence of CIL.').

89 *Prosecutor v Aleksovski (Judgment)* (International Criminal Tribunal for the former Yugoslavia, Trial Chamber, Case No IT-95-14/1-T, 25 June 1999) [75] (*Aleksovski Trial Judgment*); *Prosecutor v Delalić et al. (Judgment)* (International Criminal Tribunal for the former Yugoslavia, Trial Chamber, Case No IT-96-21-T, 18 November 1998) [377]–[378] (*Delalić Trial Judgment*); *Prosecutor v Jelisić (Judgment)* (International Criminal Tribunal for the former Yugoslavia, Trial Chamber, Case No IT-95-10-T, 14 December 1999) [61] n 1085 (*Jelisić Trial Judgment*); *Prosecutor v Jokić (Judgment)* (International Criminal Tribunal for the former Yugoslavia, Trial Chamber, Case No IT-01-42/1-T, 18 March 2004) [624] (*Jokić Trial Judgment*). *Kunarac Trial Judgment* (n 59) [541]; *Prosecutor v Tadić (Judgment)* (International Criminal Tribunal for the former Yugoslavia, Trial Chamber, Case No IT-94-1-T, 7 May 1997) [697] (*Tadić Trial Judgment*).

90 *Prosecutor v Kordic (Judgement)* (International Criminal Tribunal for the former Yugoslavia, Trial Chamber, Case No T-95-14/2-T, 26 February 2001) [50]–[53] (*Kordic Trial Judgment*).

prohibition on civilian reprisals, the ICTY Trial Chamber in *Kupreškić* famously relied on the Marten's Clause to hold that 'principles of international humanitarian law may emerge through a customary process under the pressure of the demands of humanity or the dictates of public conscience, even where State practice is scant or inconsistent'.[91] The Chamber held that, in such circumstances, *opinio juris* can become the 'decisive element'.[92] It is worth noting here that the Chamber substantiated its conclusions by reference to some supporting practice, consisting of two military manuals, the ILC Draft Articles on State Responsibility, a United Nations General Assembly Resolution, and an ICRC memo related to the Iran-Iraq conflict.[93] The Chamber further contended that a lack of states positively claiming the right to reprisals in NIACs supported the customary status of the prohibition.[94] In the *Tadić* jurisdictional appeal, 'elementary considerations of humanity' also formed part of the Appeal Chamber's reasoning when it recognised the customary prohibition of certain weapons in NIACs, though it supported this conclusion by fairly extensive reference to representative forms of practice.[95]

Schlütter concludes that the ICTY relied on representative forms of practice or 'international instruments' on at least 27 occasions.[96] The second most common methodology, appearing 14 times, was the 'deductive approach',[97] while quantitative individual state practice and *opinio juris* was used on only two occasions.[98] While the ICTY's approach to custom has attracted significant criticism as a form of judicial lawmaking, it largely reflects that of the ICJ: it relies on representative practice, primarily in the form of international treaties and judicial decisions, which it takes as evidence of both state practice and *opinio juris* simultaneously. If anything, the ICTY should be commended for at least attempting to explain some of the methodological difficulties of the traditional definition of CIL when

---

91 *Kupreškić Trial Judgment* (n 85) [227].

92 Ibid.

93 Ibid.

94 Ibid.

95 Other examples of deductive reasoning at the ICTY include the prohibition on torture, command responsibility in NIACs, and joint criminal enterprise. Mahmoud Cherif Bassiouni, *Introduction to International Criminal Law: Second Revised Edition* (Martinus Nijhoff, 2013) 386.

96 Schlütter (n 15) 280 nn 544.

97 Ibid nn 545 (the deductive approach, which is also commonly employed by the ICJ, has been theorised as a means of identifying a rule of custom in spite of contrary practice or widespread breaches of the rule, as discussed in Section V).

98 Ibid nn 547.

applied to prohibitive humanitarian rules characterised by varying degrees of noncompliance.

Notwithstanding, there remain significant methodological and evidentiary issues concerning the ICTY's approach to CIL that need to be resolved. For example, what is the justification for *opinio juris* making up for a lack of state practice? How does the practice of deducing customary rules from the principles of humanity respect the principle legal certainty, especially in a criminal context? While the ILC *Draft Conclusions on Identification of Customary International Law* have taken considerable steps to address these concerns, the issue of how representative forms of practice can overcome contrary state practice on the ground requires some further refinement.

3.5 Closing the Gap between Theory and Practice: the ILC Draft Conclusions on the Identification of Customary International Law

In 2013, the ILC embarked on a project originally entitled, *Formation and Evidence of Customary International Law*, later changed to *Identification of Customary International Law*.[99] The ILC has produced five Reports and 16 Draft Conclusions with Commentary, the aim of which is to provide practical guidance to states and courts on the methodological approach to the identification of CIL, as well as clarification on the content and scope of the evidence necessary to substantiate the existence of such rules.[100] The ILC's project surveys an impressive collection of academic publications, customary studies, and international materials, and incorporates the views of states in its interim Reports and Draft Conclusions with accompanying Commentary.[101] It provides an invaluable point of reference for current scholarly debates and makes a considerable contribution to closing the gap between the theory and practice of CIL identification by courts and tribunals.

Most notably, the ILC suggests a subtle departure from the deeply ingrained terminology of 'state practice and *opinio juris*' by using the actual wording of article 38(1)(b) of the ICJ Statute; that is, 'a general practice accepted as law'.[102] This seemingly semantic change, when taken in

99 *Report of the International Law Commission, Chapter V: Identification of Customary International Law*, UN Doc A/73/10 (n 16).

100 Ibid.

101 Ibid.

102 Michael Wood, Special Rapporteur, *Second Report on Identification of Customary International Law*, UN Doc A/CN.4/672 (22 May 2014) para 17 (*Second Report on Identification of Customary International Law*).

conjunction with the other Draft Conclusions and associated Commentary, has the potential to overcome many of the issues discussed above regarding the discrepancy between the orthodox definition of CIL and its application in practice.[103] These other developments include: (I) adopting a wide interpretation of 'a general practice' that openly includes representative state practice; (II) interpreting the 'accepted as law' (*opinio juris*) element in a manner that overcomes the *opinio juris* paradox; and (III) accepting that the same piece of evidence can be used to prove the existence of both elements of CIL simultaneously.

However, the ILC Draft Conclusions fail to adequately address situations where courts and tribunals have been willing to identify a rule of CIL despite widespread contrary state practice, usually by way of deduction, or to consider what this means for the theory and practice of CIL.

3.5.1 *Representative State Practice*

The term 'a general practice accepted as law' is immediately more inclusive than state practice and *opinio juris*, particularly where the latter is defined as the quantitative conduct of states acting under a sense of legal obligation. 'A general practice accepted as law' does not require stretching the meaning of the words to accommodate representative state practice as the most persuasive evidence of CIL.[104]

The ILC Draft Conclusions and accompanying Commentary take the necessary step of explicitly acknowledging that 'general practice' includes a wide array of state conduct, from physical to verbal acts of a state's constitutive organs to, more importantly, the collective output of states' participation in international (intergovernmental) organisations and their reaction to or acceptance of the practice of non-governmental organisations and judicial organs.[105] In short, the ILC Draft Conclusions appear to accept the empirical findings referenced in this chapter that courts and tribunals predominantly rely on representative state practice when identifying rules of CIL.

3.5.2 *The* 'opinio juris *paradox'*

With regard to the *opinio juris* paradox, the ILC suggests that the term 'accepted as law' would not require the state to believe that it is already bound

103 Ibid 55–6 para 68.

104 Roozbeh Baker, 'Customary International Law: A Reconceptualization' (2016) 41(2) Brooklyn Journal of International Law 439.

105 *Report of the International Law Commission, Chapter V: Identification of Customary International Law* (n 16) 120 Conclusion 6(3), 127–8 paras 2–5.

by a rule of custom when acting in accordance with that rule (which creates the cyclical paradox), because it is sufficient that the state 'accepts' the binding nature of the rule rather than believes that it is already bound by the rule.[106] Accordingly, the ILC Commentary to the Draft Conclusions dispenses with the chronological requirement inherent in the orthodox approach; that is, that a general practice must emerge before it can be considered to have been motivated by a sense of legal obligation.[107]

This position was summarised by the representative of South Africa in the Sixth Committee, who stated that 'what mattered was that both elements should be present, rather than their temporal order'.[108] It is therefore immaterial if the accepted-as-law (*opinio juris*) element arises first in the international arena and is then confirmed by the practice of states.[109] This change is conceptually significant. The conduct of states in signing a treaty or voting in favour of a UN Resolution can establish the 'accepted-as-law element' because, even though the state knows that it is not yet bound by the rule, it is demonstrating its intention to be legally bound. This change in terminology effectively incorporates forward-looking *opinio juris* as the genesis of CIL, rather than insisting on the improbable expectation that the requisite number of states will act in conformity with a non-existent rule.

3.5.3 *Evidence of 'a General Practice' and the 'Accepted-as-Law' Elements in the Same Conduct*

Finally, the ILC's acceptance of the fact that the same conduct can be used to establish both elements of CIL ('general practice' and 'accepted as law') is a necessary consequence of relying on representative forms of practice.[110] In short, if treaties and UN Resolutions suffice as evidence of a general practice, they must also simultaneously reflect the accepted-as-law element, providing the language is of a sufficiently legal character.[111]

---

106 Ibid 129 Conclusion 3 para 9.

107 Michael Wood, Special Rapporteur, *Third Report on Identification of Customary International Law*, UN Doc A/CN.4/682 (27 March 2015) 6–7 para 16 (*Third Report on Identification of Customary International Law*). *Report of the International Law Commission, Chapter V: Identification of Customary International Law* (n 16) 129 para 9.

108 Wood, *Third Report on Identification of Customary International Law* (n 107) 6–7 para 16.

109 Ibid; *Report of the International Law Commission, Chapter V: Identification of Customary International Law* (n 16) 129 para 9.

110 Ibid; Wood, *Third Report on Identification of Customary International Law* (n 107) 6–7 para 16.

111 *Report of the International Law Commission, Chapter V: Identification of Customary International Law* (n 16) 140–1 [3]; Brian D Lepard, 'Customary International Law as a

The same conclusion has previously been reached by other international institutions charged with determining a methodology for the identification of CIL. Reflecting on the ICRC's Customary IHL Study, Jean-Marie Henckaerts states that, 'During work on the study, it proved largely theoretical to strictly separate elements of practice and legal conviction. Often, the same (official) act reflects both practice and legal conviction'.[112] Similarly, with respect to the jurisprudence of the ICJ, the International Law Association has stated that the Court 'has not in fact said in so many words that just because there are (allegedly) distinct elements in customary law the same conduct cannot manifest both. It is in fact often difficult or even impossible to disentangle the two elements'.[113]

The ILC's project on the identification of CIL is a welcome development and may come to achieve its mandate of bringing much-needed clarity to this area of law. Its open acknowledgment of the probative value of representative state practice, its abandonment of the chronological requirement, and its acceptance that the same conduct can be used as evidence of both elements simultaneously overcome the *opinio juris* paradox and help to close the gap between theory and practice in the identification of CIL.

3.5.4 *Shortcomings of the ILC Draft Conclusions*

The main shortcomings of the ILC Draft Conclusions lie in the insistence that the empirical, twin-element approach is the *only* method for the identification of CIL in the face of considerable evidence to the contrary—the majority of which is cited in the footnotes of the ILC's Reports but does not make it into the body of its analysis.[114] The ILC Draft Conclusions, Reports, and associated Commentary take the ICJ's assurance that it only applies an

---

Dynamic Process' in Curtis A Bradley (ed), *Custom's Future: International Law in a Changing World* (CUP 2016) 62, 100.

112 Jean-Marie Henckaerts, 'The ICRC Study on Customary International Humanitarin Law: Characteristics, Conclusions and Practical Relevance' (2009) 6(1–2) *Slovenian Law Review* 225, 236.

113 International Law Association, *Final Report of the Committee on the Formation of Customary (General) International Law, Statement of Principles Applicable to the Formation of General Customary International Law* (Report of the 69th Conference, 2000) 7 para 10.

114 *Report of the International Law Commission, Chapter V: Identification of Customary International Law* (n 16) 26; Michael Wood, Special Rapporteur, *First Report on Formation and Evidence of Customary International Law*, UN Doc A/CN.4/663 (17 May 2013) 47–56 paras 97–101 (*First Report on Formation and Evidence of Customary International Law*).

inductive, orthodox approach to the identification of CIL at face value. The ILC therefore fails to engage to a sufficient degree with the numerous studies that have concluded that the Court regularly relies on deductive reasoning that is devoid of empirical analysis, thus demonstrating, at the very least, a duality of methodologies.[115]

Stephen Talmon argues that the ICJ relies on a combination of induction, deduction, and assertion when identifying rules of CIL. He states that, where neither induction nor deduction is possible due a dearth of state practice or the absence of any general principles from which to deduce an applicable rule, 'assertion is the price states have to pay for the Court not to declare an epistemological *non liquet*' (no applicable law).[116]

Sir Michael Wood (Special Rapporteur for the ILC Draft Conclusions) and Omri Sender refute Talmon's claim that the ICJ relies on deduction to any significant degree, let alone that it resorts to assertion.[117] Citing the extrajudicial writings of Judge Tanaka, they contend that the Court takes a 'pragmatic approach' by substituting its own quantitative analysis of state practice and *opinio juris* for the conclusions expressed by states (presumably in treaties and UN Resolutions) and the work of the ILC. Talmon responds to this justification by citing the *Barcelona Traction Case*, in which the Court speaks of 'deducing from considerations of equity any broader right of protection';[118] the separate opinion of President Bustamante y Rivero in the *North Sea Continental Shelf Cases* that 'it is possible to deduce [other essential principles] from the accepted concept of the continental shelf';[119] and the separate opinion of Judge Fouad Ammoun that the Court 'must enquire what rule should be deduced from the principle of equity' and that it 'is from the principle [...] that the rules flow'.[120]

Indeed, a short survey of the ICJ's case law confirms that the Court adopts a deductive approach on a semi-regular basis. For example, in the

115 Petersen (n 12); Talmon (n 63); Schlütter (n 15); Choi and Gulati (n 12); Geiger (n 55); Weisburd (n 62).

116 Talmon (n 63) 442.

117 Omri Sender and Michael Wood, 'The International Court of Justice and Customary International Law: A Reply to Stefan Talmon', *EJIL: Talk! Blog of the European Journal of International Law* (Blog Post, 30 November 2015) <https://www.ejiltalk.org/the-international-court-of-justice-and-customary-international-law-a-reply-to-stefan-talmon/> accessed 15 July 2024.

118 *Barcelona Traction, Light and Power Company, Limited* (n 42) [94].

119 *North Sea Continental Shelf* (n 38) [3].

120 Ibid [48].

1949 *Corfu Channel Case*, the ICJ held that the international legal obligation to warn incoming ships of the existence of mines in the area is based 'not on the Hague Convention of 1907, No. VIII, which is applicable in time of war, but on certain general and well-recognized principles, namely: *elementary considerations of humanity*, even more exacting in peace than in war'.[121] The ICJ returned to this line of reasoning in 1986 in *Nicaragua*, in which the Court determined the customary status of common article 3 of the *Geneva Conventions* on the basis that the rules also reflect 'elementary considerations of humanity',[122] despite Judge Jennings' dissent that the majority's reasoning was 'a matter not free from difficulty' in the face of what he alleged to be a poor record of state compliance with the *Geneva Conventions* and the majority's failure to cite any evidence of state practice or *opinio juris* to support its conclusion.[123] The customary status of IHL rules arose again in the 1996 in the *Legality of the Threat or Use of Nuclear Weapons* Advisory Opinion, in which the Court held that:

> [A] great many rules of humanitarian law applicable in armed conflict are so fundamental to the respect of the human person and 'elementary considerations of humanity' [...] These rules are to be observed by all States whether or not they have ratified the conventions that contain them, because they constitute intransgressible principles of international customary law.[124]

The *ratio decidendi* of the ICJ in the *Nuclear Weapons* Advisory Opinion was cited with approval in the 2004 *Legal Consequences of the Construction of a Wall in the Occupied Palestinian Territories* Advisory Opinion, in which the Court held that article 42 of the *Hague Relations* (annexed to *Hague Convention IV* of 1907) also reflects CIL,[125] which was in turn cited with approval in the 2005 *Armed Activities on the Territory of the Congo Case*.[126] In each of these cases, the Court's identification of a rule of CIL was not based on its inclusion in a widely ratified treaty providing evidence of CIL (which

---

121 *Corfu Channel (UK v Albania) (Judgment)* [1949] ICJ Reports 4, 22 (*Corfu Channel (UK v Albania)*) (emphasis added).

122 *Military and Paramilitary Activities in and against Nicaragua (Nicaragua v United States of America) (Merits)* [1986] 14, 114 [218] (*Military and Paramilitary Activities in and against Nicaragua*).

123 Ibid.

124 *Legality of the Threat or Use of Nuclear Weapons* (n 64) 35 [79].

125 *Legal Consequences of the Construction of a Wall in the Occupied Palestinian Territory* (n 65) 136 [89].

126 *Armed Activities on the Territory of the Congo* (n 66) [172], [214], [217].

would arguably be consistent with its reliance on representative state practice). Rather, as stated by Schlütter,

> [T]he fact that certain humanitarian rules like common Article 3 of the Geneva Conventions reflect 'elementary considerations of humanity' seems to be sufficient to make this norm customary in character. Methodologically speaking, this is an entirely deductive way of reasoning.[127]

Most academic commentators acknowledge the ICJ's use of deductive reasoning.[128] Some argue that, where the inductive approach would lead to a morally untenable result due to a lack of state practice or the existence of significant contrary state practice, the Court has tended to deduce the rule from an existing legal concept or principle.[129] Others cite practical reasons for the Court's reliance on deductive reasoning. Talmon ultimately concludes that the Court relies on deduction or assertion simply 'to avoid an epistemological *non-liquet*',[130] while Petersen concludes that the Court's interest in its own legitimacy leads it to prefer dispute settlement by reference to the common ground between the parties, or at least by the most efficient means available.[131] Both authors further note that deductive reasoning may be an intentional method by the Court to avoid the inevitable selectivity that would come with inductively identifying a rule of CIL where there is conflicting state practice.[132]

It is, therefore, difficult to fault Talmon's critique that the ILC has intentionally overlooked the ICJ's use of deductive reasoning in its *Draft Conclusions on Identification of Customary International Law*. The omission

---

127 Schlütter (n 15) 154.

128 Theodor Meron, 'The Martens Clause, Principles of Humanity and Dictates of Public Conscience' (2000) 94(1) *American Journal of International Law* 78; Schlütter (n 15); Petersen (n 12); Geiger (n 55); Roozbeh Baker, 'Customary International Law in the 21st Century: Old Challenges and New Debates' (2010) 21(1) *European Journal of International Law* 173, 91; Gleider Hernández, *The International Court of Justice and the Judicial Function* (OUP 2014); Talmon (n 63); Choi and Gulati (n 12); Tom Ginsburg, 'Bounded Discretion in International Judicial Lawmaking' (2005) 45 *Virginia Journal of International Law* 631.

129 An example of this latter approach is the decision of the ICJ regarding the principle of non-intervention. *Military and Paramilitary Activities in and against Nicaragua* (n 122).

130 Talmon (n 63) 442.

131 Petersen (n 12) 363, 385.

132 Talmon (n 63) 432; Petersen (n 12) 377; Roberts (n 9) 768 ('For example, the Permanent Court cited decisive precedents in the Lotus case [often cited as an example of the inductive approach] based on actions by only six Western states.')

perpetuates the fallacy (as presented by the ICJ itself) that CIL is only identified through an inductive approach and leaves unanswered several practical and theoretical questions concerning situations where a rule of CIL is identified despite the existence of contrary state practice. As stated by Talmon:

> [W]hat about situations in which State practice is non-existent or precarious, State practice is conflicting or too disparate and thus inconclusive, the *opinio juris* of States cannot be established, or there is a discrepancy between State practice and *opinio juris* …? In all these situations the ICJ has not been prevented from finding rules of customary international law. The ILC does not attempt to explain this. […] These problems inherent in the determination of rules of customary international law do not disappear simply by not addressing them.[133]

The ILC only dedicates a few, rather ambiguous lines to the possibility that custom can be deduced.

> The two-element approach does not in fact preclude a measure of deduction as an aid, to be employed with caution … in particular when considering possible rules of customary international law that operate against the backdrop of rules framed in more general terms that themselves derive from and reflect a general practice accepted as law, or when concluding that possible rules of international law form part of an "indivisible regime".[134]

The next section sheds some light on these questions and proposes a methodology for identifying certain rules of CIL in the face of contrary state practice, without resorting to deductive reasoning. Developing such a methodology is particularly important for the adjudication of war crimes at the ICC or any other judicial body exercising war crimes jurisdiction, as most

---

133 Stefan Talmon, 'Determining Customary International Law: The ICJ's Methodology and the Idyllic World of the ILC', *EJIL: Talk! Blog of the European Journal of International Law* (Blog Post, 3 December 2015) <https://www.ejiltalk.org/determining-customary-international-law-the-icjs-methodology-and-the-idyllic-world-of-the-ilc/> accessed 15 July 2024.

134 *Report of the International Law Commission, Chapter V: Identification of Customary International Law* (n 16) 26 para 5.

prohibitive rules under IHL are considered customary despite evidence of routine non-compliance on the ground.[135]

3.6 Current Approaches to Overcoming Contrary State Practice

Two approaches have been used to justify the judicial identification of a rule of CIL despite the existence of considerable contrary state practice. The first approach is often referred to as a 'sliding-scale' theory of CIL, in which the court substitutes scant or inconsistent state practice for strong evidence of *opinio juris*.[136] The second approach is to dismiss evidence of contrary state practice as breaches of the proposed rule where the offending state seeks to deny or qualify such conduct.[137] The second approach is arguably superior from a theoretical perspective because it concerns an assessment of the quality of the evidence of state practice, rather than prioritising one element of CIL (accepted as law or *opinio juris*) over the other (a general practice), which would appear to contradict the very foundation of CIL. However, both can be said to accurately account for how custom is formed and identified by courts and tribunals in practice.

It is presumed, at least in the context of adjudicating international criminal law, that deductive reasoning is an inappropriate means of overcoming contrary state practice as it lacks an observable methodology and is devoid of empirical evidence.

3.6.1 *Substituting State Practice for* opinio juris *on a Sliding Scale*

There is strong support in the literature for recognising two categories of CIL: 'traditional' and 'modern'. Traditional CIL refers to those rules that can be readily ascertained by a process of induction because they relate to the observable practice of states in coordinating international relations or determining reciprocal rights. For example, because the delimitation of territorial boundaries or fishing zones does not carry any great moral weight or threaten the peaceful coexistence of humankind, such rules can more

---

135 Oscar Schachter, 'New Custom: Power, *Opinio Juris* and Contrary State Practice' in Krzysztof Skubiszewski (ed), *Theory of International Law at the Threshold of the 21st Century* (Springer 1996) 531, 538–39.

136 Frederic Kirgis, 'Custom on a Sliding Scale' (1987) 81(1) *American Journal of International Law* 146.

137 *Military and Paramilitary Activities in and against Nicaragua* (n 122) [186].

readily be affirmed or denied based on state practice.[138] Modern CIL, meanwhile, refers to rules of a high moral content that are necessary to give effect to fundamental principles of humanity, such as human rights, humanitarian rules, and the maintenance of international peace and security. The necessity of maintaining these rules, which are often prohibitive in nature, has led several scholars to conclude that they are formed by widespread *opinio juris* and are impervious to contrary state practice. As stated by Anthea Roberts: 'modern custom is derived by a deductive process that begins with general statements of rules rather than instances of practice. This approach emphasizes opinio juris rather than state practice because it relies primarily on statements rather than actions'.[139]

Frederic Kirgis is credited with popularising modern theories of customary international law.[140] He proposes that CIL operates on a 'sliding scale', so that, where there is virtually uniform evidence of state practice, the need for evidence of *opinio juris* is diminished, whereas overwhelming *opinio juris* in support of a particular rule will negate the need to substantiate such belief with consistent practice.[141] With regard to normative humanitarian rules and the prohibition on the use of force, Kirgis suggests that *opinio juris* is likely to take precedence over contrary state practice.

> [W]hen issues of armed force are involved, it may well be that the need for stability explains an international decision maker's primary reliance on normative words rather than on a combination of words and consistent deeds. [...] [T]he more destabilising or morally distasteful the activity — for example, the offensive use of force or the deprivation of fundamental human rights — the more readily the international decision makers will substitute one element for the other, provided that the asserted restrictive rule seems reasonable.[142]

Several authors build on Kirgis' conception that strong *opinio juris* can be substituted for contrary or inconsistent state practice, depending on the normative value of the rule. For example, Roberts states that:

> The moral content of modern custom explains the strong tendency to discount the importance of contrary state practice in the modern

---

138 Roberts (n 9) 781–82.
139 Ibid 758.
140 Kirgis (n 136).
141 Ibid 147.
142 Ibid 147–49.

> approach. Irregularities in description can undermine a descriptive law, but a normative law may be broken and remain a law because it is not premised on descriptive accuracy.[143]

By way of example, Roberts argues that the prohibition on torture is of substantive importance to the international legal order and the principle of humanity; its customary status is thus considered resistant to contrary practice.[144] A facilitative rule, such as the rule that two approaching ships must pass each other on the left, has no morally substantive content and is therefore determined by what is most fit for purpose, as evidenced by the consistent practice of states.[145]

Oscar Schachter acknowledges the conundrum inherent in a sliding-scale conception of CIL, stating that 'the notion that state practice should yield to *opinio juris* challenges the basic premise of customary law'.[146] He argues that such an approach would be unacceptable in the 'great body' of customary rules (for example, the law on jurisdiction, immunities, state responsibility, and diplomatic privileges), for which Schachter maintains that state conduct creates expectations of future behaviour and is thus indispensable to the formation of CIL.[147] With respect to substantive humanitarian rules, however, Schachter claims that:

> The legal perception is quite different in regard to prohibitions of State conduct that are strongly supported and important to international order and human values. Examples are the prohibitions of aggression, genocide, slavery, torture and systematic racial discrimination. We would also include the humanitarian law of armed conflict as a prime example of norms generally accepted as customary (as well as treaty law) even though often violated in practice.[148]

Indeed, there is strong support for the notion that the customary status of prohibitive humanitarian rules, especially those of IHL and international human rights law (IHRL), are impervious to contrary state practice.[149] Antonio Cassese argues that the twin elements of CIL play a different role in the

---

143 Roberts (n 9) 760.
144 Ibid 781.
145 Ibid 781–82.
146 Schachter (n 136) 538.
147 Ibid.
148 Ibid 538–39.
149 Ibid 531–40.

law of armed conflict and that, in accordance with the Martens Clause, a principle or rule of IHL can be formed under the laws of humanity or the 'dictates of public conscience' in the face of contrary state practice.[150] Andrew Guzman argues that, where rules are prohibitive in character and normatively desirable, the existence of non-compliance does not render that rule invalid and should not preclude its status as customary.[151] He notes that war crimes provide the archetypal example on the basis that they are committed in every conflict and yet their customary status is rarely contested.[152] As stated by Guzman, 'incomplete compliance with a desirable rule is better than not having the rule at all'.[153] Finally, as Schachter succinctly explains:

> International rules are not all equal. Some are more important than others because they express deeply-held and widely shared conviction as to the unacceptability of the prohibited conduct. [...] Contrary and inconsistent practice would not and should not defeat their claims as customary international law.[154]

This school of thought likely influenced the decision of ICTY Trial Chamber in *Prosecutor v Kupreškić*, which tackled the issue of contrary state practice head-on. In its judgement of 14 January 2000, the Trial Chamber stated that, when determining the customary status of rules of IHL, *opinio juris necessitatis*, not state practice, plays the decisive role. In discussing the customary status of the prohibition of reprisals against civilians and civilian objects in combat zones, the Trial Chamber stated:

> Admittedly, there does not seem to have emerged recently a body of State practice consistently supporting the proposition that one of the elements of custom, namely *usus* or *diuturnitas* has taken shape. This is however an area where *opinio iuris sive necessitatis* may play a much greater role than *usus*, as a result of the aforementioned Martens

150 Antonio Cassese, *International Criminal Law* (2nd ed, OUP 2008) 160-61.

151 Andrew Guzman and Jerome Hsiang, 'Reinvigorating Customary International Law' in Curtis A Bradley (ed), *Custom's Future: International Law in a Changing World* (CUP 2016) 275, 283.

152 Ibid.

153 Ibid.

154 Oscar Schachter, 'Recent Trends in International Law Making' (1989) 12 *Australian Yearbook of International Law* 1, 11.

> Clause. In the light of the way States and courts have implemented it, this Clause clearly shows that principles of international humanitarian law may emerge through a customary process under the pressure of the demands of humanity or the dictates of public conscience, even where State practice is scant or inconsistent. The other element, in the form of *opinio necessitatis*, crystallising as a result of the imperatives of humanity or public conscience, may turn out to be the decisive element heralding the emergence of a general rule or principle of humanitarian law.[155]

In this passage, the Trial Chamber in *Kupreškić* attempted to justify the selectively that is inherent in ignoring evidence of contrary state practice. In short, the Chamber decided that what states say is more important than what they do when identifying certain rules of CIL.

However, the fundamental issue with sliding-scale conceptions of CIL (along with other theories that propose ignoring the state practice element altogether or calling it by another name)[156] is that they deprive CIL of the element that denotes its binding authority: the existence of custom.[157] As stated by Karol Wolfke: 'Without practice (*consuetudo*), customary international law would obviously be a misnomer, since practice constitutes precisely the main *differentia specifica* of that kind of international law'.[158]

Substituting state practice for *opinio juris*, even if it is an accurate reflection of what courts are doing in practice, is inconsistent with the very foundation of CIL and risks diminishing its binding authority. Accordingly, it is necessary to conceptualise those rules of CIL that are impervious to contrary state practice in a different manner.

155 *Kupreškić Trial Judgment* (n 85) [227].

156 Daniel Bodansky, 'Customary (and Not So Customary) International Environmental Law' (1995) 3 *Indiana Journal of Global Legal Studies* 105, 116-19; Jonathan Charney, 'Universal International Law' (1993) 4 *American Journal Of International Law* 529, 543, 546–47; Chodosh (n 77) 88; Petersen, 'Customary Law without Custom?' (n 82) 275; George Norman and Joel Trachtman, 'The Customary International Law Game' (2005) 99(3) *American Journal of International Law* 541, 118–19; Hugh Thirlway, 'The Law and Procedure of the International Court of Justice, 1960–1989, Part Two' (1990) 61 *British Yearbook of International Law* 10; Brian Lepard, *Customary International Law: A New Theory with Practical Application* (CUP 2010).

157 Noora Arajärvi, *The Changing Nature of Customary International Law: Methods of Interpreting the Concept of Custom in International Criminal Tribunals* (Routledge 2014) 162.

158 Karol Wolfke, *Custom in Present International Law* (Martinus Nijhoff 1993) 40–41.

3.6.2 *Qualifying Contrary State Practice as a Breach of the Rule*

Another, slightly different approach to recognising the validity of certain rules of CIL in the face of contrary state practice is to qualify such contrary practice as a breach of the rule. This approach focuses more on the quality of the evidence of state practice, rather than asserting that one element of CIL is more important than the other. It is, therefore, more consistent with the theoretical foundation of CIL.

In *Nicaragua*, the ICJ held that the prohibition on unlawful interference in the territorial sovereignty of another state is a rule of CIL by reference to its inclusion in a significant number of multilateral instruments and resolutions,[159] having stated 'with all due caution'[160] that *opinio juris* may be gleaned from states' participation in UNGA Resolutions, in particular the Friendly Relations Declaration of Resolution 2625 (XXV). Consistent with the empirical studies cited in section 2.2, the ICJ relied on such representative state practice without citing the conduct of individual states. On this point, Anthony D'Amato argues that, if the ICJ had earnestly engaged in a survey of relevant state practice, it would have uncovered sufficient contrary practice to rebut the proposed customary status of the principle of non-intervention. D'Amato cites humanitarian intervention, counter-terrorism operations and reprisals, collective enforcement measures, and transboundary security operations, all of which infringe or modify the principle of non-intervention and ought to have been relevant to the customary status of the rule.[161]

On this occasion, however, the ICJ did provide some explanation of its methodology and the conceptual basis for recognising CIL in the face of contrary state practice.

> In order to deduce the existence of customary rules, the Court deems it sufficient that the conduct of States should, in general, be consistent with such rules, and that instances of State conduct inconsistent with a given rule should generally have been treated as breaches of that rule, not as indications of the recognition of a new rule. If a State acts in a way prima facie incompatible with a recognized rule, but defends its conduct by appealing to exceptions or justifications

159 *Military and Paramilitary Activities in and against Nicaragua* (n 122) 90 [189].

160 Ibid 89 [188].

161 Anthony D'Amato, 'Trashing Customary International Law' (1987) 81(1) *American Journal of International Law* 101, 103.

> contained within the rule itself, then whether or not the State's conduct is in fact justifiable on that basis, the significance of that attitude is to confirm rather than to weaken the rule.[162]

This line of reasoning was also adopted by the ICTY. In November 1998, the *Delacić* Trial Chamber held that there can be 'no doubt that torture is prohibited by both conventional and customary international law' on the basis that it was contained in several multilateral treaties and human rights instruments.[163] Although consistent with the ICTY's reliance on representative practice, this decision seemingly ignored the issue of contrary state practice. The following month, ICTY Trial Chamber in *Prosecutor v Furundžija* upheld the customary prohibition on torture, but this time provided an explanation of its methodology for overcoming contrary state practice.[164]

> [N]o State has ever claimed that it was authorised to practice torture in time of armed conflict, nor has any State shown or manifested an opposition to the implementation of treaty provisions against torture. When a State has been taken to task because its officials allegedly resorted to torture, it has normally responded that the allegation was unfounded, thus expressly or implicitly upholding the prohibition of this odious practice. … [T]he International Court of Justice has authoritatively, albeit not with express reference to torture, confirmed this customary creating process: in the *Nicaragua* case it held that common article 3 of the 1949 Geneva Convention, which *inter alia* prohibits torture against persons taking no active part in hostilities, is now well-established as belonging to the corpus of customary international law and is applicable both to international and internal armed conflicts.[165]

The ICTY Trial Chamber in *Furundžija* conforms to the ICJ's methodology in *Nicaragua* by maintaining that contrary state practice is insufficient to negate the existence of a rule of CIL where such practice is either denied or qualified. The Chamber extended this reasoning by stating that articles 57 and 58 of *AP I* (which concern the obligation to take precautions in, and against the effects of, attack) 'form part of customary international law

162 *Military and Paramilitary Activities in and against Nicaragua* (n 122) 88 [186].
163 *Delalić Trial Judgment* (n 89) [452]–[454].
164 *Furundžija Trial Judgment* (n 87) [137]–[138].
165 *Furundžija Trial Judgment* (n 87) [138].

because they specify general pre-existing norms and *because no State seems to contest them*'.[166] In other words, irrespective of whether a rule is complied with on the ground, the absence of states contesting the validity of a rule contained in a treaty may be indicative of its customary status.

The prohibition on torture is the archetypal example of a rule whose customary status is rarely questioned by academics or practitioners of international law, even though it is frequently violated by states.[167] As exemplified by the ICTY Trial Chamber in *Furundžija*, it is also a good example of a rule in which instances of contrary state practice are denied or qualified by the offending state, thereby tending to confirm the existence of the rule.[168]

The benefit of treating contrary state practice as a breach of a rule is that it does not rely on preferencing the 'acceptance-as-law' (*opinio juris*) element over state practice, which would seem to contradict the foundations of CIL. Instead, it examines the quality of the evidence in its specific context to determine whether the behaviour can be classified as rule-forming or simply as a violation of an existing rule.

Focusing on the weight of evidence can help overcome inconsistent or contrary practice and is an approach that can be further refined in light of the ILC's Draft Conclusions, as demonstrated in the next section.

3.7 A New Proposal: a Hierarchy of Evidence for Identifying Customary International Law

Another way to overcome contrary state practice when identifying prohibitive humanitarian rules is to prioritise representative forms of practice (what states say) over evidence of non-compliance occurring on the ground (what states do). This suggestion is not exactly new. Indeed, as stated by

166 Ibid (emphasis added).

167 Amnesty International (n 44); Roberts (n 9) 769.

168 Roberts (n 9) 776 ('[I]nconsistent state practice can be interpreted as a breach of an existing custom or a seed for a new custom, which is a particularly important consideration in modern customs such as human rights obligations, where breaches seem reasonably common and widespread.'); Katie Johnston, 'Nature and Context of Rules and the Identification of Customary International Law' (2021) 32(4) *European Journal of International Law* 1167, 1183 ('The [ICJ in Nicaragua] was therefore [due to the ILC's acceptance of representative state practice] correct to tolerate the existence of some contrary practice, characterizing it as mere breaches of the prohibition on force that do not undermine the existence of the customary rule.')

Richard Baxter in 1965, 'The firm statement by the State of what it considers to be the rule is far better evidence of its position than what can be pieced together from the actions of that country at different times and in a variety of contexts'.[169] Nor is this proposal conceptually very different from the sliding-scale theories of CIL, which prioritise evidence of *opinio juris* over state practice. However, in light of the ILC's acceptance that evidence of both elements of CIL can be found in representative forms of state practice (for example, multilateral treaties and UN Resolutions), prioritising what states say over what they do in certain contexts can be reformulated as a hierarchy of evidence.

3.7.1 *Support for a Contextually Dependent Hierarchy of Evidence in the ILC Draft Conclusions*

The ILC Draft Conclusions lend weight to the proposed hierarchy of evidence for identifying rules of CIL in specific contexts. During the debates on the Third Report of the Draft Conclusions, ILC member Kriangsak Kittichaisaree queried whether 'by going forward with a strict separation between evidence of practice and opinio juris, the Special Rapporteur was rejecting Kirgis's "sliding scale" approach, in other words, the notion that the weight accorded to each element could vary according to circumstances'.[170] In response, Sir Michael Wood affirmed the supremacy of the traditional approach, declaring that the abundance of one element cannot compensate for the absence of the other, as otherwise it would no longer meet the definition of CIL.[171]

There are multiple reasons for the ILC's unwavering insistence on the two-element approach, not the least of which is the fact that states have almost unanimously claimed that CIL is exclusively defined by state practice and *opinio juris* (or a general practice accepted as law). As a group of international legal experts working in conjunction with states to codify and progressively develop the law, the ILC is effectively beholden to the views of

169 Richard Baxter, 'Multilateral Treaties as Evidence of Customary International Law' (1965) 41 *British Yearbook of International Law* 275, 300.

170 Summary of the statement by Kriangsak Kittichaisaree, ILC 67th session, provisional summary record of the 3251st meeting, A/CN.4/SR.3251.

171 Summary of the statement by Sir Michael Wood, ILC 67th session, provisional summary record of the 3254th meeting, A/CN.4/SR.3254 ('Les deux éléments doivent être présents, chacun ayant un rôle propre à jouer; l'abondance de l'un ne peut pas compenser l'absence de l'autre, sans quoi il ne s'agirait tout simplement pas de droit international coutumier.').

states and could not have proceeded down any other path in the face of such opposition to alternate theories. The other is the one acknowledged by Sir Michael Wood himself; namely, that CIL without the actual practice of states is inherently contradictory and would seem to undermine its legally binding status. In rejecting the notion that different rules on the identification of CIL could apply to different fields of law, such as IHL or IHRL, Sir Michael Would writes in the Fourth and final Report:

> The two-element approach applies to the identification of the existence and content of rules of customary international law in all fields of international law. This is confirmed in the practice of States and in the case law, and is consistent with the unity and coherence of international law, which is a single legal system and is not divided into separate branches, each with its own approach to sources.[172]

However, despite some resistance in its earlier Reports,[173] the ILC eventually acknowledged that the same act can provide evidence of both the 'general practice' and 'accepted-as-law' elements simultaneously.[174] This decision reflects the reality that courts have frequently relied on representative forms of practice (such as public statements, treaties, and UN resolutions) as evidence of both state practice and *opinio juris*. As stated in the ILC Commentary to Draft Conclusion 6:

> While some have argued that it is only what stated "do" rather than what they "say" that counts as practice for the purpose of identifying customary international law, it is now generally accepted that verbal conduct (whether written or oral) may also count as practice; indeed, practice may at times consist of entirely verbal acts, for example diplomatic protests.[175]

---

172 Ibid Draft Conclusion 2, para 6, 126.

173 Wood, *Second Report on Identification of Customary International Law* (n 102) 59 para 74 ('[T]he same conduct should not serve in a particular case as evidence of both practice and acceptance of that practice as law.')

174 *Report of the International Law Commission, Chapter V: Identification of Customary International Law* (n 16) Conclusion 10, 141 para 3 ('There is some common ground between the forms of evidence of acceptance as law and the forms of State practice; in part, this reflects the fact that the two elements may at times be found in the same material.')

175 *Report of the International Law Commission, Chapter V: Identification of Customary International Law* (n 16) 133.

As a result, one form of practice (what states say) can be given greater probative weight in a specific context than another form of practice (what states do on the ground). Categorising the evidence in this way can enable a court to determine, for example, that the extensive practice of states affirming the prohibition on torture through treaties, resolutions, domestic laws, and public statements outweighs the (less probative) evidence of states acting in violation of this rule.

Indeed, the ILC commentary explicitly provides that the weight of different forms of evidence needed to prove a rule of CIL may depend on the relevant context.

> Paragraph 3 clarifies that in principle no form of practice has a higher probative value than others in the abstract. In particular cases, however, as explained in the commentaries to draft conclusions 3 and 7, it may be that different forms (or instances) of practice ought to be given different weight when they are assessed in context.[176]

The ILC Commentary does not go so far as to provide specific examples of where a certain type of practice might prevail over another, nor does it explicitly state that verbal practice could trump physical practice with respect to prohibitive humanitarian rules. Indeed, where the ILC does address the issue of contrary state practice, it seems to take a different route. As stated in the ILC Commentary to Conclusion 3:

> The nature of the rule in question may also be of significance when assessing evidence for the purpose of ascertaining whether there is a general practice that is accepted as law (accompanied by *opinio juris*). In particular, where prohibitive rules are concerned (such as the prohibition of torture) it may sometimes be difficult to find positive State practice (as opposed to inaction); cases involving such rules will most likely turn on evaluating whether the practice (being deliberate inaction) is accepted as law.[177]

Treating the inaction of states as a means of offsetting those who act contrary to a proposed rule of CIL is a novel and potentially effective means of dealing with contrary state practice. In theory, it allows a court to consider that for every state that practices torture, for example, there is a greater

176 Ibid Conclusion 6(3), 134 para 8.

177 Ibid Conclusion 3, 128 para 4. See also Johnston (n 168) 1174–76.

number of states who do not engage in torture because they have accepted its prohibition as law. With the ILC's conception of state inaction in mind, Katie Johnston argues that the ICJ in *Nicaragua* was correct to dismiss contrary state practice as violations of the customary rule of non-intervention.

> Balanced against the considerable supportive practice of states that do abstain from using force in the acceptance that this conduct is required by law, the Court was justified in concluding that there is nevertheless both a widespread and representative practice and opinio juris supporting the existence of a customary prohibition on force.[178]

The ILC explicitly recognises 'deliberate' inaction as a form of practice and *opinio juris* in Draft Conclusions 6 and 10, respectively, which enables such inaction to be assessed alongside evidence of contrary state practice when determining the existence of CIL.[179] The problem with this conception is that evidence of 'inaction' is intangible and may be difficult to quantify, as there is usually no way of inferring whether the reason behind a state's inaction is a belief that the conduct is prohibited as opposed to mere convenience or indifference.[180]

Noora Arajärvi notes that 'a considerable number of States (Chile, France, Indonesia, Ireland, the Republic of Korea, Romania, Slovakia, Slovenia, Spain, Turkey) called for clarification of the requirements of inaction for the purposes of CIL formation'.[181] Japan expressed 'caution in viewing inaction as evidence of opinio juris due to the practical difficulty of distinguishing the inaction that contributes to CIL from all other kinds of non-actions', while Iran explicitly rejected the idea that inaction in respect of a violation of international law can be seen as relevant practice.[182] The general view appeared to be that deliberate inaction must be limited to situations that called for a response from the relevant state for it to qualify as evidence of CIL.[183]

---

178 Johnston (n 168) 1167, 1183.

179 *Report of the International Law Commission, Chapter V: Identification of Customary International Law* (n 16) 133.

180 Roberts (n 9) 778–79.

181 Noora Arajärvi, 'The Requisite Rigour in the Identification of Customary International Law: A Look at the Reports of the Special Rapporteur of the International Law Commission' (2017) 19 *International Community Law Review* 9, 22.

182 Ibid 23.

183 Ibid 22–3. El Salvador, Mexico, Peru, Japan, Netherlands each expressed the need for limitations when treating inaction as practice. Johston argues that inaction must be

Relying on inaction also creates the somewhat uncomfortable suggestion that states are only refraining from violating certain rules of CIL (such as the prohibition on torture or rape) because they are prohibited from doing so, as opposed to the understanding that states create CIL rules through positive conduct (such as signing treaties that prohibit torture or rape). It would therefore seem preferable to accommodate deliberate inaction as a form of practice where appropriate, as suggested by the ILC, while also categorising different forms of practice along a contextually dependent hierarchy of evidence. In other words, the two proposals can work together.

So, how might the evaluation of different forms of practice work when determining the customary status of a prohibitive rule? Take the war crime torture as an example. The representative forms of practice seen in treaties, resolutions, public condemnations, and other instruments prohibiting torture would constitute highly probative evidence of both state practice and *opinio juris* (or a general practice accepted as law). The fact that many states do not practice torture, on its own, would lack the necessary specificity to qualify as practice through inaction. By contrast, 'deliberately' refraining from engaging in torture against detained prisoners of war with sensitive information, for example, might form relevant evidence of its customary prohibition. Examples in which states practice torture but seek to deny or qualify their conduct can be seen as breaches of the rule that reinforce its customary status, consistent with the ruling in *Nicaragua*. Finally, general evidence of noncompliance with the prohibition on torture must be acknowledged as relevant practice, but can be ascribed relatively low probative value when pitted against the weight of representative practice confirming the existence of the prohibitive rule.

The ILC determined that 'different forms (or instances) of practice ought to be given different weight when they are assessed in context'.[184] In the context of prohibitive humanitarian rules that are essential to the functioning of a just and sustainable international order, including war crimes, crimes against humanity, human rights violations, and the prohibition on the use of force, the firm evidence of what states accept as law, as demonstrated in treaties, resolutions, public statements, and other international instruments, should be treated as more probative than evidence of contrary state practice occurring on the ground. Noncompliance with a prohibitive

---

supported by strong *opinio juris* so that it is clear the state is acting deliberately in view of its legal obligations.

184 *Report of the International Law Commission, Chapter V: Identification of Customary International Law* (n 16) Conclusion 6(3), 134.

rule should not diminish its customary status where states widely affirm the existence the rule through their verbal practice, deliberate inaction, and acceptance of its legal character.

3.7.2 *Support for a Contextually Dependent Hierarchy of Evidence in the Alternative Theories of Customary International Law*

It is worth reiterating that this proposed hierarchy of evidence is broadly consistent with the alternative approaches to CIL. Kirgis' sliding scale enables strong evidence of the accepted-as-law element (*opinio juris*) to overcome inconsistent or contrary practice. The ICJ in *Nicaragua* and the ICTY in *Furundžija* held that contrary practice is to be treated as a violation of a rule where such conduct is denied or qualified, providing there is sufficiently robust *opinio juris* to confirm that rule's existence. The change that is proposed here is about the categorisation and prioritisation of different forms of evidence in specific contexts. For prohibitive humanitarian rules, representative forms of practice, such as treaties, resolutions, public statements, and other instruments, should be viewed as more probative than examples of contrary state practice on the ground.

The main critique of sliding-scale or 'modern' theories of CIL is that substituting state practice for *opinio juris* can no longer be said to be a source of law that is based on the practice (custom) of states. Karol Wolfke argued in 1993 that relying on *opinio juris* 'neglects the very essence of every kind of custom, which for centuries has been based upon material deeds and not words [...] customs arise from acts of conduct and not from promises of such acts'.[185] The attempts to mould CIL to fit the rise in the identification of prohibitive humanitarian rules by international criminal tribunals led Schabas to comment that '[i]t might be better if it was simply acknowledged that [CIL] in the context of international criminal law means something different than [CIL] in the context of traditional public international law'.[186] However, in light of the ILC's rejection of the notion that CIL can have different meanings for different fields of law,[187] such an approach is unlikely to gain favour. Instead, buoyed by the ILC's acknowledgement that oral or 'representative' forms of practice constitute evidence of both practice

---

185 Karol Wolfke, *Custom in Present International Law* (2nd ed, Martinus Nijhoff, 1993) 42.

186 Schabas 'Customary or "Judge-Made" Law' (n 6) 101.

187 *Report of the International Law Commission, Chapter V: Identification of Customary International Law* (n 16) Conclusion 2, para 6, 126.

and *opinio juris*, it is possible to replace the sliding-scale theories of CIL with a contextually dependent hierarchy of evidence.

Focusing on different forms of evidence allows the identification of CIL to remain grounded in the broadly defined 'practice' of states, while still benefiting from the normative value of the alternative theories of CIL. These alternative theories highlight that what states say in prohibiting inhumane conduct is more important than their unfortunate inability to live up to their own standards. Indeed, it is well noted that prohibitive humanitarian rules do not lend themselves to widespread compliance. Josef Kunz commented in 1934 that the very nature of prohibitive rules presupposes that they will be violated, which is why criminal laws have punishments inbuilt.[188] In contrast to facilitative rules of international law that arise through states acting in a virtually uniform manner, prohibitive humanitarian rules arise because states get together to sign treaties and declarations prohibiting certain conduct with the knowledge that such rules will be violated and their perpetrators will need to be punished. It is logical to treat such violations as a less probative form of evidence than the practice of states in agreeing that the conduct should be prohibited in the first place.

Of course, this approach is already reflected in judicial practice to varying degrees. International courts and tribunals will continue to recognise war crimes as customary even though they are violated on the ground. What the contextually dependent hierarchy of evidence enables them to do is to identify such rules as customary by inductively compiling evidence of representative state practice, while explaining the comparatively low probative value of contrary practice. Adopting this approach can help courts and tribunals avoid entirely deductive forms of reasoning – and the naturalist law critique that that such reasoning invites – thereby bringing greater clarity and evidentiary certainty to the identification of CIL in the international criminal context.

3.8 Conclusion

The disparity between theory and practice in the judicial identification of CIL is a likely reason behind the ICC's reluctance to apply the principle of

188 Josef Kunz, 'Plus de Lois de la Guerre?' (1934) 41 *Revue Générale de Droit International Public* 22, 29.

systemic integration and interpret the definition of war crimes consistently with customary IHL. Analysis of the jurisprudence of both the ICJ and the ICTY reveals that CIL it is not evidenced in the quantifiable practice of individual states acting under a sense of pre-existing legal obligation, as the traditional approach would suggest, but in the collective output of states in the international diplomatic arena concerning their desire for what the law should be. On this point, the ILC Draft Conclusions have helped close the gap between theory and practice. The ILC openly acknowledges the evidentiary value of representative state practice, abandons the chronological requirement inherent in the *opinio juris* paradox, and accepts the fact that the same conduct can be used as evidence of both elements of CIL simultaneously.

However, the ILC Draft Conclusions fail to address the fact that both the ICJ and the ICTY have resorted to deductive reasoning and other alternative approaches when identifying rules of CIL in the face of considerable contrary state practice. The omission is particularly problematic for courts seeking to identify customary rules of IHL, including the ICC, as these rules are 'a prime example of norms generally accepted as customary [...] even though often violated in practice'.[189] Indeed, the general acceptance by both courts and academics that prohibitive humanitarian rules retain their customary status despite routine non-compliance has not been met with a theoretically or methodologically sound approach to identifying such rules in practice.

Building on the dictum in *Nicaragua* and *Furundžija*, courts should adopt a contextually dependent hierarchy of evidence when identifying customary rules that are widely supported in the international discourse but subjected to routine non-compliance on the ground. Evidence of representative forms of state practice, such as the participation of states in signing treaties, UN Resolutions, and other international instruments, should carry greater probative value in the identification of prohibitive humanitarian rules of CIL than evidence of non-compliance with such rules on the ground, especially where such non-compliance is qualified or denied.

Taken together with the ILC Draft Conclusions, this Chapter has aimed to provide greater clarity on the methodology for identifying CIL. Clarifying the evidence needed to prove the constituent elements of CIL, particularly

189 Schachter, 'New Custom: Power, *Opinio Juris* and Contrary State Practice' (n 135) 538–39.

in the face of contrary state practice, has the potential to increase transparency. It is hope that this approach will, in turn, facilitate the ICC's compliance with the principle of systemic integration by allowing it to more confidently engage in the judicial identification of CIL when interpreting the definition of crimes.

CHAPTER 4

Assessing the International Criminal Court's Compliance with the Principle of Systemic Integration

4.1 Introduction

In this book, I have examined why judges of the International Criminal Court (ICC) appear reluctant to comply with the principle of systemic integration and interpret the war crimes provisions of the *Rome Statute* consistently with customary international humanitarian law (customary IHL). I hypothesised that three factors influence this reluctance.

1. The judges tend to view the *Elements of Crimes* as obviating the need to ascertain the definition and scope of an offence under customary international law (CIL).
2. The judges tend to view the codification of the principle of legality and its concomitant rules of strict construction in article 22(2) of the *Statute* as limiting or precluding interpretive reliance on CIL.
3. The judges are discouraged from identifying rules of CIL for the purpose of interpreting the *Statute* due to the lack of clarity surrounding the constituent elements of CIL and the evidence necessary to prove their existence in a court of law.

From a legal perspective, I have argued that none of these reasons provides sufficient legal justification for failing to apply the principle of systemic integration. This chapter is dedicated to determining whether these hypotheses are empirically true.

Hypothesis 3 cannot be tested against the ICC's jurisprudence because its assumptions are not explicitly stated or inferable from the Court's reasoning; it is therefore excluded from the present analysis. Testing Hypotheses 1 and 2 against the ICC's interpretation of the definition of crimes and modes of liability in the *Rome Statute*, however, led to three conclusions on the ICC's adherence to the principle of systemic integration.

First, the Court rarely refers to article 3(1)(3)(c) of the *Vienna Convention on the Law of Treaties* (VCLT) or the principle of systemic integration. However, this lack of formal observance does not necessarily provide an accurate representation of the Court's compliance with the principle in practice.

 | DOI:10.1163/9789004690042_005

Second, broader analysis reveals that the Court is also not complying with the principle of systemic integration in practice. The Court refers to CIL or an equivalent term in approximately 15 per cent of cases when interpreting the definition of crimes or modes of liability. However, qualitative analysis of a select sample suggests that the interpretive value of CIL is limited to situations where the *Elements of Crimes* has not provided its own definition of the relevant offence.[1] The sample cases were selected because they contained the most references to the *VCLT*, and because they were the only cases to have formally relied on the principle of systemic integration. Consistent with Hypothesis 1, the fact that these only relied on external sources of law to interpret the *Statue* where the *Elements of Crimes* do not provide a definition suggests that judges tend to view CIL as subservient to the *Elements of Crimes*.

Third, the Court's tendency to rely exclusively on the *Elements of Crimes* is usually justified by reference to the principle of legality in article 22(2) of the *Statute*. Consistent with Hypothesis 2, this suggests that judges tend to view the codification of the principle of legality and its concomitant rules of strict construction in article 22(2) of the *Statute* as limiting or precluding interpretive reliance on CIL.

Following on from these findings, I engage in a qualitative analysis of three Appeals Chambers decisions in which, despite not mentioning the principle of systemic integration, the Court determined that certain war crimes 'must' be interpreted consistently with customary IHL (section 4.4).[2] On the one hand, these cases highlight the potential for the principle of systemic integration to prevent fragmentation and contribute to the incremental development of the law. On the other hand, the failure of multiple ICC

1 *Prosecutor v Germain Katanga and Mathieu Ngudjolo Chui* (*Judgment*) (International Criminal Court, Trial Chamber II, Case No ICC-01/04-01/07, 7 March 2014) [47], [1100], [1395] nn 1394, [1625] ('*Katanga Trial Judgment*'); *Prosecutor v Jean-Pierre Bemba Gombo* (*Judgment*) (International Criminal Court, Trial Chamber III, Case No ICC-01/05-01/08, 21 March 2016) [78]–[79] ('*Bemba Trial Judgment*').

2 *Prosecutor v Thomas Lubanga Dyilo* (*Judgment*) (International Criminal Court, Appeals Chamber, Case No ICC-01/04-01/06 A5, 1 December 2014) [322] ('*Lubanga Appeals Judgement*'); *Prosecutor v Bosco Ntaganda* (*Judgement on the appeal of Mr Ntaganda against the "Second decision on the Defence's challenge to the jurisdiction of the Court in respect of Counts 6 and 9*) (International Criminal Court, Appeals Chamber, Case No ICC-01/04-02/06 OA5, 15 June 2017) [52]–[53] ('*Appeals Chamber's Second Decision on Mr Ntaganda's Jurisdictional Appeal*'); *Prosecutor v Bosco Ntaganda* (*Judgment*) (International Criminal Court, Appeals Chamber, Case No ICC-01/04-02/06 A A2, 30 March 2021) [564] ('*Ntagnanda Appeals Judgment*').

Trial Chambers to implement the same approach reflects the methodological mayhem at the ICC.

While the ICC's record of compliance with the principle of systemic integration in its war crimes jurisprudence is inconsistent, certain decisions reflect the true potential of this principle. Beyond preventing fragmentation, interpreting the definition of war crimes in accordance with customary IHL serves to clarify the content of such rules when applied to novel scenarios. In doing so, it contributes to legitimate, incremental development of the law.

4.2 Quantitative Analysis

In 2014, ICC Trial Chamber II in *Katanga* stated that, 'The chambers of the Court have unanimously and systematically based their interpretation of the Statute on the principles established by the Vienna Convention'.[3] Quantitative analysis of the ICC's jurisprudence reveals that this is not the case.[4] Instead, the data shows, there is very rarely any formal reference to the general rule of interpretation in article 31 of the *VCLT* when interpreting the definition of crimes.

There are even fewer formal references to the principle of systemic integration under article 31(3)(c) of the *VCLT*. Indeed, of the 190 ICC decisions analysed in this study, only two refer to article 31(3)(c) or the principle of systemic of systemic integration.[5] Of course, lack of formal reference to the principle of systemic integration does not necessarily mean that it has not been complied with in substance. However, the ICC's limited reference to terms like 'customary' or 'international humanitarian law' also suggest limited substantive compliance with the principle of systemic integration. The data from this approach, when combined with qualitative analysis of select cases, sheds some light on the Court's methodology but suggests that its substantive compliance with the principle of systemic integration is still, at best, inconsistent.[6]

3 *Katanga Trial Judgment* (n 1) [43].
4 See Figure 4.1.
5 *Katanga Trial Judgment* (n 1) [47], [1100], [1395] nn 1394, [1625]; *Bemba Trial Judgment* (n 1) [78]–[79].
6 See Figure 4.2.

4.2.1 *Methodology*

In compiling the quantitative data, all ICC decisions written in English on the confirmation of charges, trial and appeal judgements, decisions on jurisdiction and admissibility, and decisions to authorise investigations were examined for reference to the general rule of interpretation in article 31 of the *VCLT* and the principle of systemic integration more specifically.[7] These categories of decisions were selected because they are the most likely to involve substantive interpretations of the definition of crimes.

To determine whether the decision mentions the general rule of interpretation directly, all decisions were scanned for any reference to the *VCLT*. To try and account for situations in which the general rule may have been applied substantively though not formally, all decisions were also searched for 'ordinary meaning', 'object and purpose', 'good faith', and 'in its context'. These results are displayed in Figure 4.1, below.

The same approach was applied to determine the Court's adherence to the principle of systemic integration. All decisions were scanned for formal reference to 'article 31(3)(c)' and 'systemic integration'. To get an impression of the reliance on CIL as a source of law more generally, the decisions were then scanned for reference to 'customary', 'international humanitarian law, 'established framework [of the international law of armed conflict]', 'laws of war', and 'law of armed conflict'. These results are in Figure 4.2.

To gain a more accurate picture, every positive match was analysed using the 'legal findings' search option on the ICC database to determine whether the reference to the *VCLT* rules of interpretation or reliance on customary law pertained to an interpretation of the definition of crimes, as opposed to an interpretation of other provisions or procedures in the *Rome Statute*. This distinction between a positive match and the more specific determination of whether the relevant search term is being used to interpret the definition of crimes is reflected in both Figures 4.1 and 4.2 by comparing 'total hits' with 'relevant hits'.

7 The International Criminal Court database can be found here: <https://legal-tools.org/cld>. The terms were searched under the 'decisions' tab and filtered by the following categories of decisions: 'Appeal Judgment 82 RC – interlocutory appeals'; 'Decision 61 RC – confirmation of charges'; 'Decision 74 RC – conviction or acquittal'; 'Decision 18–19 RC – jurisdiction or admissibility'; 'Appeal Judgment 81 RC – conviction, acquittal or sentence'; and 'Decision 15 RC – authorisation of investigation'.

4.2.2 *Results*

As demonstrated in Figure 4.1, below, approximately 19 per cent of all decisions analysed referred directly to the VCLT (36 out of 190 decisions). Compliance with the general rule of interpretation was similar when searching for reference to the substantive rules contained within article 31 of the VCLT. Approximately 24 per cent of decisions referred to the term 'object and purpose', 20 per cent to 'good faith', 16 per cent to 'ordinary meaning', and seven per cent to 'in its context'.

However, when these results were limited to instances in which the VCLT rules were used to interpret the definitions of crimes or modes of liability, compliance with the general rule of interpretation was significantly reduced. Fewer than nine per cent of decisions referred to the VCLT directly, eight per cent to the term 'object and purpose', six per cent to 'good faith', seven per cent to 'ordinary meaning', and three percent to 'in its context'. Several significant decisions, including those in which an accused was acquitted or convicted at trial or on appeal, made no reference these customary rules of interpretation when construing the definition of crimes.[8]

As demonstrated in Figure 4.2, below, less than one per cent of all decisions examined made reference to article 31(3)(c) or the principle of systemic integration directly (2 out of 190 decisions). These decisions are Trial Chamber III's 2016 Judgment in *Prosecutor v Bemba* and Trial Chamber II's 2014 Judgment in *Prosecutor v Katanga*, both of which provided a tailored approach to interpretation that combines article 31 of the VCLT with the rules of strict construction in article 22(2) and confirmed that article 31(3)(c) requires the Court to consider CIL in the interpretation of the *Rome Statute*.[9]

8 *Prosecutor v Ahmad Al Faqi Al Mahdi (Judgment and Sentence)* (International Criminal Court, Trial Chamber VIII, Case No ICC-01/12-01/15, 27 September 2016) (*'Al Mahdi Trial Judgment'*); *Prosecutor v Jean-Pierre Bemba Gombo (Judgment)* (International Criminal Court, Appeals Chamber, Case No ICC-01/05-01/08 A, 8 June 2018) (*'Bemba Appeals Judgment'*); *Appeals Chamber's Second Decision on Mr Ntaganda's Jurisdictional Appeal* (n 2); *Prosecutor v Bosco Ntaganda (Judgment)* (International Criminal Court, Trial Chamber, Case No ICC-01/04-02/06, 8 July 2019) (*'Ntagnada Trial Judgment'*); *Ntagnanda Appeals Judgment* (n 2); *Prosecutor v Dominic Ongwen (Judgment)* (International Criminal Court, Trial Chamber IX, Case No ICC-02/04-01/15, 4 February 2021) (*'Prosecutor v Dominic Ongwen'*).

9 *Katanga Trial Judgment* (n 1) [47], [1100], [1395] nn 1394, [1625]; *Bemba Trial Judgment* (n 1) [78]–[79]. See also: *Prosecutor v William Samoei Ruto (Decision on Mr Ruto's Request for Excusal from Continuous Presence at Trial)* (International Criminal Court, Trial Chamber V(A), Case No ICC-01/09-01/11, 18 June 2013) [101]–[102] (*Decision on Mr Ruto's Request for Excusal*) (note that the *Ruto* decision was not within the categories choses in the

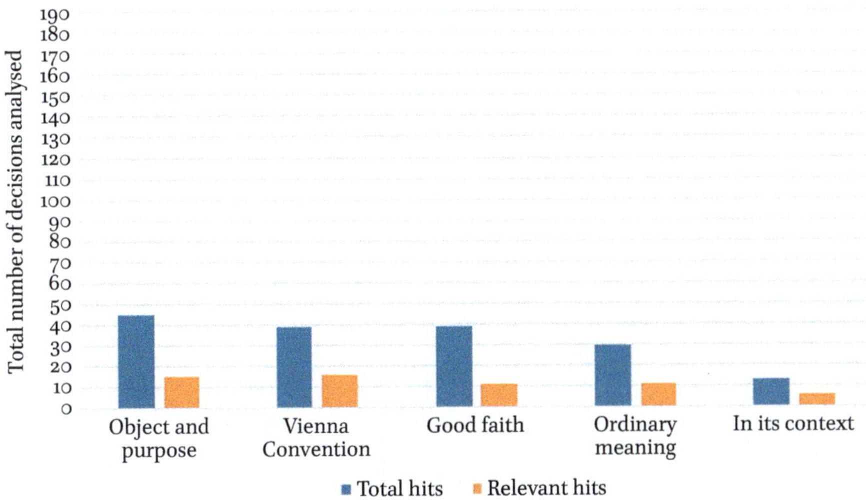

FIGURE 4.1 References to the general rule of interpretation
The x-axis shows the search terms relating to the general rule of interpretation. The y-axis shows the 'total hits' out of the 190 decisions analysed, as well as 'relevant hits', which reflects the number of decisions in which the terms were used to interpret the definition of crimes or modes of liability.

To demonstrate the extent to which the ICC is relying on customary international law or equivalent terms, Figure 4.2 shows that approximately 15 per cent of decisions referred to the term 'customary' or 'international humanitarian law', ten per cent to 'law of armed conflict', and three per cent to 'laws of war'. These numbers reduced when limited to interpretations of the definitions of crimes or modes of liability specifically, though not to the same extent as the *VCLT* rules of interpretation.

4.2.3 *Discussion*

The clearest result from the quantitative analysis is that the ICC makes very few formal references to the general rule of interpretation in article 31 of the *VCLT*, and even fewer references to the principle of systemic integration in article 31(3)(c). These results stands in contrast to the statement in *Katanga* that the Court has 'systematically' based its interpretation of the *Statute* on such rules.[10] The results also contrast the jurisprudence of the International

---

dataset, and the reference to article 31(3)(c) was not in relation to interpreting the definition of crimes. Nonetheless, it does provide a valuable, and accurate, account of the principle of systemic integration generally.).

10 *Katanga Trial Judgment* (n 1) [43].

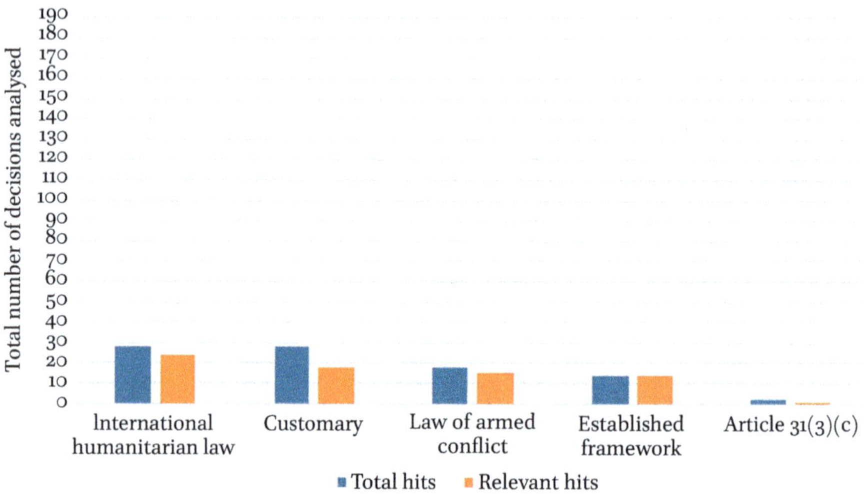

FIGURE 4.2 References to the principle of systemic integration or customary international law
The x-axis shows the search terms relating to the principle of systemic integration. The y-axis shows the 'total hits' out of the 190 decisions analysed, as well as 'relevant hits', which reflects the number of decisions in which the terms were used to interpret the definition of crimes or modes of liability.

Criminal Tribunal for the former Yugoslavia (ICTY), which confirmed the applicability of the *VCLT* to the interpretation of the ICTY Statute, even though it was the product of a United Nations Security Council Resolution and not a multilateral treaty.[11] The lack of reference to article 31 of the *VCLT* or its constituent rules of interpretation undermines the customary status of these rules and likely contributes to methodological inconsistency across ICC Chambers.

In terms of the extent to which the ICC adheres to the principle of systemic integration in substance, the quantitative data does not provide a definitive answer. However, looking at those decisions that refer to 'customary international law' or an equivalent term, there is generally no evidence that the Court sees itself as obliged to take applicable treaties and CIL 'into account' in the interpretation of the *Statute*, even though this is explicitly required by article 31(3)(c). Indeed, given the fact that fewer than 15 per cent of decisions referred to the terms 'customary', 'international humanitarian

11 William Schabas, 'Interpreting the Statutes of the Ad Hoc Tribunals' in Lal Chand Vohrah (ed), *Man's Inhumanity to Man: Essays in International Law in Honour of Antonio Cassese* (Kluwer Law International 2003) 847, 849–52.

law', or 'established framework [of international law]', it is reasonable to conclude that the ICC does not generally see itself as being under an obligation to interpret the definition of war crimes consistently with customary IHL. Given that the content and drafting history of the *Rome Statute* generally confirms the presumption of interpretive consistency with custom, these results demonstrate a general lack of compliance with the principle of systemic integration and a tendency to view the ICC as a self-contained regime.[12]

It is difficult to assess the significance of those cases that refer to external sources of law but without explaining a methodology for interpreting the *Statute*. Many cases appear to make cursory reference to external law to support a conclusion that had already been reached by reference to the *Statute* and *Elements of Crimes*; some provided a more detailed analysis of sources that could be argued to reflect an attempt to ground the interpretation in CIL. Closer analysis of the 'applicable law' sections of these cases revealed a pattern in which significant reliance on external sources of law tended to be evident only where the *Elements of Crimes* does not provide its own definition.[13] These examples included interpretations of terms such as 'attack',[14] 'armed conflict',[15] and 'active participation in hostilities'.[16] By contrast, where the *Elements of Crimes* does provide a definition of the relevant offence, there appeared to be little or no reference to external law.[17] This

12 Leena Grover, *Interpreting Crimes in the Rome Statute of the International Criminal Court* (CUP 2014) 246–344.

13 For example, see: *Katanga Trial Judgment* (n 1) [47] ('Where the founding texts do not specifically resolve a particular issue, the Chamber must refer to treaty or customary humanitarian law and the general principles of law.').

14 *Ntagnada Trial Judgment* (n 8) [916] (the Trial Chamber prefaced its reliance on external law by stating that 'neither the Statute nor the Elements of Crimes include a definition of the term "attack" before going on to rely on external sources of law').

15 Ibid [701] ('[T]he Court's legal framework does not define the term "armed conflict not of an international character". [...] However, noting that paragraph 2(e) and the Elements of Crimes explicitly refers to "the established framework of the international law of armed conflict", the Chamber adopts the definition [...] introduced by the ICTY Appeals Chamber in 1995.').

16 *Lubanga Appeals Judgement* (n 2) [322] (here, the Appeals Chamber prefaced its reliance on external law by stating that 'the range of activities that may constitute "use to participate actively in hostilities" under article 8 (2) (e) (VII) of the Statute is not explicitly set out in the Statute, the Rules of Procedure and Evidence or the Elements of Crimes').

17 For example, see: *Katanga Trial Judgment* (n 1) [961]–[972] (Trial Chamber II relies exclusively on the *Elements of Crimes* for the definition of 'rape' as a war crime).

pattern suggests that the Court views the interpretive value of CIL as subservient to that of the *Elements of Crimes*.

To properly grasp the Court's understanding of the relationship between CIL and the *Elements of Crimes*, I provide a qualitative analysis of the Trial Chamber Judgments in *Katanga* and *Bemba*. In doing so, I test Hypothesis 1, that ICC judges view the *Elements of Crimes* as obviating the need to rely on CIL in the interpretation of an offence, and Hypothesis 2, that the ICC justifies this approach as required by the principle of legality in article 22(2) of the *Statute*. Trial Chamber Judgments in *Katanga* and *Bemba* offer the best examples of the ICC's compliance with the principle of systemic integration, at least formally.[18] The rationale of choosing these cases is that, if the pattern of treating the *Elements* as subservient to CIL is evident in cases in which the ICC explicitly upholds the principle of systemic integration, then it is likely to be replicated in cases which do not refer to systemic integration explicitly and which make fewer and less-reasoned references to external sources of law. The results of the qualitative study and their wider impact on the ICC's compliance with the principle of systemic integration are discussed in 4.3.

There is an exception to the conclusion that the ICC does not see itself as bound to interpret war crimes consistently with customary IHL. In three ICC decisions, the Court explicitly stated that all war crimes falling under articles 8(2)(b) and 8(2)(e) 'must' be interpreted consistently with customary IHL.[19] Notably, the Court did not reach this conclusion by reference to the principle of systemic integration under article 31(3)(c). Rather, it deemed that interpretive consistency with customary IHL was mandated by the construction the relevant text of the *Statute*. I provide a qualitative analysis of these decisions and their potential impact in section 4.4.

4.3 Qualitative Analysis: Article 31(3)(c), Custom, and the *Elements of Crimes* in the Jurisprudence of the ICC

This section tests Hypotheses 1 and 2 against two ICC cases: the decision of Trial Chamber II in *Katanga* and that of Trial Chamber III in *Bemba*. These cases represent the Court's most thorough application of the principle of systemic integration under article 31(3)(c). Indeed, they are the only two

18 Ibid [47], [1100], [1395] footnote 1394, [1625]; *Bemba Trial Judgment* (n 1) [78]–[79].

19 *Lubanga Appeals Judgement* (n 2) [322]; *Appeals Chamber's Second Decision on Mr Ntaganda's Jurisdictional Appeal* (n 2) [52]–[53]; *Ntagnanda Appeals Judgment* (n 2) [564].

cases in which the ICC has explicitly relied on article 31(3)(c) when interpreting the definition of crimes as a means of drawing on external sources of law.[20] Yet, despite being the best examples of the ICC's formally complying with article 31(3)(c), a qualitative analysis shows that, in practice, Hypotheses 1 and 2 are borne out. That is to say, where the *Elements of Crimes* provides the definition of an offence, the Court has either refrained from referring to CIL or otherwise treated such external sources of law as subservient to the *Elements of Crimes*. In support of its approach, the Court has cited the principle of legality.

Consistent with the findings of Chapter 2, in which it was argued that neither the *Elements of Crimes* nor the principle of legality justify ignoring CIL, it is submitted that the correct approach is to reconcile the *Elements of Crimes* with the definition of the offence under CIL to the greatest possible extent.

4.3.1 *Prosecutor v Katanga*

Trial Chamber II's 2014 decision in *Katanga* is one of two decisions in which the ICC undertook a thorough analysis of article 31 of the *VCLT* and considered its operation alongside the principle of legality, as codified in article 22(2) of the *Rome Statute*.[21] In this case, the Court explicitly relied on article 31(3)(c) of the *VCLT* when using external sources of law to interpret the *Statute*, stating that 'consideration shall be given to any relevant rules of international law applicable in the relations between the parties' and therefore confirmed that the Court 'may rely on rules extraneous to the text concerned'.[22] The Trial Chamber subsequently used stronger language when introducing its approach to the interpretation of crimes against humanity under article 7 of the *Statute*.

> [T]he interpretation of the terms of art 7 and, where necessary, the Elements of Crimes *requires* that reference be had to the jurisprudence of the ad hoc tribunals insofar as that jurisprudence identifies a pertinent rule of custom, in accordance with article 31(3)(c) of the Vienna Convention.[23]

---

20 There are examples in which the ICC has referred to article 31(3)(c) when interpreting other parts of the *Rome Statute*. For example, see: *Decision on Mr Ruto's Request for Excusal* (n 9) [101]–[102].

21 *Katanga Trial Judgment* (n 1) [43]–[57].

22 Ibid [47].

23 Ibid [1100] (emphasis added).

In a footnote discussing its method of interpreting the applicable mode of liability, Trial Chamber II stated that it is allowed, where necessary, 'to draw on customary law in the course of systemic interpretation'.[24] Later, Trial Chamber II applied the principle of systemic integration by interpreting the definition of 'common purpose' liability under article 25(1)(d) of the *Statute* in accordance with the comparable 'joint criminal enterprise' mode of liability used by the ad hoc tribunals.[25] The Trial Chamber stated that it is entitled to draw on such jurisprudence to 'best ascertain the meaning of a statutory phrase or expression, such as the phraseology "common purpose", and in so doing, recourse to the systemic method of interpretation may be had', noting that the definition adopted by ad hoc tribunals is 'based on an analysis of customary international law'.[26]

In contrast to the majority of ICC cases, in which there is no reference to article 31(3)(c) at all and minimal reliance on CIL,[27] Trial Chamber II made a concerted effort to recognise CIL's role in achieving systemic integration, even if the language oscillates between treating it as an obligatory and a discretionary interpretive aid.

However, closer analysis of *Katanga* reveals the ICC's reluctance to apply the principle of systemic integration under article 31(3)(c) to the interpretation of an offence where the *Elements of Crimes* provides its own definition. The Chamber clearly viewed the interpretive value of CIL as subservient to the *Elements of Crimes*, consistent with hypothesis 1.

In interpreting the war crime of intentionally directing attacks against civilians, Trial Chamber II noted the absence of a definition of the term 'attack' and 'civilians' in either the *Statute* or *Elements of Crimes*. The judges proceeded to interpret these terms by reference to article 13 of *Additional Protocol II* (*AP II*) and the associated International Committee of the Red Cross (ICRC) Commentary, 15 ICTY cases, the ICRC Customary IHL Study, and scholarly literature.[28] Similarly, when interpreting the war crime of 'destroying [...] the property of an adversary unless such destruction [...] be imperatively demanded by the necessities of the conflict', Trial Chamber II interpreted the definition of 'property', 'military necessity', and the rule of proportionality (none of which are defined in the *Elements*) by reference to

24 Ibid [1395] nn 1394.

25 Ibid [1625].

26 Ibid.

27 See Figure 4.1. Only two out of the 203 decisions analysed referenced article 31(3)(c) of the *VCLT*.

28 *Katanga Trial Judgment* (n 1) [797]–[803].

article 57 of *Additional Protocol I* (*AP I*) and associated ICRC Commentary, article 47 of *Geneva Convention IV*, article 14 of the *Lieber Code*, four ICTY cases, the ICRC Customary IHL Study, and scholarly literature.[29]

These examples demonstrate the willingness of Trial Chamber II to comply with the principle of systemic integration where the *Elements of Crimes* has not provided its own definition. However, as demonstrated below by reference to the war crimes of rape and pillage, where the *Elements* does provide its own definition, Trial Chamber II ceases to apply the principle of systemic integration.

Element 2 of article 8(2)(e)(VI) in the *Elements of Crimes* defines the war crime of rape in the following terms:

> The invasion was committed by force, or by threat of force or coercion, such as that caused by fear of violence, duress, detention, psychological oppression or abuse of power, against such person or another person, or by taking advantage of a coercive environment, or the invasion was committed against a person incapable of giving genuine consent.

Former ICTY Judge David Hunt notes that the inspiration for this definition comes from a combination of two Trial Chamber decisions (one from the ICTY and one from the International Criminal Tribunal for Rwanda (ICTR)),[30] as is made clear in the unofficial record of the negotiations leading to the *Elements of Crimes*.[31] However, it is arguable that this definition in the *Elements of Crime* is no longer reflective of CIL.

The ICTY Trial Chamber in *Prosecutor v Kunarac et al.* subsequently conducted a more extensive analysis of domestic definitions of rape and concluded that the Prosecution need only prove the absence of consent, as opposed to force, the threat of force, or coercion.[32] This broader definition

29 Ibid [893]–[896].

30 *Prosecutor v Furundžija* (*Judgment*) (International Criminal Tribunal for the former cYugoslavia, Trial Chamber, Case No IT-95-17/1-T, 10 December 1998) [185] ('*Furundžija Trial Judgment*'); *Prosecutor v Furundžija* (*Appeal Judgment*) (International Criminal Tribunal for the former Yugoslavia, Appeals Chamber, Case No IT-95-17/1-A, 21 July 2000) [597]–[598] ('*Prosecutor v Furundžija*').

31 Eve La Haye, 'Article 8(2)(b)(XXII)' in Roy S Lee (ed), *The International Criminal Court: Elements of Crimes and Rules of Procedure and Evidence* (Kluwer Law International 1999) 187.

32 *Prosecutor v Kunarac et al.* (*Judgment*) (International Criminal Tribunal for the former Yugoslavia, Trial Chamber, Case No IT-96-23-T and IT-96-23/1-T, 22 February 2001) [460] ('*Kunarac Trial Judgment*') ('In light of the above considerations, the Trial Chamber understands that the actus reus of the crime of rape in international law is

was confirmed on appeal,[33] and, according to Hunt, 'is now the authoritative definition of that crime for the purpose of the Tribunal, as well as under customary international law'.[34] In line with his overall criticism that the *Elements of Crimes* risks freezing the definition of crimes at a time when they were undergoing evolution and clarification, Hunt has lamented that:

> The drafters of the ICC Statute, by adopting almost verbatim a narrow definition given in two trials without waiting for the Appeals Chamber to give detailed consideration to the issue, have discouraged the judges of the ICC from taking those recent developments into account. It is to be hoped that the judges will accept a responsibility to see that international criminal law continues to develop in the future and does not stand still and therefore become obsolete.[35]

Nevertheless, in *Katanga*, ICC Trial Chamber II applied the definition of rape in the *Elements of Crimes* without mentioning the decision of the ICTY Appeals Chamber in *Kunarac* or, indeed, without a single reference to external sources of law.[36] The contours of rape as a war crime were interpreted exclusively by reference to the *Elements of Crimes*.

For the war crime of pillage, Element 2 of the *Elements of Crimes* states that, 'The perpetrator intended to deprive the owner of the property and to appropriate it for *private or personal use*'. This 'novel' limitation regarding private or personal use[37] is inconsistent with customary IHL because it excludes the unlawful appropriation of resources to fuel the war effort (that is, a public use).

---

constituted by: the sexual penetration, however slight: (a) of the vagina or anus of the victim by the penis of the perpetrator or any other object used by the perpetrator; or (b) of the mouth of the victim by the penis of the perpetrator; where such sexual penetration occurs without the consent of the victim. Consent for this purpose must be consent given voluntarily, as a result of the victim's free will, assessed in the context of the surrounding circumstances. The mens rea is the intention to effect this sexual penetration, and the knowledge that it occurs without the consent of the victim.').

33 *Prosecutor v Kunarac et al (Judgment)* (International Criminal Tribunal for the former Yugoslavia, Appeals Chamber, Case No T-96-23 & IT-96-23/1-A, 12 June 2002) [127]–[128] ('*Prosecutor v Kunarac et al*').

34 David Hunt, 'The International Criminal Court: High Hopes, Creative Ambiguity and an Unfortunate Mistrust in International Judges' (2004) 2(1) *Journal of International Criminal Justice* 56, 60.

35 Ibid 60–1.

36 *Katanga Trial Judgment* (n 1) [961]–[972].

37 Yutaka Arai, *The Law of Occupation: Continuity and Change of International Humanitarian Law, and its Interaction with International Human Rights Law* (Martinus Nijhoff 2009) 1250.

Under CIL, the crime of pillage extends to the taking of property for military (public) purposes, providing such appropriation is not justified by military necessity. The International Military Tribunal (IMT) in Nuremberg held that Germany's economic exploitation of the occupied territories 'without consideration of the local economy, and in consequence of a deliberate design and policy' amounted to systematic 'plunder of public or private property', contrary to the Nuremberg Charter.[38] There was no requirement that the property be plundered for private or personal use.[39] Instead, the Nuremberg and Tokyo Tribunals held that the appropriation of property is only lawful where it falls within the limited exceptions provided in the *Hague Regulations*, which stipulate that property may only be seized where it is justified by military necessity.[40]

The same approach was adopted by the ICTY and the Special Court for Sierra Leone (SCSL). The ICTY Trial Chamber in *Prosecutor v Martić* held that 'the appropriation of private or public property must not be done without lawful basis or legal justification [...] [a]ccording to the Hague Regulations'.[41] The ICTY Trial Chamber in *Hadžihasanović* further clarified that the laws and customs of war 'do not allow arbitrary and unjustified pillage for army purposes *or* for the individual use of army members', thereby confirming that appropriation for both public and private use can constitute the war crime of pillage, providing it is not justified by the laws of war.[42] And, in addressing submissions influenced by the *Elements of Crimes*, the SCSL held in *Brima* that 'the requirement of "private or personal use" is unduly restrictive and ought not to be an element of the crime of pillage'.[43]

---

38 Nuremberg International Military Tribunal, 'Trial of the Major War Criminals Before the International Military Tribunal, Official Documents' (1947) vol I, 239.

39 Note that 'plunder' and 'pillage' are treated as synonymous under IHL. *Prosecutor v Delalić et al. (Judgment)* (International Criminal Tribunal for the former Yugoslavia, Trial Chamber, Case No IT-96-21-T, 18 November 1998) [591] (*'Delalić Trial Judgment'*).

40 Nuremberg International Military Tribunal (n 38) Volume VIII, 1133 (*United States v. Krauch et al. (IG Farben)*); 'N.V. De Bataafsche Petroleum Maatschappij and Others v The War Damage Commission' (1957) 51(4) *American Journal of International Law* 802, 808, 811.

41 *Prosecutor v Martić (Judgment)* (International Criminal Tribunal for the former Yugoslavia, Trial Chamber, Case No IT-95-11-T, 10 June 2007) [102] (*'Prosecutor v Martić'*).

42 *Prosecutor v Hadžihasanović (Judgment)* (International Criminal Tribunal for the former Yugoslavia, Trial Chamber, Case No IT-01-47-T, 15 March 2006) [52] (*'Prosecutor v Hadžihasanović'*).

43 *Prosecutor v Brima, Kamara and Kanu (Trial Judgment)* (Special Court of Sierra Leone, Trial Chamber II, Case No SCSL-2004-16-PT, 29 June 2007) [754] (*'Prosecutor v Brima, Kamara and Kanu'*). See also: *Prosecutor v Fofana and Kondewa (Trial Judgment)* (Special Court for Sierra Leone, Trial Chamber I, Case No SCSL-04-14-T, 2 August 2007) [160] (*'Prosecutor v Fofana and Kondewa'*). However, the SCSL Appeals Chamber came

Scholarly literature also highlights the discrepancy between the *Elements of Crimes* and CIL in the definition of 'pillage'. In a thorough study on the applicability of prosecuting corporations for the pillage of natural resources during armed conflict, James Stewart concludes that the 'private or personal use' restriction is not part of customary IHL.[44]

Given the discrepancy between the definitions of 'pillage' under the *Elements of Crimes* and CIL, one might have expected Trial Chamber II in *Katanga* to attempt to reconcile them in light of the principle of systemic integration or at least acknowledge the departure. However, Trial Chamber II upholds the 'private or personal use' requirement in the *Elements of Crimes* without any reference to external sources of law.

4.3.2 *Prosecutor v Bemba*

Trial Chamber III's 2016 decision in *Prosecutor v Bemba* is the second of only two decisions to provide a thorough analysis of article 31 of the *VCLT* and explain its operation alongside the rules of strict construction.[45] Unlike the decision of Trial Chamber II in *Katanga*, Trial Chamber III in *Bemba* did not restrict the interpretive value of CIL under article 31(3)(c) to situations where the *Elements of Crimes* does not provide a definition; however, it does treat CIL as subservient to the *Elements of Crimes* in cases of interpretive conflict.

When interpreting the definition of rape as a war crime, Trial Chamber III in *Bemba* relied on the definition in the *Elements of Crimes* noted above. It also cited the decision of the ICTR Trial Chamber in *Prosecutor v Akayesu*[46] to provide a detailed analysis third limb, which prohibits rape 'by taking advantage of a coercive environment'.[47] Interestingly, although Trial Chamber III did not reference the ICTY Appeals Chamber's definition of rape in *Kunarac* (which Hunt argues is reflective of CIL), it held that 'lack of

---

to a different conclusion: *Prosecutor v Fofana and Kondewa* (*CDF Case*) (*Judgment*) (International Criminal Tribunal for the former Yugoslavia, Appeals Chamber, Case No SCSL-04-14-A, 28 May 2008) [392] nn 770 ('*Prosecutor v Fofana and Kondewa* (*CDF Case*)') ('Seizure is distinct from pillage because seizure is the appropriation of property for public purposes, whereas pillage is for private purposes.').

44 James Stewart, *Corporate War Crimes: Prosecuting the Pillage of Natural Resources* (Open Society Foundations 2011) para 18. See also: Arai (n 37) 1250.

45 *Bemba Trial Judgment* (n 1) [75]–[86].

46 *Prosecutor v Jean-Paul Akayesu* (*Judgment*) (International Criminal Tribunal for Rwanda, Appeals Chamber, Case No ICTR-96-4-T, 2 September 1998) ('*Prosecutor v Jean-Paul Akayesu*').

47 *Bemba Trial Judgment* (n 1) [103].

consent is not a legal element of the crime of rape under the Statute',[48] noting further that:

> The preparatory works of the Statute demonstrate that the drafters chose not to require that the Prosecution prove the non-consent of the victim beyond reasonable doubt, on the basis that such a requirement would, in most cases, undermine efforts to bring perpetrators to justice.[49]

In other words, the definition of rape in the *Elements of Crimes* was analysed against an external source of law. Although one could argue that the extent of that analysis fell short of what would be expected under the principle of systemic integration, there appears to have been a concerted effort to situate the definition in the *Elements of Crimes* with broader international law.

When interpreting the war crime of pillage, Trial Chamber III in *Bemba* made extensive references to external sources of law[50] and explicitly addressed the discrepancy between the *Elements of Crimes* and CIL.

> In relation to the concept of the appropriation of property for private or personal use, the Chamber notes that this requirement is not explicitly expressed in customary or conventional international humanitarian law and has not been established, as such, in the jurisprudence of other international criminal tribunals. However, given the explicit inclusion of this concept in the Elements of Crimes, the Chamber considers that this requirement must be met for the appropriation of property to amount to pillaging as a war crime under Article 8(2)(e)(v).[51]

Ultimately, Trial Chamber III applied the definition of pillage in the *Elements of Crimes* despite the inconsistency with CIL. The rationale for this decision is provided earlier in the judgment, where the judges stated that, although the *Elements* 'shall assist' in the interpretation of the *Statute* (and is therefore non-binding),[52]

---

48 Ibid [105].
49 Ibid.
50 Ibid [114–7], [123–5].
51 Ibid [120].
52 Ibid [67].

> [t]he Chamber is of the view that the Elements of Crimes form an integral part of the primary sources of applicable law provided for in Article 21(1)(a) and, as such, in accordance with the principle of strict legality provided for in Article 22, should be applied subject to any conflict with the provisions of the Statute.[53]

Trial Chamber III's decision in *Bemba* challenges Hypothesis 1, that the ICC relies exclusively on the *Elements of Crimes* where it provides the definition of the relevant offence, as the Chamber refers to external sources of law on each occasion. However, the Chamber proceeds to treat the interpretive value of CIL as subservient to that of the *Elements of Crimes* without attempting to reconcile the two. Confirming Hypothesis 2, the *Bemba* Trial Chamber cites the principle of legality to justify this approach.

4.3.3 *Discussion*

In *Katanga* and *Bemba*, despite being the only cases to formally cite article 31(3)(c) when interpreting the definition of crimes, CIL was either ignored or treated as subservient to the *Elements of Crimes* where the latter provided its own definition of the relevant offence (Hypothesis 1). The justification for this interpretive approach was the principle of legality (Hypothesis 2).

The approach of Trial Chamber II in *Katanga* of ignoring CIL and relying exclusively on the *Elements of Crimes* for the interpretation of the war crimes of rape and pillage risks fragmenting international law. It will be recalled that situating the interpretation of a treaty in its broader context in accordance with the principle of systemic integration is not discretionary, as dictated by the term 'shall take into account' in article 31(3)(c) of the *VCLT*. Even if Trial Chamber II were ultimately inclined to preference the *Elements of Crimes* over CIL, the principle of systemic integration requires the Court to highlight the discrepancy and explicitly justify the departure (fragmentation) by reference to the text of the treaty.[54]

Explaining the Court's decision to fragment international law in this manner is essential to give the Assembly of States Parties the opportunity to rectify the inconsistency if they so choose, or to give other ICC Chambers

53 Ibid [58].

54 International Law Commission, Martti Koskenniemi, *Report on Fragmentation of International Law: Difficulties Arising from the Diversification and Expansion of International Law*, UN Doc A/CN.4/L.682 (13 April 2006) 243–44 paras 79–80 (*Fragmentation of International Law Study*).

the opportunity to adopt a different interpretation. After all, part of the rationale for the principle of systemic integration is the presumption against such normative conflict.

In *Bemba*, Trial Chamber III went a long way towards rectifying this oversight. With respect to interpreting the war crime of rape, it at least situated its interpretation by reference to external sources of law. For the war crime of pillage, the Chamber explicitly acknowledged that the *Elements of Crimes* departs from the accepted definition under CIL. Contrary to that of Trial Chamber II in *Katanga*, this approach shines a spotlight on the fragmentation of international law and gives those within the ICC's institutional framework the opportunity either to rectify this fragmentation or knowingly decide that this is the direction they would like the law to take. Specific to the war crime of pillage, it gives occasion to consider whether the 'private or personal use' restriction in the *Elements of Crimes* is a desirable departure from CIL. A brief argument is provided below for why such a departure is not desirable.

The International Court of Justice (ICJ) has held that exploitation of natural resources not justified by military necessity constitutes pillage in violation of IHL.[55] Excluding appropriations for military (i.e., 'public') purposes from the crime of pillage would, as Stewart points out, allow impunity for illegal resource exploitation.[56] Matthew Gillett concurs, noting that, 'Warring factions will regularly use misappropriated property to fund their military campaigns, rather than for personal ends',[57] while Olivia Radics argues that:

> Based on the ICC Elements of Crime's limitation regarding personal or private gain, it seems that natural resource exploitation to finance rebellions would not fall under the purview of Article 8(2)(b)(XVI) [or

55 *Armed Activities on the Territory of the Congo (Democratic Republic of the Congo v Uganda) (Judgment)* [2005] ICJ Rep 168, [245]–[246] (*Armed Activities on the Territory of the Congo*). See also: Aaron Ezekiel, 'The Application of International Criminal Law to Resource Exploitation: Ituri, Democratic Republic of The Congo' (2007) 47(1) *Natural Resources Journal* 225; Michael Lundberg, 'The Plunder of Natural Resources During War: A War Crime(?)' 39 *Georgetown Journal of International Law* 495.

56 Stewart (n 44) para 18.

57 Matthew Gillett, 'Eco-Struggles: Using International Criminal Law to Protect the Environment During and After Non-International Armed Conflict' in Carsten Stahn, Jens Iverson and Jennifer Easterday (eds), *Environmental Protection and Transitions from Conflict to Peace: Clarifying Norms, Principles, and Practices* (OUP 2017) 231.

> article 8(2)(e)(v)] … This means that one of the most important nexuses between conflict and natural resources – the financing of conflict through illegal or illicit natural resource exploitation – would be unaddressed by the war crime of pillage in the ICC.[58]

The *Elements of Crimes*' departure from the CIL definition of pillage also creates evidentiary issues. As stated by Olivia Radics and Carl Bruch, 'It is challenging to disentangle the symbiotic relationship that often exists between exploitation activities that are done in furtherance of an armed conflict – either by government or rebel groups – or for strictly personal gain and enrichment'.[59] Yulia Nuzban similarly argues that the distinction between private and public use is especially difficult to maintain with respect to non-state armed groups 'with more fluid structures and fewer resources' and those in which 'private and public life are merged into one'.[60] Accordingly, the 'private or personal use' requirement in the *Elements of Crimes* should be removed.

It is worth considering whether Trial Chamber III in *Bemba* could have chosen not to apply the 'private or personal use' requirement, given its inconsistency with CIL. After all, the *Elements of Crimes* is a non-binding interpretive guide. Trial Chamber III's justification for preferring the *Elements of Crimes* is that it is required by the principle of legality and should be applied 'subject to any conflict with the provisions of the Statute'.[61] While numerous scholars have pointed out that applying the *Elements of Crimes* is not actually required by the principle of legality,[62] overriding the written word of the *Elements of Crimes* in favour of unwritten CIL to the detriment

58 Olivia Radics and Carl Bruch, 'The Law of Pillage, Conflict Resources, and Jus Post Bellum' in Carsten Stahn, Jens Iverson and Jennifer Easterday (eds), *Environmental Protection and Transitions from Conflict to Peace: Clarifying Norms, Principles, and Practices* (OUP 2017) 151. See also Daniëlla Dam-de Jong, 'From Engines for Conflict into Engines for Sustainable Development: The Potential of International Law to Address Predatory Exploitation of Natural Resources in Situations of Internal Armed Conflict' (2013) 82(1) *Nordic Journal of International Law* 155, 165–66.

59 Radics and Bruch (n 58) 150–1.

60 Yulia Nuzban, '"For Private or Personal Use": The Meaning of the Special Intent Requirement in the War Crime of Pillage under the Rome Statute of the International Criminal Court' (2020) 102(915) *International Review of the Red Cross* 1249, 1264–5.

61 *Bemba Trial Judgment* (n 1) [58].

62 Grover (n 12) 365; Gudrun Hochmayr, 'Applicable Law in Practice and Theory: Interpreting Article 21 of the ICC Statute' (2014) 12(4) *Journal of International Criminal Justice* 655, 658.

of the accused does not sit well with the *Rome Statute*'s emphasis on strict legality. Indeed, it could perhaps be argued that an irreconcilable conflict between the *Elements of Crimes* and CIL amounts to residual ambiguity that must be resolved 'in favour of the person being investigated, prosecuted, or convicted'.[63] In any event, Trial Chamber III's approach in *Bemba* supports the analysis that judges would be unlikely to preference CIL over the *Elements of Crimes* where it would broaden the criminal responsibility of the accused (see Chapter 2).

Notwithstanding this conclusion, Trial Chamber III in *Bemba* explicitly acknowledged that the *Elements* should only be applied 'subject to any conflict with the provisions of the Statute'. As examined in the next section, a series of decisions by the ICC Appeals Chamber between 2017 and 2021 determined that the *chapeaux* to war crimes under articles 8(2)(b) and 8(2)(e) of the *Statute* (which includes the war crimes of rape and pillage) 'must' be interpreted consistently with customary IHL. It could therefore be argued that the definition of pillage in the *Elements of Crimes* is inconsistent with the *Rome Statute.*

4.4 Systemic Integration in the *Chapeaux* to War Crimes and Its Implications for the *Elements of Crimes*

The ICC Appeals Chamber has determined – once in *Lubanga* and twice in *Ntaganda* – that war crimes falling under the *chapeaux* to articles 8(2)(b) and 8(2)(e) '*must* be consistent with international law, and international humanitarian law in particular'[64] for the reason that the *chapeaux* to these provisions define the impugned offences as 'other serious violations of the laws and customs of war [...] within the established framework of the international law of armed conflict'. Although neither *Lubanga* nor *Ntaganda* were decided by reference to article 31(3)(c) of the *VCLT*, the Appeals Chamber's approach effectively confirms the principle of systemic integration for the interpretation of all war crimes in article 8(2)(b) and 8(2)(e), which together comprise 51 separate offences.

63 *Rome Statute of the International Criminal Court*, opened for signature 17 July 1998, 2187 UNTS 38544, art 22(2) (entered into force 1 July 2002) (*Rome Statute of the International Criminal Court*).

64 *Lubanga Appeals Judgement* (n 2) [322]; *Appeals Chamber's Second Decision on Mr Ntaganda's Jurisdictional Appeal* (n 2) [43]–[46]; *Ntagnanda Appeals Judgment* (n 2) [548]–[550], [563] (emphasis added).

The qualitative analysis of the ICC's approach in *Lubanga* and *Ntaganda* (below) argues that, while the Appeals Chamber's reasoning for applying the principle of systemic integration to articles 8(2)(e) and 8(2)(b) of the *Statute* is methodologically sound, it should be supplemented by drawing on article 31(3)(c) of the *VCLT*. Furthermore, the failure of Trial Chamber IV in *Ntaganda* to implement the Appeals Chamber's approach demonstrates 'methodological mayhem' across the various chambers of the ICC. Finally, it is argued, the application of the principle of systemic integration by the Appeals Chamber demonstrates how this principle can contribute to the incremental development of the law by unifying the disparate sources of CIL and clarifying the content of the law.

4.4.1 *Prosecutor v Lubanga*

The Appeals Chamber's 2014 decision in *Lubanga* makes no reference to article 31 of the *VCLT* or to the principle of systemic integration. Unlike the Trial Chamber decisions in *Katanga* and *Bemba*, there is no attempt to reconcile the general rule of interpretation in article 31 with the *Elements of Crimes* or the rules of strict construction. The *Lubanga* appeal is significant, however, for providing one of the most through applications of the principle of systemic integration in substance, with the decision even going so far as to say that the interpretation of certain war crimes 'must' be consistent with customary IHL – rather than the discretionary language used in *Katanga* and *Bemba*.

4.4.1.1 Background

On 14 March 2012, ICC Trial Chamber I found Mr Thomas Lubanga Dyilo, former President of the *Union des Patriotes Congolais* (UPC) and Commander-in-Chief of its military wing the *Force Patriotique pour la Libération du Congo* (FPLC), guilty of recruiting child soldiers and using them to participate actively in hostilities, contrary to article 8(2)(e)(VII) of the *Rome Statute*.[65] Mr Lubanga was held individually criminally responsible under article 25(3)(a) of the *Statute* as an indirect co-perpetrator of the crimes.

One of the central legal issues in the case was the definition and scope of the phrase 'to participate actively in hostilities'.[66] While using children in combat functions is expressly criminalised under article 8(2)(e)(VII), it was

65 *Prosecutor v Thomas Lubanga Dyilo (Judgment)* (International Criminal Court, Trial Chamber I, Case No ICC-01/04-01/06, 14 March 2012) (*Lubanga Trial Judgment*).

66 Ibid [282]–[288].

less clear whether more indirect modes of participation in the war effort fell within the scope of prohibited conduct. The Chamber held that:

> The use of the expression 'to participate actively in hostilities', as opposed to the expression 'direct participation' (as found in Additional Protocol I to the Geneva Conventions) was clearly intended to import a wide interpretation to the activities and roles that are covered by the offence of using children under the age of 15 actively to participate in hostilities.[67]

Trial Chamber I found that the scope of activities falling within the definition of 'to participate actively in hostilities' is to be determined primarily by reference to whether the activity exposed the child to danger by rendering him or her a potential target.[68] Accordingly, the Court assessed the child's contribution to the war effort but held that the 'level of consequential risk' to which the child is exposed is the 'decisive factor'.[69]

On appeal, Mr Lubanga argued that the international law of armed conflict does not distinguish between the concepts of 'to participate actively in hostilities' and 'direct participation in hostilities',[70] referring to the interchangeable use of the terms in the French and English texts of common article 3 and the fact that they were treated as 'synonymous concepts' in the case law of the ICTY and ICTR.[71] Mr Lubanga further submitted that Trial Chamber I's reliance on the concept or 'risk' is unsupported in international law,[72] and that culpability should instead be limited to those 'activities which have a direct part in the conduct of hostilities'.[73]

4.4.1.2 Systemic Integration in Lubanga by Reference to the Chapeau to Article 8(2)(e)

In response, the Appeals Chamber noted that neither the *Statute* nor *Elements of Crimes* defines the term 'to participate actively in hostilities'.[74] To justify its reliance on customary IHL to interpret the impugned provision,

67 Ibid [627].
68 Ibid [628].
69 Ibid.
70 *Lubanga Appeals Judgement* (n 2) [256].
71 Ibid [256]–[257].
72 Ibid [255].
73 Ibid [267].
74 Ibid [322].

the Chamber pointed out that article 8(2)(e) of the *Statute* is criminalised under the *chapeau* of 'Other serious violations of the laws and customs applicable in armed conflicts not of an international character, within the established framework in international law'.[75] Furthermore, it noted that the *Introduction* to article 8 of the *Elements of Crimes* provides that 'the elements for war crimes under article 8, paragraph 2, of the Statute *shall* be interpreted within the established framework of the international law of armed conflict'.[76] The Chamber concluded that 'the interpretation of article 8(2)(e)(VII) of the Statute *must* be consistent with international law, and international humanitarian law in particular'.[77] Although the Appeals Chamber in *Lubanga* did not rely on article 31(3)(c) of the *VCLT* in confirming the principle of systemic integration, the end result is the same: the definition of crimes in article 8(2)(e) and, by extension, those in 8(2)(b) – which together comprise 51 separate offences – must be interpreted consistently with customary IHL.

In interpreting the prohibition on using children to actively participate in hostilities by reference to customary IHL, the *Lubanga* Appeals Chamber held that the concept of active/direct participation in the conduct of hostilities under common article 3 is for the specific purpose of determining when a civilian loses his or her protection under IHL and becomes a lawful target,[78] whereas the purpose of the term 'active participation' under article 8 (2)(e)(VII) of the *Rome Statute* is to remove children from all situations connected with armed conflict. Thus, according to the Chamber, 'the interpretation given to Common Article 3 of the Geneva Conventions in the context of the principle of distinction cannot be simply transposed to that of article 8(2)(e)(VII) of the Statute'.[79]

The Chamber made reference to articles 77(2) of *AP I* and 4(3)(c) of *AP II*, ICRC Commentary, and the ICRC's Customary IHL Study in concluding that the prohibition on using children to participate in the conflict does not employ the same test as that used under common article 3 or the principle of distinction more generally.[80] In doing so, it determined that the appropriate test for proving that a child was used to participate actively in

---

75 Ibid.
76 Ibid (emphasis added).
77 Ibid (emphasis added).
78 Ibid [324].
79 Ibid.
80 Ibid [325]–[328].

hostilities contrary to article 8(2)(e)(VII) of the *Rome Statute* is that of establishing a sufficient 'link' between the activity and the armed conflict.[81] The Chamber said it would be guided by the list of activities set out the ICRC commentary on the *Additional Protocols* and the *Draft Statute* of the Preparatory Commission, which must be considered on a case-by-case basis.[82]

The significance of this decision in clarifying the law and contributing to its incremental development is discussed in section 4.4.

4.4.2 *Prosecutor v* Ntaganda

Working chronologically, this section analyses the ICC's approach to the principle of systemic integration in the *Ntaganda* jurisdictional appeal, trial judgment, and appeals judgment. The Appeals Chamber in *Ntaganda* upheld the approach taken in the *Lubanga* appeals judgment by ruling that war crimes under articles 8(2)(b) and 8(2)(e) must be interpreted consistently with customary IHL and applied this approach to those war crimes that were the subject of the appeal. The Trial Chamber, while of course implementing the Appeals Chamber's substantive rulings on those crimes subject to appeal, made no reference the Appeals Chambers interpretive methodology and did not apply it elsewhere in the Trial Chamber decision. This puzzling sequence reveals the 'methodological mayhem' across the different chambers of the ICC when interpreting the *Rome Statute*.

4.4.2.1 Background

On 9 June 2014, Pre-Trial Chamber II found 'substantial grounds to believe' that Mr Ntaganda committed, *inter alia*, the war crimes of pillage, intentionally directing attacks against the civilian population, rape and sexual slavery, and forcible transfer of the civilian population during his tenure as the Deputy Chief of Staff of the FPLC (the armed wing of the UPC) from 2002 to 2003.[83] From a legal perspective, the most compelling charge against Mr Ntaganda was that of 'rape, sexual slavery [...] and any other form of sexual violence *also* constituting a serious violation of article 3 common to the four Geneva Conventions' contrary to article 8(2)(e)

81 Ibid [333]–[335].

82 Ibid.

83 *Prosecutor v Bosco Ntaganda (Decision Pursuant to Article 61(7)(a) and (b) of the Rome Statute on the Charges of the Prosecutor Against Bosco Ntaganda)* (International Criminal Court, Pre-Trial Chamber II, Case No ICC-01/04-02/06, 9 June 2014) (*Prosecutor v Bosco Ntaganda*).

(VI) of the *Rome Statute*, even though both victim and perpetrator were members of same armed group, the FPLC.[84]

Mr Ntaganda challenged the jurisdiction of the Court with respect to this charge on the basis that war crimes cannot be committed by and against members of the same armed force and that, in the context of a non-international armed conflict (NIAC), the victims of war crimes must be protected persons within the meaning of common article 3, due to the use of the term 'also' in article 8(2)(e)(VI).[85] That is to say, Mr Ntaganda argued that victims of war crimes in a NIAC must satisfy the 'status requirement' under common article 3, which limits its protection to 'persons taking no active part in the hostilities, including members of armed forces who have laid down their arms and those placed *hors de combat* by sickness, wounds, detention or any other cause'.[86] Given that the victims of rape and sexual slavery in *Ntaganda* were members of the FPLC armed group, the defence claimed that they were not protected persons under common article 3.[87]

4.4.2.2 Systemic Integration in *Ntaganda* Jurisdictional Appeal by Reference to the Chapeau to Article 8(2)(e)

In its decision on the defence's jurisdictional challenge, the ICC Appeals Chamber confirmed that it had subject-matter jurisdiction over the crime of rape and sexual slavery when committed by and against members of the same armed force. In doing so, it confirmed the approach taken in *Lubanga* with respect to the *chapeau* in article 8(2)(e) imposing an obligation to interpret the definition of crimes consistently with customary IHL.[88] It also went a step further in deciding that such consistency with customary IHL is not limited to interpretation and may require imposing additional elements.

The Appeals Chamber responded to Mr Ntaganda's jurisdictional appeal in two parts.[89] First, it determined that the internal provisions of the *Statute* do not impose a status requirement on the victims of sexual violence contrary article 8(2)(e)(VI).[90] Second, the Appeals Chamber considered

84 Ibid [76]–[82].

85 *Appeals Chamber's Second Decision on Mr Ntaganda's Jurisdictional Appeal* (n 2) [26]–[32].

86 *Rome Statute of the International Criminal Court* (n 63) art 8(2)(c).

87 *Appeals Chamber's Second Decision on Mr Ntaganda's Jurisdictional Appeal* (n 2) [26]–[32].

88 *Lubanga Appeals Judgement* (n 2) [322].

89 *Appeals Chamber's Second Decision on Mr Ntaganda's Jurisdictional Appeal* (n 2) [34]–[54].

90 Ibid [46]–[51].

whether it was obliged to apply the status requirement to fulfil its obligation to interpret article 8(2)(e)(VI) consistently with customary IHL.[91]

The Prosecution had submitted that the reference to the 'established framework of international law' in the *chapeau* to article 8(2)(e) obliged the Court to make recourse to customary IHL for interpretive purposes only.[92] It argued that to use the established framework of international law to impose additional elements not contained within the *Statute* would offend the principle of legality as codified in article 22.[93] In support of its position, the Prosecution referenced the Introduction to article 8 of the *Elements of Crimes*, which provides that war crimes 'shall be *interpreted* within the established framework of international law'.[94] The Prosecution maintained that using customary IHL to impose additional elements was limited to situations in which the Court had identified a *lacuna* that could not be resolved by reference to the *Statute* and *Elements of Crimes*, pursuant to article 21(1)(a)–(b).[95]

The Appeals Chamber disagreed. It held that 'clearly distinguishing between interpreting the existing elements on the one hand and introducing additional elements on the other when examining the "established framework of international law" may not always be possible'.[96] It determined that the obligation to ensure interpretive consistency with customary IHL may require the Court to impose additional elements irrespective of whether there was a *lacuna* in the *Statute*.[97] Given that including additional elements from customary IHL would create extra hurdles for the Prosecution to overcome and thus benefit the accused, the Chamber stated that it did not offend the principle of legality in article 22.[98]

Ultimately, the Appeals Chamber determined that IHL does not impose additional status requirements on the victims of rape and sexual violence in the context of a NIAC.[99] In rejecting Mr Ntaganda's submission that IHL only protects against mistreatment by the opposing armed force, the Chamber referenced the fact that *Geneva Conventions I* and *II* protect the

---

91 Ibid [52]–[53].

92 Ibid [36].

93 Ibid.

94 *Prosecution Submissions on Ntaganda Jurisdictional Appeal* (n 2) [46] (emphasis in original).

95 Ibid [30], [42].

96 *Appeals Chamber's Second Decision on Mr Ntaganda's Jurisdictional Appeal* (n 2) [54].

97 Ibid [53].

98 Ibid [54].

99 Ibid [63].

wounded and sick on land and at sea 'in all circumstances [...] without any adverse distinction founded on sex, race, nationality' and irrespective of the side to which they belong.[100] This stands in contrast to *Geneva Conventions III* and *IV*, which require that 'protected persons' find themselves in the hands of the enemy. The Chamber concluded that 'international humanitarian law does not contain a general rule that categorically excludes members of an armed group from protection against crimes committed by members of the same armed group'.[101]

As for whether IHL imposes a status requirement specifically for victims of sexual violence, the Chamber found 'no conceivable reason for reaching such a conclusion'.[102] It agreed with the Trial Chamber that 'there is never a justification to engage in sexual violence against any person' and that there is no basis for imposing a rule that would preclude victims of intra-armed force sexual violence from redress.[103] Although not explicitly endorsed by the Appeals Chamber, the Trial Chamber had also pointed out that the absolute prohibition on sexual violence is consistent with IHL's fundamental purpose of balancing humanitarian protection against military necessity. As stated by the Trial Chamber, 'Raping and sexually enslaving children under the age of 15 years, or indeed any persons would never bring any accepted military advantage, nor can there ever be a necessity to engage in such conduct'.[104]

4.4.2.3 Rejecting Systemic Integration in the *Ntaganda* Trial Judgement

In 2019, following the 2017 jurisdictional appeal, Trial Chamber VI convicted Mr Ntaganda as an indirect co-perpetrator of war crimes and crimes against humanity.[105] While the Trial Chamber was bound to implement the Appeals Chamber's substantive rulings on the war crime of rape and sexual slavery, it ignored its findings on the obligation to interpret the definition of all war crimes under the *chapeau* to article 8(2)(e) consistently with customary IHL.

Trial Chamber VI in *Ntaganda* only referred to 'the established framework of international law' on two occasions – once to construe the definition of the phrase 'armed conflict not of an international character',[106]

100 Ibid [57]–[60].
101 Ibid [63].
102 Ibid [64].
103 Ibid [65].
104 Ibid [48].
105 *Ntagnada Trial Judgment* (n 8) [1199].
106 Ibid [701].

and once to determine the meaning of the term 'attack' under article 8(2)(e)(i).[107] On both occasions, Trial Chamber VI prefaced its examination of the established framework of international law by noting that neither the *Statute* nor the *Elements of Crimes* includes a definition of the relevant term, implying that interpretive reference to CIL is only required to fill gaps or resolve ambiguity in the text.

This inference is equally apparent where Trial Chamber VI does *not* refer to the established framework of international law. When interpreting the definition of rape and pillage under the *Statute*, Trial Chamber VI relied exclusively on the *Elements of Crimes* and made no attempt to determine whether the definition in the *Elements of Crimes* is consistent with customary IHL,[108] despite the Appeals Chamber's ruling on three occasions that all offences falling under this provision 'must' be interpreted consistently with customary IHL. As noted in the previous section (and as accepted by Trial Chamber III in *Bemba* with respect to pillage), the evidence suggests that the *Elements of Crimes* for rape and pillage are not consistent with customary IHL.

It is not explicitly stated why Trial Chamber VI ignored the Appeals Chamber's direction to interpret war crimes under articles 8(2)(b) and 8(2)(e) consistently with customary IHL. However, the implication is that the obligation to ensure interpretive consistency with CIL only applies where the *Elements of Crimes* has not provided its own definition.[109] No justification is given for why the *Elements of Crimes* should supersede a direction in the *Statute* to ensure interpretive consistency with customary IHL.

When Mr Ntaganda appealed his conviction, the Appeals Chamber was able to reassert its approach, but only with respect to those crimes mentioned in the appeal, which did not include the war crimes of rape or pillage.

4.4.2.4 Reaffirming Systemic Integration in the *Ntaganda* Appeals Judgment

In 2021, the Appeals Chamber in *Ntaganda* confirmed its approach that war crimes under article 8(2)(e) of the *Statute* 'must' be interpreted consistently with customary IHL, quoting from the obligatory language used in both the

107 Ibid [916], [1136].

108 Ibid [932]–[935], [1026]–[1030].

109 However, the Appeals Chamber in *Lubanga* also prefaced its reliance on customary IHL by stating that neither the *Statute* nor *Elements of Crimes* defines the term 'to participate actively in hostilities'. *Lubanga Appeals Judgement* (n 2) [322].

Lubanga Appeals Judgement and its earlier jurisdictional appeal.[110] The Appeals Chamber expressly deferred to the established framework of the international law of armed conflict to interpret the war crimes of '[o]rdering the displacement of the civilian population' and 'intentionally directing attacks against protected objects' under articles 8(2)(e)(VIII) and 8(2)(e)(IV) of the *Statute*, respectively. It must be noted, however, that the *Elements of Crimes* does not provide a definition for the components of these offences that were the subject of the appeal.

In interpreting the war crime of ordering the displacement of the civilian population, the Appeals Chamber unanimously determined, contrary to Mr Ntaganda's submissions, that 'territorial control' is not a precondition under customary IHL.[111] In reaching this conclusion, the Appeals Chamber carefully analysed the relationship between article 17 of *AP II* and article 49 of the *Geneva Convention IV* alongside the ICRC Commentary to these provisions, rule 129B of the ICRC's Study on Customary International Humanitarian Law, and two commentaries on the *Elements of Crimes* and the negotiations leading to its adoption.[112]

With respect to the war crime of intentionally directing attacks against protected objects, the Appeals Chamber was split on the question of whether the established framework of international law limits the concept of the term 'attack' to actions taken in offence or defence during the actual conduct of hostilities, as determined by Trial Chamber VI. Two of the five appellate judges, Judge Howard Morrison and Judge Piotr Hofmański, strongly stated that interpreting the term 'attack' consistently with CIL limits the war crime of intentionally directing attacks against protected objects to the conduct of hostilities.[113] In her separate opinion, Judge Solomy Balungi Bossa determined on the facts that the impugned conduct did take place during the conduct of hostilities and therefore did not expressly determine whether this limitation is a legal requirement of the term 'attack'.[114] Judge Chile Eboe-Osuji[115] and Judge Ibáñez Carranza,[116]

---

110 *Ntagnanda Appeals Judgment* (n 2) [548].

111 Ibid [564].

112 Ibid [549]–[564].

113 Ibid [1164]; (Majority Judgment; Annex 1, Separate Opinion of Judge Howard Morrison and Judge Piotr Hofmański.)

114 Ibid; (Annex 4, Separate opinion of Judge Solomy Balungi Bossa.)

115 Ibid; (Annex 5, Partly concurring opinion of Judge Chile Eboe-Osuji.)

116 Ibid [1165]–[1168].

for different reasons, determined the term 'attack' is not limited to actions taken during the conduct of hostilities.

4.4.3 *Discussion*

Although imperfect, the ICC Appeals Chamber's decisions in *Lubanga* and *Ntaganda* demonstrate the benefit that comes from complying with the principle of systemic integration. First, while the Appeals Chamber's reliance on the *chapeaux* to articles 8(2)(b) and 8(2)(e) in applying the principle of systemic integration is otherwise methodologically sound, it should be supplemented by reference to article 31(3)(c) of the *VCLT*. Second, Trial Chamber IV's failure to implement the Appeals Chamber's ruling in this regard is indicative of the 'methodological mayhem' inherent across ICC chambers. Finally, the application of the principle of systemic integration in the *Lubanga* and *Ntaganda* appeals shows the potential of this principle to prevent fragmentation and contribute to the progressive development of the law by clarifying its scope in novel situations.

4.4.3.1 Analysis of the ICC Appeals Chamber's Approach in *Lubanga* and *Ntaganda*

The Appeals Chamber's decisions in *Lubanga* and *Ntaganda* demonstrate substantive compliance with the principle of systemic integration for war crimes under articles 8(2)(b) and 8(2)(e) of the *Rome Statute* without mentioning it formally. In its Report on Fragmentation of International Law, the International Law Commission (ILC) explicitly stated that such formality is not required.

> It may of course often be the case that no formal reference to article 31(3)(c) is needed because other techniques provide sufficiently the need to take into account the normative environment. As we have seen, customary law, general principles of law and general treaty provisions form the interpretative background for specific treaty provisions and it often suffices to refer to them to attain systemic integration.[117]

This statement accurately reflects the approach of the ICC Appeals Chamber in relying on the *chapeaux* provisions to articles 8(2)(b) and 8(2)(e) to interpret the crimes consistently with CIL, rather than article 31(3)(c) of the

117 International Law Commission, *Fragmentation of International Law Study* (n 54) 86 para 421.

VCLT. As implied in the ILC Report, one might argue, it is only substantive compliance with the principle of systemic integration that matters. Yet, there are reasons to lament the fact that the ICC Appeals Chamber did not supplement its reasoning by reference to article 31(3)(c) and to argue that subsequent Chambers should adjust their approach accordingly.

First, reliance on the *chapeaux*'s reference to the 'established framework of international law' only covers those war crimes in article 8(2)(b) and 8(2)(c), as there is no such reference in the *chapeaux* to war crimes under articles 8(2)(a) or 8(2)(c). These provisions are copied almost *verbatim* from grave breaches of the *Geneva Conventions* and common article 3, the customary status of which is not in question. The principle of systemic integration is, therefore, equally applicable to the interpretation of these provisions; yet, there has been no equivalent of the Appeals Chamber's ruling in *Lubanga* or *Ntaganda* that they 'must' be interpreted consistently with customary IHL.

Second, others have concluded that the principle of systemic integration should equally apply to the interpretation of the crime of genocide and crimes against humanity under articles 6 and 7 of the *Rome Statute*, respectively.[118] There is no reference to CIL in the *chapeaux* to these articles and so the ICC would, instead, have to provide some other justification for interpreting their respective provisions consistently with CIL, presuming it were so inclined. It would be preferrable for the Court to simply apply the principle of systemic integration under article 31(3)(c) to all crimes in the *Rome Statute*, unless there is evidence of a clear legislative intent to the contrary.

Third, using article 31(3)(c) of the *VCLT* when interpreting the definition of crimes in the *Rome Statute* would signal a return to the approach most notably reflected in the *Katanga* and *Bemba* Trial Judgments. In those decisions, the Court explicitly relied on the general rule of interpretation in article 31 of the *VCLT* and, although its use of article 31(3)(c) left something to be desired, it made a concerted effort to harmonise such rules of interpretation with the specific requirements of the *Rome Statute* and *Elements of Crimes*.[119] This wholistic approach to interpretation, which recognises the *Rome Statute*'s unique position as both a criminal code and a multilateral treaty that must be interpreted in accordance with international law, is the

118 Grover (n 12) 246–344.

119 *Katanga Trial Judgment* (n 1) [47], [1100], [1395] nn 1394, [1625]; *Bemba Trial Judgment* (n 1) [78]–[79].

best way to foster consistency in judicial reasoning and to prevent the unnecessary fragmentation of international law.

4.4.3.2 'Methodological Mayhem' across ICC Chambers

The Appeals Chamber's ruling in *Lubanga* and *Ntaganda* is clear: war crimes under articles 8(2)(b) and 8(2)(e) 'must' be interpreted consistently with CIL. However, ICC Trial Chambers have not complied with this approach. Trial Chamber III's Judgment in *Bemba* was decided in 2016, two years after the *Lubanga* Appeal, and yet made no mention of the obligation to interpret war crimes under articles 8(2)(e) and 8(2)(b) consistently with customary IHL. The *Bemba* Trial Judgment is among the best examples of the application of the principle of systemic integration at the ICC. It grounded its interpretation of the definition of every offence in broader international law and, when faced with the inconsistency between the definition of 'pillage' in the *Elements of Crimes* and CIL, it explicitly highlighted this discrepancy for the benefit of the Assembly of States Parties and the wider international community.[120] However, the war crime of pillage falls under the *chapeau* to article 8(2)(e) and therefore, according to the Appeals Chamber, 'must' be interpreted consistently with CIL. Accordingly, the definition of pillage in the *Elements of Crimes* is not only inconsistent with CIL, but also with the *chapeau* to article 8(2)(e) of the *Rome Statute*. As is made clear by article 9(3) of the *Statute*, the *Statute* prevails over the *Elements of Crimes*.

So, what should Trial Chamber III have done when faced with this situation? One option would have been to declare that, because the *Elements of Crimes*' limitation on the definition of pillage to appropriations for 'private or personal use' is inconsistent with CIL (and therefore inconsistent with the *chapeau* to article 8(2)(e) of the *Rome Statute*), this component of the *Elements of Crimes* must be declared void. Given that there had been no charges brought against Bemba for 'pillaging' property for a public purpose not justified by military necessity, such a ruling would have been *obiter dicta* and not detrimental to the accused in the case at hand. Accordingly, this would have been an appropriate time to jettison the 'private or personal' use element of pillage.[121] The same approach could be applied to the

120 *Bemba Trial Judgment* (n 1) [120].

121 Formally, the Assembly of States Parties, by two-thirds majority, can adopt amendments to the *Elements of Crimes* that have been proposed by any State Party, the judges acting by absolute majority, or the Prosecutor under art 9(2). However, the

definition of rape as a war crime, although the inconsistency between the *Elements of Crimes* and CIL is arguably not as clear-cut for that offence.

If Trial Chamber III's decision to ignore the Appeals Chamber's ruling in *Lubanga* was surprising, Trial Chamber VI's decision in *Ntaganda* was even more so. In the *Ntaganda* Jurisdictional Appeal, the Appeals Chamber unanimously confirmed the *Lubanga* Appeals Chamber's ruling that the definition of crimes under articles 8(2)(b) and 8(2)(e) must be interpreted consistently with customary IHL.[122] It applied this approach to the definition of rape and sexual slavery under article 8(2)(e)(VII) to determine that such conduct committed by and against members of the same armed force is a war crime. However, when the case returned to trial, Trial Chamber IV did not apply this approach to any of the other six crimes falling under article 8(2)(e) with which Mr Ntaganda was charged, including the war crime of pillage. Instead, it relied on the *Elements of Crimes*.

The unwillingness of the Trial Chambers in *Bemba* and *Ntaganda* to apply the Appeals Chamber's approach to systemic integration highlights the methodological mayhem across ICC chambers. Recalling that the *Bemba* and *Ntaganda* are otherwise among the better examples of ICC cases that referred to external sources of law when interpreting the definition of crimes, there are many more cases where the Court has relied on the *Elements of Crimes* without any significant attempt to base its interpretation on applicable customary IHL.

4.4.3.3 The Principle of Systemic Integration and the Incremental Development of the Law in *Lubanga* and *Ntaganda*

Despite the unwillingness of Trial Chambers to apply the Appeals Chamber's ruling, the *Lubanga* and *Ntaganda* Appeals demonstrate the potential of the principle of systemic integration to incrementally develop the law by clarifying its scope in novel situations.

Prior to the *Lubanga* Appeal, it had not been explicitly stated that the concept of using children to actively or directly participate in hostilities was different from the concept of active or direct participation in hostilities under the principle of distinction. A reasonable person may well have applied the same legal test, notwithstanding the distinct purposes of each rule. This was the approach adopted by the *Lubanga* Trial Chamber, for which it

Court could also simply declare that an element is inconsistent with the *Statute* contrary to art 9(3) and not apply it.

122 *Appeals Chamber's Second Decision on Mr Ntaganda's Jurisdictional Appeal* (n 2) [53].

received widespread criticism on the basis that it had unwittingly increased the scope of activities for which children could be lawfully targeted under common article 3 by conflating that test with a broad definition of the war crime of using children to participate actively in hostilities.[123]

While the ICRC had gone to considerable lengths to explain when a civilian would lose the protection of IHL under its *Interpretive Guidance on the Notion of Direct Participation in Hostilities*,[124] there had previously been no separate legal test to determine those activities that would violate the prohibition on using children to participate in hostilities. The *Lubanga* Appeals Chamber, in carefully considering the scope, object, and purpose of each rule under contemporary customary IHL and interpreting article 8(2)(e)(VII) accordingly, was able to clarify the status of customary IHL and contribute to its progressive development by ensuring greater protection for children in armed conflict.[125]

Prior to the decision in *Ntaganda*, the most that can be said about IHL's regulation over intra-armed force violence is that the law was indeterminate. The ICRC's updated (2016) commentary on common article 3 stated that, 'The fact that [...] the abuse [is] committed by their own Party *should not* be a ground to deny such persons the protection of common Article 3',[126] thereby indicating a soft or hortatory obligation under international law. Furthermore, the only legal authority provided in support of this claim, beyond the fundamental humanitarian purpose of common article 3 itself,

---

123 Mark Drumbl, 'The Effects of the Lubanga Case on Understanding and Preventing Child Soldiering' (2012) 15 *Yearbook of International Humanitarian Law* 87, 121; Chris Jenks, 'Law as Shield, Law as Sword: The ICC's Lubanga Decision, Child Soldiers and the Perverse Mutualism of Direct Participation in Hostilities' (2013) 3 *University of Miami National Security and Armed Conflict Law Review* 106; Nicole Urban, 'Direct and Active Participation in Hostilities: The Unintended Consequences of the ICC's decision in Lubanga' *EJIL: Talk! Blog of the European Journal of International Law* (Blog Post, 11 April 2012) <https://www.ejiltalk.org/direct-and-active-participation-in-hostilities-the-unintended-consequences-of-the-iccs-decision-in-lubanga/> accessed 15 July 2024; Natalie Wagner, 'A Critical Assessment of Using Children to Participate Actively in Hostilities in Lubanga: Child Soldiers and Direct Participatio' (2013) 24 *Criminal Law Forum* 181.

124 Nils Melzer, *Interpretive Guidance on the Notion of Direct Participation in Hostilities under International Humanitarian Law* (ICRC 2009).

125 In this regard, the Appeals Chamber also confirmed that the *Rome Statute* should be interpreted consistently with contemporary CIL pursuant to the intertemporal rule.

126 International Committee of the Red Cross, 'Commentary on Geneva Convention III Relative to the Treatment of Prisoners of War, Second Edition' (ICRC 2020) (*ICRC 2020 Commentary on Common Article 3*) para 744.

was the *Ntaganda* Pre-Trial Chamber decision of 2014. The only other case to have considered the issue was the *Sesay* Judgment of the SCSL in 2009, in which the Court reached the opposite conclusion. Accordingly, the law was in a state of flux. In deciding that customary IHL does not impose a status requirement on the victims of sexual violence, the Appeals Chamber in *Ntaganda* clarified the status of customary IHL and, as is often the case with the judicial identification of customary rules, it simultaneously contributed to the progressive development of the law.

It is also worth mentioning the broader humanitarian implications of the Appeals Chamber's decision in *Ntaganda*. The case provides clear judicial support for the absolute prohibition on all forms of sexual violence, helping to confirm its status as a rule of *jus cogens*. As stated by the Trial Chamber, 'As a consequence of the prohibition against rape and sexual slavery being peremptory norms, such conduct is prohibited at all times, both in times of peace and during armed conflicts, and against all persons, irrespective of any legal status'.[127]

The decision thus represents a significant moment in the international community's quest to end impunity for crimes of sexual violence in armed conflict. It also had the specific consequence of ensuring that forcible recruitment into an armed force or group could not be used as a means of avoiding criminal liability for subsequent acts of abuse; a perverse consequence in which the act of raping a civilian would cease to be a war crime if, prior to engaging in the prohibited conduct, the soldier first conscripted the victim into the armed force or group. The insidiousness of such a result is amplified where the act of conscription is itself prohibited under IHL and is a crime within the jurisdiction of the ICC, as was the case with the Mr Ntaganda's rape and sexual slavery of children forcibly recruited into the FPLC. The Appeals Chamber's decision to interpret article 8(2)(e)(VI) consistently with customary IHL thus brought much-needed clarity to this area of law.

4.5 Conclusion

The ICC's adherence to the principle of systemic integration in its war crimes jurisprudence is inconsistent. Despite the attempts of earlier decisions (2012–2016) to highlight the importance of article 31(3)(c) of the *VCLT*,

---

127 *Trial Chamber VI's Second Decision on Mr Ntaganda's Jurisdictional Appeal* (n 2) [52].

those same cases abandoned or diminished the principle of systemic integration when faced with a definition in the *Elements of Crimes*, often influenced by an arguably overzealous interpretation of the principle of legality.

More recent cases (2016–2021) have discarded article 31 of the *VCLT* altogether, without explanation. However, of these same cases, those in the Appeals Chamber have applied the principle of systemic integration to war crimes under articles 8(2)(b) and 8(2)(e) of the *Rome Statute* – not because of the operation of article 31(3)(c) of the *VCLT*, but due to reference in the *chapeaux* to these provisions that all crimes contained therein constitute 'serious violations of the laws and customs of war […] within the established framework of international law'.

Although this reasoning is sound, it should be supplemented by the obligation in article 31(3)(c) of the *VCLT*. One of the reasons for this is that the principle of systemic integration is equally applicable to war crimes under articles 8(2)(a) and 8(2)(c), for which there is no equivalent reference to CIL in their respective *chapeaux*. Moreover, this approach has so far been applied to cases where there is no direct inconsistency between the *Elements of Crimes* and CIL. Accordingly, the question of which interpretive aid takes priority in case of an irreconcilable conflict has not been dealt with by the Appeals Chamber.

While the *Lubanga* and *Ntaganda* Appeals demonstrate the potential for the principle of systemic integration to prevent fragmentation and contribute to the incremental development of the law, the fact that subsequent ICC Trial Chambers have not applied the Appeals Chamber's approach further demonstrates the 'methodological mayhem' that is inherent across ICC chambers. The ICC should return to its earlier adherence to article 31 of the *VCLT*. To do so would ensure greater consistency and provide further justification for applying the principle of systemic integration in the interpretation of all war crimes in the *Rome Statute*.

CHAPTER 5

Systemic Integration and the Definition of a 'Regularly Constituted Court' under Customary International Humanitarian Law

5.1 Introduction

Article 8(2)(c)(IV) of the *Rome Statute* of the International Criminal Court (ICC) criminalises the 'passing of sentences and the carrying out of executions without previous judgment pronounced by a regularly constituted court'. The 2019 decision of Pre-Trial Chamber I in *Al Hassan* was the first time an international court had considered the definition of a 'regularly constituted court'.[1] It was also only the second time that any court had attempted to apply this prohibition to courts established by a non-state armed group (NSAG).[2] Consistent with the general practice of the ICC, neither Pre-Trial Chamber I nor Trial Chamber X in *Al Hassan* attempted to ascertain the meaning of the term 'regularly constituted' under customary international humanitarian law (IHL). Instead, both Chambers relied exclusively on the definition provided in the *Elements of Crimes*, which only requires that regularly constituted courts be 'independent and impartial'.[3]

This chapter critiques the ICC's approach in *Al Hassan*. It argues that subsequent Chambers should interpret the meaning of the term 'regularly constituted court' in accordance with the general rule off interpretation in article 31 of the *Vienna Convention on the Law or Treaties* (VCLT), paying special attention to its meaning under customary IHL in accordance with the principle of systemic integration. When this approach is followed, it is revealed that a regularly constituted court contains the following definitional prerequisites: (I) it has a pre-existing legal basis authorising its

1 *The Prosecutor v Al Hassan Ag Abdoul Aziz Ag Mohamed Ag Mahmoud* (Corrected version of *Décision relative à la Confirmation des Charges Portées contre Al Hassan Ag Abdoul Aziz Ag Mohamed Ag Mahmoud*) (International Criminal Court, Pre-Trial Chamber I, Case No ICC-01/12-01/18, 13 November 2019) (English Translation) (*Al Hassan Pre-Trial Judgment*).

2 The first occasion on which this rule was applied to courts established by a NSAG was in *Prosecutor v Omar Haisam Sakhanh (Judgement)* (Stockholms Tingsrätt (Stockholm District Court), Case No 3787–16, 16 February 2017) 2401–16 (*Omar Haisam Sakhanh*).

3 *Al Hassan Pre-Trial Judgment* (n 1) [376]; *Prosecutor v Al Hassan* (International Criminal Court, ICC-01/12-01/18, Trial Judgment, 26 June 2024) [1169] (*Al Hassan Trial Judgment*).

 | DOI:10.1163/9789004690042_006

establishment; (II) its jurisdictional competence is limited by the scope of that legal basis; and (III) it operates with independence and impartiality. As argued throughout this book, compliance with article 31 of the *VCLT* and the principle of systemic integration promotes methodological consistency, contributes to the unity of international criminal law (ICL), and upholds the rationale behind the prohibition of irregularly constituted courts.

If the ICC continues to rely exclusively on the requirements of 'independence and impartiality' in the *Elements of Crimes*, it will fail to criminalise special courts with irregular jurisdiction, which were expressly outlawed by the *Geneva Conventions of 1949*. Alternatively, if the ICC wishes to limit responsibility for this crime to situations where the impugned courts are not independent or impartial, it should acknowledge that it is applying a standard beyond that which is required under customary IHL.

5.2 *Al Hassan* and the ICC's Interpretation of a 'Regularly Constituted Court'

5.2.1 *Background to the Al Hassan Case*

On 17 January 2012, the *Mouvement national de libération de l'Azawad* (National Movement for the Liberation of Azawad (MNLA)) launched an attack on a military base in the town of Menaka in the Gao region of Northern Mali, sparking a complex non-international armed conflict (NIAC) involving several NSAGS.[4] The MNLA is a secular nationalist movement comprised of ethnic Tuaregs seeking political autonomy in the North. By 2 April 2012, it seized control of the main cities and military bases of Gao, Kidal, and Timbuktu, forcing the Malian armed forces to retreat to the South.[5] The rebellion was soon overrun by Ansar Dine, a Tuareg jihadist Salafist movement that sought to impose a strict interpretation of Sharia law in Mali with the help of al-Qaeda in the Islamic Maghreb (AQIM) and the *Mouvement pour l'unicité et le jihad en Afrique de l'Ouest* (Movement for Unity and Jihad in West Africa (MUJAO)). The MNLA was forced to withdraw from all major centres; by the end of June 2012, Ansar Dine and AQIM controlled Timbuktu and Kidal, while MUJAO controlled the Gao region.[6]

---

4 Office of the Prosecutor of the International Criminal Court, *Situation in Mali: Article 53(1) Report* (ICC 2013), 9, paras 26–29.

5 Ibid.

6 Ibid.

Ansar Dine informed the civilian population over radio of its alliance with AQIM and the groups' shared objective of implementing their own variant of Sharia law. The armed groups brutally enforced their religious ideology through the Islamic Police and Tribunals, frequently resorting to public floggings, amputations, and arbitrary imprisonment for failure to adhere to the religious dress code, smoking cigarettes, drinking alcohol, adultery, homosexuality, or any form of resistance.[7] Human Rights Watch reported several instances in which persons were either stoned to death or summarily executed.[8]

On 18 July 2012, Mali referred the situation to the ICC; by the end of January 2013, the Malian armed forces had regained control of the major centres of Northern Mali with the support of the French army. Three separate United Nations (UN) Security Council Resolutions between July and December 2012 declared the situation in Mali a threat to international peace and security under Chapter VII, proclaiming that perpetrators of human rights and IHL violations shall be held accountable and authorising the deployment of the African-led International Support Mission in Mali (AFISMA) to support the Malian forces in regaining control.

Mr Al Hassan was an inhabitant of Timbuktu prior to the arrival of Ansar Dine. On 7 May 2012, almost immediately following Ansar Dine's involvement in the armed insurrection, he joined the regime as an interpreter and administrative member of the Islamic Police force, mediating between the Police and the civilian population, drafting reports, participating in patrols, arrests, detentions, and security cordons.[9] He eventually became the *de facto* Chief of the Islamic Police. Mr Al Hassan is alleged to have been involved in the physical and psychological mistreatment of detainees, including death threats and the intentional deprivation of food and water, and to have personally engaged in flogging on one occasion.[10] He was in direct contact with the leaders of Ansar Dine and is alleged to have been involved, in an administrative capacity, in facilitating the rape, torture, sexual slavery, persecution, and denial of a fair trial against the civilian population of Timbuktu. He is also alleged to have contributed to the war crime of

---

7 Human Rights Watch, *Mali Conflict and Aftermath. Compendium of Human Rights Watch Reporting 2012–2017* (Human Rights Watch, 2017) <https://www.hrw.org/sites/default/files/supporting_resources/malicompendium0217.pdf> accessed 30 July 2024.

8 Ibid 10, 17, 140, 148.

9 *Al Hassan Pre-Trial Judgment* (n 1) [723]–[762].

10 Ibid [765].

intentionally directing attacks against buildings dedicated to religion and historic monuments. Mr Al Hassan worked for Ansar Dine until its defeat in January 2013. He was surrendered to the ICC on 31 March 2018.

On 13 November 2019, Pre-Trial Chamber I found 'substantial grounds to believe' that Al Hassan contributed, as part of a 'common purpose', to several war crimes and crimes against humanity within the jurisdiction of the Court, including rape, torture, outrages upon personal dignity, and the passing of sentences without previous judgment pronounced by a regularly constituted court; and was convicted by Trial Chamber X on 27 July 2024.[11]

5.2.2 *Interpreting the Definition of a 'Regularly Constituted Court'*

When interpreting the definition of a 'regularly constituted court', neither Pre-Trial Chamber I nor Trial Chamber X followed the rule of strict construction in article 22(2) of the *Rome Statute* or the general rule of interpretation in article 31 of the *VCLT*. They neglected to consider the ordinary meaning of the words and did not refer to their context or to the object and purpose of either the *Rome Statute* as a whole or article 8(2)(c)(IV) in particular. Moreover, there was no attempt to ascertain the definition and scope of the term 'regularly constituted court' in customary IHL, in violation of the principle of systemic integration.

5.2.2.1 Exclusive Reliance on the Elements of Crimes

Both Chambers in *Al Hassan* relied exclusively on the *Elements of Crimes*, which provides that 'the court that rendered the judgement was not "regularly constituted", *that is*, it did not afford the essential guarantees of independence and impartiality'.[12] It is clear from the use of the conjunctive phrase 'that is' that the *Elements* defines a regularly constituted court as one that affords the essential guarantees of independence and impartiality. It emphasises the fairness of the court's operation rather than the legal basis of the court's establishment.[13]

The Prosecution had submitted to the Pre-Trial Chamber that, in addition to the requirements of independence and impartiality, the term 'regularly constituted' imposes limitations on the jurisdictional competence of the court in question. Courts established by NSAGs, it argued, could only be

11 Ibid; *Al Hassan Trial Judgment* (n 3).

12 *International Criminal Court, Elements of Crimes*, art 8(2)(c)(IV), 34 (emphasis added) (*International Criminal Court, Elements of Crimes*).

13 *Al Hassan Pre-Trial Judgment* (n 1) [376].

considered 'regularly constituted' if they enforced the pre-existing law of the state, save for examples where the laws of the NSAG ensure better compliance with IHL and international human rights law (IHRL).[14] (This point will be discussed in detail in the Chapter 6.)

Pre-Trial Chamber I rejected this submission outright, holding that, 'independence and impartiality are the requisite attributes for a court to be regarded as "regularly constituted" within the meaning of the Statute'.[15] It refused to consider whether this term imposed any additional requirements under IHL or IHRL, contrary to the principle of systemic integration in article 31(3)(c) of the *VCLT*, and instead focused only on the meaning of 'independence and impartiality'.[16] Trial Chamber X adopted the same approach with respect to the meaning of the term 'regularly constituted'. Indeed, the Trial Chamber made it quite explicit that it would only need to refer to customary IHL where the *Elements of Crimes* do not provide a definition.[17]

5.2.2.2 The Ordinary Meaning of the Words 'Regularly Constituted' in Their Context and in Light of the Object and Purpose of the *Rome Statute*

Had the Chambers complied with the obligation to give the words their ordinary meaning, they would have determined that the term 'regularly constituted court' denotes something more than the requirements of independence and impartiality. Using dictionary definitions of the term 'regularly constituted', it may be said that courts in armed conflicts must be 'establish[ed] by law' or '[g]ive[n] legal or constitutional form' in 'a regular

14 *Document Contennant les Charges contre M. Al Hassan* (*Version amendée et corrigée du Document contenant les charges contre M. Al Hassan Ag Abdoul Aziz Ag Mohamed Ag Mahmoud*) (International Criminal Court, Case No ICC-01/12-01/18, 2 July 2019) (*Prosecution Document Containing the Charges against Al Hassan*).

15 Ibid [376].

16 *Al Hassan Pre-Trial Judgment* (n 9) [375]–[382]. Pre-Trial Chamber I noted at [377] that the Preparatory Commission for the *Elements of Crimes* had chosen not to retain the Belgian draft proposal, which had left 'regularly constituted' undefined, and instead opted for the current wording. The Chamber inferred from this sequence of events that the Preparatory Committee intended that a 'regularly constituted court' is to be defined exclusively by reference to the requirements of independence and impartiality. While the decision to reject the Belgian draft proposal may indeed shed light on the Committee's intention, there is no record of the debate. In any event, speculations over drafter's intent do not relieve the Court of its obligation to interpret war crimes in the *Statute* in accordance with their plain and ordinary meaning and in a manner consistent with applicable customary IHL.

17 *Al Hassan Trial Judgment* (n 3) [1171].

manner',[18] which is defined as 'constituted, conducted, scheduled, or done in conformity with established or prescribed usages, rules, or discipline'.[19] These definitions stress that a regularly constituted court is one with a 'legal basis' (that is either 'established by law' or given a 'legal or constitutional form') and is created in accordance with ordinary legal rules and procedures.

The 'context' in which the words must be interpreted in accordance with their natural meaning includes the surrounding treaty text, preamble, annexes, and any other agreement or instrument made in connection with the treaty. The fact that the term 'regularly constituted court' derives from common article 3(1)(d) of the *Geneva Conventions* stipulates that the relevant 'context' is customary IHL applicable to NIACs, of which common article 3 is an indisputable component. The phrase 'regularly constituted court' is also a treaty term of 'special meaning', pursuant to article 31(4) of the *VCLT*, to which the drafters are presumed to have intended to refer. The meaning of this under customary IHL will be discussed in the following section, but it is worth noting that it is broadly consistent with its ordinary meaning and stipulates that the court must have an authorised legal basis and defined jurisdictional competence.

With respect to the obligation to interpret treaties in light of their object and purpose, it will be recalled that the principle of *in dubio pro reo* (when in doubt, favour the accused) precludes the Court from relying on broad interpretations of the *Rome Statute*'s object and purpose when interpreting the definition and scope of an offence. Instead, it is necessary to bear in mind that the *Rome Statute*'s objective is to ensure fair trials in accordance with the rule of law and to focus on the object and purpose of the specific provision to understand its true meaning. The drafting of article 8(2)(c)(IV) of the *Statute* and the origins of this provision in common article 3(1)(d) of the *Geneva Conventions* confirm that the object and purpose of article 8(2)(c)(IV) is to prohibit summary justice and to criminalise the denial of a fair trial in a NIAC by prohibiting the establishment of special tribunals with irregular jurisdiction.[20] Its goal is to prohibit summary executions, criminal

18 'Constituted', *Lexico Oxford Online Dictionary* <https://www.lexico.com/definition/constitute> accessed 30 July 2024.

19 'Regular', *Merriam-Webster Online Dictionary* <https://www.merriam-webster.com/dictionary/regular> accessed 30 July 2024.

20 Otto Triffterer and Kai Ambos, 'Jurisdiction, Admissibility and Applicable Law' in Otto Triffterer and Kai Ambos (eds), *Rome Statute of the International Criminal Court: A Commentary* (Bloomsbury 2016) 111, 554 para 907 ('Given the fact that the Statute,

punishment from the executive branch, sham trials, the denial of fair trial guarantees, and the creation of special courts whose jurisdiction is not limited by a constitutional or other appropriate legal basis. Indeed, given that the term 'regularly constituted court' has a technical meaning under IHL, the ICC could equally have relied on article 31(4) of the *VCLT* to give the term its 'specialised meaning', as previously mentioned.

Neither Chamber in *Al Hassan* made any reference to these rules of interpretation. Its approach can be criticised on this basis alone, as it promotes methodological inconsistency and undermines the customary status of the general rule of interpretation in article 31 of the *VCLT*. However, the ICC's approach also affects the substantive outcome. The Court's interpretation of the term 'independence and impartiality' achieves some of the object and purpose behind article 8(2)(c)(IV), but is ultimately unsatisfactory as it overlooks key aspects of the customary definition of a regularly constituted court.

5.2.3 *The Definition of 'Independence and Impartiality'*

Despite failing to apply the general rule of interpretation to the term 'regularly constituted court', both ICC Chambers drew on external law when interpreting the terms 'independence and impartiality'. In doing so, the ICC makes a valuable contribution to the law by clarifying the meaning of these terms when applied to courts established by NSAGs. The *Al Hassan* case is the first time that an international court has considered the independence

unlike the chapeau of article 6 para. 2 of Add. Prot. II, has verbatim retained the language of common article 3, also non-governmental armed groups are, notwithstanding the problems involved, bound to set up 'regularly constituted Courts' before a sentencing might take place, thereby prohibiting special courts set up on an ad hoc-basis.'); Dieter Fleck and Michael Bothe, *The Handbook of International Humanitarian Law* (3rd edn, OUP 2013) para 576; Knut Dörmann, *Elements of War Crimes under the Rome Statute of the International Criminal Court: Sources and Commentary* (CUP 2003) 412 ('Given the fact that the Statute has verbatim retained the language of common Art. 3 GC, dissident armed groups are also bound to set up "a regularly constituted court" before a sentencing can take place. Thus, special courts set up on an ad hoc basis by rebel groups are prohibited.'); International Committee of the Red Cross, *Commentary on Convention (IV) relative to the Protection of Civilian Persons in Time of War* (ICRC 1958) 340 ('The courts are to be "regularly constituted". This wording definitely excludes all special tribunals. It is the ordinary military courts of the Occupying Power which will be competent. Such courts will, of course, be set up in accordance with the recognized principles governing the administration of justice.').

and impartiality of NSAG courts.[21] It is therefore worth examining the Court's interpretation of these terms in some detail.

5.2.3.1 Interpreting 'Independence and Impartiality' in Accordance with External Sources of International Law

Following its determination that 'regularly constituted' means 'independent and impartial', both Chambers stated that they must refer to external sources of international law, 'as the concepts of independence and impartiality are not defined in the Statute or the Elements of Crimes'.[22] This approach is consistent with Hypothesis 1; namely, that the ICC tends to rely on external sources of law only where the *Elements of Crimes* does not provide its own definition.

Neither Chamber justified reliance on external sources of law by reference to the principle of systemic integration. Pre-Trial Chamber I cited article 21(3) of the *Rome Statute* to draw exclusively on IHRL.[23] Article 21(3), which falls under the 'Applicable Law' provisions of the *Rome Statute*, states that, 'The application and interpretation of law pursuant to this article must be consistent with internationally recognized human rights'.[24] There is debate over whether article 21(3) superimposes interpretive consistency with IHRL on all crimes in the *Rome Statute*. From a methodological perspective, requiring interpretive consistency with IHRL would appear to contradict the *lex specialis* nature of IHL in the interpretation of war crimes in article 8 of the *Statute*.[25] Moreover, using IHRL to broaden the definition of crimes could be considered contrary to the rule of strict construction in article 22(2). Consistent with the writings of Grover and others,[26] the present study adopts the position that article 21(3) requires *procedural* consistency with international human rights in the application of the *Rome Statute*, not *substantive* consistency. Several cases appear to confirm this interpretation by

---

21 The European Court of Human Rights has considered a similar issue in terms of recognising the effects of courts operated by non-state entities. *Cyprus v Turkey* [2001] Application No 25781/94, IV Eur Court HR, [231] (*Cyprus v Turkey*).

22 *Al Hassan Pre-Trial Judgment* (n1) [378]; *Al Hassan Trial Judgment* (n 3) [1171].

23 *Al Hassan Pre-Trial Judgment* (n 1) [378].

24 *Rome Statute of the International Criminal Court*, opened for signature 17 July 1998, 2187 UNTS 38544 (entered into force 1 July 2002) (*Rome Statute*).

25 Leena Grover, *Interpreting Crimes in the Rome Statute of the International Criminal Court* (CUP 2014) 132.

26 Ibid; Stephen Bailey, 'Article 21(3) of the Rome Statute: A Plea for Clarity' (2014) 14 *International Criminal Law Review* 513.

applying article 21(3) to issues concerning the procedural rights of the accused,[27] though at times the language used is broad enough to suggest that the definition of crimes themselves must be interpreted consistently with human rights law.[28]

Pre-Trial Chamber I relied on the *International Covenant on Civil and Political Rights* (*ICCPR*), the jurisprudence of the European Court of Human Rights (ECtHR), the Inter-American Human Rights Commission, and the African Human Rights Commission.[29] The only reference to IHL comes at the end of a long citation of human rights cases and instruments in support of the prohibition of actual (subjective) judicial bias, in which the reader is directed to 'see equally' the *Customary International Humanitarian Law* study prepared by the International Committee of the Red Cross (ICRC *Customary IHL Study*).

In accordance with the human rights instruments and judicial decisions listed above, Pre-Trial Chamber I concluded that 'independence' means judicial independence from the executive or legislative branches of the relevant state or NSAG.[30] It stated that there will be a violation of the principle of independence where it is impossible to distinguish between the two exercises of power or where the executive is controlling the judiciary.[31] The Chamber interpreted 'impartiality' to mean freedom from bias and prejudice in which the judge must not presume the guilt or innocence of the accused or act in a manner that promotes the interest of one of the parties.[32]

---

27 *Prosecutor v Thomas Lubanga Dyilo* (*Appeal of the Prosecutor against the decision of Trial Chamber I entitled 'Decision on the release of Thomas Lubanga Dyilo'*) (International Criminal Court, Appeals Chamber, Case No ICC-01/04-01/06 OA 12, 21 October 2008) [12]; *Prosecutor v Jean-Pierre Bemba Gombo* (*Judgment*) (International Criminal Court, Trial Chamber III, Case No ICC-01/05-01/08, 21 March 2016) [36] (*Bemba Trial Judgment*).

28 *Prosecutor v Lubanga* (*Judgment on the Appeal of Mr. Thomas Lubanga Dyilo against the Decision on the Defence Challenge to the Jurisdiction of the Court pursuant to article 19(2)(a)*) (International Criminal Court, Appeals Chamber, Case No ICC-01/04-01/06-772, 14 December 2006) [37] (*Decision on the Defences Challenge to Jurisdiction*) ('Human rights underpin the Statute; every aspect of it, including the exercise of the jurisdiction of the Court. Its provisions must be interpreted and more importantly applied in accordance with internationally recognized human rights.'). However, this case also applied article 21(3) to a procedural issue.

29 *Al Hassan Pre-Trial Judgment* (n 1) [379–382].

30 Ibid [379].

31 Ibid.

32 Ibid [380].

As it turns out, the definition of 'independence and impartiality' under IHL is broadly consistent with IHRL. Indeed, the ICRC *Customary IHL Study* draws heavily on the same IHRL sources cited by Pre-Trial Chamber I when defining each term. However, the ICRC *Customary IHL Study* considers the exigencies of armed conflict and the need for contextualising the requirements of independence and impartiality where trial by a military judge or tribunal is the only viable option. For example, the ICRC *Customary IHL Study* notes that 'independence' requires a court to 'perform its functions without interference from any other branch of government, especially the executive'[33] but, where the armed conflict necessitates the use of military judges that form part of the executive branch, there must be specific 'procedures in place to ensure they perform their judicial functions independently and impartially'.[34] Similarly, the decision of the United States (US) Supreme Court in *Hamdan* explained the need for provisions that 'insulat[e] military judges from the effects of command influence' and thus 'preserve judicial impartiality',[35] and concluded that the Military Commissions used to try Guantánamo Bay detainees unjustifiably 'remove[d] safeguards that are important to the fairness of the proceedings and the independence of the court'.[36]

Accordingly, while the core meaning of 'independence and impartiality' with respect to judicial institutions is consistent across IHL and IHRL,[37] as confirmed in the jurisprudence of the *ad hoc* international criminal tribunals with respect to their own proceedings,[38] the application of these rules

---

33 Jean-Marie Henckaerts and Louise Doswald-Beck, *Customary International Humanitarian Law (Rules)* (International Committee of the Red Cross/CUP 2005), vol 1 (Rules), 355–356.

34 Ibid.

35 *Hamdan v Rumsfeld* 548 U.S. 557, Separate Opinion of Kennedy J [11] (Quoting Weiss v United States (1994) 510 U.S. 163 [179]–[181] (United States Supreme Court, 2006) (*Hamdan v Rumsfeld*).

36 Ibid [16].

37 International Committee of the Red Cross, 'Commentary on Geneva Convention III Relative to the Treatment of Prisoners of War, Second Edition' (ICRC 2020) para 703.

38 *Prosecutor v Ferdinand Nahimana, Jean-Bosco Barayagwiza, and Hassan Ngeze (Appeal Judgment)* (International Criminal Tribunal for Rwanda, Appeals Chamber, Case No ICTR-99-52-A, 28 November 2007) [19] (*Prosecutor v Ferdinand Nahimana, Jean-Bosco Barayagwiza, and Hassan Ngeze*); *Prosecutor v Furundžija (Appeal Judgment)* (International Criminal Tribunal for the former Yugoslavia, Appeals Chamber, Case No IT-95-17/1-A, 21 July 2000) [189–191] (*Prosecutor v Furundžija*); *Prosecutor v. Stanilav Galić (Appeal Judgment)* (International Criminal Tribunal for the former

in the IHL context demonstrates its *lex specialis* function. The rules of IHRL remain relevant to construing the definition of 'independence and impartiality', but IHL ought to provide the primary source of interpretation. Methodologically speaking, therefore, Pre-Trial Chamber I's almost exclusive reliance on IHRL under article 21(3) is cause for concern. The prohibition on denying a fair trial under article 8(2)(c)(IV) is a war crime. The ICC's war crimes jurisdiction under article 8 was intended to reflect and be interpreted consistently with customary IHL. The Introduction to the elements of war crimes in the *Elements of Crimes* (which is where the reference to 'independence and impartiality' is found) states that the elements 'shall be interpreted consistently with the established framework of the international law of armed conflict'. Accordingly, IHL should have been the primary source of law guiding Pre-Trial Chamber I's interpretation as supplemented by IHRL, not the other way round.

For its part, Trial Chamber X appeared to have acknowledged the need for its interpretation to be grounded in IHL. Rather than rely on Article 21(3) to invoke IHRL, the Trial Chamber cited Article 21 in its entirety to state that it 'can refer to 'customary and conventional international law regardless of whether any lacuna exists, to ensure an interpretation of Article 8 of the Statute that is fully consistent with international law".[39] The Chamber proceeded to rely on a combination of IHL and IHRL sources, in particular the updated ICRC commentary to Common Article 3 of the *Geneva Conventions*. Importantly, the Chamber was 'mindful that a court established by a non-state actor may not be able to successfully comply with the same level of independence required of a State court' and therefore considered that 'reasonable flexibility should be applied in assessing non-state armed groups' capacity to adhere' to the requirement of judicial independence from the executive.[40] Indeed, the *lex specialis* of IHL with respect to the legality of state courts during armed conflict is especially relevant to the regulation of NSAG courts that are unlikely to have the same resources,

---

Yugoslavia, Appeals Chamber, Case No IT-98-29-A, 30 November 2006) [37–41] (*Prosecutor v Stanilav Galić*).

39 *Al Hassan Trial Judgment* (n 3) [1171]. In this passage, Trial Chamber is quoting directly from the Appeals Chamber in *Prosecutor v Bosco Ntaganda* (*Judgement on the appeal of Mr Ntaganda against the "Second decision on the Defence's challenge to the jurisdiction of the Court in respect of Counts 6 and 9*) (International Criminal Court, Appeals Chamber, Case No ICC-01/04-02/06 OA5, 15 June 2017) ('*Appeals Chamber's Second Decision on Mr Ntaganda's Jurisdictional Appeal*') at [53].

40 *Al Hassan Trial Judgment* (n 3) [1173].

sophistication, or degree of separation from the executive branch of the NSAG, if there is one.[41] This passage from the *Al Hassan* Trial Chamber reflects an important understanding that certain rules may have 'common but differentiated' responsibilities depending on the capacity of the NSAG, a point which is explored further in Chapter 7.

Trial Chamber X's ruling that it may refer to 'customary or conventional international law' to 'ensure an interpretation of Article 8 of the Statute that is fully consistent with international law' represents a significant step towards compliance with the principle of systemic integration but is undercut by the fact that interpretive reliance on customary IHL is limited to situations where the *Elements* do not provide a definition. Ultimately, the Trial Chamber interprets the term 'independence and impartiality' in accordance with customary IHL, but does not examine whether the term 'regularly constituted' has any special meaning beyond what is provided in the *Elements of Crimes*.

Turning to the substantive outcome, both Chambers concluded that the Islamic Tribunals operated under the influence of executive members of Ansar Dine and AQIM and were therefore neither independent nor impartial, noting that several witnesses had described the judicial proceedings as a 'façade'.[42] Certain decisions were considered 'too important' for the Islamic Tribunal and were instead handed to an executive member of the NSAG, before returning to the Tribunal for an official determination in accordance with the view of the executive.[43] Trial Chamber X determined that the 'functions and competencies' of the Islamic Tribunal cannot be distinguished from the groups political and military leadership 'because the latter was able to control the former, thereby rendering the Islamic Court not independent'.[44] In finding against impartiality, the Trial Chamber held that judges would 'improperly promote the interests of Ansar Dine/AQIM and created the unacceptable appearance of bias'.[45]

41 The concept of a sliding scale of obligations imposed on NSAGs depending on their capacity, also referred to as 'common but differentiated responsibilities', is discussed in Chapter 7 of this thesis. See also Marco Sassòli and Yuval Shany, 'Should the Obligations of States and Armed groups under International Humanitarian Law Really be Equal?' (2011) 93(882) *International Review of the Red Cross* 425.

42 *Al Hassan Pre-Trial Judgment* (n 1) [419].

43 Ibid [420].

44 *Al Hassan Trial Judgment* (n 3) [1512].

45 Ibid [1514].

5.2.3.2 Systemic Lack of Independence and Impartiality: Political Courts

In one paragraph, seemingly *obiter dicta*, Pre-Trial Chamber I did draw specifically on IHL for the meaning of 'independence and impartiality'. This paragraph is arguably the Pre-Trial Chamber's most important ruling on the interpretation of 'independence and impartiality' in the context of armed conflict and shows the unifying potential of the principle of systemic integration, though it was not picked up on by the Trial Chamber. The Prosecution had argued that 'the interference of members of the executive in the judicial process was systematic'[46] and that the Islamic Courts were 'instrumentalised' by the armed group Ansar Dine as a means of imposing their ideology and religious vision on the civilian population, often through violent punishment.[47] Pre-Trial Chamber I appeared to agree. It stated that a systemic violation of the 'independence and impartiality' requirement in the 'structure and operation' of the court would violate article 8(2)(c)(IV), without necessarily requiring proof of violations of individual fair trial guarantees on a case-by-case basis.[48] According to the Chamber, the evidence capable of proving this 'instrumentalization' of the judicial system included: (I) accelerated proceedings; (II) the 'enactment of specific and discriminatory laws and decrees'; (III) executive influence over the judiciary; and (IV) the 'application of measures by judges in violation of procedural and regulatory guarantees'.[49]

In support, Pre-Trial Chamber I cited with approval the post-World War II decision of the United States Military Tribunal in Nuremberg in *United States of America v Josef Altstötter and others*, also known as the *Justice Case*.[50] As demonstrated below, the Chamber's reliance on the *Justice Case* incorporated the notion that the entire judicial system of a state or NSAG could be deemed to be in violation of 'independence and impartiality' due to its misuse as a tool of persecution. Practically speaking, this modality may be important where it is difficult or impractical to prove that independence and impartiality were denied on a case-by-case basis. Furthermore, it touches on the notion that the enforcement of discriminatory laws, even if

---

46 *Prosecution Document Containing the Charges against Al Hassan* (n 14) [429].

47 Ibid [428].

48 *Al Hassan Pre-Trial Judgment* (n 1) [372].

49 Ibid.

50 *United States of America v Josef Altstötter and others* (*The Justice Case*) (United States Military Tribunal Trials of War Criminals Before the Nuernberg Military Tribunals Under Control Council Law No. 10, Volume III) (*The Justice Case*).

enacted in accordance with the laws of the authority in question, can render such courts irregularly constituted.

The *Justice Case* was prosecuted on the basis that the 12 accused were responsible for the 'distortion and denial of the judicial and penal process', and 'the superimposition of extraordinary courts of a predominantly political nature ... with wide and arbitrary criminal jurisdiction upon the ordinary court system; and the use of the judicial process as a powerful weapon for persecution and extermination'.[51] The structural lack of independence and impartiality of the Nazi courts is best exemplified by the discretion afforded to individual judges,[52] who were empowered to 'refuse any evidence if they deemed it not necessary for the resolution of the case'[53] and who, under the direction of the Reich Minister of Justice, could deviate from any existing law.[54]

Most post-World War II cases dealing with the war crime of denying a fair trial turned on the denial of specific individual fair trial guarantees, such as the right to legal counsel or the right to be informed of the charges.[55] By contrast, it was the substance of the laws themselves in the *Justice Case* that transformed the judicial system into a tool of persecution and ultimately precluded those accused from relying on the defence that they were applying the existing law. As stated by the Tribunal:

> The defendants contend that they should not be found guilty because they acted within the authority and by the command of the German

51 Ibid [1063].

52 Ibid [988]–[994]. For example, article 2 of the Law to Change the Penal Code reads: 'Whoever commits an act which the law declares as punishable or which deserves punishment according to the fundamental idea of a penal law and the sound concept of the people, shall be punished. If no specific penal law can be directly applied to this act, then it shall be punished according to the law whose underlying principle can be most readily applied to the act'.

53 Ibid [999]–[1001].

54 Ibid [988].

55 See, for example, Trial of General Tanaka Hisakasu and Five Others, 'US Military Commission, Shanghai, 13 August–3 September 1946', *Law Reports of Trials of War Criminals, Volume VI* (United Nations War Crimes Commission, 1948) 66; Trial of Lieutenant General Shigeru Sawada and Three Others, 'US Military Commission, Shanghai, 27 February–15 April 1946', *Law Reports of Trials of War Criminals, Volume V* (United Nations War Crimes Commission, 1948) 1; Trial of Lieutenant Harukei Isayama and Seven Others, 'US Military Commission, Shanghai, 1–25 July 1946', *Law Reports of Trials of War Criminals, Volume V* (United Nations War Crimes Commission, 1947) 60.

> laws and decrees … The very essence of the prosecution case is that the laws, the Hitler decrees and the Draconic, corrupt, and perverted Nazi judicial system themselves constituted the substance of war crimes and crimes against humanity and that participation in the enactment and enforcement of them amounts to complicity in crime. … It can scarcely be said that governmental participation, the proof of which is necessary for conviction [of crimes against humanity], can also be a defence to the charge.[56]

The *Justice Case* provides the precedent, as accepted by Pre-Trial Chamber I in *Al Hassan*, that the systematic enforcement of discriminatory laws by the judicial system can result in a systematic denial of the requirements of independence and impartiality. As noted by Jennifer DePiazza, the Prosecution in the *Justice Case* 'pleaded systemic denial of fair trial against thousands of victims and sought to show that the system for the administration of justice was, as such, incapable of delivering fair trials'.[57] The evidence tendered by the Prosecution therefore consisted of 'the applicable laws themselves, orders, directives and correspondence between various actors within the Reich system for the administration of justice, showing the behind the scenes rigging of the system'.[58]

This approach has the potential to shift focus away from the structure of the court and its separation from the executive to an analysis of the content of the laws themselves. Pre-Trial Chamber I's statement in *Al Hassan* that the 'enactment of specific and discriminatory laws and decrees' could amount to a systemic lack of independence and impartiality explicitly references this connection. While the Islamic Tribunal's lack of independence and impartiality in *Al Hassan* was ultimately decided on different grounds, Pre-Trial Chamber I's willingness to incorporate post-World War II war crimes jurisprudence, in what amounted to an application of the principle of systemic integration, provides ripe ground for discussion on the scope of the obligation to provide judicial independence and impartiality.

---

56 *The Justice Case* (n 50) 984.

57 Jennifer DePiazza, 'Denial of Fair Trial as an International Crime: Precedent for Pleading and Proving it under the Rome Statute' (2017) 15 *Journal of International Criminal Justice* 257, 274.

58 Ibid. DePiazza observes that the Selection Policy of the Office of the Prosecutor of the ICC is likely to favour allegations of a systemic denial of the right to a fair trial involving a substantial number victims over individual cases, due to the gravity requirement.

5.2.4 *Summary of the ICC's Interpretation of a 'Regularly Constituted Court'*

In sum, the ICC's approach to interpreting the definition of a 'regularly constituted court' in *Al Hassan* was unsatisfactory. It relied exclusively on the *Elements of Crimes* to determine that the words 'regularly constituted' mean 'independent and impartial', which plainly contradicts the ordinary meaning of the words and their specialised meaning under customary IHL. While both the Chambers provided useful insights on the meaning of the term 'independence and impartiality' by drawing on external sources of law, they failed to consult customary IHL to determine the meaning of a regularly constituted court and therefore missed an important opportunity to promote the principle of systemic integration and bring further clarity to this area of law.

5.3 The Definition of a 'Regularly Constituted Court' under Customary International Humanitarian Law

Under customary IHL, there is no doubt that courts in armed conflict must be regularly constituted. The ICRC's updated commentary to common article 3 states that the 'regularly constituted' requirement 'is part of customary international law'.[59] Beyond its codification in common article 3, whose customary status has been confirmed by the International Court of Justice on multiple occasions,[60] the term is replicated both in article 75(4) of *Additional Protocol I* (*AP I*)[61] and article 66 of *Geneva Convention IV*,[62] the latter of which uses 'properly constituted' in the text of the treaty and 'regularly constituted' in the official commentary, thereby treating the terms as synonymous.[63] It is codified in the international criminal statutes of the

---

59 International Committee of the Red Cross, *Commentary on Geneva Convention III Relative to the Treatment of Prisoners of War, Second Edition* (n 37) para 710.

60 *Military and Paramilitary Activities in and against Nicaragua (Nicaragua v United States of America) (Merits)* [1986] 14, [218] (*Military and Paramilitary Activities in and against Nicaragua*); *Legality of the Threat or Use of Nuclear Weapons (Advisory Opinion)* [1996] ICJ Rep 226, [79] (*Legality of the Threat or Use of Nuclear Weapons*).

61 *Protocol Additional to the Geneva Conventions of 12 August 1949, and Relating to the Protection of Victims of International Armed Conflicts*, opened for signature 8 June 1977, 1977, 1125 UNTS 3 (entered into force 7 December 1978) (*AP I*).

62 International Committee of the Red Cross, *Commentary on Convention (IV) relative to the Protection of Civilian Persons in Time of War* (n 20).

63 Ibid 340.

International Criminal Tribunal for Rwanda (ICTR), the Special Court of Sierra Leone (SCSL), and the *Rome Statute*. Of the 125 states party to the *Rome Statute*, 65 have enacted domestic legislation incorporating the 'regularly constituted' requirement.[64] As recorded in the ICRC's *Customary IHL Study*, the term is used in the military manuals of 23 states,[65] is explicitly codified in the national legislation of at least 15 states,[66] and is incorporated into the national legislation of those that have classified violations of the *Geneva Conventions* as domestic crimes.

In contrast to the widespread use of the term 'regularly constituted', there have been few attempts to define its meaning. The ICRC 2005 Customary IHL study defined a regularly constituted court as one that 'has been established and organised in accordance with the laws and procedures already in force in a country'.[67] However, this definition has been challenged in more recent times due to the fact that it would appear to exclude NSAG courts altogether. By examining the practice and legal opinions of states in prohibiting courts that are not regularly constituted (or 'established by law' under IHRL), this section concludes that customary IHL imposes three requirements for a court to be considered regularly constituted in situations of armed conflict: (I) it has a pre-existing legal basis authorising its establishment; (II) its subject-matter jurisdiction is limited by the scope of its legal basis; and (III) it affords the essential guarantees of independence and impartiality.

5.3.1 *The Court Has a Pre-existing Legal Basis Authorising its Establishment*

The first definitional component of a regularly constituted court under customary IHL is that it must have a *pre-existing* legal basis authorising its establishment. The purpose of this rule is to prohibit the convening of special tribunals for a particular situation or individual. For example, rule 100 of the ICRC's *Customary IHL Study*, entitled 'Fair Trial Guarantees', defines a regularly constituted court as one that 'has been established and organised

64 Jean-Marie Henckaerts and Louise Doswald-Beck, *Customary International Humanitarian Law (Practice)* (International Committee of the Red Cross, CUP 2005), vol 2 (Practice), 2401–2416.

65 Ibid.

66 Ibid.

67 Henckaerts and Doswald-Beck, *Customary International Humanitarian Law (Rules)* (n 33) 355 (emphasis added).

in accordance with the laws and procedures *already in force in a country*'.[68] The official commentary to article 66 of the *Geneva Convention IV*, applicable to civilians under the control of an Occupying Power, states that the 'regularly constituted' requirement 'definitely excludes all special tribunals' and that all such courts must be 'non-political' so as to prohibit the use of the judicial system as 'an instrument of political or racial persecution'.[69]

Both of these sources were cited with approval by the US Supreme Court in *Hamdan v Rumsfeld*,[70] which determined that the Military Commission established to try Salim Hamdan (a Guantánamo Bay detainee), which had been established pursuant to a Presidential Executive Order,[71] was a special tribunal and not regularly constituted because 'the regular courts in [the US] system are the courts-martial established by congressional statutes'.[72] A Presidential Executive Order does not amount to a pre-existing legal basis; therefore, the Military Commission was deemed irregularly constituted. Although the US Congress subsequently passed the *Military Commissions Act* (MCA) of 2006 (amended in 2009) – giving congressional authority for the convening of military commissions to try Guantánamo Bay detainees (which are described in the legislation as 'regularly constituted courts') – it is doubtful that such commissions are in fact 'regularly constituted' under common article 3. The Congressional authority provides a 'legal basis' for the establishment of the commissions, but it is not a *pre-existing* legal basis. As stated by one commentator:

> The military commissions created under the MCAs were not 'already in force' or 'chosen in advance.' They were created in order to try merely some of those captured during the war in Afghanistan ... and the laws establishing them were enacted years after detainees at Guantanamo entered U.S. custody.[73]

---

68 Ibid.

69 International Committee of the Red Cross, *Commentary on Convention (IV) relative to the Protection of Civilian Persons in Time of War* (n 20) 340.

70 *Hamdan v Rumsfeld* (n 35) 69 per Stevens J.

71 International Committee of the Red Cross, 'United States, President's Military Order, 13 November 2001' *How Does Law Protect in War? Online Casebook* (Web Page, 2024) <https://casebook.icrc.org/case-study/united-states-presidents-military-order> accessed 30 July 2024.

72 *Hamdan v Rumsfeld* (n 35) 70 per Stevens J.

73 Jordan Paust, 'Still Unlawful: The Obama Military Commissions, Supreme Court Holdings, and Deviant Dicta in the D.C. Circuit' (2012) 45(2) *Cornell International Law Journal* 367, 370.

The US Supreme Court has not had the opportunity to review the legality of commissions established pursuant to the *MCA*. However, it did seem to anticipate the illegality of such a move when in noted in *Hamdan* that the International Military Tribunal for the Far East in *Yamashita* had condemned a military commission as a court 'specially constituted for a particular trial',[74] which is clearly distinct from the concept of a regular court with a pre-existing legal basis.

The requirement of a pre-existing legal basis for the establishment of courts is also reflected in IHRL, which uses the phrase 'established by law' rather than 'regularly constituted'.[75] Although the content of IHRL cannot be automatically transferred to that of IHL, the basic definitional components of both 'regularly constituted' and 'established by law' are synonymous and, in such circumstances, a general practice accepted as law in the IHRL context may influence and clarify the content of customary IHL. Indeed, human rights jurisprudence examining the 'established by law' requirement, in the context of reviewing the legality of military tribunals, forms a substantial part of the evidence relied upon in the ICRC's *Customary IHL Study*, thereby confirming the symbiotic relationship between the two bodies of law.[76]

Under IHRL, a court that is 'established by law' must have a pre-existing legal basis authorising its establishment and its jurisdiction must be limited by the scope of that legal basis. As described by Manfred Nowak in the *Commentary to the UN Covenant on Civil and Political Rights*, a court 'established by law' must be created independent of the particular case and pursuant to 'law' in a strict parliamentary sense.[77] It has been noted that, 'The expression "established by law" concerns the "predictability" according to law of the very existence of the tribunal and the way it is organised. The law must cover the *creation* and *competence* of the judicial body'.[78]

---

74 *Hamdan v Rumsfeld* (n 35) 69 per Stevens J.

75 See, for example, *International Covenant on Civil and Political Rights*, opened for signature 16 December 1966, 999 UNTS 171, art 9(1) (entered into force 23 March 1976) (*ICCPR*); *European Convention for the Protection of Human Rights and Fundamental Freedoms, as amended by Protocols Nos. 11 and 14*, opened for signature 4 November 1950, ETS 5, art 6(1) (entered into force 3 September 1953) (*ECHR*).

76 Henckaerts and Doswald-Beck, *Customary International Humanitarian Law (Practice)* (n 64) 2401–2416.

77 Manfred Nowak, *UN Covenant on Civil and Political Rights: CCPR Commentary* (Kehl 2005) 319.

78 García Roca and Vidal Zapatero, 'The Right to an Independent and Impartial Tribunal (Art. 6.1 ECHR): A Specific Minimum Standards Guarantee Rather than a Rule of

The ECtHR has confirmed on several occasions that a court 'established by law' must have a pre-existing legal basis. For example, in *Guðmundur Andri Ástráðsson v Iceland*, the ECtHR stated that, 'The phrase "established by law" covers not only the legal basis for the very existence of a "tribunal" but also the compliance by that tribunal with the particular rules that govern it',[79] and noted that, 'The nature and scope of the cases that have so far come before the Court in respect of the "tribunal established by law" requirement have mostly called for a determination as to whether a court overseeing a case had any legal basis in domestic law'.[80] In *Coëme and Others v Belgium*, the ECtHR similarly stated that, 'According to the case-law, the object of the term "established by law" in Article 6 of the Convention is to ensure "that the judicial organisation in a democratic society [does] not depend on the discretion of the Executive, but that it [is] regulated by law emanating from Parliament"',[81] quoting with approval a report from the European Commission on Human Rights.[82] In *Guðmunder Andri Ástráðsson v Iceland*, the ECtHR also found that the domestic law and practice of 29 of the 40 member states surveyed specifically interpret the term 'established by law' as requiring 'a legal basis for the existence of the tribunal'.[83] For its part, article 8(1) of the American Convention on Human Rights provides that 'every person has the right to a hearing, with due guarantees and within a reasonable time, by a competent, independent, and impartial tribunal, *previously established by law*', while article 26 of the American Declaration of the Rights and Duties of Man states that, 'Every person accused

---

Justice' in Javier García Roca and Pablo Santolaya (eds), *Europe of Rights: A Compendium on the European Convention of Human Rights* (Brill-Nijhoff 2012) 219, 223. See also Ulrike Muessig and Née Seif, 'The Common Legal Tradition of a Court Established by Law: Historical Foundations of Art. 6 para. 1 European Convention on Human Rights' (2005) 47(2) *American Journal of Legal History* 161, 162: '[A] basic aspect of justice [is that] justice is done by ordinary courts and their judges governed by law'.

79 *Guðmundur Andri Ástráðsson v Iceland* [2020] Application No 26374/18, Eur Court HR (Grand Chamber), [213] ('*Guðmundur Andri Ástráðsson v Iceland*').

80 Ibid [229].

81 *Coëme and Others v Belgium* [2000] Applications Nos 32492/96, 32547/96, 32548/96, 33209/96 and 33210/96, Eur Court HR, [98] (*Coëme and Others v Belgium*). This passage is also quoted with approval in *Richert v Poland* [2011] Application No 54809/07, Eur Court HR (*Richert v Poland*).

82 *Zand v Austria* [1978] Application No 7360/76, Eur Court HR (Decisions and Reports), 70, 80 (*Zand v Austria*).

83 *Guðmundur Andri Ástráðsson v Iceland* (n 79) [150] (emphasis added).

of an offence has the right [...] to be tried by courts previously established in accordance with *pre-existing laws*'.[84]

Based on the definition of a regularly constituted court in the ICRC *Customary IHL Study* and the human rights law commentary and jurisprudence on the equivalent 'established by law' requirement, the first definitional component of a regularly constituted court is that it must have a pre-existing legal basis authorising its establishment.

5.3.2 *The Jurisdiction of Courts Is Limited by the Scope of Its 'Legal Basis'*

The second definitional component of a regularly constituted court under customary IHL is that its jurisdiction must be limited by the scope of the legal basis authorising its establishment. Put another way, a court that exceeds its jurisdictional competence is not a regularly constituted court. As stated by Louise Doswald-Beck, the term 'regularly constituted' means that 'the tribunal has been established by law in order to decide cases relating to certain subject matters', meaning that the 'jurisdictional power of a tribunal is not created for a specific case, nor by an arbitrary administrative act'.[85] While this interpretation has yet to receive explicit judicial attention in the IHL context, the Chairman of the post-World War II United Nations War Crimes Commission has stated that:

> [T]he customary law of war requires that before anyone, a combatant or non-combatant, should be executed or otherwise punished as for an offence against the laws of war, he should first be tried and sentenced by a court whose jurisdiction is recognized by international law.[86]

The principle that a regularly constituted court is one whose jurisdiction is confined to the scope of its legal basis has been confirmed numerous times by the ECtHR in addressing the equivalent IHRL obligation that courts must be 'established by law'. The ECtHR has repeatedly stated that courts or tribunals must operate within the procedural and jurisdictional limitations of

84 Inter-American Commission on Human Rights, *American Declaration of the Rights and Duties of Man* (2 May 1948) (emphasis added).

85 Louis Doswald-Beck, 'Judicial Guarantees under Common Article 3' in Andrew Clapham, Paola Gaeta and Marco Sassòli (eds), *The 1949 Geneva Conventions: A Commentary* (OUP 2016) 469, 471.

86 United Nations War Crimes Commission, *Law Reports of the Trials of War Criminals* (UNWCC 1948), vol V, viii.

the law authorising their establishment.[87] In *Sokurenko and Strygun v Ukraine*, the ECtHR stated:

> In the Court's view, having overstepped the limits of its jurisdiction, which were clearly laid down in the Code of Commercial Procedure, the Supreme Court could not be considered the 'tribunal established by law' within the meaning of Article 6 § 1 of the Convention in respect of the impugned proceedings.[88]

Even the Joint Dissenting Opinion of Judges Lorenzen and Maruste in the *Sokurenko and Strygun v Ukraine*, which disagreed with the majority's conclusion that a violation of domestic law renders a court 'not established by law', found that, 'A literal interpretation of that expression leads in our opinion to the result that what is required is a legal basis for the existence and organisation of a tribunal, *including a determination of what matters come within the jurisdiction of that court*'.[89]

In *Gorguiladzé v Georgia*, the ECtHR stated that a tribunal cannot be 'established by law' where it 'goes beyond its jurisdictional competencies which are clearly vested in it by law'.[90] The Court in *Guðmunder Andri Ástráðsson v Iceland* found that 37 (of 40) member states surveyed interpret the term 'established by law' to include 'the jurisdiction and competence of a court or tribunal to rule in a particular case'.[91] Overall, the ECtHR and other regional bodies have found a violation of the 'established by law' requirement: where the court has not been created in accordance with ordinary rules and procedures;[92] where the tenure, recusal, or composition of

87 See, for example, *Gorguiladzé v Georgia* [2009] Application No 4313/04, Eur Court HR, [68] (*Gorguiladzé v Georgia*); *Pandjikidzé and Others v Georgia*, [2009] Application No 30323/02, Eur Court HR (*Pandjikidzé and Others v Georgia*); *Zeynalov v Azerbaijan* [2013] Application No 31848/07, Eur Court HR (*Zeynalov v Azerbaijan*).

88 *Sokurenko and Strygun v Ukraine* [2006] Applications Nos 29458/04 and 29465/04, Eur Court HR [28] (*Sokurenko and Strygun v Ukraine*).

89 Ibid 12, Joint Dissenting Opinion of Judges Lorenzen and Maruste (emphasis added).

90 *Gorguiladzé v Georgia* (n 87) [69].

91 *Guðmundur Andri Ástráðsson v Iceland* (n 79) [150].

92 *Case of Castillo Petruzzi et al. v Peru* (*Merits, Reparations and Costs*) (Inter-American Court of Human Rights Series L/V/III.47, 30 May 1999) [129] (*Case of Castillo Petruzzi et al. v Peru*): 'A basic principle of the independence of the Judiciary is that every person has the right to be heard by regular courts, following procedures previously established by law. States are not to create "[t]ribunals that do not use the duly established

the bench is not in accordance with the prescribed law;[93] where a court has breached the applicable procedural rules;[94] and where a court has exceeded its jurisdictional limitations.[95] The European Court of Justice has stated that, according to the 'settled' jurisprudence of the ECtHR, the 'established by law' criterion was introduced 'to ensure that the organisation of the judicial system does not depend on the discretion of the executive, but that it is regulated by law emanating from the legislature in compliance with the rules governing its jurisdiction'.[96]

Although there is limited guidance on this point in the IHL context, expert commentary and IHRL jurisprudence provide persuasive authority that a regularly constituted court is one whose jurisdictional competence is limited by the scope of its legal basis.

5.3.3 *The Court Affords the Essential Guarantees of Independence and Impartiality*

The third definitional component of a regularly constituted court under customary IHL is that it affords the essential guarantees of independence and impartiality. The 'independence and impartiality' requirement is, of course, included in the *Elements of Crimes* and was recognised by the ICC in *Al Hassan*. What the ICC failed to do was explain whether 'independence and impartiality' is part of the definition of a regularly constituted court under customary IHL. While 'independence and impartiality' was not always associated with the definition of a regularly constituted court, it has become an inseparable component of this term, predominantly under the influence of human rights law.

Traditionally, the term 'independence and impartiality' is associated with the court's operation, while the 'regularly constituted' requirement concerns the legal basis of the court's establishment and its jurisdictional competence. For example, rule 100 of the ICRC's *Customary IHL Study* concludes that a 'fair trial' under customary IHL requires an 'independent, impartial

---

procedures of the legal process […] to displace the jurisdiction belonging to the ordinary courts or judicial tribunals"' (citations omitted).

93 *Sokurenko and Strygun v Ukraine* (n 88) [24]; *Zeynalov v Azerbaijan* (n 87) [30].

94 *Coëme and Others v Belgium* (n 81) [98]; 67, Partly Concurring, Partly Dissenting Opinion of Judge Baka.

95 *Sokurenko and Strygun v Ukraine* (n 88) [28]; *Coëme and Others v Belgium* (n 81) [99]; *Zeynalov v Azerbaijan* (n 87) [30].

96 *Judgment of the Court of Justice of the European Union* [2020] (Grand Chamber) Review of Erik Simpson and HG v Council of the European Union and European Commission Joined Cases C-542/18 RX-II and C-543/18 RX-II (*Judgment of the Court of Justice of the European Union*).

and regularly constituted court',[97] clearly distinguishing between each concept. The same pattern is reflected in IHRL, as every international and regional human rights instrument separates the concept of a tribunal 'established by law' from the requirement that it must operate with independence and impartiality.[98] This distinction has led commentators to observe that the *Elements of Crimes* appears to 'confuse' the legal basis requirement with the rules regulating the court's operation,[99] as the requirements of 'independence and impartiality' are usually considered among the essential fair trial guarantees that a regularly constituted court must afford.

There is, nevertheless, evidence to suggest that the requirements of 'independence and impartiality' can be read into the definition of a regularly constituted court under customary IHL, such that a court must be 'independent and impartial' in both its establishment and operation. The reason is that the 1949 *Geneva Conventions*, which were drafted before the advent of human rights law, only included the term 'regularly constituted' when discussing the establishment and operation of courts. When the *Additional Protocols* were drafted in 1977 to 'supplement and develop' the *Geneva Conventions*, all provisions concerning the administration of justice in armed conflict included the requirements of independence and impartiality. As stated by the ICRC in its updated commentary to common article 3, independence and impartiality have since become the 'touchstones' for interpreting the meaning of a regularly constituted court.[100] In a similar fashion, the US Supreme Court in *Hamdan* stated that 'independence from the executive is necessary to render a [military court] "regularly constituted"'.[101] For its part, the ECtHR has noted on multiple occasions that, while the two requirements are legally distinct,

---

97 Henckaerts and Doswald-Beck, *Customary International Humanitarian Law (Practice)* (n 63) 2363–2488 (emphasis added).

98 See, for example, *ICCPR* (n 75) art 14(1); *ECHR* (n 75) art 6(1); Organization of American States, *American Convention on Human Rights* ('Pact of San Jose', Costa Rica, 22 November 1969) art 8(1). See also Paweł Filipek, 'Only a Court Established by Law Can Be an Independent Court: The ECJ's Independence Test as an Incomplete Tool to Assess the Lawfulness of Domestic Court' *Verfassungsblog On Matters Constitutional* (Blog Post, 23 January 2020) <https://verfassungsblog.de/only-a-court-established-by-law-can-be-an-independent-court/> accessed 30 July 2024.

99 Knut Dörmann, 'Article 8' in Otto Triffterer (ed), *Commentary on the Rome Statute of the International Criminal Court* (Beck-Hart 2008) 275; Jonathan Somer, 'Jungle Justice: Passing Sentence on the Equality of Belligerents in Non-International Armed Conflict' (2007) 89 *International Review of the Red Cross* 655, 675.

100 International Committee of the Red Cross, *Commentary on Geneva Convention III Relative to the Treatment of Prisoners of War, Second Edition* (n 37) para 714.

101 *Hamdan v Rumsfeld* (n 35) 9–10, Partly Concurring Opinion of Kennedy J.

> a very close interrelationship had been formulated in the Court's case-law between [the right to be heard by a tribunal 'established by law'] and the guarantees of "independence" and "impartiality"', such that a structural lack of independence and impartiality could violate the rule that the tribunal must be 'established by law.[102]

The close relationship between the terms 'regularly constituted' and 'independence and impartiality' does not mean that they are interchangeable. In its commentary to *AP II*, the ICRC suggested that the need for a regularly constituted court in common article 3 '*is replaced by*' one that affords the essential guarantees of independence and impartiality by virtue of article 6(2) *AP II*.[103] While the shift in language in *AP II* was certainly influenced by concern that NSAGs may not be able to meet the 'regularly constituted' requirement, the suggestion that independence and impartiality 'replaced' this requirement is not supported by the language or legal effect of the treaty. *AP II* was explicitly drafted to 'supplement and develop' common article 3 'without modifying its existing conditions of application'. Common article 3 applies as a 'minimum yardstick' in all NIACs, while *AP II* applies in addition and under a narrower set of circumstances. As a result, *AP II* cannot replace any legal requirements under common article 3. As stated by Réne Provost:

> Additional Protocol II was not adopted to amend or change the Geneva Conventions but rather to supplement them. There is nothing in the text or in the travaux préparatoires of Protocol II that suggests an intent to delete the regularly constituted requirement found in Common Article 3.[104]

The ICRC's updated commentary to common article 3, as opposed to the 1987 commentary to *AP II*, takes a more nuanced and correct approach, noting that the definition of a regularly constituted court was 'fleshed out' in

---

102 *Reczkowicz v Poland* [2021] Application No 43447/19, Eur Court HR, [220] (*Reczkowicz v Poland*); *Guðmundur Andri Ástráðsson v Iceland* (n 79) [231].

103 International Committee of the Red Cross, Commentary on the Additional Protocols of 8 June 1977 to the Geneva Conventions of 12 August 1949 (ICRC/ Martinus Nijhoff, 1987) para 4600 (emphasis added).

104 René Provost, "Regularly Constituted' Courts of Non-State Armed Groups Between Rome and Geneva' in Martin Faix and Ondřej Svaček (eds) *ICC Jurisprudence and the Development of International Humanitarian Law* (Springer, 2024) 191, 206.

AP II and that independence and impartiality have since become the 'touchstones' for interpreting this term.[105]

In summary, there is no justification under customary IHL for treating independence and impartiality as the exhaustive definition of a regularly constituted court. Customary IHL dictates that a regularly constituted court is threefold: (I) it has a pre-existing legal basis; (II) its jurisdictional competence is limited by the scope of that legal basis; and (III) it is established in accordance with the fundamental guarantees of independence and impartiality.

5.4 Reconciling the Customary Definition of a 'Regularly Constituted Court' with the *Elements of Crimes*

To ensure compliance with the principle of systemic integration, the definition of war crimes in the *Rome Statute* must be interpreted consistently with customary IHL. But what if there is apparent conflict between the definition in the *Elements of Crimes* and that which applies under customary IHL? Which definition should take priority? As discussed in Chapter 2, there are, on the one hand, good reasons for preferring an interpretation consistent with custom. The *Elements of Crimes* is explicitly non-binding and must be consistent with the *Statute*, whereas the terms in the *Statute* should be interpreted in accordance with their meaning under customary IHL. On the other hand, in cases of direct conflict, it is difficult to envision an ICC judge overruling the *Elements of Crimes* in favour of customary IHL where this would broaden the criminal responsibility of the accused. The fact that the *Elements* are technically non-binding is unlikely to overcome the appearance that such an approach is inconsistent with the rights of the accused.

However, the above analysis is strictly limited to cases of irreconcilable conflict. The situation is very different where it is possible to harmonise the *Elements of Crimes* with customary IHL. Indeed, it is worth recalling that the 'Introduction' to Article 8 in the *Elements of Crimes* states that the elements for war crimes 'shall be interpreted within the established framework of the international law of armed conflict'.[106] Wherever it is possible to interpret

---

105 International Committee of the Red Cross, *Commentary on Geneva Convention III Relative to the Treatment of Prisoners of War, Second Edition* (n 37) paras 710, 714.

106 *Elements of Crimes*, Article 8 'Introduction'.

the *Elements of Crimes* consistently with customary IHL to avoid unnecessary fragmentation, it is obligatory to do so. As stated by Mauro Politi,

> [B]y providing that the elements for war crimes 'shall be interpreted within the established framework of the international law of armed conflict', the text simply indicates … a hermeneutic criterion according to which, when facing doubts about the exact content of certain elements, the Court should give preference to the interpretation that appears to be more consistent with the customary rule of international law that the definition of the offence at issue is meant to reflect.[107]

The definition of a regularly constituted court in the *Elements of Crimes* is not irreconcilable with that which is applicable under customary IHL. The former only refers to 'independence and impartiality', while the latter imposes two additional requirements concerning the legal basis of the court's establishment and the limits of its jurisdictional competence. The simplest way to reconcile the two is to treat the *Elements* as emphasising one component of a broader definition that exists under customary IHL.

The 'regularly constituted' requirement in common article 3 is replicated in Article 8(2)(c)(IV), but neither provision contains any reference to independence and impartiality. To reflect the fact that independence and impartiality have since become the 'touchstones' for interpreting the meaning of the term 'regularly constituted', as reflected in the *Additional Protocols* and human rights law,[108] they have been emphasised in the *Elements of Crimes*. Accordingly, to reconcile the *Elements of Crimes* with customary IHL, the Court simply needs to apply the traditional definition of a regularly constituted court – requiring a legal basis and limited jurisdictional scope – in addition to the requirements of independence and impartiality contained in the *Elements of Crimes*, as the latter reflects an important development in this area of law.

Some may be tempted to argue that the sole reference to 'independence and impartiality' in the *Elements of Crimes* limits the scope of this offence under the *Rome Statute*, without prejudice to the fact that regularly

---

107 Mauro Politi 'Elements of Crimes' in Cassese et al (eds) *The Rome Statute of the International Criminal Court: A Commentary* (OUP 2002) 459–60.

108 *Case of Castillo Petruzzi et al. v Peru* (n91) [128]; *Case of Cantoral Benavides v Peru (Judgment)* (Inter-American Court of Human Rights, Series C No. 69, 8 August 2000) [112] (*Case of Cantoral Benavides v Peru*).

constituted courts under customary IHL require a preexisting legal basis. Indeed, this appears to be the implication of the ICC's decisions in *Al Hassan*. Pre-Trial Chamber I stated that 'independence and impartiality are the requisite attributes for a court to be regarded as "regularly constituted" *within the meaning of the Statute*'.[109] In very similar fashion, Trial Chamber X stated that 'independence and impartiality are viewed as the requisite attributes for a court to be regarded as 'regularly constituted' *within the meaning of the Court's statutory framework*'.[110] Such language could be taken to mean that the ICC is aware that a regularly constituted court means something different under customary IHL, but is restricting the war crime in the *Rome Statute* to the language of the *Elements of Crimes*. This approach could be seen as consistent with Article 10 of the *Statute*, which states that nothing within the ICC's subject matter jurisdiction 'shall be interpreted as limiting or prejudicing in any way existing or developing rules of international law for purposes other than this Statute'.

However, such an approach is not tenable. In the simplest of terms, the *Rome Statute* requires courts in NIAC to be 'regularly constituted', and that phrase has an explicit meaning under customary IHL. In *Al Hassan*, the ICC held that the drafters of the *Elements of Crimes* 'departed' from the regularly constituted requirement in common article 3 in favour of independence and impartiality.[111] However, the *Elements* cannot depart from the regularly constituted requirement, as this requirement is contained in Article 8(2)(c)(IV) of the *Statute* itself. Article 9(3) of the *Statute* provides that the *Elements of Crimes* must be consistent with the *Statute*. Using the *Elements* to depart from the *Statute* is 'something the Elements of Crimes manifestly cannot lawfully do'.[112]

To put it bluntly, if the drafters of the *Rome Statute* wanted to limit this war crime to violations of independence and impartiality only, they could have framed article 8(2)(c)(IV) as prohibiting the passing of sentences by a court that is not 'independent and impartial', but they did not. Instead, they prohibited courts that are not 'regularly constituted', which naturally imports the meaning of this term under customary IHL. The customary definition of a regularly constituted court has arguably incorporated the

109 *Al Hassan Pre-Trial Judgment* (n 1) [376] (emphasis added).

110 *Al Hassan Trial Judgment* (n 3) [1169] (emphasis added).

111 *Al Hassan Pre-Trial Judgment* (n 1) [377].

112 Provost (n 104) 208.

requirements of independence and impartiality, but necessarily continues to require a preexisting legal basis and limited jurisdictional competence.

5.5 Conclusion

The *Al Hassan* case before the ICC was the first time that an international court had considered the definition of a regularly constituted court since the term was codified in 1949 in common article 3(1)(d) of the *Geneva Conventions*. The fact that the Islamic Tribunals belonged to a NSAG made it an even more important opportunity to clarify the state of the law in accordance with the principle of systemic integration. Yet, neither Pre-Trial Chamber I nor Trial Chamber X opted to consider the ordinary meaning of the term 'regularly constituted court' or its definition and scope under customary IHL, choosing instead to rely exclusively on the definition provided in the *Elements of Crimes*. By treating the *Rome Statute* as a self-contained regime, the decisions in *Al Hassan* undermine the ICC's potential to serve as a model international court and unnecessarily risk fragmenting international law.

This chapter has attempted to rectify the ICC's approach. Consistent with the methodology outlined in Chapter 2, it has combined the general rule of interpretation in article 31 of the *VCLT* with the rules of strict construction codified in article 22(2) of the *Statute*, thereby interpreting the term 'regularly constituted court' in accordance with the ordinary meaning of the words, in their context and in light of the object and purpose of the *Rome Statute*, and in a manner consistent with their definition and scope under customary IHL. Based on this analysis, the definition of a regularly constituted court is threefold: (I) it has a pre-existing legal basis authorising its establishment; (II) its subject-matter jurisdiction is limited by the scope of its legal basis; and (III) it affords the essential guarantees of independence and impartiality.

By relying exclusively on the *Elements of Crime*, the ICC in *Al Hassan* ignored the first two definitional components of a regularly constituted court. This critique is not simply methodological, but also substantive. The post-World War II military tribunals, the US Supreme Court in *Hamdan*, and the ICRC *Customary IHL Study* each confirms that the rule that courts must be regularly constituted is designed to prohibit the convening of 'special' courts with irregular jurisdiction. The rule aims to ensure that individuals are not subject to *ad hoc* military justice. The requirements of 'independence and impartiality' are essential for ensuring a fair trial. On their own, however, they do not fulfil the limitations imposed by the obligation that all courts in armed conflict be regularly constituted. If the ICC's interpretation of a regularly constituted court were to influence the development of customary IHL, it would significantly undermine the protection afforded by this term as it is currently understood under common article 3(1)(d) of the *Geneva Conventions*.

Accordingly, the definition of a regularly constituted court in the *Elements of Crimes* should be reconciled with that provided under customary IHL by supplementing the former's reference to 'independence and impartiality' with the latter's requirement that courts in armed conflict have a pre-existing legal basis and limited jurisdictional scope. For states, this means that courts must be organised and operated in accordance with the state's pre-existing constitutional authority and jurisdictional limitations, thereby preventing *ad hoc* military courts from being convened with a special jurisdictional mandate to target a specific situations or group of people. For courts established by NSAGs, there is currently no agreement on how to apply the customary definition of a regularly constituted court. The next chapter explores this issue in detail.

CHAPTER 6

Applying the Customary Definition of a 'Regularly Constituted Court' to the Courts of Non-state Armed Groups

6.1 Introduction

For courts established by non-state armed groups (NSAGs), there is currently no agreement on how to apply the customary definition of a 'regularly constituted court'. Can NSAGs, which possess no recognised constitutional authority to create law, nonetheless provide a legal basis for the establishment of their own courts and determine their own jurisdictional scope? Are NSAGs limited to applying the pre-existing law of the state, as some have suggested, or are they subject to any other limitations on their jurisdictional competence?

In accordance with the principle of systemic integration, Chapter 5 argued that the International Criminal Court (ICC) should interpret the term 'regularly constituted court' under article 8(2)(c)(IV) of the *Rome Statute* consistently with customary IHL. As we have seen, customary IHL stipulates a three-pronged definition. First, the court must have a pre-existing legal basis authorising its establishment. Second, it must operate within the jurisdictional scope of that legal basis. Third, the court must afford the essential guarantees of independence and impartiality.

This chapter focuses on the definition of a regularly constituted court under customary IHL as it applies to courts established by NSAGs. While the core meaning of each of the three definitional components outlined above must remain the same, debate continues over the 'legal basis' of NSAG courts and, therefore, the limits of their jurisdictional competence. This is an area of customary IHL in need of judicial clarification, and the ICC is the most appropriate forum to address this challenge.

One approach is to declare that all NSAG courts are illegal under IHL. NSAG courts appear to lack the requisite legal basis to regularly constitute courts because, unlike state courts, there is no pre-existing legal authority in the state constitutional system that would authorise their establishment. NSAGs are considered illegal under the state's domestic law and possess no sovereign authority under international law. There are, however, several (by

 | DOI:10.1163/9789004690042_007

now well-versed)[1] legal and practical reasons to recognise NSAG courts as regularly constituted courts for the purposes of IHL. They are necessary: (I) to maintain law and order in the territory under the control of the NSAG to fulfil the obligation of humane treatment; (II) to give effect to the relevant treaty provisions to ensure the equal application of the law under the 'equality of belligerents' principle; and (III) to fulfil the obligation to prosecute alleged violations of international criminal law (ICL) perpetrated by members of the NSAG under the doctrine of command responsibility. It is, therefore, untenable to treat NSAG courts as *prima facie* unlawful under IHL.

Another approach, as adopted by the ICC in *Al Hassan*, is to ignore the requirements under customary IHL that a regularly constituted court must have a legal basis and limited jurisdictional scope, and instead define it by exclusive reference to 'independence and impartiality'.[2] Chapter 5 showed that this approach violates the general rule of interpretation in article 31 of the *Vienna Convention on the Law of Treaties* (VCLT) and undermines the very purpose of the 'regularly constituted' requirement, which was developed to prohibit the establishment of special courts with irregular jurisdiction. Failing to regulate the jurisdictional competence of NSAG courts in a non-international armed conflict (NIAC) arguably carries an even greater risk of abuse and poses unique challenges to civilian populations subjected to the 'laws' of the NSAG exercising territorial control.

Consistent with the principle of systemic integration, the correct approach is to ascertain the legal basis for the establishment of NSAG courts and define the limits of their jurisdictional competence under customary IHL. To this end, the International Committee of the Red Cross (ICRC) has proposed two possible solutions: (I) NSAG courts may be regularly constituted in accordance with the 'laws' of the armed group; or (II) NSAG courts could be regularly constituted by applying the pre-existing law of the state in which they operate. While both these proposals have merit, neither can be said to adequately resolve the issue without further refinement.

1 International Committee of the Red Cross, 'Commentary on Geneva Convention III Relative to the Treatment of Prisoners of War, Second Edition' (ICRC 2020), paras 725–731.

2 *The Prosecutor v Al Hassan Ag Abdoul Aziz Ag Mohamed Ag Mahmoud* (Corrected version of *Décision relative à la Confirmation des Charges Portées contre Al Hassan Ag Abdoul Aziz Ag Mohamed Ag Mahmoud*) (International Criminal Court, Pree-Trial Chamber I, Case No ICC-01/12-01/18, 13 November 2019) [376] (English Translation) (*Al Hassan Pre-Trial Judgment*); *Prosecutor v Al Hassan* (International Criminal Court, ICC-01/12-01/18, Trial Judgment, 26 June 2024) [1169] (*Al Hassan Trial Judgment*).

In short, state practice does not recognise NSAGs as possessing unfettered legislative authority to establish courts according to their own 'laws' or to determine the limits of their own jurisdictional competence. Restricting NSAGs to enforcing the pre-existing law of the state, meanwhile, would be impractical in most contexts and finds only limited support by analogy to other legal regimes. Instead, I argue that IHL provides the legal basis for the establishment of NSAG courts, as it is the only body to explicitly regulate their operation. By virtue of this position, IHL also provides the outer limit of their jurisdictional competence in accordance with its fundamental rules applicable in NIAC. This conception of the legal basis of NSAG courts recognises the reality that such courts must be able to function within their own legal frameworks, but imposes necessary limits on their establishment and operation.

Given the frequency with which NSAGs have used the judicial system to subjugate civilian populations through intimidation and violence, on the one hand, and the necessity of using NSAG courts to maintain order and prohibit summary execution, on the other, it is fundamentally important to determine their limitations.

6.2 The Phenomenon of Non-state Courts in Non-international Armed Conflict

The legal status of NSAG courts is unclear and in need of judicial clarification. Indeed, the prevalence with which NSAGs resort to establishing and operating courts during NIAC highlights the need for legal regulation. Similarly, the practical necessity for such courts to fill the legal and political vacuum in the absence of state control demonstrates that they cannot simply be ignored or rendered illegal *ab initio*. The risk that unregulated NSAG justice poses to civilian populations living under their authority demands greater legal protection than that which has been offered by the ICC ruling in *Al Hassan*.

6.2.1 *The Prevalence of Non-state Courts*

NSAGs routinely establish courts with varying degrees of sophistication and operational capacity. In situations where NSAGs control territory to the exclusion of the state, it is inevitable that they will be required to apply some form of governance, whether military or civilian, in the form of policing, dispute resolution, and enforcement.[3] The extent to which NSAGs achieve these functions is generally an indicator of their overall capacity.[4] Megan Stewart suggests that one-third of all NSAGs since 1945 have attempted governance strategies as a means of achieving their long-term goals of independence, while Cyanne Loyle and Helga Binningsbø confirm that judicial processes increase with the relative strength of the armed group.[5] Reyko Huang's empirical study of 126 NSAGs shows that, while there is no statistically significant correlation between the use of courts and military victory, 28 per cent of those 126 NSAGs used judicial enforcement as a governance strategy (as distinguishable from the unregulated use of armed violence or mere internal regulation).[6] The fact that NSAG courts 'exist and will continue to exist regardless of the views of third parties'[7] requires a practical response to regulate their operation and facilitate their compliance with IHL. As stated by Sandesh Sivakumaran, an overly idealistic approach 'sacrifices real protection for the sake of paper standards'.[8]

The enforcement of NSAG 'law' can be the underlying cause of a rebellion, due to the inadequacy or oppressive nature of the laws promulgated by the state. This was initially the case with, for example, the Islamic Tribunals in Northern Mali (as a response to widespread banditry),[9] the Taliban Courts in Afghanistan (due to insecurity and corruption),[10] Kurdish forces in North-East Syria (establishing ethnically and religiously inclusive People's Courts in accordance with international human rights law (IHRL)),[11] and

3 Tom Ginsburg, 'Rebel Use of Law and Courts' (2019) 15 *Annual Review of Law and Social Science* 495, 496.

4 Zachariah Cherian Mampilly, *Rebel Rulers: Insurgent Governance and Civilian Life during War* (Cornell UP 2011) 44.

5 Cyanne Loyle and Helga Binningsbø, 'Justice during Armed Conflict: A New Dataset on Government and Rebel Strategies' (2016) 62(2) *Journal of Conflict Resolution* 442.

6 Reyko Huang, *The Wartime Origins of Democratization: Civil War, Rebel Governance, and Political Regimes* (CUP 2016), as interpreted by Ginsburg (n 3) 501–502.

7 Sandesh Sivakumaran, 'Courts of Armed Opposition Groups: Fair Trials or Summary Justice?' (2009) 7(3) *Journal of International Criminal Justice* 489.

8 Ibid 503.

9 Human Rights Watch, *Mali Conflict and Aftermath. Compendium of Human Rights Watch Reporting 2012–2017* (Human Rights Watch 2017) 129–130 <https://www.hrw.org/sites/default/files/supporting_resources/malicompendium0217.pdf> accessed 30 Jluy 2024.

10 Ashley Jackson and Florian Weigand, 'Rebel Rule of Law: Taliban Courts in the West and North-West of Afghanistan' (Humanitarian Policy Group 2020).

11 International Legal Assistance Consortium, *ILAC Rule of Law Assessment Report: Syria 2017* (ILAC 2017) 114–127.

Hamas (in prioritising civilian security in Gaza in response to corrupt practices of the Palestinian Authority).[12] As an extreme example, the Islamic Courts Union in Somalia, established to address the lack of judicial regulation, subsequently assumed a governance function in the 'complete absence of state power'.[13]

Huang's empirical data (as interpreted by Ginsburg) provides three main determinants of whether NSAGs are likely to establish or operate courts.[14] First, where NSAGs enjoyed a degree of political autonomy before the outbreak of the conflict, the use of a judicial system is more prevalent.[15] Sophisticated governance mechanisms, including courts, were also more likely where they received support from civilian populations, external funding, or collected taxes.[16] Second, the legal tradition of the host state is a statistically significant variable, with 46 per cent of NSAGs operating in countries with a common law or British legal tradition using courts, compared with the overall average of 28 per cent.[17] The third determinant is ideology. A little over 37 per cent of the Marxist groups identified used courts, as did 36 per cent of the Islamic NSAGs.[18]

From Huang's data and other secondary sources, Ginsburg extrapolates the tentative conclusion that ideologically motivated NSAGs are more likely to try to *change* the existing legal structure and enforce their own laws during the conflict. While NSAGs whose short-term goals are more pragmatically aimed at consolidating political power may be content to use the pre-existing legal structure, groups with a more immediate ideological imperative will seek to enforce their own legal vision during the conflict. Examples of the former include Marxist NSAGs (whose manifestos permit a delay in realising the full legal-political ambitions of the group until the war is won) and certain NSAGs in Myanmar (who defer to existing village-level leadership instituting local customary law).[19] Examples of the latter range from the Liberation Tigers of Tamil Eelam (LTTE) in Sri Lanka (whose penal

12 Benedetta Berti, 'Rebel justice? Rule of law and Law Enforcement by Non-State Armed Groups' in Linda Hamid and Jan Wouters (eds), *The Rule of Law and Areas of Limited Statehood* (Edward Elgar 2019) 119.

13 Ginsburg (n 3) 501.

14 Ibid 501–502.

15 Ibid.

16 Ibid.

17 Ibid.

18 Ibid.

19 Ibid 498.

code abolished the caste system and generally saw a reduction in crime)[20] and Kurdish Syrian Democratic Forces (SDF) in North-East Syria (whose constitution purports to incorporate all major international human rights treaties),[21] to ISIS (whose penal code provided for the torture, enslavement, and mutilation of captured non-believers).[22]

6.2.2 *The Necessity and Risks of NSAG Courts*

NSAG courts fill a legal and political vacuum and are necessary for maintaining law and order in the absence of state authority. Ginsburg argues that the use of courts – particularly for the enforcement of the NSAG's own 'laws' – 'can serve to send signals to domestic and international audiences and consolidate symbolic authority' as 'law and courts are associated with statehood, meaning that they convey symbolic legitimacy, even when they are repressive'.[23] NSAG military courts are also an essential means of maintaining discipline and complying with the group's obligations under IHL.

From a humanitarian perspective, the practical concern of NSAG courts is not so much that they are created and used by a non-state entity. Rather, it is the risk that the enforcement of NSAG law leaves the civilian population vulnerable to reactionary legislation influenced by the nature of the NIAC, much of which emerges in conflicts characterised by ethnic, religious, and/or political division. There are also reports of NSAG courts issuing excessive punishments for fear of appearing too weak and losing control over the civilian population.[24]

By far the most reported concern of NSAG courts is that they routinely violate fair trial guarantees.[25] Even those NSAGs which have instituted substantive laws that are more in line with international human rights have attracted criticism for failing to afford essential judicial guarantees. For example, the LTTE courts have been criticised by the US Department of

20 Ibid 504; Sivakumaran (n 7) 493–495.

21 *Charter of the Social Contract in Rojava (Syria)* (Web Page, 2014) <https://www.kurdishinstitute.be/en/charter-of-the-social-contract/> accessed 30 July 2024. However, see Human Rights Watch, *Under Kurdish Rule: Abuses in PYD-run Enclaves in Syria* (Human Rights Watch 2014).

22 International Legal Assistance Consortium (n 11) 131.

23 Ginsburg (n 3) 497.

24 René Provost, 'FARC Justice: Rebel Rule of Law' (2018) 8(2) *UC Irvine Law Review* 227, 251.

25 Sandesh Sivakumaran, *The Law of Non-International Armed Conflict* (OUP 2012) 550–555.

State as operating 'essentially as agents of the LTTE rather than as an independent judiciary',[26] while Human Rights Watch has criticised the Kurdish People's Courts for allowing arbitrary detention and failing to uphold the right to a lawyer in criminal proceedings.[27] The groups themselves have sometimes responded by arguing for a pragmatic approach to upholding fair trial guarantees that reflect their operational and resource constraints in the context of an armed conflict. As stated by a member of the LTTE,

> [T]he contours of the space within which our legal system has to function is quite limited by political, economic and military pressures. But as this space expands in the future we would be in a position to adopt measures that would perfect our legal system to match international standards.[28]

The *Farabundo Martí National Liberation Front* (FMLN) has similarly stated that international fair trial standards must be 'adapted to the conditions and capacity' of the group in response to criticisms from the United Nations Observer Mission in El Salvador.[29] While pragmatism is certainly not foreign to IHL, and prominent scholars such as Marco Sassòli have suggested a 'sliding-scale' of fair trial obligations depending on the capacity of the NSAGs, the ICRC has maintained the bare minimum approach that, 'No trial should be held, whether by State authorities or by non-State armed groups, if [the guarantees of independence and impartiality] cannot be provided'.[30]

6.2.3 *Punishments in Violation of International Humanitarian Law*

Beyond the question of the capacity of NSAGs to comply with judicial guarantees, there is the problem of NSAG courts applying laws and punishments that are inconsistent with both IHL and IHRL. In Mali, the NIAC is fought between government forces and three Islamist NSAGs: Ansar Dine;

---

26 Ibid.

27 Human Rights Watch, *Under Kurdish Rule: Abuses in PYD-run Enclaves in Syria* (n 21).

28 Sivakumaran, *The Law of Non-International Armed Conflict* (n 25) 494–495 (citing Interview with E Pararajasingham, 'Tamil Eelam - A De Facto State: Tamil Eelam Legal System' (Web Page, 30 October 2003) <www.tamilnation.org/tamileelam/defacto/index.htm> accessed 30 July 2024.

29 FMLN Secretariat for the Promotion and Protection of Human Rights, *The Legitimacy of Our Methods of Struggle* (FMLN 1988).

30 International Committee of the Red Cross (n 1) para 730.

the Movement for Unity and Jihad in West Africa (MUJAO); and al-Qaeda in the Islamic Maghreb (AQIM). These groups, which appear to be closely coordinated to the extent that they are often indistinguishable to the civilian population, have exercised *de facto* territorial control in the Northern regions of Gao, Kidal, and Timbuktu since April 2012.[31] They have demonstrated a significant degree of organisation and governmental capacity, establishing fundamentalist Islamic Courts and the Islamic Police to enforce a radical interpretation of Sharia law.[32] Sectors of the civilian population in Northern Mali initially welcomed the NSAG governance for helping to restore order and security. Human Rights Watch notes that, early on, the NSAGs 'took several measures to protect civilians from the widespread looting, sexual violence, and other abuses perpetrated by the *Mouvement national de libération de l'Azawad* (MNLA), Arab militias, and common criminals' who had previously competed for territorial control or committed acts of banditry in the North of the country.[33] The situation thus initially reflected the necessity for NSAG governance in what would otherwise have been a legal and political vacuum.

Civilians soon bore the brunt of the NSAGs' extreme ideology, however. Each of the NSAGs prohibited, under their own laws, all conduct they declared *haraam* (forbidden), including: failing to adhere to a strict dress code; listening to music on portable audio devices; failing to attend daily prayers; smoking or selling cigarettes; consuming or selling alcohol; and adultery.[34] Women were specifically prohibited from wearing perfume or jewellery and from having contact with men other than their husbands or family members.[35] Punishments included beatings, floggings, detention, amputation for theft, and, in the case adultery, death by stoning.[36]

In the Aleppo and Idlib regions of Syria, the Islamist NSAG *Jabhat al-Nusra* established a number of fundamentalist Islamic courts and tribunals.[37] The courts purported to enforce their own law based on the Unified Arab Code, a set of Sharia-inspired rules, that was endorsed by the Arab

31 Office of the Prosecutor of the International Criminal Court, *Situation in Mali: Article 53(1) Report* (ICC 2013) 9.

32 Human Rights Watch, *Mali Conflict and Aftermath* (n 9) 116–1167.

33 Ibid 130.

34 Ibid 140.

35 Ibid.

36 Ibid 129.

37 Amnesty International, *Torture was My Punishment: Abductions, Torture and Summary Killings Under Armed Group Rule in Aleppo and Idleb* (Amnesty International 2016) 20

League between 1988 and 1996 but never applied in any context until the Syrian uprising.[38] The Code's punishments included death by stoning, amputation, and flogging for *hudud* (fixed punishment) crimes under Sharia law. Human Rights Watch further reported that many judges were left to apply their own 'radical interpretations' of Sharia law and were thus not limited to imposing punishments in accordance with the Code.[39] The United Nations Human Rights Commission has reported that the courts did not respect due process guarantees and occasionally resorted to summary executions.[40] In one case, Human Rights Watch reported that the 'House of Justice in Hreitan', one of *Jabhat al-Nusra*'s courts in North Aleppo, sentenced two men and a 17-year-old boy to death for homosexuality.[41] Death sentences in *Jabhat al-Nusra* courts have also been issued against: persons suspected of adultery; persons suspected of being 'infiltrators';[42] businessmen alleged to have provided financial support to the enemy;[43] judges who applied Syrian rather than Sharia law;[44] and persons suspected of creating and distributing pornography.[45]

Meanwhile, ISIS courts operating in Syria have 'published a 136 page document, meticulously buttressed with Quranic verses, setting out rules according to which Muslim and non-believer prisoners may be killed, decapitated, tortured, enslaved, or mutilated'.[46] It further published 'rules for having sex with captured and enslaved non-Muslim women and girls' and provided 'legal justification for the extermination of certain non-Muslim

---

<https://www.amnestyusa.org/wp-content/uploads/2017/04/embargoed5july-torturewasmypunishment-finalversion.pdf>.

38 Ibid 29.

39 Ibid 20.

40 United Nations, *Report of the Independent International Commission of Inquiry on the Syrian Arab Republic*, UN Doc A/HRC/30/48 (13 August 2015) 13, para 97 (*Report of the Independent International Commission of Inquiry on the Syrian Arab Republic*); United Nations, *Report of the Independent International Commission of Inquiry on the Syrian Arab Republic*, UN Doc A/HRC/33/55 (11 August 2016) 12, para 71 (*Report of the Independent International Commission of Inquiry on the Syrian Arab Republic*).

41 Amnesty International, *Torture was my Punishment* (n 37) 28.

42 Ibid.

43 The New Humanitarian, '"Sometimes you cannot apply the rules" – Syrian rebels and IHL' (Web Page, 13 May 2013) <https://www.thenewhumanitarian.org/analysis/2013/05/13/sometimes-you-cannot-apply-rules-syrian-rebels-and-ihl> accessed 30 July 2024.

44 International Legal Assistance Consortium (n 11x`x) 93.

45 Ibid 95 (however, the report notes that the local population appeared to support punishing this particular conduct).

46 Ibid 131.

minorities within the Caliphate's territory, such as the Yazidis'.[47] *Hudud* crimes punishable by death under ISIS rule included blasphemy, adultery, sodomy, spying, and apostasy.[48]

Many of the above punishments would independently constitute the war crimes of 'mutilation, cruel treatment and torture' or 'outrages upon personal dignity' under IHL in violation of common article 3, irrespective of whether they were issued by a court of law. However, IHL does not *per se* prohibit the death penalty or criminal detention, both of which could, *arguendo*, be 'legislated' by the NSAG as a punishment for any crime. Such a law would not necessarily violate the guarantees of independence and impartiality.

A related concern is that NSAG law would invariably create two competing legal systems with which it may be impossible for the civilian population to comply.[49] This is especially the case where an NSAG engages in campaigns of forcible recruitment, while both the state and NSAG have passed laws prohibiting insurrection,[50] equally highlighting the need for clarification of their legal status and competence to punish certain conduct.

The above examples in which NSAGs have instituted disproportionate punishments, often in violation of both IHL and IHRL, must be balanced against those in which NSAG governance has replaced inadequate or oppressive state law, such as the LTTE in Sri Lanka and the Kurdish People's Courts in North-East Syria. Similarly, it must be remembered that NSAG law is often viewed by the civilian population as preferable to anarchy. For example, 'Taliban judges have generally been successful at positioning themselves as a faster, fairer, and more efficient alternative than either the moribund governmental justice or the opportunistic and often predatory "tribal" courts propped up by international actors'.[51]

---

47 Ibid 130.

48 René Provost, *Rebel Courts: The Administration of Justice by Armed Insurgents* (OUP 2021) 112; Pouria Askary and Katayoun Hosseinnejad, 'Non-State Courts: Illegal or Conditional? The Case of Da'esh Courts' (2019) 10 *Journal of International Humanitarian Legal Studies* 240, 248–253.

49 Jonathan Somer, 'Jungle Justice: Passing Sentence on the Equality of Belligerents in Non-International Armed Conflict' (2007) 89 *International Review of the Red Cross* 655, 663.

50 Matias Thomsen, 'Forcible Recruitment of Adults by Non-State Armed Groups in Non-International Armed Conflict', *Diakonia International Humanitarian Law Centre* (Web Page, May 2019) 15 <https://apidiakoniase.cdn.triggerfish.cloud/uploads/sites/2/2021/05/Forcible-Recruitment-EN-May-2019.pdf> accessed 30 July 2024.

51 Provost, *Rebel Courts: The Administration of Justice by Armed Insurgents* (n 48) 126.

Despite the evidence that many NSAG courts breach international law requirements protective of individual rights, the reality that NSAGs will continue to establish courts and enforce their own 'laws' means that 'international law must address and regulate this phenomenon rather than pretend it just doesn't exist'.[52] The precursor to addressing this problem under both IHL and ICL is to establish that the 'regularly constituted court' requirement applies to the courts of NSAGs. More specifically, the legal basis authorising the establishment of NSAG courts must be identified, so that limitations on the jurisdictional competence of such courts can be determined and imposed.

6.3 Applying the Customary Definition of a 'Regularly Constituted Court' to the Courts of Non-state Armed Groups

Several reasons support the *necessity* of recognising NSAG courts. First, numerous NSAGs control territory to the exclusion of the state and are, *de facto*, responsible for maintaining the safety of the civilian population. In such situations, NSAGs are obliged to use courts to fulfil the obligation of humane treatment under IHL.[53] Second, states have signed treaties governing their reciprocal relationship with NSAGs during NIACs, in which they recognise the existence of NSAG courts and the need to regulate them.[54] As confirmed by the drafting history to *Additional Protocol II* (*AP II*) and the commentary to common article 3, these treaties implicitly authorise NSAG

52 Ibid 192.

53 Common article 3(1). See also ICRC 2019 Report: International Committee of the Red Cross, 'International Humanitarian Law and the Challenges of Contemporary Armed Conflict: Report' (Published Report, 22 November 2019) <https://www.icrc.org/en/document/icrc-report-ihl-and-challenges-contemporary-armed-conflicts> accessed 30 July 2024.

54 Article 3 Common to *Geneva Convention for the Amelioration of the Condition of the Wounded and Sick in Armed Forces in the Field*, opened for signature 12 August 1949, 75 UNTS 31 (entered into force 21 October 1950) (*Geneva Convention I*; *Geneva Convention for the Amelioration of the Condition of the Wounded, Sick and Shipwrecked Members of Armed Forces at Sea*, opened for signature 12 August 1949, 75 UNTS 85 (entered into force 21 October 1950) (*Geneva Convention II*); *Geneva Convention Relative to the Treatment of Prisoners of War*, opened for signature 12 August 1949, 75 UNTS 135 (entered into force 21 October 1950) (*Geneva Convention III*); *Protocol Additional to the Geneva Conventions of 12 August 1949, and Relating to the Protection of Victims of Non-International Armed Conflicts*, opened for signature 8 June 1977, 1977, 1125 UNTS 609 (entered into force 7 December 1978) (*Additional Protocol II*).

courts under the principle of the equal application of the law.[55] Third, states and intergovernmental bodies have consistently called upon NSAGs to 'end impunity' for international crimes, which implicitly recognises the legal status of NSAG courts, as punishment without trial is prohibited under IHL.[56] Finally, under the doctrine of command responsibility, NSAG commanders can be found individually criminally responsible for 'failing to submit [alleged violations of IHL] to the competent authorities for investigation and prosecution', which almost invariably requires the NSAG to operate some sort of military justice system.[57] Accordingly, it must be accepted that IHL does not 'rule out, a priori, the initiation of criminal proceedings by armed groups'.[58]

These justifications for recognising the existence of NSAG courts do not, on their own, demonstrate *how* NSAG courts satisfy the definitional prerequisites of a regularly constituted court; namely, the pre-existing legal basis authorising their establishment and a defined jurisdictional competence in accordance with the scope of that legal basis. Building on the principle that

55 Howard S Levie, *The Law of Non-International Armed Conflict: Protocol II to the 1949 Geneva Conventions* (Martinus Nijhoff 1987) 258–303 (This volume collates the Official Records of the Diplomatic Conference on the Reaffirmation and Development of International Humanitarian Law Applicable in Armed Conflicts, Geneva, 1978); Antonio Cassese, *International Criminal Law* (2nd edn, OUP 2008). Cassese notes that the equal application of treaty obligations also finds support in the principle *ut res magis valeat quam pereat*, which provides that a treaty must be given an interpretation that allows its provisions to be effective and useful. Furthermore, the notion that a treaty cannot be given an interpretation that a priori excludes its application by one of the parties is reflected in the obligation to interpret treaties in good faith under article 31(1) of the Vienna Convention on the Law of Treaties; International Committee of the Red Cross, *Commentary on Geneva Convention III Relative to the Treatment of Prisoners of War, Second Edition* (n 1) para 728.

56 See the practice cited in Section 6.3.1.2 and associated analysis.

57 International Committee of the Red Cross, *Commentary on Geneva Convention III Relative to the Treatment of Prisoners of War, Second Edition* (n 1) para 726; *Prosecutor v Bemba Gombo (Decision Pursuant to Article 61(7)(a) and (b) of the Rome Statute)* (International Criminal Court, Pre-Trial Chamber II, Case No ICC01/05-01/08, 15 June 2009) [501] (*Prosecutor v Bemba Gombo Decision on the Confirmation of Charges*). The Pre-Trial Chamber in Bemba noted that the MLC maintained a 'functional military judicial system' that could fulfil the commander's duty to punish violation of IHL under article 28 of the *Rome Statute*.

58 Anne-Marie La Rosa and Carolin Wuerzner, 'Armed Groups, Sanctions and the Implementation of International Humanitarian Law' (2008) 90 *International Review of the Red Cross* 327, 336.

the rules of IHL must apply equally to all parties to a conflict,[59] the ICRC poses two hypothetical solutions:

> [T]o give effect to [common article 3], it may be argued that courts are regularly constituted as long as they are constituted in accordance with the 'laws' of the armed group. Alternatively, armed groups could continue to operate existing courts applying existing legislation.

Both suggestions will now be considered in turn. While there is merit in each, a third approach is to be preferred on the basis that it more accurately reflects customary IHL; namely, that IHL provides an implied legal basis for the establishment of NSAG courts in armed conflict and stipulates the outer limit on their jurisdictional competence.

6.3.1 *The Law of the Armed Group as the Legal Basis and Jurisdictional Competence of Non-state Courts*

The ICRC's first hypothetical solution is that NSAG courts be considered regularly constituted so long as they are constituted in accordance with the 'laws' of the armed group. In other words, the laws of the NSAG provide the legal basis for the establishment of its own courts, comparable to the inherent constitutional authority of the state. Taken to its logical conclusion, allowing the laws of the NSAG to provide the requisite legal basis would mean that NSAGs can also determine the jurisdictional competence of their own courts.

Proponents of this view usually find support in the *Official Records of the Diplomatic Conference* for the drafting of *AP II* (*Diplomatic Conference*) and associated material.[60] However, neither the drafting history of *AP II* nor the subsequent practice and legal opinions of states supports the notion that NSAGs have any sort of constitutional authority to establish courts according to their own laws or to determine their jurisdictional competence. Rather, these sources suggest the willingness of states to recognise NSAG

---

59 The principle that IHL binds each party to the conflict equally in NIAC is often referred to as a version of the 'equality of belligerents' principle. See Marco Sassòli, 'Ius ad Bellum and Ius in Bello – The Separation between the Legality of the Use of Force and Humanitarian Rules to be Respected in Warfare: Crucial or Outdated?' in Michael Schmitt and Jelena Pejic (eds), *International Law and Armed Conflict: Exploring the Faultlines – Essays in Honour of Yoram Dinstein* (Brill-Nijhoff 2007) 241, 255–257; Somer (n 49) 659–664.

60 Sivakumaran, *The Law of Non-International Armed Conflict* (n 25) 557–562.

courts for the limited purpose of fulfilling the group's obligations under IHL. In some cases, this may extend to recognising the practical effect of such courts in maintaining law and order in the absence of state authority.

6.3.1.1 Additional Protocol II Drafting History

For several reasons, the drafting history of *AP II* does not support the ICRC's proposal that NSAG courts could be regularly constituted in accordance with the laws of the armed group, and least not without further limitations on the legal basis and jurisdictional competence of such courts.

It is true that the debates at the *Diplomatic Conference* demonstrated states' recognition of the necessity of NSAG courts, but this recognition was explicitly restricted to the punishment of crimes 'connected with the conflict' and without prejudice to the right of states to deny the legal effect of NSAG courts under domestic law. Moreover, the legal basis for establishing such courts was only accepted as a necessary means of ensuring the equal application of the Protocol. These factors strongly indicate that the legal basis and jurisdictional competence of NSAG courts is limited to the exceptional circumstances of armed conflict under the exclusive auspices of IHL, and militate against any interpretation that would afford NSAGs unfettered authority to establish courts in accordance with their own laws. Beginning with the text of the relevant provision, article 6 of *AP II* states that:

> No sentence shall be passed and no penalty shall be executed on a person found guilty of an offence except pursuant to a conviction pronounced by a court offering the essential guarantees of independence and impartiality.[61]

Even though *AP II* 'supplements and develops' common article 3 'without modifying its existing conditions of application',[62] article 6 of *AP II* does not replicate the term 'regularly constituted court' from article 3(1)(d) of common article 3. The ICRC Commentary on the Additional Protocols of 8 June 1977 notes that 'some experts argued that it was unlikely that a court could be "regularly constituted" under national law by an insurgent party' and therefore proposed an alternate wording based on article 84 of *Geneva*

61 *Additional Protocol II* (n 54) art 6(2).

62 Ibid art 1(1).

Convention III.[63] The debate over the legal basis for the establishment of NSAG courts was therefore the explicit reason for choosing different terminology, even though it does not change the fact that *all* courts in NIAC must still be 'regularly constituted' under common article 3, which applies to all NIACS 'as a minimum'.[64]

In recognising that article 6 of *AP II* would implicitly authorise the establishment of NSAG courts, significant concern arose during the *Diplomatic Conference* as to what 'law' such courts would be expected to apply.[65] It was clear that NSAG courts could not offend the principle of *nullum crimen sine lege* (no crime without law) and therefore could not purport to prosecute acts that were not already prohibited under existing legislation. But could such courts enforce criminal 'laws' that had been 'legislated' by the NSAG? The *Official Record of the Diplomatic Conference* shows that states were only prepared to entertain the notion of NSAG courts subject to three conditions. First, from a legal perspective, NSAG courts would only be recognised as a necessary means of ensuring the equal application of the Protocol.[66] Second, such recognition extended only to the prosecution of crimes 'connected with the conflict'. Third, states reserved the right to afford such courts and their decisions no legal effect. With these qualifications in mind, the ICRC delegate confirmed that the effect of article 6 would be to recognise the existence and operation of NSAG courts.

> It was therefore no longer hypothetical to admit that the insurgent forces would be in a position to apply [what would become article 6] if they intended to try those who were in their power. The insurgent party could for that purpose make use of the courts existing within the part of the territory under its control ... or set up people's courts.[67]

Only the Nigerian delegate explicitly contemplated the proposal that NSAGS could derive the legal basis for the establishment of courts from their own

63 International Committee of the Red Cross, *Commentary on the Additional Protocols of 8 June 1977 to the Geneva Conventions of 12 August 1949* (Martinus Nijhoff 1987) para 4600.

64 This is the language used in common article 3(1)(d) of the *Geneva Conventions* to highlight that this provision applies in all NIACS as a minimum threshold. *Additional Protocol II*, meanwhile, supplements and develops common article 3 and, as a matter of treaty law, only applies in certain NIACS where a higher threshold is met.

65 Levie (n 55) 250–290.

66 Ibid (Volume VIII, para 24, CDDH/I/SR.33, para 23, page 346 of the Reports).

67 Ibid.

laws, while highlighting the need to define the jurisdictional competence of such courts.

> Mr. ABDUL – MALIK (Nigeria) ... had serious reservations about paragraph 1. Rebels could certainly set up courts with a genuine legal basis, but to ensure that such a basis was established he wished to propose the insertion of the words, 'whose jurisdiction is based on a recognizable body of law' after the word 'court', in paragraph 1. It was only logical that if rebels could organize themselves sufficiently to observe the Protocols, and thereby enjoy their protection, they could also organize a recognizable body of law.[68]

This statement is frequently cited as authority for the ICRC's proposal that NSAG courts could potentially be considered regularly constituted in accordance with their own laws.[69] However, the response of other states was considerably more muted and does not support this conclusion. The United Kingdom simply stated that the principle of equal application of the law 'must clearly be given special consideration when provisions concerning penal law were being drafted',[70] while Ukraine specified that the provisions 'must be implemented by both Parties to an armed conflict'.[71] Iraq criticised any recognition of NSAG 'law' and its implications for assessing the legality of the rebellion.[72] The United States,[73] India,[74] Pakistan,[75] Mexico,[76] Argentina,[77] and Iran[78] shared similar concerns. Pakistan sought to ensure that

---

68 Ibid (Official Records of the Diplomatic Conference of 1974–1979, Volume VIII, CDDH/I/SR.34, para 20, p 360).

69 Sivakumaran, 'Courts of Armed Opposition Groups: Fair Trials or Summary Justice?' (n 7) 507; Ezequiel Heffes, 'Generating Respect for International Humanitarian Law: The Establishment of Courts by Organized Non-State Armed Groups in Light of the Principle of Equality of Belligerents' in Terry D Gill (ed), *Yearbook of International Humanitarian Law* (TMC Asser Press 2016) vol 18, 81.

70 Levie (n 55) (Official Records of the Diplomatic Conference of 1974–1979, Volume XIII, CDDH/I/SR.33, at 350, para 45).

71 Ibid para 48.

72 Ibid (CDDH/I/SR.33, 351, para 52).

73 Ibid para 55.

74 Ibid para 60.

75 Ibid para 67.

76 Ibid (CDDH/I/SR.34, para 8).

77 Ibid para 22. Argentina 'shared the doubts already expressed by some delegations with regard to the courts that would pronounce the sentences and apply the penal procedures in every case that a State considered with difficulty such courts as being the decisive organs as regards rebels'.

78 Ibid para 32.

any recognition of NSAG courts was without prejudice to the right of the state to prosecute those involved under its domestic laws, while the United States proposed that the provisions concerning penal prosecutions should be limited 'to offences committed in connexion with the armed conflict' so as to avoid any interpretation that it was of general application.[79] The US proposal is reflected almost *verbatim* in article 6(1), while Pakistan's concern is assuaged in article 3, which precludes any invocation of the Protocol as a means of limiting the state's sovereign right to re-establish law and order.[80] This latter principle is also covered by the rule in common article 3 that the laws of NIAC 'shall not affect the legal status of the Parties to the conflict'.

These statements show that any recognition of NSAG courts was strongly tapered by states' determination to reassert their sovereignty and to limit the legality of such courts to that which is required under IHL. Indeed, draft article 5, the provision which enshrined the principle of the equal rights and duties of the parties to the conflict, was subsequently removed, along with 'any provision which made it appear that the two sides were on the same level or had equal rights', in order to save *AP II* from being abandoned altogether.[81] As stated by Jonathon Somer:

> [N]one of the state delegate statements referred to above indicated whether they agreed with the ICRC delegate on the legal basis issue. It was only the Nigerian delegate who explicitly recognized that rebels 'could certainly set up courts with a genuine legal basis'. The general warnings in connection with draft Article 5, and the subsequent jettisoning of that article, suggest that many states recognized with apprehension that their monopoly on the legislative and judicial branches of government was at stake.[82]

The other common source of evidence for the ICRC's proposal that NSAG courts could be regularly constituted in accordance with laws of the armed group comes from the English text of article 6(2)(c) of *AP II*. The original draft of this provision limited criminal punishment to conduct that was criminalised at the time of the commission 'under *national or international law*', but the text was subsequently amended such that the offence only had

79 Ibid para 55.
80 *Additional Protocol II* (n 63) art 3.
81 Somer (n 49) 660.
82 Ibid 678.

to have been criminalised 'under *law*'; that is, without further qualification regarding the source of the law. While some have suggested that this change was instituted to encompass the laws of NSAGs, the *Official Record of the Diplomatic Conference* reveals that this was not the case. States were generally wary of conflating the concept of national law with NSAG law. For example, Argentina claimed that 'It was indeed unlikely that a Government which was a party to a non-international armed conflict would recognize the idea of rebel law as "national law"'.[83] Accordingly, a proposal was made to remove the reference to 'national or international' and leave the word 'law' unqualified. This proposal was rejected by a vote of 35 to three, with four abstentions.[84] However, in what appears to have been a clerical error,[85] the final draft of the English text used the bare word 'law', while the French draft maintained the qualifier '*le droit national ou international*' ['national or international law']. As stated by Provost, 'No one seems to have noticed the discrepancy, and both English and French versions were adopted by consensus by the Conference Plenary without any discussion of this issue', resulting in 'two equally authentic versions of Protocol II that diverge in a critical manner'.[86]

Support for the ICRC's proposal that NSAGs can regularly constitute courts in accordance with their own laws is often based on the English draft of article 6(2)(c). For example, Sivakumaran argues that the substitution of 'national or international law' for 'law' (perhaps irrespective of whether it was intentional) implicitly incorporates the 'law' of NSAGs.[87] The 2004 UK Manual on the Law of Armed Conflict similarly states that the 'use of the bare word "law" [in article 6(2)(c) of *AP II*] could also be wide enough to cover "laws" passed by an insurgent authority'.[88] For its part, the 1987 ICRC commentary to *AP II* is noncommittal, simply stating that, 'The possible co-existence of two sorts of national legislation, namely, that of the State

83 Levie (n 55) 282 (Meeting of Committee I, 7 June 1976, CDDH/I/SR.64, para 54).

84 Ibid 290 (proposed amendment rejected by a vote of 35 to 3, with 4 abstentions: Report of Committee I, Third Session, CDDH/I/Rev.1, Official Records, vol 10, 131).

85 Provost, *Rebel Courts: The Administration of Justice by Armed Insurgents* (n 48) 190 nn 447, noting that a subsequent amendment from Pakistan on a separate issue happened to omit the reference to 'national or international', which may have been the source of the error.

86 Ibid.

87 Sivakumaran, 'Courts of Armed Opposition Groups: Fair Trials or Summary Justice?' (n 7) 507–508.

88 UK Ministry of Defence, *The Manual of the Law of Armed Conflict* (OUP 2004) 404.

and that of the insurgents, makes the concept of national law rather complicated in this context'.[89] However, the fact that the unqualified use of the word 'law' in the English text appears to have been a mistake, coupled with the fact that the French text retains the qualifier 'national or international', suggests that the text of article 6(2)(c) of *AP II* is a weak basis on which to assert that NSAGs can regularly constitute courts in accordance with their own laws.

The *Official Record of the Diplomatic Conference* of *AP II* provides support for recognising the legality of NSAG courts, but it does not support the ICRC's suggestion that NSAGs could regularly constitute courts in accordance with their own 'laws'. The debates over article 6 of *AP II* were dominated by reassertions of state sovereignty and only took place under three provisos: (I) that NSAGs be capable of equally applying the law (a provision which was itself jettisoned due to the mere suggestion that it might be used to legitimate such groups); (II) that NSAG courts be limited to enforcing crimes 'connected with the conflict'; and (III) that states be under no obligation to recognise the legitimacy or effect of the decisions of NSAG courts.

It is, therefore, necessary to adopt a more nuanced interpretation of the *Diplomatic Conference*. States were willing to accept the reality that NSAGs would establish and operate courts, which, in turn, implies a reluctant acceptance that NSAGs would legislate their own laws, but only through the lens of ensuring the equal application of IHL and compliance with its rules. It follows that the legal basis for the establishment of NSAG courts does not come from the laws of the NSAG – as they possess no recognised authority to govern – but from the limited authority provided by IHL. Subsequent state practice appears to confirm this more nuanced interpretation.

6.3.1.2 Evidence of a General Practice Accepted as Law

While state practice has evolved in favour of recognising the legality of NSAG courts under certain conditions, it is limited to an acceptance that NSAGs must use courts to maintain law and order and prosecute alleged violations of international criminal law (ICL). Contrary to the ICRC's suggestion that NSAGs may be able to regularly constitute courts in accordance with their own laws, there is no evidence in the practice or legal opinion of states that they are willing to recognise NSAGs as possessing a state-like legislative

89 International Committee of the Red Cross, *Commentary on the Additional Protocols of 8 June 1977 to the Geneva Conventions of 12 August 1949* (n 63) para 4605.

capacity to determine the jurisdictional competence of their own courts beyond that which is authorised under IHL.

Turning first to the practice of the territorial state in which the NSAG operates, it is unsurprising that territorial states tend to reject the laws of the NSAG against which they are fighting. Louis Doswald-Beck states that 'the creation of a criminal justice system is a fundamental function of government, and states are vehement in their rejection of any kind of status for rebel groups'.[90] René Provost argues that NSAG attempts to administer criminal justice 'have been vigorously resisted by territorial states in the name of sovereignty',[91] while Andrew Clapham asserts that, 'No state really accepts that armed groups are entitled to detain or try anyone'.[92] While there are exceptions to the rule,[93] the territorial state tends to systematically deny the legality and legal effect of NSAG courts operating within its borders.[94] As stated by the Chief Justice of the Sri Lankan Supreme Court on the LTTE, '[T]hey have no judicial authority. ... Judicial power is part of the sovereignty of the people and it cannot be exercised by any other person than those who are vested with it'.[95]

Looking beyond the affected state, the practice of the United Nations (UN) appears to oscillate from outright condemnation of NSAG justice to a more nuanced position that promotes and in some cases demands the use of NSAG courts to prosecute international crimes. For example, the UN

90 Louis Doswald-Beck, 'Judicial Guarantees under Common Article 3' in Andrew Clapham, Paola Gaeta and Marco Sassòli (eds), *The 1949 Geneva Conventions: A Commentary* (OUP 2016) 469, 469, 491.

91 Provost, *Rebel Courts: The Administration of Justice by Armed Insurgents* (n 48) 274.

92 Andrew Clapham, 'The Limits of Human Rights in Times of Armed Conflict and Other Situations of Armed Violence' in Bardo Fassbender and Knut Traisbach (eds), *The Limits of Human Rights* (OUP 2019) 315.

93 Provost, *Rebel Courts: The Administration of Justice by Armed Insurgents* (n 48) 435–445.

94 Ibid 11, noting that the 'mainstream' view of states having exclusive legislative authority "is systematically adopted by governments confronted with armed opposition groups that claim to establish judicial bodies".

95 Laila Nasry, 'Interview with Chief Justice Sarath N de Silva: LTTE Has No Judicial Authority – CJ', *Sunday Times* (Sri Lanka) (online, 14 November 2004) <https://sundaytimes.lk/021208/news/courts.html> cited in Sivakumaran, 'Courts of Armed Opposition Groups: Fair Trials or Summary Justice?' (n 7) 507. See also *Yesid Arteta Davila* (Supreme Court of Colombia, Penal Chamber, Case No 23438, 2 July 2008) [33] (*Yesid Arteta Davila*). 'This was a case of private justice, carried out by an outlawed armed group [...] which amounts to a grave breach of public order and public security with a view to instill fear or terror among the public.'

Special Rapporteur on the Independence of the Judiciary stated in 2006 stated that, 'The administration of justice is a function that clearly belongs to the State of Afghanistan. It is entirely unacceptable for a non-state entity, such as the Taliban, to exercise a State function by trying and punishing an alleged criminal'.[96] Similarly, the UN Office of the High Commissioner for Human Rights in Nepal stated in 2006 that the Communist Party of Nepal-Maoist (CPN-M) courts 'cannot substitute for criminal investigations by police, independent investigations and prosecutions carried out in a state court',[97] while the UN Security Council stated in 2012 that it 'condemns the attempts by the M23 [March 23 Movement] to establish an illegitimate parallel administration and to undermine state authority of the Government of the DRC'.[98] The UN Assistance Mission in Afghanistan (UNAMA), meanwhile, urged NSAGs in 2017 'to immediately cease running parallel justice structures, which have no basis under Afghan law, and stop imposing punishments on civilians', reiterating that 'the Government bears the ultimate responsibility to protect fundamental human rights in Afghanistan and must prioritize the suppression of all such illegal procedures'.[99]

On other occasions, however, the UN has focused its attention on the obligation for NSAGs to uphold fair trial guarantees and has actively promoted the use of NSAG courts to end impunity for international crimes. To take a few illustrative examples, in the 1990s, the UN Mission in El Salvador (ONUSAL) evaluated the penal code developed by the FMLN for its consistency with IHL, rather than disregarding the notion of NSAG justice altogether.[100] In 1996, the Special Rapporteur for Sudan stated that the relevant armed groups 'should take the necessary measures without delay to prevent

96 UN Special Rapporteur Leandro Despouy, 'UN Special Rapporteur on Independence of Judiciary Condemns Public Execution following Illegal Trial in Afghanistan, Statement by Leandro Despouy, the Special Rapporteur on the Independence of Judges and Lawyers' *United Nations Press Release* (Web Page, 8 June 2006) <https://www.ohchr.org/en/statements/2009/10/un-special-rapporteur-independence-judiciary-condemns-public-execution-following> accessed 30 July 2024.

97 United Nations Officer for the High Commissioner of Human Rights in Nepal, 'Human Rights Abuses by the CPN-M: Summary of Concerns' (UN Document, September 2006) 3–4, 8.

98 SC Res 2076, UN Doc S/RES/2076 (20 November 2012) para 3.

99 United Nations Assistance Mission in Afghanistan, 'Afghanistan Annual Report 2017: Protection of Civilians on Armed Conflict' (UN Office of the High Commissioner for Human Rights, February 2018).

100 FMLN, *Principios, Normativos y Medidas Dispuestas por el FMLN en el Transcurso de la Guerra* (1991).

future violations by investigating the cases brought to their attention and holding the perpetrators responsible'.[101] In 2002, the UN Security Council stated that the 'RCD [Rally for Congolese Democracy]-GOMA must [...] ensure an end to all violations of human rights and to impunity in all areas under its control',[102] echoing several other Security Council Resolutions that have specifically called on NSAGS to ensure respect for IHL by bringing perpetrators to justice.[103] In 2009, the UN Fact Finding Mission on the Gaza Conflict noted that there is 'an obligation for "State-like" entities to prosecute and try perpetrators',[104] while the Group of Eminent Experts on Yemen recommended that all parties to the conflict 'ensure accountability for the perpetrators'.[105] In 2011, the Commission of Inquiry for Libya recommended that the Libyan National Transitional Council (a NSAG) 'conduct exhaustive, impartial and public investigations into all allegations of international human rights law and international humanitarian law violations [...] with full respect of judicial guarantees',[106] while in 2015, the Special Rapporteur on human rights and terrorism stated that ISIS 'is bound under international law to respect core human rights obligations', emphasising that '[t]he right to a fair trial should also be guaranteed'.[107]

---

101 Gáspár Bíró, Special Rapporteur, *Report on Situation of Human Rights in the Sudan*, UN Doc E/CN.4/1996/62 (20 February 1996) para 87 (*Report on Situation of Human Rights in the Sudan*).

102 United Nations Security Council, *Statement by the President of the Security Council*, S/PRST/2002/22 (23 July 2002) para 4 (*Statement by the President of the Security Council*).

103 SC Res 1479, UN Doc S/RES/1479 (13 May 2003) para 8; SC Res 1509, UN Doc S/RES/1509 (19 September 2003) para 10; SC Res 1962, UN Doc S/RES/1962 (20 December 2010) para 9; SC Res 1933, UN Doc S/RES/1933 (30 June 2010) para 13; SC Res 2041, UN Doc S/RES/2041 (22 March 2012) para 32; SC Res 2139, UN Doc S/RES/2139 (22 February 2014) para 3. See also the practice cited by Sivakumaran, *The Law of Non-International Armed Conflict* (n 25) 550–555.

104 Report of the United Nations Fact-Finding Mission on the Gaza Conflict, UN Doc A/HRC/12/48 (25 September 2009) paras 1962–1963.

105 Report of the Group of Eminent International and Regional Experts as submitted to the United Nations High Commissioner for Human Rights, *Situation of Human Rights in Yemen, Including Violations and Abuses since September 2014 – 9 August 2019*, UN Doc A/HRC/42/17 (3 Sep 2019) para 98(g) (*Situation of Human Rights in Yemen, Including Violations and Abuses since September 2014 – 9 August 2019*).

106 Report of the International Commission of Inquiry to Investigate All Alleged Violations of International Human Rights Law in the Libyan Arab Jamahiriya, UN Doc A/HRC/17/44 (1 June 2011) paras 60–65.

107 Ben Emmerson, Special Rapporteur, *Report of the Special Rapporteur on the Promotion and Protection of Human Rights and Fundamental Freedoms while Countering*

The individual practice of third-party states is more difficult to quantify. Direct statements in condemnation or support of NSAG justice are not as common, and, in any event, it could be argued that any such examples are motivated by political factors rather than a legal assessment of the jurisdictional competence of NSAG courts. For example, the US Supreme Court held that providing support in the form of legal advice and training in IHL to the LTTE in Sri-Lanka or the Kurdistan Workers Party (PKK) in Turkey could constitute the provision of 'material support to terrorist groups' in violation of US law,[108] even though the LTTE courts are among the most advanced of any NSAG. Several states have similarly condemned the justice mechanisms of NSAGs which they designate as terrorist organisations or otherwise oppose politically.[109]

On the other hand, there is a trend of third-party states of recognising the legality of NSAG courts where it is politically convenient. In the Syrian civil war, several European and other foreign states have refused to repatriate their nationals imprisoned by the primarily Kurdish SDF for alleged affiliation with ISIS,[110] implicitly accepting that they will be prosecuted at the hands of a NSAG. The French government explicitly declared a preference for its nationals held in detention in Syria (totalling approximately 100 persons) to be tried by the courts of the Kurdish rebels in Rojava, Syria.[111] In

---

Terrorism, UN Doc A/HRC/29/51 (16 June 2015) paras 30–1 (*Report of the Special Rapporteur on the Promotion and Protection of Human Rights and Fundamental Freedoms while Countering Terrorism*). See also Human Rights Council, *Report of the Special Rapporteur on Extrajudicial, Summary or Arbitrary Executions on Armed Non-State Actors: The Protection of the Right to Life*, UN Doc A/HRC/38/44 (5 June 2018) paras 74–75 (*Report of the Special Rapporteur on Extrajudicial, Summary or Arbitrary Executions on Armed Non-State Actors: The Protection of the Right to Life*).

108 *Holder Attorney General et al v Humanitarian Law Project et al* (United States Supreme Court, Case No 08–1498, 21 June 2010) (*Holder Attorney General et al v Humanitarian Law Project et al*).

109 For example, when the FMLN in El Salvador announced that it would prosecute several of its own members for the murder of American servicemen in 1991, the US Assistant Secretary of State for Inter-American Affairs announced that 'the FMLN lacks the legal authority to carry out a proper investigation, prosecution or appellate process that would deserve recognition or legitimacy under international law or the law of any sovereign state'. Quoted in Theodor Meron, 'Application of Humanitarian Law in Non-International Armed Conflicts: Remarks by Theodor Meron' (1991) 85 *American Society of International Law Proceedings* 83, 83–85.

110 Matias Thomsen, 'Legal Status of ISIS-Affiliated Foreign Nationals in Syria' *Diakonia International Humanitarian Law Centre* (Legal Brief, August 2019) 40–42.

111 Provost, *Rebel Courts: The Administration of Justice by Armed Insurgents* (n 48) 416.

Thailand, it is reported that the Thai authorities have been willing to transfer alleged offenders to the Karen National Union (KNU), a NSAG that administers territory in South-East of Myanmar.[112] In Libya, the United States, France, and the United Kingdom issued a joint statement in which they 'welcome the announcement by the [...] LNA [Libyan National Army] that it will investigate reports of unlawful killings in Benghazi', calling upon the armed group to ensure that '[t]hose suspected of committing, ordering, or failing to prevent unlawful killings and torture on all sides must be fully investigated and held accountable, as appropriate'.[113] And in the Democratic Republic of Congo, although the US condemned the *Mouvement de Libération du Congo* (MLC) trials, it did so for their 'inadequate' due process guarantees, 'disregard for the serious nature of the crimes', and 'the failure to charge anyone with crimes against humanity or war crimes'.[114]

The practice referred to above confirms that NSAG courts are not *a priori* prohibited under international law. In addition to the fact that NSAG courts are a necessary means for such groups to fulfil their obligations under IHL and benefit from the equal application of the law, their use is actively encouraged by UN bodies and, at times, third-party states. Such acceptance of NSAG courts by the international community, both explicit and implicit, is recognised as a valid form of state practice and *opinio juris* (or a general practice accepted as law) in the formation and identification of customary international law (CIL).[115] As stated by Hannes Jöbstl:

> Whereas the state practice observed above does not necessarily seem to extend the duty to prosecute war crimes onto [NSAGs], it can and

112 Brian McCartan and Kim Jolliffe, *Ethnic Armed Actors and Justice Provision in Myanmar* (Asia Foundation 2016) 20.

113 UK Foreign & Commonwealth Office, 'Joint Statement by the Governments of France, the United Kingdom, and the United States of America: ICC Arrest Warrant for Major Mahmoud Al-Werfalli in Libya' (Press Release, 9 August 2017) <https://shorturl.at/KJmH4> accessed 30 July 2024.

114 Hannes Jöbstl, 'Bridging the Accountability Gap: Armed Non-state Actors and the Investigation and Prosecution of War Crimes' (2020) 18(3) *Journal of International Criminal Justice* 567, 584–585, citing Statement by Mr Williamson (USA) (UNSC 4784th Meeting, UN Doc. S/PV.4784, 7 July 2003) para 19.

115 *Report of the International Law Commission, Chapter V: Identification of Customary International Law*, UN GAOR, 73rd sess, Supp No 10, UN Doc A/73/10 (2018) 129 Conclusion 3 para 9 (*Report of the International Law Commission, Chapter V: Identification of Customary International Law*).

> should be interpreted and conceptualized as growing evidence of an obligation of [NSAGs] to ensure accountability for war crimes.[116]

However, state practice does not go so far as to recognise a jurisdictional competence for NSAG courts beyond the exigencies of the armed conflict. On the contrary, most of the examples cited above refer to an obligation on NSAGs to prosecute alleged violations of international crimes, seemingly under the customary obligation in article 1 of the *Geneva Conventions* to ensure respect for IHL or, in some cases, based on the developing norm that NSAGs exercising territorial control incur human rights obligations.[117] It is relatively clear from such practice that, whatever jurisdictional competence NSAG courts possess, it does not come from the group itself but from IHL as the body of law that authorised the existence of such courts in the first place. Before considering this point further, it is necessary to examine the ICRC's second proposal that the jurisdiction of NSAG courts is limited to enforcing the pre-existing law of the territorial state.

6.3.2 *The Pre-existing Law of the State as the Legal Basis and Jurisdictional Competence of Non-state Courts*

The ICRC's second proposal is that NSAG courts be considered regularly constituted where they 'continue to operate existing courts applying existing legislation'.[118] The Prosecution raised a similar argument before the *Al Hassan* Pre-Trial Chamber, when it submitted that NSAGs are not regularly constituted where they depart from the laws of the territorial state in question.[119] In a footnote, the Prosecution made the following qualification.

> The prosecution holds two cases in which a tribunal allegedly established by a non-state armed group may depart from the laws already in force in the territory in which it acts: 1) when international law humanitarian authority authorizes it to do so and 2) when the law it is supposed to apply is more compatible with internationally recognized

116 Jöbstl (n 114) 596.

117 Provost, *Rebel Courts: The Administration of Justice by Armed Insurgents* (n 48) 284.

118 International Committee of the Red Cross, *Commentary on Geneva Convention III Relative to the Treatment of Prisoners of War, Second Edition* (n 1) para 728.

119 *Document Contennant les Charges contre M. Al Hassan* (*Version amendée et corrigée du Document contenant les charges contre M. Al Hassan Ag Abdoul Aziz Ag Mohamed Ag Mahmoud*) (International Criminal Court, Case No ICC-01/12-01/18, 2 July 2019) [486] (*Prosecution Document Containing the Charges against Al Hassan*).

> human rights than are the laws already in force in the territory in question.[120]

In support of this submission, the Prosecution cited a recent case before the Stockholm District Court, in which it was held that NSAGs have the authority to establish criminal courts on the proviso that they apply the pre-existing law of the state, or at least law that is not 'considerably' stricter.[121] The Prosecution also cited two cases before the European Court of Human Rights (ECtHR) which have upheld the principle that courts established by a non-state entity can be considered 'established by law', insofar as they reflect the existing legal tradition of the state or human rights law.[122] Pre-Trial Chamber I rejected this argument outright,[123] and it was not raised at trial. However, the Pre-Trial Chamber did so because it relied exclusively on the 'independence and impartiality' requirement in the *Elements of Crimes* and did not consider the legal basis or jurisdictional competence of the Islamic Tribunals. As shown in Chapter 5, Pre-Trial Chamber I and Trial Chamber X ignored the customary definition of a regularly constituted court and their approach should not be followed. The notion that NSAG courts may be limited to enforcing the law of the territorial state under customary IHL therefore remains judicially untested at the ICC and, as stated by Diletta Marchesi, 'is a question that cannot be overlooked'.[124]

6.3.2.1 *Prosecutor v Omar Haisam Sakhanh*

In *Prosecutor v Haisam Sakhanh*, the accused, a member of the Syrian NSAG *firqat suleiman el-muqatila* [Sulemain's Company], admitted to having

120 Ibid nn 1190.

121 *Prosecutor v Omar Haisam Sakhanh (Judgement)* (Stockholms Tingsrätt (Stockholm District Court), Case No 3787–16, 16 February 2017) (*Omar Haisam Sakhanh*). For an English translation of this case (referred to hereafter), see Mark Klamberg, 'On the Establishment of Courts in Non-International Armed Conflict by Non-State Actors' (2018) 16(2) *Journal of International Criminal Justice* 403.

122 *Ilaşcu and others v Moldova and Russia* [2004] VII Eur Court HR 179 (*Ilaşcu and others v Moldova and Russia*).

123 *The Prosecutor v Al Hassan Ag Abdoul Aziz Ag Mohamed Ag Mahmoud* (Corrected version of *Décision relative à la Confirmation des Charges Portées contre Al Hassan Ag Abdoul Aziz Ag Mohamed Ag Mahmoud*) (International Criminal Court, Pree-Trial Chamber I, Case No ICC-01/12-01/18, 13 November 2019) [375], [482] (English Translation) (*Al Hassan Pre-Trial Judgment*).

124 Diletta Marchesi, 'The War Crimes of Denying Judicial Guarantees and the Uncertainties Surrounding their Material Elements ' (2021) 54(2) *Israel Law Review* 174, 198.

jointly executed seven unidentified persons *hors de combat* from the Syrian Armed forces. The soldiers were forced onto their hands and knees and shot several times in the head and body, including by the defendant.[125] However, the defendant denied criminal responsibility on the basis that the executions amounted to a lawful death sentence issued by a regularly constituted court pursuant to the rules of IHL.[126] In its judgment of 16 February 2017, the Swedish District Court rejected Haisam Sakhanh's defence, but recognised the legality of NSAG courts under certain conditions, as advocated by expert IHL witness, Mark Klamberg.[127] These conditions are as follows:

> In a non-international armed conflict, a nonstate actor can establish tribunals to (1) maintain discipline among the group's own armed units and (2) to maintain law and order in a given territory which the group controls provided that the court is staffed by personnel which before the outbreak of the conflict, in a regular manner, were appointed as judges or officials of the judicial system, and that the court *applies the law that existed before the outbreak of the conflict*, or at least not laws that differ considerably in stricter direction from the legislation that existed before the outbreak of the conflict.[128]

The Court specifically noted that, 'In the event that the requirement that a court would be regularly constituted is interpreted strictly in relation to the principle of sovereignty, it would be impossible to maintain such control of military units',[129] before holding that 'the requirement that a court shall be regularly constituted must be seen as fundamentally paired with [i.e., not *replaced by*] the issue [of] whether the court offers essential judicial guarantees such as independence and impartiality'.[130] The decision

125 Klamberg (n 121) 404.

126 Ibid 406.

127 Ibid.

128 *Omar Haisam Sakhanh* (n 121) [38] (emphasis added); Klamberg, 'On the Establishment of Courts in Non-International Armed Conflict by Non-State Actors' (n 121) 416. Regarding the Swedish Court's determination that NSAG courts must be staffed by judges who were appointed before the outbreak of the conflict, Klamberg later clarified that in his submission this was an ideal situation rather than a strict legal requirement. See Mark Klamberg, 'The Legality of Rebel Courts during Non-International Armed Conflicts' (2018) 16(2) *Journal of International Criminal Justice* 235, 257 fn 106.

129 Klamberg, 'On the Establishment of Courts in Non-International Armed Conflict by Non-State Actors' (n 121) 414 (at [29] of the judgment).

130 Ibid at [30] of the judgment.

was subsequently upheld by the Swedish Court of Appeal and leave to appeal to the Supreme Court of Sweden was denied due to the failure to identify legal error.[131]

The Stockholm Court appeared to accept that IHL provides an inherent legal basis for the establishment of NSAG courts in NIAC and instead focused on the jurisdictional limitation to apply the pre-existing law of the state, or at least to not apply laws that are considerably stricter. The Court justified its approach on the basis of the necessity of recognising NSAG courts to maintain internal discipline and a system of law and order in the territory under the control of the armed group. However, it balanced this fact against its interpretation of article 6(2)(c) of *AP II* that 'it is only states in accordance with their respective constitutional rules that by law may impose criminal law'.[132]

Somer criticises the Swedish Court's narrow interpretation of the word 'law' in article 6(2)(c) of *AP II*, arguing that, while state legislative monopoly is absolute under human rights law in times of peace, competing legal authority is the 'name of the game' under the law of NIAC.[133] In support, Somer cites the ICRC's contemplation of the 'law' of NSAGs in its commentaries to both *AP II* and common article 3 and the ambivalent statements of a few states during the *AP II Diplomatic Conference*.[134] However, in accordance with the analysis of the *Diplomatic Record* in section 6.3.1.1, the unqualified use of the word 'law' in the English text of *AP II* appears to have been a clerical error and the equally authentic French text explicitly retains the qualifier 'national or international' before the use of the word 'law'. The French text of article 6(2)(c) could therefore be said to lend credibility to the argument that NSAGs are limited to applying the pre-existing criminal laws of the state ('national law') or international criminal law ('international law').

---

131 *Prosecutor v Omar Sakhanh Haisam Sakhanh* (Svea hovratt (Svea Appeal Court), Case No B 2259-17, 31 May 2017) (*Prosecutor v Omar Sakhanh Haisam Sakhanh*).

132 Klamberg, 'On the Establishment of Courts in Non-International Armed Conflict by Non-State Actors' (n 121) 414 (at [30] of the judgment).

133 Jonathan Somer, 'Opening the Floodgates, Controlling the Flow: Swedish Court Rules on the Legal Capacity of Armed Groups to Establish Courts' *EJIL: Talk! Blog of the European Journal of International Law* (Blog Post, 10 March 2017) <https://www.ejiltalk.org/opening-the-floodgates-controlling-the-flow-swedish-court-rules-on-the-legal-capacity-of-armed-groups-to-establish-courts/> accessed 30 July 2024.

134 Ibid.

However, even though states at the *Diplomatic Conference* were uncomfortable with the prospect that NSAG 'law' would be conflated with 'national law', Somer is correct to point out that states appeared to accept that NSAGs would be required to pass their own laws to effectively manage the territory under their control and operate courts. Furthermore, what the debates at the *Diplomatic Conference* seemed to suggest is that states saw the authority for such courts as strictly limited to that which is afforded to them by the equal application of IHL's rules.

Somer points out that there are several understandable policy reasons in favour of restricting NSAGs to applying the pre-existing law of the state, such as maintaining the 'core the state's monopoly on violence; mitigating against vigilantism; reducing the likelihood of unqualified or partial judges; ensuring that 'populations will not be subjected to partisan laws, or for example religious laws that deviate from the state's legal foundations'; and ensuring that such persons 'will not find themselves under two competing sets of law with which it is impossible to comply'.[135] At the same time, Somer argues that imposing the pre-existing law of the state on NSAGs may reduce positive engagement with NSAGs which may in turn reduce their compliance with IHL. Furthermore, he argues that such a limitation assumes that the law of the state is more in line with internationally recognised human rights which, Somer argues, is 'often' not the case.[136]

The argument that the Swedish Court's decision rested more on policy than legal grounds in imposing the pre-existing law of the state as a jurisdictional limitation on NSAG courts is valid. The Swedish Court appears to have begun with the notion that the jurisdiction of NSAG courts must be limited to uphold the abovementioned policy considerations and worked backwards from there, rather than clearly identifying the legal basis for the establishment of NSAG courts and using that legal basis to determine the outer limits of their jurisdictional competence.

As an alternative to the Swedish Court's approach, Somer suggests analogising the jurisdictional competence of NSAG courts with the restrictions imposed on an occupying power under articles 64–67 of *Geneva Convention IV* (*GC IV*). However, as will be demonstrated below, there are also problems with using occupation law as the legal basis for the establishment of NSAG courts.

135 Somer, 'Opening the Floodgates, Controlling the Flow' (n 133).
136 Ibid.

6.3.2.2 Analogy with the Law of Occupation

Another argument that has been proposed as a means of restricting NSAGs to applying the pre-existing law of the state is by drawing an analogy with the law of occupation, under which the occupying power may only displace the law of the occupied territories in exceptional circumstances. However, as the law of occupation is expressly limited to situations of international armed conflict (IAC), the analogy is useful for illustrative purposes only.

Appliable only in IAC, the law of occupation limits courts established by the occupying power to applying the pre-existing law of the occupied state, with a few notable exceptions. Article 64 of *GC IV* provides that, 'The penal laws of the occupied territory shall remain in force'.[137] As express exceptions to this rule, article 64 states that the occupying power may: (I) repeal or suspend the laws of the occupied territory where they 'constitute a threat to its national security or an obstacle to the application of the present Convention'; and (II) legislate new provisions that are 'essential to enable the Occupying Power to fulfil its obligations under the present Convention, to maintain the orderly government of the territory, and to ensure the security of the Occupying Power'.[138] Articles 65–67 of *GC IV* circumscribe this power further by obliging the occupying power to: (I) publish any new offences to the civilian population in a language they understand prior to their enforcement; (II) use 'properly constituted, non-political military courts'; and (III) respect the principles of legality and proportionality, respectively.

The reason that the law of occupation has been proposed as an appropriate analogy to the situation of NSAG judicial enforcement is that it recognises the necessity of law as a form of governance that is 'dissociated from sovereignty'.[139] In other words, it gives practical legal effect to an otherwise illegal situation and recognises that the exercise of law can be legal notwithstanding the illegitimacy of the actor. René Provost makes a compelling argument that, at a minimum, the law of occupation should apply to NSAGs exercising territorial control over civilian populations whose allegiance is to the opposing side, which is usually the state.[140] This proposal follows the reasoning of the International Criminal Tribunal for the former Yugoslavia

---

137 *Geneva Convention Relative to the Protection of Civilian Persons in Time of War, opened for signature 12 August 1949, 75 UNTS 287 art 4 (entered into force 21 October 1950) ('Geneva Convention IV').*

138 Ibid.

139 Provost, 'FARC Justice: Rebel Rule of Law' (n 4) 264.

140 Ibid 275–6.

(ICTY) Appeals Chamber in *Tadić*, which concluded that 'ethnicity may become determinative of national allegiance' for the purpose of interpreting the 'nationality' status requirement in *GC IV*.[141] It could be more generally applied to all NSAGs exercising territorial control where the relationship with the civilian population can be characterised as belligerent.[142]

Most recently, ICC judge Antoine Keisa-Mbe Minuda in his partially dissenting judgment in the *Al Hassan* Trial Chamber decision declared that 'it is quite clear' that the obligations of an occupying power apply to Ansar Dine/AQIM in Northern Mali.[143] The judgment is remarkable for the confidence with which it asserts that the law of occupation, applicable only in IAC as a matter of treaty law, also applies to NSAGs exercising territorial control in the context of a NIAC. Judge Minuda canvases the right of the Tuerag peoples of Mali to self-determination,[144] the distinction between *jus ad bellum* (which regulates the legality of going to war) and *jus in bello* (which regulates conduct in war),[145] the manner in which NSAGs are bound by international law,[146] and the international law obligations of Ansar Dine/AQIM, which he characterises as an occupying power. Unfortunately, there is virtually no authority provided for this novel interpretation of the law.

In asserting that occupation can occur at the hands of a 'non-state entity', Judge Minuda cites a 1984 article by Adam Roberts and a 2012 article by Kenneth Watkin. The Roberts article posits that a non-state entity fighting a war of liberation may 'occupy territory of a neighbouring State', using Yugoslav partisans in Trieste in the Second World War, the National Liberation Front of South Vietnam in Cambodia in 1975, and the Palestine Liberation Organization in part of Lebanon in the 1970s and early 1980s as examples.[147] Roberts continues that the 'general applicability of the laws of war to certain liberation movements is clear enough', citing the recognition of such conflicts as international under *Additional Protocol I* (*API*).[148] He

141 *Prosecutor v Tadić* (*Judgment*) (International Criminal Tribunal for the former Yugoslavia, Appeals Chamber, Case No IT-94-1-A, 15 July 1999) [166] (*Tadić Appeals Judgment*).

142 Ibid.

143 *Al Hassan Trial Judgment*, Separate and Partially Dissenting Judgment of Judge Antoine Keisa-Mbe Minuda [34]–[38].

144 Ibid [1]–[18].

145 Ibid.

146 Ibid [19]–[25].

147 Adam Roberts, 'What is Military Occupation' (1984) 55(1) *British Yearbook of International Law* 249, 292.

148 Ibid 293.

concludes that while occupation law should apply to non-state groups exercising territorial control, some provisions 'might be hard to implement in cases where the occupant lacks some of the resources which a State enjoys'.[149] The Watkin article, meanwhile, simply makes reference to Roberts' typologies of occupation.[150]

Although interesting, the value of this reference is unclear. Roberts is referring to a non-state entity fighting a war of national liberation that proceeds to occupy part of the territory of *another state*. He is not referring to a rebel faction within a state occupying part of that same state's territory. Moreover, this entire discussion takes place under the premise that the conflict has qualified as an IAC because the non-state entity is engaged in a war of national liberation. While Judge Minuda in *Al Hassan* speaks of the Tuerag peoples' right to self-determination, he continues under the premise that Ansar Dine/AQIM are engaged in a NIAC against the Malian state, not an IAC by virtue of a war of liberation.

There are certainly practical and normative reasons for recognising NSAG territorial control as a form of occupation, as noted above. The civilian population are subjected to the authority of the NSAG and, to the extent that civilians are unsympathetic to that group and see their exercise of control as belligerent, the situation shares many of the same features as hostile occupation by a foreign state. It may, therefore, be perfectly reasonable to refer to NSAG control as a form of occupation in descriptive terms, but it is another thing altogether to assert that the law of occupation applies. To substantiate this proposed development of the law, the judgment should have at least provided a detailed examination of the primary sources of international law and scholarly debates on the issue, as was the case in *Tadić* where the ICTY recognised that certain war crimes applicable in IAC should apply in NIAC under customary international law.[151] Unfortunately, such engagement with the sources of international law was not forthcoming.

It is, perhaps, a missed opportunity that Judge Minuda did not delve further into the possible justifications for applying occupation law to NSAGs exercising territorial control in NIACs. The law of occupation provides

149 Ibid

150 Kenneth Watkin, 'L'emploi de la Force en Période d'Occupation: Maintien de l'Ordre Public et Conduite des Hostilités' (2012) 94 (Séléction Francaise) *Revue International du Croix-Rouge* 179, 181.

151 *Prosecutor v Tadić (Decision on the Defence Motion for Interlocutory Appeal)* (International Criminal Tribunal for the former Yugoslavia, Appeals Chamber, Case No IT-94-1, 2 October 1995) [97]–[127] ('*Tadić Jurisdictional Appeal*').

fertile ground for further discussion on imposing limitations on NSAG governance, including possible limitations on the jurisdiction of NSAG courts. The legal regulation of NSAGs would have benefited from a well-reasoned judicial pronouncement on this issue. The partially dissenting judgment of Judge Minuda, while touching on this important topic, is unlikely to yield much influence due to its lack of engagement with the sources of international law.

Nevertheless, it is self-evident that NSAG governance requires some form of regulation. While the application of human rights obligations to NSAGs is gaining traction, it does not make up for the gap in IHL. As stated by Sivakumaran, 'It is difficult to comprehend that, once a territory falls under the control of a non-state armed group, international humanitarian law has little or nothing to offer.'[152] In response, Sivakumaran advocates for a piecemeal approach in which the law of occupation could be applied by analogy to NSAGs on a case-by-case basis, depending on their governance capacity.[153] Speaking on the subject of NSAGs legislating their own laws to promote compliance with IHL or human rights standards, Deborah Casalin argues that it would be appropriate to apply the limitations imposed on occupying powers to keep the laws of the state in force, 'especially regarding subject matter and retroactivity'.[154]

However, there are quite specific reasons why an occupying power is limited to enforcing the pre-existing law of the state, and these justifications are not easily transposed to NSAGs exercising territorial control. Most notably, an occupation is a temporary (and unlawful) state of affairs in which the occupying power is effectively administering the territory without displacing the sovereign. While this might describe some NSAG-controlled territories, the motivations of most NSAGs are to liberate the territory, reclaim it, or overthrow an oppressive regime. Marco Sassoli notes the armed groups that liberated parts of Syria from the Bashar Al-Assad regime refused in principle to apply pre-existing Syrian law, including certain rules of the penal code that were perfectly consistent with human rights, because any law emanating from the oppressive Syrian regime was to them 'tinged with injustice'.[155]

152 Sivakumaran, *The Law of Non-International Armed Conflict* (n 5) 529.

153 Ibid.

154 Deborah Casalin, 'Taking Prisoners: Reviewing the International Humanitarian Law Grounds for Deprivation of Liberty by Armed Opposition Groups' (2011) 93 *International Review of the Red Cross* 743, 756–7.

155 Marco Sassòli, 'L'administration d'un Territoire par un Groupe Armé, Peut-elle être Régie par le Droit?', in M. Hottelier et al (eds), *Études en l'Honneur du Professeur Thierry Tanquerel* (Schulthess, 2019) 267, 270.

This example serves as a reminder that restricting NSAGs to applying the pre-existing law of the state, whether derived from occupation law or elsewhere, is fundamentally impractical in most NIACs. If the pre-existing law of the state were considered a jurisdictional limitation, any enforcement of NSAG 'law' would render the court irregularly constituted for the purpose of the relevant decision. Such a limitation 'seems inconsistent with the thrust of the analysis of [IHL] up to this point' and would impose unrealistic standards on NSAG courts.[156] Forcing such standards on groups whose *raison d'être* is to challenge the state's sovereign monopoly is asking the impossible and is, therefore, likely to reduce compliance with IHL. In short, from an IHL perspective, limiting NSAG courts to enforcing the pre-existing law of the state has no direct legal basis in IHL and would be impractical in most cases.

6.3.2.3 Analogous Jurisprudence of Regional and International Courts

Moving away from the realm of IHL, the ECtHR and the ICJ have both been prepared to recognise the exercise of law by non-state courts subject to two provisos: (I) the law enforced by the non-state court must be compatible with the legal tradition of the territorial state and/or international human rights; and (II) recognition of the effect of such judicial decisions must be necessary to avoid causing detriment to the civilian population under its *de facto* jurisdiction. On the one hand, these decisions could be viewed as lending support to the argument that NSAGs are limited to enforcing the pre-existing law of the state. On the other hand, they could be seen as international law providing an outer limit on the jurisdictional competence of non-state courts. In light of the preceding analysis, the latter interpretation should be preferred when it comes to determining the 'regular constitution' of NSAG courts under IHL.

In *Cyprus v Turkey*, the ECtHR held that the civil courts of the Turkish Republic of Northern Cyprus (TRNC) could be considered 'established by law' in accordance with the 'law' of the TRNC to the extent that they operated 'for the benefit' of the civilian population, notwithstanding the regime's unlawful claim to statehood.[157] However, the ECtHR's decision was premised on the fact that 'the court system in its functioning and procedures reflects the judicial and common-law tradition of Cyprus'.[158] This conclusion

---

156 Provost, *Rebel Courts: The Administration of Justice by Armed Insurgents* (n 48) 191–192.

157 *Cyprus v Turkey* [2001] Application No 25781/94, IV Eur Court HR, [231], [237] (*Cyprus v Turkey*).

158 Ibid. See also *Mitrovic v Serbia* [2017] Application No 52142/12, Eur Court HR (*Mitrovic v Serbia*). Provost argues that the *Mitrovic v Serbia* judgment suggests that detention

was informed by the Commission's findings that the TRNC courts 'were in substance based on the Anglo-Saxon tradition and were not essentially different from the courts operating before the events of 1974 and from those which existed in the southern part of Cyprus'.[159] With regards to the purpose of the courts, the ECtHR stated:

> It appears evident to the Court, despite the reservations the Greek-Cypriot community in northern Cyprus may harbour regarding the 'TRNC' courts, that the absence of such institutions would work to the detriment of the members of that community. Moreover, recognising the effectiveness of those bodies *for the limited purpose of protecting the rights of the territory's inhabitants* does not, in the Court's view and following the Advisory Opinion of the International Court of Justice, legitimise the 'TRNC' in any way.[160]

The Advisory Opinion to which this passage refers is that of *Legal Consequences for States of the Continued Presence of South Africa in Namibia (South West Africa) notwithstanding Security Council Resolution 276 (Namibia)*.[161] The circumstances of that case were that, in response to South Africa's illegal administration of the independent territory of Namibia, the UN Security Council prohibited member states from recognising any legal consequences arising from the illegality of South Africa's rule. However, the international community appealed to the necessity of recognising certain administrative powers by South African authorities for the benefit of the civilian population of Namibia.[162] The ICJ held that the illegality of the regime does not necessarily preclude recognition of their laws provided those laws are necessary to maintain the rights of the civilian population.[163] Over 100 years earlier, a similar principle was espoused by the US Supreme Court

pursuant to a conviction by a regularly constituted NSAG court affording judicial guarantees would not necessarily violate IHRL. See Provost, *Rebel Courts: The Administration of Justice by Armed Insurgents* (n 48) 430–431.

159 *Cyprus v Turkey* (n 157) [231].

160 Ibid [92] (emphasis added).

161 *Legal Consequences for States of the Continued Presence of South Africa in Namibia (South West Africa) notwithstanding Security Council Resolution 276 (Advisory Opinion)* [1971] ICJ Rep 16, [125] (*Legal Consequences for States of the Continued Presence of South Africa in Namibia (South West Africa) notwithstanding Security Council Resolution 276*).

162 Ibid Pleadings, Vol II, 130, 503.

163 Ibid [125].

with regards to the recognition of 'legislation' emanating from rebel Confederate states.[164]

6.3.2.4 Summary: NSAG Courts Are Not Limited to the Pre-existing Law of the State

The decision of the Stockholm District Court in *Sakhanh*, the analogy to the law of occupation, and the above case excerpts each start with the presumption that the legal basis and jurisdictional competence of non-state courts is the pre-existing law of the state, and then proceed to accept certain exceptions to the state's legislative monopoly: (I) where the 'law' of the non-state entity is necessary to maintain law and order for the benefit of the civilian population; (II) where it is necessary to ensure the immediate security of the non-state entity; and (III) where it is more consistent with internationally recognised human rights.

While international law may indeed limit the jurisdictional scope of NSAG courts in a manner similar what has been proposed above, it is submitted that the starting point is incorrect: the legal basis and jurisdictional competence of NSAG courts does not derive from the pre-existing law of the state. The reasons for reaching this conclusion are twofold.

First, NSAG courts are illegal under the territorial state's domestic law, irrespective of whether the group purports to enforce a broadly similar legal tradition. Second, there does not appear to be any explicit legal justification for restricting NSAGs to applying the pre-existing law of the state, as occupation law is not directly applicable. Any attempt to argue that an individual is criminally responsible for administering NSAG justice on the basis that it deviated from the law of the state is therefore contrary to the rights of the accused and doomed to fail. Accordingly, the better approach is that IHL provides the legal basis for the establishment of NSAG courts and limits the jurisdictional competence of such courts in accordance with IHL's fundamental rules applicable in NIAC. Such rules are already binding on NSAGs and therefore satisfy the obligations of legal certainty and fair warning.

164 *Texas v White* (United States Supreme Court, No 74 US 700, 1868) [733] (*Texas v White*): '[A]cts necessary to peace and good order among citizens [...] which would be regarded as valid if emanating from a lawful government, must be regarded in general as valid when proceeding from an actual, though unlawful government; and [...] acts in furtherance or support of rebellion [...] or intended to defeat the just rights of citizens, and other acts of the like nature, must, in general, be regarded as invalid and void'.

6.3.3 *International Humanitarian Law as Providing the Legal Basis for Non-state Courts and Determining Their Jurisdictional Competence*

As we have seen, there is insufficient support in the practice and legal opinions of states for the proposition that NSAGs can establish courts in accordance with their own 'laws' and determine the limits of their own jurisdictional competence. There is also insufficient support for the position that the pre-existing law of the state provides the legal basis for NSAG courts and pre-determines their jurisdictional competence, and that such a limitation would be impractical in NIACs where the NSAG is challenging the legal authority of the state. Instead, IHL provides the legal basis for the establishment of NSAG courts and sets the outer limit of their jurisdictional competence, as it is the only body of law to explicitly recognise the existence NSAG courts and regulate their conduct.

6.3.3.1 Legal Basis

Each of the justifications put forward in favour of recognising the legality of NSAG courts – the equal application of IHL treaties in NIAC, the doctrine of command responsibility, and the necessity of maintaining law and order in situations created by armed conflict – derives its legitimacy from IHL. If IHL were removed from the equation, there would be no legal authority on which to assert a recognised legal basis for NSAG courts; they would simply constitute a domestic crime entirely unregulated by international law.

States' tacit acceptance of NSAG courts during the negotiations for *AP II* was predicated on the fact that it was a necessary means of ensuring the equal application of the treaty. These states ensured that the acknowledgement of NSAG courts was limited to the judicial enforcement of crimes 'connected with the conflict' and without prejudice to the right of states to deny the legal effect of such courts under domestic law, thereby confirming that the legal basis of such courts is limited to the exceptional circumstances of armed conflict under the exclusive auspices of IHL. It is therefore logical to conclude that IHL provides the legal basis for NSAG courts.

Some authors resist this conclusion. Monika Hakim notes that, unlike the implied right of NSAGs to detain for imperative reasons of security, the ICRC has not expressly claimed that IHL authorises trials, arguing that common article 3 'simply requires that criminal trials be fair and in regularly constituted courts when they are conducted'.[165] Sivakumaran makes the

165 Monica Hakimi, 'Fair Trial Guarantees in Armed Conflict' *Lawfare* (Blog Post, 23 September 2016) <https://www.lawfareblog.com/joint-series-international-law-and-armed

point in a more tentative fashion, stating that: 'International humanitarian law may not *explicitly* create a right for armed opposition groups to set up courts; neither does it prohibit their establishment. Rather, it regulates their creation and operation should armed opposition groups decide to convene them'.[166] Somer, Sassòli, and Hannes Jöbstl also look at common article 3 as not prohibiting NSAG courts, as opposed to providing an explicit legal basis.[167]

Other scholars, meanwhile, proceed under the direct assumption that IHL provides the legal basis for the establishment of NSAG courts. Alessandro Amoroso argues that common article 3 'vests NSAGs with an inherent power to conduct proceedings in NIACs', as neither ICL nor human rights law provides 'the necessary legal basis to lawfully exercise criminal jurisdiction'.[168] Ezequel Heffes argues that common article 3 and *AP II* 'unequivocally grant armed opposition groups the possibility to "regularly" constitute courts … and to "legislate" in order to meet the judicial guarantees component',[169] while Darragh Murray contends that states 'implicitly (but necessarily)' granted NSAGs with the authority to establish courts by regulating their operation under the law of NIAC.[170]

-conflict-hakimi-fair-trial-guarantees-armed-conflict> accessed 30 July 2024. However, Hakimi accepts that the legal basis of NSAG courts must be resolved: 'The question then remains: under what authority would nonstate groups establish their own criminal courts? IHL might have nothing to say about this question, but international lawyers probably should. And unlike for state trials, the authority for nonstate groups is unlikely to be a state's domestic law and is not self-evidently human rights law'.

166 Sivakumaran, 'Courts of Armed Opposition Groups: Fair Trials or Summary Justice?' (n 7) 498 (emphasis added).

167 Somer, 'Jungle Justice: Passing Sentence on the Equality of Belligerents in Non-International Armed Conflict' (n 49) 670; Jöbstl (n 114) 576, quoting Marco Sassòli.

168 Alessandro Mario Amoroso, 'Should the ICC Assess Complementarity with Respect to Non-State Armed Groups? Hidden Questions in the Second Al-Werfalli Arrest Warrant' (2018) 16(5) *Journal of International Criminal Justice* 1063, 1077.

169 Ezequiel Heffes, 'Armed Opposition Groups' Courts: Challenging the Lawfulness of Detentions in Light of the Serdar Mohammed Appeals Judgment' *Just Security* (Blog Post, 2 September 2015) <https://www.justsecurity.org/25775/armed-opposition-groups-courts-challenging-lawfulness-detentions-light-serdar-mohammed-appeals-judgment/> accessed 30 July 2024.

170 Darragh Murray, 'Non-State Armed Groups in NIAC: Does IHL Provide Legal Authority for the Establishment of Courts?' *EJIL: Talk! Blog of the European Journal of International Law* (Blog Post, 4 June 2014) <https://www.ejiltalk.org/non-state-armed-groups-in-niac-does-ihl-provide-legal-authority-for-the-establishment-of-courts/> accessed 30 July 2024.

Whether one views IHL as expressly or impliedly authorising NSAG courts, either should suffice as the legal basis for the establishment of NSAG courts, as IHL is the *only* authorisation to be found. The practice and legal opinion of states consistently suggest that NSAG courts are only recognised to the extent they are necessary under IHL, as IHL is the only body of law to explicitly regulate their establishment and operation. As stated by Provost, NSAGs 'do not have an existence separate from the conflict as far as law goes'.[171] It follows that IHL should be viewed as providing the legal basis and jurisdictional competence of NSAG courts.

If we accept this premise, there are two types of law for which IHL provides the necessary legal basis and corresponding jurisdictional limitations: NSAG 'military' courts and NSAG 'criminal' courts.[172] The legal basis for NSAG military courts is clearly provided by the obligations of maintaining internal discipline and discharging command responsibility under both treaty and customary IHL. The requisite 'connection to the conflict' is less clear regarding NSAG criminal courts but is generally accepted on the basis that the territorial control of the armed group over the civilian population provides the requisite nexus to the conflict. As stated by the ICRC:

> [T]he way in which non-State armed groups exercise control over, and interact with, persons living in territory under their de facto control is inherently linked to the conflict in question. The armed conflict plays a substantial part in the group's ability to control the lives of those living under its control and the manner in which such control is exercised.[173]

The nexus between the armed conflict and the administration of NSAG justice can be explained by analogy to the law of IAC. In IACs, how a state

---

171 René Provost, 'Book Launch: Rebel Courts' *Geneva Acadamy: IHL Talks* (Web Video, 1 December 2021) <https://www.geneva-academy.ch/event/all-events/detail/312-book-launch-rebel-courts> accessed 30 July 2024.

172 Provost, *Rebel Courts: The Administration of Justice by Armed Insurgents* (n 48) 274–281. Provost argues that IHL should also regulate NSAG civil courts. However, this argument is not based on common article 3(1)(d) and is therefore not relevant to the interpretation of article 8(2)(c)(IV), which only regulates 'the passing of sentences'.

173 International Committee of the Red Cross, 'International Humanitarian Law and the Challenges of Contemporary Armed Conflict: Report' (n 53) 53. See also *Al Hassan Pre-Trial Judgment* (n 123) [415]. The Pre-Trial Chamber held that the enforcement of ordinary crimes was 'associated with the armed conflict' because it took place in the territory controlled by the NSAG.

treats its own nationals generally has no nexus to the conflict, but persons who find themselves in the hands of a party of which they are not nationals benefit from IHL's protection. Any exercise of judicial power over such persons in IAC necessarily carries a nexus to the armed conflict, and the same can be said of those who are prosecuted by NSAGs. Tilman Rodenhäuser notes that 'This is particularly the case if the NSAG decides to change the previously existing legal order and imposes new rules'.[174] In support, Rodenhäuser cites the drafting history of *AP II* in which the ICRC commented that situations of NSAG governance are precisely when IHL must apply to protect civilians 'against the arbitrary authority of the Parties to the conflict when constitutional guarantees ha[ve] been generally suspended or … no longer appl[y] effectively'.[175]

It may, therefore, be concluded that IHL provides the pre-existing legal basis for the establishment of NSAG military and criminal courts.

6.3.3.2 Jurisdictional Competence

The customary definition of a regularly constituted court is that it must have a pre-existing legal basis authorising its establishment and its jurisdictional competence must be limited by the scope of that legal basis. Given that IHL provides the pre-existing legal basis for the establishment of NSAG courts, we must look to applicable rules of IHL to determine the necessary jurisdictional limitations.

At a minimum, NSAGs are bound by treaty and customary IHL applicable in NIAC. Therefore, the enforcement of any law in violation of the law of NIAC will render the court irregularly constituted for the purpose of that decision. Provost comes to a similar conclusion in his 2021 book, *Rebel Courts*:

> [R]ebel jurisdiction *ratione materia* remains subject to the constraints of [IHL] and especially [IHRL]. Thus, the more disproportionate or discriminatory use of criminal law by armed groups […] would run afoul of such binding international legal standards. […] The limits thus imposed by international human rights and humanitarian law mark the

---

174 Tilman Rodenhäuser, 'The Legal Protection of Persons Living under the Control of Non-State Armed Groups' (2020) 102 *International Review of the Red Cross* 991, 1003.

175 Official Records of the Diplomatic Conference on the Reaffirmation and Development of International Humanitarian Law applicable in Armed Conflicts, Vol. 8, CDDH/I/SR.22 (Geneva, 1974–77) 201, cited in Rodenhäuser (n 173) 1003.

> outer boundaries of what may be regulated by criminal law [...] leaving a vast area in which an armed group can adopt and implement its own penal standards to the extent that it wields effective authority over a territory and population.[176]

Leaving aside for a moment the question of whether IHRL directly binds NSAGs, it is first necessary to consider which rules of NIAC would limit the jurisdictional competence of NSAG courts. The obvious starting point is common article 3, which provides that all protected persons, including civilians taking no active part in hostilities, 'shall in all circumstances be treated humanely, without any adverse distinction founded on race, colour, religion or faith, sex, birth or wealth, or any other similar criteria'. Immediately, it becomes clear that the enforcement of NSAG criminal laws that discriminate against civilians on the basis of any one of the abovementioned characteristics would violate the jurisdictional competence of the court. Furthermore, the deliberately open-textured reference to 'any other similar criteria' permits the inclusion of other traits within the prohibition on adverse distinction, such as sexual orientation or political affiliation. Indeed, common article 3 has been confirmed as a 'minimum yardstick' of humanitarian protection in armed conflict and would thus incorporate other limitations on NSAG 'law' for the protection of the civilian population.[177]

The other obvious point of reference is the 'Fundamental Guarantees' in article 4 of *AP II*, whose customary status is not in doubt. Of relevance to the present discussion, article 4(2)(b) prohibits 'collective punishment' (which some have argued is implied into common article 3 anyway) and reaffirms the prohibition on adverse distinction.[178] Both treaties prohibit any punishment amounting to torture, mutilation, or cruel, inhumane, or degrading treatment. Instituting such punishments through court proceedings would therefore exceed the court's jurisdiction and render it irregularly constituted, in addition to constituting independent war crimes. Beyond treaty provisions applicable in NIAC, rules of customary IHL applicable in both IAC and NIAC would equally determine the outer limit of NSAG

176 Provost, *Rebel Courts: The Administration of Justice by Armed Insurgents* (n 48) 264.

177 *Military and Paramilitary Activities in and against Nicaragua* (*Nicaragua v United States of America*) (*Merits*) [1986] 14, [218] (*Military and Paramilitary Activities in and against Nicaragua*).

178 *Prosecutor v Brima, Kamara and Kanu* (*Trial Judgment*) (Special Court of Sierra Leone, Trial Chamber II, Case No SCSL-2004-16-PT, 29 June 2007) [675] (*Prosecutor v Brima, Kamara and Kanu*).

jurisdiction, which would include, *inter alia*, those rules related to the treatment of persons in detention,[179] respect for religious practices,[180] and the prohibition on forced labour.[181]

With respect to the detailed set of rules applicable under the law of occupation, following Sivakumaran's suggestion that they should be applied to NSAGs controlling territory in a 'piecemeal' fashion, it is submitted that, as and when such rules are considered binding on NSAGs under customary IHL, they would impose jurisdictional limitations on NSAG courts.[182]

As explained in the previous section, it is impractical to restrict NSAGs to enforcing the pre-existing law of the state under article 64 of *GC IV*, even if states have interpreted the exceptions contained within this rule rather liberally.[183] One rule that may already have achieved customary status, not least because it is also a general principle of law, is the obligation in article 67 of *GC IV* that 'the penalty shall be proportioned to the offence'.[184] The commentary to article 67 states that this rule was introduced 'because of certain abuses committed during the Second World War, when heavy punishments, and even the death penalty, were inflicted for minor offences such as listening to enemy radio programmes or coming out on strike'.[185] As detailed at the beginning of this chapter, the same phenomenon has been observed in the practice of NSAG courts.[186] It is therefore essential to

---

179 See, for example, Jean-Marie Henckaerts and Louise Doswald-Beck, *Customary International Humanitarian Law (Rules)* (International Committee of the Red Cross, CUP 2005) vol 1 (Rules), 299–384, 428–457.

180 Ibid 375–379 (Rule 104).

181 Ibid 330–334 (Rule 95).

182 Sivakumaran, 'Courts of Armed Opposition Groups: Fair Trials or Summary Justice?' (n 7) 530; Provost, *Rebel Courts: The Administration of Justice by Armed Insurgents* (n 48) 76; Michael Kelly, *Restoring and Maintaining Order in Complex Peace Operations* (Martinus Nijhoff 1999) vol 2, 151; Adam Roberts, 'What is a Military Occupation' (1985) 55 *British Yearbook of International Law* 249, 253.

183 Provost, *Rebel Courts: The Administration of Justice by Armed Insurgents* (n 48) 259; Yutaka Arai, *The Law of Occupation: Continuity and Change of International Humanitarian Law, and its Interaction with International Human Rights Law* (Martinus Nijhoff 2009) 115–36; Marco Sassòli, 'Legislation and Maintenance of Public Order and Civil Life by Occupying Powers' (2005) 16 *European Journal of International Law* 661.

184 See, for example, *Charter of Fundamental Rights of the European Union*, 2012/C 326/02, art 49(3) (entered into force 1 December 2009) (*Charter of Fundamental Rights of the European Union*).

185 International Committee of the Red Cross, *Commentary on Convention (IV) relative to the Protection of Civilian Persons in Time of War* (ICRC 1958) 341.

186 See Section 6.2.3 of this chapter.

incorporate this rule, as disproportionate punishments that are indiscriminately applied might otherwise remain within the jurisdictional limitations of the law of NIAC.

Finally, there is the question of whether the jurisdictional competence of NSAG courts is limited by IHRL. Provost emphatically answers this question in the affirmative:

> [T]he whole rebel administration of criminal justice remains subject to the requirements of international human rights law. As such, the creation of any crime violating established fundamental rights and freedoms, whether by discrimination or otherwise, would amount to the illegal exercise of subject-matter jurisdiction by a non-state armed group.[187]

There is certainly a developing norm of international law that NSAGs controlling territory are directly bound by IHRL *vis-à-vis* the civilian population.[188] Indeed, as noted by the UN Human Rights Committee Special Rapporteur on extrajudicial, summary or arbitrary executions in her 2020 Report on armed non-state actors:

> Over the past two decades, there have been over 125 Security Council resolutions, approximately 65 General Assembly resolutions and over 50 statements by the President of the Security Council pertaining to the human rights obligations or other related responsibilities of armed non-State actors, prompting researchers to conclude that the Council and the Assembly 'have recognized, at a minimum, that the conduct of at least some [armed non-State actors] – in contexts as diverse as the DRC to Syria – can amount to violations or abuses of human rights'.[189]

---

187 Provost, *Rebel Courts: The Administration of Justice by Armed Insurgents* (n 48) 274.

188 Andrew Clapham, 'Human Rights Obligations of Non-State Actors in Conflict Situations' (2006) 88(863) *International Review of the Red Cross* 491; Zakaria Daboné, *Le Droit International Public Relatif aux Groupes Armés Non Étatiques* (Schulthess 2012) 322–332; Tilman Rodenhäuser, *Organizing Rebellion: Non-State Armed Groups under International Humanitarian Law, Human Rights Law, and International Criminal Law* (OUP 2018).

189 Human Rights Council, *Report of the Special Rapporteur on Extrajudicial, Summary or Arbitrary Executions on Armed Non State Actors: The Protection of the Right to Life*, UN Doc A/HRC/38/44 (7 December 2020) 3 para 10 (*Report of the Special Rapporteur on Extrajudicial, Summary or Arbitrary Executions on Armed Non State Actors: The Protection of the Right to Life*).

The parameters of this developing norm are beyond the scope of the present study. Suffice it to say that, to the extent that a rule of IHRL is considered customary, binding on NSAG groups, and non-derogable in times of armed conflict, it too would constitute an outer limit on the jurisdictional competence of NSAG courts.

6.4 Conclusion

The ICRC has proposed two possibilities for the legal basis establishing NSAG courts: NSAG courts could be regularly constituted in accordance with their own laws, or they could operate existing state courts applying existing state legislation. While there is merit in both suggestions, neither is satisfactory without further refinement. Suggesting that the legal basis comes exclusively from the laws of the armed group implies that NSAGs possess the legislative capacity to determine the jurisdictional competence of their own courts – something which is not reflected in the practice or legal opinion of states. Operating state courts and applying state law, meanwhile, would certainly *satisfy* the legal basis requirement, but there is insufficient evidence that this is required under IHL.

Instead, this chapter has argued that IHL provides the legal basis for the establishment of NSAG courts, as it is the only body of law to explicitly recognise their legality and regulate their operation. Every argument put forward in favour of recognising the legality of NSAG courts – from the equal application of IHL's rules and the need for NSAGs to discharge command responsibility obligations, to the maintenance of law and order in the territory under the control of the NSAG – is entirely dependent on IHL's regulation of NSAGs. IHL is therefore the only source of authority for the establishment of NSAG courts and must be recognised as providing the requisite legal basis.

Contrary to the principle of systemic integration, the ICC's decision in *Al Hassan* neglected to consider the customary definition of a regularly constituted court. Relying exclusively on the *Elements of Crimes*, it concluded that a regularly constituted court is an independent and impartial court and nothing more.[190] Subsequent ICC decisions should apply the customary definition of a regularly constituted court, which requires a legal basis to establish the court's authority and determine the limits of its jurisdictional

190 *Al Hassan Trial Judgment* (n 2) [1169].

competence. Following on from this, IHL should be recognised as providing the legal basis for the establishment of NSAG courts and the IHL rules applicable in NIAC should determine the outer limit of their jurisdictional competence. As courts and other institutions continue to delineate the obligations on NSAGs under customary IHL (and IHRL), these rules will regulate the administration of justice by NSAGs in a manner that better protects the lives of civilians living under their territorial control.

CHAPTER 7

'Judicial Guarantees Recognized as Indispensable'

7.1 Introduction

Under article 8(2)(c)(iv) of the *Rome Statute*, a regularly constituted court must afford 'all judicial guarantees generally recognized as indispensable'. It is not possible for judges of the International Criminal Court (ICC) to rely on 'strict construction' to interpret this requirement. Rather, the wording of the offence requires judges to identify the applicable law, using the secondary sources of law referred to in article 21(1)(b); namely, applicable treaties and customary international law (CIL). This reliance on CIL as an external source of law is to be distinguished from its role as an aid to interpretation in accordance with the principle of systemic integration under article 31(3)(c) of the *Vienna Convention on the Law of Treaties* (*VCLT*).[1] Instead, ICC judges must apply CIL as a secondary source of law to fill an intentional gap in the *Statute*.

This chapter forms the final instalment of a three-part case study on the war crime of denying a fair trial in NIAC, and argues that the ICC should interpret the term 'all judicial guarantees recognized as indispensable' in article 8(2)(c)(iv) consistently with the six-step methodology outlined in Chapter 2. Significantly, the relevant 'context' in which these judicial guarantees must be identified limits such guarantees to those considered indispensable under customary international humanitarian law (customary IHL), rather than the more expansive guarantees that might be applicable under international human rights law (IHRL). This finding is contrary to the approach of ICC Pre-Trial Chamber I in *Al Hassan*, which relied almost exclusively on human rights instruments,[2] and that of Trial Chamber X, which

1 *Vienna Convention on the Law of Treaties*, opened for signature 23 May 1969, 1155 UNTS 331 (entered into force 27 January 1980) (*VCLT*).

2 *The Prosecutor v Al Hassan Ag Abdoul Aziz Ag Mohamed Ag Mahmoud* (Corrected version of *Décision relative à la Confirmation des Charges Portées contre Al Hassan Ag Abdoul Aziz Ag Mohamed Ag Mahmoud*) (International Criminal Court, Pre-Trial Chamber I, Case No ICC-01/12-01/18, 13 November 2019) [383]–[386] (English Translation) (*Al Hassan Pre-Trial Judgment*).

 | DOI:10.1163/9789004690042_008

limited indispensable guarantees to those codified in *Additional Protocol II* (*AP II*).[3]

Pre-Trial Chamber I's approach was too broad, as judicial guarantees under IHRL may not necessarily be regarded as 'indispensable' in situations of armed conflict, as ordinary standards may need to be adjusted to account for the realities of war. By contrast, Trial Chamber X's approach was too narrow, as it relied exclusively on *AP II* and did not consider whether any other guarantees have become recognised as indispensable under customary IHL applicable in non-international armed conflict (NIAC). This chapter argues that future ICC Chambers should look to customary IHL to determine which judicial guarantees are recognised as indispensable in the context of a NIAC, which requires an examination of a general practice accepted as law (or state practice and *opinio juris*).

Using the list of judicial guarantees contained in the International Committee of the Red Cross (ICRC) 2005 study entitled 'Customary International Humanitarian Law' (*Customary IHL Study*),[4] this chapter examines the contemporary practice and legal opinion of states to determine which guarantees may be recognised indispensable in NIAC. In doing so, it employs the finding of Chapter 3 this book by applying the 'contextually dependent hierarchy of evidence' to treat the widespread support of such guarantees in treaties and other forms of representative practice as more probative than evidence of states failing to comply with these rules in practice. Finally, it considers whether there are legitimate arguments for adjusting the standard of compliance with judicial guarantees when applied to non-state armed groups (NSAGs) with varying capabilities, ultimately concluding that prosecutorial and judicial discretion should play an important role in ensuring that only substantive violations of the judicial guarantees requirement constitute war crimes.

3 *Prosecutor v Al Hassan* (International Criminal Court, Trial Chamber X, Case No ICC-01/12-01/18, 26 June 2024) [1176]–[1178] (*Al Hassan Trial Judgment*).

4 Jean-Marie Henckaerts and Louise Doswald-Beck, *Customary International Humanitarian Law* (*Rules*) (International Committee of the Red Cross, CUPCUP 2005) vol 1, 352–371; Jean-Marie Henckaerts and Louise Doswald-Beck, *Customary International Humanitarian Law* (*Practice*) (International Committee of the Red Cross/CUPCUP 2005) vol 2.

7.2 Interpreting the Term 'All Judicial Guarantees Recognized as Indispensable' under Article 8(2)(c)(iv) of the *Rome Statute*

To assist in the interpretation of the term 'all judicial guarantees recognized as indispensable' it is worth recalling steps one and four of the six-step methodology outlined in Chapter 2 of this book.

1. The definition of crimes must be strictly construed in accordance with article 22(2) of the *Rome Statute* and article 31(1) of the *VCLT*; however, open-textured language, terms with specialised meaning under CIL, and directions to fill gaps in the *Statute* each require judges to identify and apply CIL directly.
4. The definition of crimes must be interpreted in accordance with the object and purpose of the *Rome Statute* in accordance with article 31(1) of the *VCLT*; however, consistent with the [...] application of *in dubio pro reo*, object and purpose interpretations should be limited in the following way: (I) the object and purpose of the *Rome Statute* includes ensuring a fair trial in accordance with the principle of legality; and (II) it is necessary to refer to the object and purpose of the specific provision to understand its meaning.

Applying these steps to the interpretation of the term 'all judicial guarantees recognized as indispensable' raises two critical points. First, the use of this term amounts to an express direction to judges to fill the gap in the *Statute* by determining which guarantees are recognised as indispensable under CIL. As there is no list of judicial guarantees provided in the *Statute*, judges are required to directly apply CIL as a secondary source of law under article 21(1)(b). Second, interpreting this term in its context and in light of the object and purpose of the *Rome Statute* requires judges to identify those judicial guarantees that have been recognised as indispensable under customary IHL, as opposed to the potentially more expansive list of judicial guarantees applicable under IHRL.

7.2.1 *Ordinary Meaning of the Term 'All Judicial Guarantees Generally Recognized as Indispensable' in Its Context*

Article 22(2) of the *Rome Statute* requires that the definition of crimes must be 'strictly construed'. Often referred to as 'textualism', this rule corresponds with the obligation under article 31(1) of the *VCLT* to give treaty terms their ordinary meaning. However, the term 'all judicial guarantees recognized as indispensable' cannot be 'strictly construed' using the principle of textualism. Instead, it requires the direct application of external law.

The ordinary meaning of the term 'all judicial guarantees generally recognized as indispensable' is not controversial. Standard dictionary definitions stipulate that this phrase means 'assurances'[5] relating to 'the administration of justice'[6] that are 'legally or morally exactable'[7] and that have been, 'as a rule',[8] 'accept[ed] or approve[d] as having legal or official authority, that is "not subject to being set aside or neglected"'.[9] However, the *Rome Statute* does not specify which judicial guarantees are 'accepted as having legal authority' which is 'not subject to be being set aside' (i.e., 'recognized as indispensable'). Accordingly, there is a gap in the *Statute*. It is not possible to rely solely on textualism where there are gaps in the *Statute* that must be filled to avoid situations of *non liquet* (no applicable law).[10] In these situations, it is necessary to apply the secondary sources of law under article 21(1)(b) of the *Statute*, which includes applicable treaties and CIL.[11] However, it is not specified whether the 'applicable' treaties and CIL with respect to judicial guarantees should derive from IHL or IHRL.

Given the significant degree of overlap between the two sources of law when it comes to the recognition of judicial guarantees, it is reasonable to question whether it matters if judges rely on those under IHL or IHRL. It does matter – for two reasons. First, the evidence suggests that the list of judicial guarantees under customary IHL is narrower than that under IHRL. Even if that difference only comes down to a very small number of judicial

5 'Guarantees', *Merriam-Webster Online Dictionary* <https://www.merriam-webster.com/dictionary/guarantees>.

6 'Judicial', *Merriam-Webster Online Dictionary* <https://www.merriam-webster.com/dictionary/judicial>.

7 'Rights', *Merriam-Webster Online Dictionary* <https://www.merriam-webster.com/dictionary/rights> (on the basis that the terms 'judicial guarantees' and 'fair trial rights' are used synonymously).

8 'Generally', *Merriam-Webster Online Dictionary* <https://www.merriam-webster.com/dictionary/generally>.

9 'Indispensable', *Merriam-Webster Online Dictionary* <https://www.merriam-webster.com/dictionary/indispensable>.

10 For example, see: William Lietzau, 'Checks and Balances and Elements of Proof: Structural Pillars for the International Criminal Court' (1999) 32 *Cornell International Law Journal* 477, 482; Jared Wessel, 'Judicial Policy-Making at the International Criminal Court: An Institutional Guide to Analyzing International Adjudication' (2006) 44 *Columbia Journal of Transnational Law* 377, 413–4.

11 Caroline Davidson, 'How to Read International Criminal Law: Strict Construction and the Rome Statute of the International Criminal Court' (2017) 91(1) *St John's Law Review* 37, 89; Leena Grover, *Interpreting Crimes in the Rome Statute of the International Criminal Court* (CUP 2014) 129.

guarantees, that distinction could prove pivotal for a particular trial and must be acknowledged by the Court. Second, the application of the obligatory rules of interpretation dictates that the list of judicial guarantees must derive from IHL. Compliance with the correct approach has several important consequences, especially when applied to the courts of NSAGS.

The 'context' in which a treaty term must be interpreted includes the surrounding treaty text, preamble, annexes, and any other agreement or instrument made in connection with the treaty.[12] Article 8(2)(c)(IV) falls under the Court's war crimes jurisdiction in NIAC and replicates almost *verbatim* common article 3(1)(d) of the *Geneva Conventions*, which was part of a deliberate attempt to limit such jurisdiction to war crimes recognised under customary IHL.[13] Given the *lex specialis* nature of the laws of armed conflict, in which several rules of IHRL and domestic law are suspended or augmented, it is reasonable to conclude that only a violation of those judicial guarantees recognised as indispensable under IHL would constitute a war crime, as opposed to the more expansive list of protections that may be afforded under either domestic or international human rights law.[14] As stated by one delegate during the drafting process of the *Rome Statute*,

> The judicial guarantees must be those recognized by international humanitarian law which takes into consideration the nature of the war; it would be inappropriate to adopt those of international human rights law, which are intended to apply during peacetime.[15]

Interpreting this term in its context and in light of the object and purpose of the *Rome Statute* also requires the Court to consider the rights of the

---

12 Richard Gardiner, *Treaty Interpretation* (OUP 2008) 177–89.

13 Michael Cottier, 'Article 8' in Otto Triffterer (ed), *Commentary on the Rome Statute of the International Criminal Court* (Beck-Hart, 2nd ed, 2008) 275, 283, 287–8.

14 Note that while the *Elements of Crimes* for article 8(2)(c)(IV) refers to guarantees recognised as indispensable 'under international law', which could be interpreted more broadly, the introduction to the war crimes division of the *Elements* states that the elements for war crimes 'shall be interpreted within the established framework of the law of armed conflict'. *International Criminal Court, Elements of Crimes*, 13, 34 ('*International Criminal Court, Elements of Crimes*').

15 Preparatory Commission for the International Criminal Court, *Colombia: Comments on the proposal submitted by Costa Rica, Hungary and Switzerland on Article 8, paragraph 2 (c), of the Rome Statute of the International Criminal Court*, UN Doc PCNICC/1999/WGEC/DP.15 (29 July 1999) ('*Colombia on Article 8(2)(c)*') <https://legal-tools.org/doc/9c032f/pdf>.

accused. Simply put, if the list of judicial guarantees under IHRL is more expansive, it would broaden the possible situations in which an accused may be found guilty of the war crime of denying a fair trial contrary to article 8(2)(c)(IV). As stated by Diletta Marchesi, 'This approach may expand the material element of the war crime, in tension with the *nullum crimen sine lege* principle as protected under Article 22 of the ICC Statute'.[16] Similarly, if there is any lingering ambiguity about whether judicial guarantees should derive from IHL or IHRL, the principle of *in dubio pro reo* dictates that the accused must be given the more favourable interpretation.

A further argument in favour of restricting the term 'all judicial guarantees recognized as indispensable' to those recognised as such under IHL is to focus on the context of the word 'indispensable'. The right to a fair trial under article 14 of the *ICCPR* is not part of the non-derogable rights listed in article 4, which means that states could derogate from these rights during armed conflict, subject to the obligation that such derogation is 'strictly required by the exigencies of the situation' and does not 'circumvent non-derogable rights', such as the right to life or the prohibition on torture.[17] However, the Human Rights Committee has clarified that the judicial guarantees that are enshrined in IHL are *non-derogable*.[18] In other words, judicial guarantees under customary IHL are those that have explicitly been recognised as 'indispensable' in times of armed conflict.[19] This conclusion is bolstered by the fact that, during the drafting of the *Additional Protocols*

16 Diletta Marchesi, 'The War Crimes of Denying Judicial Guarantees and the Uncertainties Surrounding their Material Elements ' (2021) 54(2) *Israel Law Review* 174, 187. See also: Yutaka Arai, *The Law of Occupation: Continuity and Change of International Humanitarian Law, and its Interaction with International Human Rights Law* (Martinus Nijhoff, 2009) 510.

17 UN Human Rights Committee (HRC), *General Comment No 32, Article 14: Right to Equality Before Courts and Tribunals and to Fair Trial*, UN Doc CCPR/C/GC/32 (23 August 2007) para 6 ('*General Comment No 32, Article 14: Right to Equality Before Courts and Tribunals and to Fair Trial*'); UN Human Rights Committee (HRC), *CCPR General Comment No 29: Article 4: Derogations during a State of Emergency*, UN Doc CCPR/C/21/Rev.1/Add.11 (31 August 2001) para 15 ('*CCPR General Comment No 29: Article 4: Derogations during a State of Emergency*').

18 UN Human Rights Committee (HRC), UN Doc CCPR/C/GC/32 (n 17) para 6; UN Human Rights Committee (HRC), UN Doc CCPR/C/21/Rev.1/Add.11 (n 17) para 16.

19 Mark Klamberg, 'The Legality of Rebel Courts during Non-International Armed Conflicts' (2018) 16(2) *Journal of International Criminal Justice* 235, 246 (noting that the derogability of IHRL guarantees 'reinforces the argument, as set out above, that the primary regulatory framework when it comes to the conduct of trials during armed conflicts is international humanitarian law').

(which occurred after the entry into force of the *ICCPR*), states opted to include a list of judicial guarantees that would remain applicable in times of armed conflict, thereby choosing to render these rules non-derogable or 'indispensable'. Notably, the list is more constrained than that which is applicable during peacetime under the *ICCPR*.

In sum, the ordinary meaning of the words 'judicial guarantees generally recognized as indispensable', in their context and in light of the object and purpose of the *Statute*, requires ICC judges to identify and apply those judicial guarantees that have been recognised as indispensable under customary IHL.

7.2.2 *Judicial Guarantees under International Humanitarian Law and Human Rights Law: Is There Any Difference?*

As there is no definitive list of guarantees recognised as indispensable under customary IHL applicable in NIAC, it is not easy to make a direct comparison with IHRL. The customary status of common article 3 is well established,[20] but it does not provide a list of guarantees. *AP II*, which was drafted to supplement and develop common article 3,[21] does provide a list and is arguably the starting point for determining those which are recognised as indispensable under customary IHL in NIAC.[22] Beyond that, it would be reasonable to ask whether the additional judicial guarantees codified in IHL treaties applicable to international armed conflict (IAC) are now recognised under customary IHL applicable in NIAC, as determined by the ICRC *Customary IHL Study*.[23]

If we compare article 6(2) of *AP II* with the full suite of judicial guarantees codified under IHRL in article 14 of the *International Covenant on Civil and Political Rights* (*ICCPR*),[24] *AP II* does not protect the right to examine

20 *Military and Paramilitary Activities in and against Nicaragua* (*Nicaragua v United States of America*) (*Merits*) [1986] 14, [218] ('*Military and Paramilitary Activities in and against Nicaragua*'); *Legality of the Threat or Use of Nuclear Weapons* (*Advisory Opinion*) [1996] ICJ Rep 226, 79 ('*Legality of the Threat or Use of Nuclear Weapons*').

21 *Protocol Additional to the Geneva Conventions of 12 August 1949, and Relating to the Protection of Victims of Non-International Armed Conflicts*, opened for signature 8 June 1977, 1977, 1125 UNTS 609, art 1(1) (entered into force 7 December 1978) ('*Additional Protocol II*').

22 Ibid art 6(2).

23 Henckaerts and Doswald-Beck, *Customary International Humanitarian Law* (*Rules*) (n 4) 352–71.

24 *International Covenant on Civil and Political Rights*, opened for signature 16 December 1966, 999 UNTS 171 (entered into force 23 March 1976) ('*ICCPR*').

witnesses, the right to public proceedings, the right of *ne bis in idem* (i.e., the right not to be prosecuted twice for the same offence, also known as the prohibition on double jeopardy), the right to be tried without undue delay, or the right to appeal. The ICRC's *Customary IHL Study* concludes that all judicial guarantees in *AP II* and *Additional Protocol I* (*AP I*),[25] as well as six additional guarantees taken from *Geneva Convention III* and *Geneva Convention IV*, are now recognised as customary in both IACs and NIACs.[26] If this were accepted, the list of judicial guarantees under customary IHL would be practically identical to that under IHRL.[27] Yet, careful analysis reveals that this may not be the case.

7.3 Judicial Guarantees under Customary International Humanitarian Law: an Assessment of the ICRC Study

The list of judicial guarantees included in the ICRC *Customary IHL Study* combines those codified in both *AP I* and *AP II* with six additional guarantees derived from *Geneva Convention III* and *Geneva Convention IV*.[28] An evaluation of the ICRC's approach is necessary to determine whether each of the guarantees included in the *Customary IHL Study* finds sufficient support in state practice and *opinio juris* (or a general practice accepted as law) in the context of NIAC.

7.3.1 *Assessing the Customary Status of Judicial Guarantees in Relevant Treaties*

The ICRC's methodology for identifying judicial guarantees under customary IHL is broadly consistent with that of most courts and tribunals,

25 Article 75(4) of *AP I* recognises three guarantees that are additional to those under article 6(2) of *AP II* are: the right to examine witnesses, the right to public proceedings, and the right of *non bis in idem*

26 As discussed in more detail in Section III, four of these additional guarantees are arguably incorporated in *AP I* and *AP II* by the right to 'necessary means and rights of a defence' (namely, the right to defend oneself or to be assisted by a lawyer of one's own choice, the right to free legal assistance if the interests of justice so require, the right to sufficient time and facilities to prepare the defence, and the right of the accused to communicate freely with counsel). The other two are the right to be tried without undue delay and the right to appeal.

27 There are no differences between that list and *AP II*, but the interpretation in the IHRL context by human rights bodies may still differ from the interpretation in the IHL context.

28 Henckaerts and Doswald-Beck, *Customary International Humanitarian Law* (*Rules*) (n 4) 352–71.

and is largely endorsed by The International Law Commission (ILC) *Draft Conclusions on Identification of Customary International Law* (Draft Conclusions). The most common source of evidence relied upon the identification CIL is multilateral treaties (see Chapter 3).[29] The ILC Draft Conclusions confirms the validity of treaties as representative forms of state practice and 'forward looking' *opinio juris* in the identification of CIL,[30] and accepts that evidence of both elements can be found in the same source.[31] When it comes to the *opinio juris* ('accepted as law') element, states must express their intention to be bound by the rule, whether immediately or at such a time as it is recognised by other states.

The ICRC relies primarily on the existence of judicial guarantees in one or more of *AP I*, *AP II*, *Geneva Convention III*, or *Geneva Convention IV*, and supplements this with evidence of states upholding such guarantees in the post-World War II jurisprudence, IHRL treaties, judicial decisions of regional human rights courts, national legislation, and military manuals.[32] With the exception of *AP II*, none of these treaties is applicable in NIAC; *Geneva Convention III* and *Geneva Convention IV* are only applicable to Prisoners of War (PoWs) and civilians, respectively, who find themselves in the hands of a hostile occupying power. Therefore, it is necessary to determine whether there is sufficient evidence that states accept that they are obliged to uphold such guarantees in situations of NIAC.

Borrowing from the work of Yutaka Arai, the best way to determine if states view a judicial guarantee as binding in all situations of armed conflict under customary IHL is by reference to the status of its derogability under IHRL. The rationale for this approach is relatively straightforward. Judicial guarantees that are viewed as *derogable* may be derogated from in an

29 Niels Petersen, 'The International Court of Justice and the Judicial Politics of Identifying Customary International Law' (2017) 17(2) *European Journal of International Law* 357, 372–5; Stephen J Choi and Mitu Gulati, 'Customary International Law: How Do Courts Do It?' in Curtis A Bradley (ed), *Custom's Future: Customary International Law in a Changing World* (2016) 117, 146–7.

30 *Report of the International Law Commission, Chapter V: Identification of Customary International Law*, UN GAOR, 73rd sess, Supp No 10, UN Doc A/73/10 (2018) 120 Conclusion 6(3), 127–8 paras 2–5 ('*Report of the International Law Commission, Chapter V: Identification of Customary International Law*').

31 Ibid 129 Conclusion 3 para 9.

32 Henckaerts and Doswald-Beck, *Customary International Humanitarian Law* (*Practice*) (n 4) 2363–493. To view the ICRC's updates to state practice since 2005, see: International Committee of the Red Cross, 'Practice Relating to Rule 100: Fair Trial Guarantees', *ICRC Customary International Humanitarian Law Database* (*Practice*) (Web Page, Updated Database) <https://ihl-databases.icrc.org/customary-ihl/eng/docs/v2_rul_rule100>.

emergency, which includes situations of armed conflict. By contrast, judicial guarantees that are viewed as *non-derogable* cannot be derogated from during armed conflict of any description, which makes such guarantees applicable in all situations and therefore confirms their customary status in NIAC. As stated by Arai, '[All] the fair trial guarantees of a non-derogable nature are *ipso facto* customary [IHL] norms'.[33] The Human Rights Committee has reached the same conclusion in reverse, stating that all judicial guarantees recognised under customary IHL are, by definition, non-derogable.[34] By comparing the list of judicial guarantees in the ICRC *Customary IHL Study* with the views of states as to the derogability of such guarantees, whether at the time of signing the treaty or in subsequent practice, it is possible to draw some conclusions about their customary status in NIAC.

7.3.1.1 Additional Protocol II

As the only IHL treaty to provide a list of judicial guarantees applicable in NIAC, *AP II* provides the clearest evidence as to the non-derogability of such guarantees. Indeed, the drafting history of the *Additional Protocols* reveals that states were intent on including a list of codified guarantees 'for the purpose of precluding state parties invoking the derogation clause under Article 4 of the *ICCPR*, which came into force a year before the adoption of [the *Additional Protocols*]'.[35] While *AP II* is not universally ratified, no state expressed any opposition to the list of judicial guarantees and there is strong evidence to suggest that they are viewed as 'indispensable' in NIAC, as evidenced by a general practice accepted as law.[36] As a result, all judicial guarantees contained in *AP II* are included in the ICRC *Customary ICRC Study*.

---

33 Arai (n 16) 545.

34 UN Human Rights Committee (HRC), UN Doc CCPR/C/GC/32 (n 17) para 6; UN Human Rights Committee (HRC), UN Doc CCPR/C/21/Rev.1/Add.11 (n 17) paras 15–6.

35 Michael Bothe, Karl Partsch and Waldemar Solf, *New Rules for Victims of Armed Conflicts* (Martinus Nijhoff, 1982) 463. See also: International Committee of the Red Cross, *Commentary on the Additional Protocols of 8 June 1977 to the Geneva Conventions of 12 August 1949* (Marinus Nijhoff, 1987) 4597 ('[A] number of delegates supported what was to become Article 6 [of AP II] for the very reason that it reflected provisions of the ICCPR.').

36 International Committee of the Red Cross, 'Practice Relating to Rule 100: Fair Trial Guarantees' (n 32); UN Human Rights Committee (HRC), UN Doc CCPR/C/GC/32 (n 17) para 6; UN Human Rights Committee (HRC), UN Doc CCPR/C/21/Rev.1/Add.11 (n 17) paras 15–6.

7.3.1.2 Additional Protocol I

The list of judicial guarantees in *AP I* includes three judicial guarantees that are not contained in *AP II*; namely, right to examine witnesses, the right to public proceedings, and the right not to be prosecuted twice for the same offence (*ne bis in idem*). For the same reasons as with *AP II*, states party to *AP I* clearly viewed these additional guarantees as non-derogable in IAC. Given that the two treaties were drafted contemporaneously, an argument could be made, however, that the decision of the drafters to include these guarantees in *AP I* – while excluding them from *AP II* – suggests that states viewed them as *derogable* in situations of NIAC.

For its part, the ICRC commentary to common article 3 notes that the right to examine witnesses and the right to public proceedings were not included 'in response to the wish of some delegates to keep the list as short as possible', suggesting that the final text is not determinative of their customary status.[37] This position is supported by the fact that article 6(2) of *AP II* prefaces the list of judicial guarantees with the term 'in particular', suggesting that other guarantees may also be considered indispensable in NIAC. Moreover, bearing in mind evolution of the law,[38] and the practice and legal opinion of states with respect to these specific rights collated in the ICRC Customary IHL Study,[39] there is sufficient evidence to support their status as customary in NIAC.[40]

The third additional rule in *AP I* – the right of *ne bis in idem* – requires special attention because it was explicitly excluded by the drafters of *AP II*

---

37 International Committee of the Red Cross, *Commentary on Geneva Convention III Relative to the Treatment of Prisoners of War, Second Edition* (ICRC, 2020) para 723.

38 *Prosecutor v Tadić (Decision on the Defence Motion for Interlocutory Appeal)* (International Criminal Tribunal for the former Yugoslavia, Appeals Chamber, Case No IT-94-1, 2 October 1995) [97] (*'Tadić Jurisdictional Appeal'*) ('[T]he distinction between interstate wars and civil wars is losing its value as far as human beings are concerned', concluding that 'international legal rules have increasingly emerged or have been agreed upon to regulate internal armed conflict').

39 International Committee of the Red Cross, 'Practice Relating to Rule 100: Fair Trial Guarantees' (n 2).

40 Arai notes that a distinction must sometimes be drawn between the non-derogability of a right and its modification in certain circumstances to protect the right to life of those involved. Arai (n 16) 530–1 ('[A] word of caution ought to be added. In contrast to Article 75(4)(g) API, which does not contain any escape clause, the Report notes that the right to examine witnesses present in courts can be derogated from where there is no alternative to secure witnesses' anonymity and lives.').

'due to the special situation of such conflicts'.[41] Concerned with any limitation on their right to restore law and order following an insurgency and to prosecute rebels for taking up arms, states rejected the applicability of *ne bis in idem* as they thought NSAGs might hold trials for the sole purpose of 'prevent[ing] a future procedure before the courts of the other side'.[42] This concern is misplaced. As noted in the ICRC's updated commentary on common article 3, the right of *ne bis in idem* is formulated in *AP I* as a prohibition on being 'prosecuted or punished *by the same party* for an offence in respect of which a final judgement acquitting or convicting that person has been previously pronounced'.[43] This formulation does not preclude the state from prosecuting an individual who had previously been tried by a NSAG court, as they are opposing parties to the conflict. Given that subsequent state practice with respect to the prosecution of the same conduct by courts with different jurisdiction has been accepted as consistent with the right of *ne bis in idem*, it could be argued that the impediment to recognising its non-derogability in NIAC is no longer present. This and other relevant practice suggest that the right of *ne bis in idem* is equally recognised as customary in NIAC.[44] In sum, there is sufficient evidence to justify including the three additional judicial guarantees in *AP I* in the ICRC's *Customary IHL Study* as applicable in both IAC and NIAC.

7.3.1.3 Geneva Conventions III and IV

The list of judicial guarantees in the ICRC *Customary IHL Study* also includes six guarantees contained in *Geneva Convention III* and *Geneva Convention IV* that do not appear in *AP I* or *AP II*. As a rule, extrapolating general rules of customary IHL from *Geneva Convention III* and *Geneva Convention IV* should be treated with caution on account of their specialised fields of application. The *Geneva Conventions* were drafted in 1949, almost 20 years before the *ICCPR*, so the question of the derogability or otherwise of human rights in times of armed conflict was not yet apparent. Rather,

---

41 Pouria Askary and Katayoun Hosseinnejad, 'Non-State Courts: Illegal or Conditional?: The Case of Da'esh Courts' (2019) 10 *Journal of International Humanitarian Legal Studies* 240, 257; Bothe, Partsch and Solf (n 35) 745.

42 Askary and Hosseinnejad (n 41) 257.

43 International Committee of the Red Cross, *Commentary on Geneva Convention III Relative to the Treatment of Prisoners of War, Second Edition* (n 37) para 723, citing art 75(4)(h) of *AP I* (emphasis added).

44 Henckaerts and Doswald-Beck, *Customary International Humanitarian Law* (*Practice*) (n 4) 2488–93.

each of these conventions sought to regulate very specific issues of IAC. *Geneva Convention III*, applicable to the treatment of PoWs, provides a detailed list of protections, including judicial guarantees, that are afforded exclusively to PoWs as a specially protected category of persons in IAC.[45] Similarly, the provisions of *Geneva Convention IV* relating to judicial guarantees are exclusively applicable to civilians who find themselves in the hands of a belligerent occupying power as a special category of persons requiring extra protection.[46] To justify the customary status of the relevant judicial guarantees contained within these treaties, it would need to be shown that states currently view them as non-derogable in all situations of armed conflict. Despite this high threshold, four of the six judicial guarantees in the ICRC *Customary IHL Study* that are taken from *Geneva Convention III* and/or *Geneva Convention IV* (and which are not included in either of the *Additional Protocols*) appear to be recognised as non-derogable by states and are therefore 'recognised as indispensable' under customary IHL applicable in all conflicts:

(i) the right to defend oneself or to be assisted by a lawyer of one's own choice;
(ii) the right to free legal assistance if the interests of justice so require;
(iii) the right of the accused to communicate freely with counsel; and
(iv) the right to an interpreter.[47]

For the remaining two judicial guarantees – the right to be tried without undue delay and the right to appeal a conviction – there appears to be insufficient evidence of a general practice accepted as law to assert that states view them as non-derogable, thereby casting doubt on their customary status in all situations of armed conflict.

Regarding the right to be tried without undue delay, neither General Comment 29 of the United Nations Human Rights Committee nor any of

---

45 *Geneva Convention Relative to the Treatment of Prisoners of War*, opened for signature 12 August 1949, 75 UNTS 135, arts 4–5 (entered into force 21 October 1950) ('*Geneva Convention III*').

46 *Geneva Convention Relative to the Protection of Civilian Persons in Time of War*, opened for signature 12 August 1949, 75 UNTS 287 art 4 (entered into force 21 October 1950) ('*Geneva Convention IV*').

47 International Committee of the Red Cross, 'Practice Relating to Rule 100: Fair Trial Guarantees' (n 32); Arai (n 16) 536–45 (Arai cites additional practice tending to affirm the non-derogability and resultant customary status of the right to defend oneself or to be assisted by a lawyer, the right to legal assistance, the right to sufficient time and facilities to prepare a defence, and the right to the assistance of an interpreter or translator).

the documents prepared by other human rights treaty bodies claim that it is non-derogable. Indeed, the Inter-American Commission on Human Rights (IACmHR) Report on Terrorism and Human Rights (regarded as the 'most liberal') expressly acknowledges its derogability in a public emergency.[48] For its part, the ICRC updated commentary to common article 3 states that 'undue delay could also taint a trial in the context of a non-international armed conflict and *should* thus be taken into account to assess the fairness of such a trial', while conceding that, 'The right to be tried 'within a reasonable time' may involve a specific assessment in the 'exceptional circumstances'.[49]

As for the right to appeal a conviction, the ICRC *Customary IHL Study* reaches the following conclusion.

> [T]he influence of human rights on this issue is such that it can be argued that the right of appeal proper – and not only the right to be informed whether appeal is available – has become a basic component of fair trial rights in the context of armed conflict.[50]

Arai contends, however, that 'the Study's assertion is not backed by the empirical evidence in a rigorous manner that otherwise characterises its meticulous survey in many respects', noting that the Study's reliance on national constitutional provisions, human rights treaties, and military manuals does not actually support its conclusion.[51] While Arai tapers this criticism with the observation that it 'does not negate the possibility that this right may be entering the domain of customary IHL',[52] others have similarly noted that 'it is difficult to state that current international humanitarian law requires the right to appeal even though such a right exists under human rights'.[53]

---

48 Arai (n 16) 541 ('However, the Report emphasises that a delay exceptionally longer than would otherwise be acceptable in non-emergency situations can be recognised only pursuant to two specific conditions: (I) the delay must be subordinated "at all times" to judicial review; and (II) it must not be prolonged or indefinite.').

49 International Committee of the Red Cross, *Commentary on Geneva Convention III Relative to the Treatment of Prisoners of War, Second Edition* (n 37) para 724 (emphasis added).

50 Henckaerts and Doswald-Beck, *Customary International Humanitarian Law (Rules)* (n 4) 369–70.

51 Arai (n 16) 544.

52 Ibid.

53 Klamberg (n 19) 244; See also: Louis Doswald-Beck, 'Judicial Guarantees under Common Article 3' in Andrew Clapham, Paola Gaeta and Marco Sassòli (eds), *The 1949*

Irrespective of whether this is, or continues to be, the case, the ICC should identify the list of judicial guarantees recognised as indispensable by reference to customary IHL, rather than relying on IHRL or *AP II* in isolation. Not only is this correct from a methodological standpoint, but it will also provide necessary clarification on this area of law.

7.3.2 *Applying the 'Hierarchy of Evidence': Judicial Guarantees Recognised under Customary International Humanitarian Law Despite Contrary State Practice*

The ICRC *Customary IHL Study* does not explain how it deals with widespread support for prohibitive humanitarian rules on paper and significant evidence of contrary state practice on the ground.[54] This phenomenon is no less prevalent with respect to judicial guarantees. Consistent with the 'contextually dependent hierarchy of evidence' (see Chapter 3), evidence of states violating judicial guarantees in practice – especially where such violations are denied or qualified – is not detrimental to proving the existence of a rule of CIL,[55] for the reason that such contrary state practice is afforded less probative weight compared with the representative forms of what states say and do in the international diplomatic arena. To repeat Richard Baxter's 1965 assessment, 'The firm statement by the State of what it considers to be the rule is far better evidence of its position than what can be pieced together from the actions of that country at different times and in a variety of contexts'.[56]

Fair trial guarantees recognised as customary are routinely violated by states. In the context of judicial review, the right to a fair trial has 'long been the most heavily-litigated' of the provisions of the *European*

Geneva Conventions: A Commentary (OUP 2016) 469, 483; Andrew T Guzman and Jerome Hsiang, 'Reinvigorating Customary International Law' in Curtis A Bradley (ed), *Custom's Future: International Law in a Changing World* (CUP 2016) 275, 283.

54 Oscar Schachter, 'New Custom: Power, *Opinio Juris* and Contrary State Practice' in Krzysztof Skubiszewski (ed), *Theory of International Law at the Threshold of the 21st Century* (Springer, 1996) 531, 538–9.

55 *Military and Paramilitary Activities in and against Nicaragua* (n 20) [186]; *Prosecutor v Furundžija (Judgment)* (International Criminal Tribunal for the former Yugoslavia, Trial Chamber, Case No IT-95-17/1-T, 10 December 1998) [137]–[138] ('*Furundžija Trial Judgment*'); Anthea Roberts, 'Traditional and Modern Approaches to Customary International Law: A Reconciliation' (2001) 95(4) *American Journal of International Law* 757, 776.

56 Richard Baxter, 'Multilateral Treaties as Evidence of Customary International Law' (1965) 41 *British Yearbook of International Law* 275, 300.

Convention on Human Rights.[57] Indeed, one study found more violations of the right to a fair trial than of the ten other *Convention* rights combined.[58] A similar trend has been observed before the IACMHR.[59] Amnesty International's 2021 Report, meanwhile, documented violations of the right to a fair trial, extrajudicial killings, or obtaining confessions through torture in 48 of 149 countries reviewed.[60] It concluded that in Russia and in much of Eastern Europe and Central Asia, 'violations of the right to a fair trial remained widespread',[61] while in 'countries including Egypt, Iran, Israel and the Occupied Palestinian Territories (OPT), Libya, Saudi Arabia and Syria, exceptional courts, such as military, revolutionary and security courts, were used extensively, and trials grossly violated fair trial standards'.[62]

With the possible exception of a few states attempting to modify certain fair trial norms with respect to terrorism offences, states do not claim that they have the right to violate judicial guarantees that have been recognised as indispensable. Examples in which states have been criticised for denying a fair trial during armed conflict and other emergency situations tend to have been met with denial or equivocation.[63] As with most prohibitive humanitarian rules contained in widely ratified treaties (see Chapter 3), the examples of contrary state practice 'on the ground' can be contrasted with broad acceptance and compliance in representative forms of state practice

---

57 Ryan Goss, 'The Undermining of Article 6 ECHR' in Gerd Oberleitner and others (eds), *European Yearbook on Human Rights 2019* (Intersentia, 2019) 295, 296.

58 Ibid. See also: René Provost, *Rebel Courts: The Administration of Justice by Armed Insurgents* (OUP 2021) 308 ('In the European human rights regime, for example, more than half of all cases from 1959 to 2019 dealt with Article 6 on the right to a fair trial, more than those dealing with all other rights combined.').

59 Christian Steiner and Marie-Christine Fuchs, *Comentario Convención Americana Sobre Derechos Humanos* (Konrad Adenauer Stiftung, 2nd ed, 2019) 263.

60 Amnesty International, 'Amnesty International Report 2020/21: The State of the World's Human Rights' (Published Report, 7 April 2021) <https://www.amnesty.org/en/documents/pol10/3202/2021/en/> (report was manually searched for references to denials of the right to a fair trial and/or extra judicial killings).

61 Ibid 44.

62 Ibid 53.

63 Leandro Despouy, Special Rapporteur, *Report on the Independence of Judges and Lawyers: Situations in Specific Countries Territories*, UN Doc A/HRC/11/41/Add.1 (19 May 2009) ('*Report on the Independence of Judges and Lawyers: Situations in Specific Countries Territories*') (the Report compiles urgent appeals sent to 52 countries concerning allegations affecting the independence of judges or violating the right to a fair trial. All countries that responded denied such allegations by presenting alternative accounts. No state claimed it was justified in denying fundamental fair trial guarantees.).

in international diplomatic fora. States and the broader international community have no appetite to deny the customary status of such rules in response to contrary state practice, no matter how widespread such contrary practice may be.[64]

Rather than ignore the phenomenon of contrary practice (which is often the approach taken by international courts) or attempt to change the theoretical foundation of CIL by prioritising *opinio juris* over state practice for certain normative rules (which is the approach advocated by many scholars), courts should transparently afford more weight to representative forms of state practice in the identification of prohibitive humanitarian rules and comparatively little weight to non-compliance with the rule, especially where it is denied or qualified. This approach would confirm the customary status of those judicial guarantees discussed so far.

In sum, there is likely to be sufficient evidence of representative state practice and *opinio juris* for all but two of the ICRC's list of judicial guarantees to be confirmed as 'indispensable' under customary IHL applicable in NIAC. The two guarantees with arguably insufficient confirmatory practice accepted as law are: the right to be tried without undue delay and the right to an appeal. For the other guarantees, evidence of contrary state practice on the ground should be treated as less probative and therefore non-detrimental to upholding their customary status.

7.4 Applying 'All Judicial Guarantees Recognized as Indispensable' to Non-state Courts

As we have seen, the rule that all courts in armed conflict be 'regularly constituted' means something different when applied to NSAGs. While core elements of the rule remain the same (i.e., that the court has a pre-existing legal basis authorising its establishment and that its jurisdictional competence is limited by the scope of that legal basis), the origin and scope of the

64 Ibid; Pieter Kooijmans, Special Rapporteur, *Report on Torture and Other Cruel, Inhuman or Degrading Treatment or Punishment*, UN Doc E/CN.4/1988/17 (12 January 1988) 23 para 76 ('*Report on Torture and other Cruel, Inhuman or Degrading Treatment or Punishment*') ('How can this remarkable discrepancy between legal opinion (opinio Juris) and practice be explained, a discrepancy which is not unknown in the field of human rights in general but is all the more remarkable with respect to torture, since here the practice is never justified by those who are alleged to have practised it but is flatly denied.').

pre-existing legal bases are different. For states, the origin and scope are determined by the state's own domestic laws and constitutional limitations. For NSAGs, it is IHL that provides the legal basis to establish courts and limits their jurisdictional competence.

We now consider whether there is any legal authority on which to assert that the obligation under IHL to 'afford all judicial guarantees recognized as indispensable' means something different for the courts of NSAGs. First, consistent with most of the literature in this field, there are strong normative reasons for accepting a different standard of compliance with judicial guarantees by NSAGs, providing the core content of such guarantees is not violated. In short, differentiated means of compliance is better than no compliance. Second, while there is no explicit rule under IHL that justifies modifying NSAG compliance with judicial guarantees, multiple proposals in the scholarship provide some legal basis and thus warrant further attention. Finally, the prosecutorial discretion inherent in both the ICC's 'gravity' requirement – and in article 8(2)(c)(IV), specifically – enable the ICC to apply a differentiated standard to NSAGs in practice by only prosecuting serious violations of judicial guarantees.

It should be noted that this discussion is largely hypothetical. Field studies reveal that NSAG courts generally fail to adequately comply with fair trial guarantees.[65] However, such studies do not pre-determine the question of whether they can fulfil the minimum legal requirements; neither do they discount the importance of determining *how* they can fulfil such requirements as a means of fostering greater compliance with IHL.

7.4.1 *Normative Arguments for Accepting Differentiated Responsibilities of Non-state Armed Groups*

The normative view, shared by most legal scholars writing on this issue, is that judicial guarantees may be adapted to make NSAG compliance with IHL possible, but only insofar as such adaptation does undermine the core

---

65 Jan Willms, 'Justice through Armed Groups' Governance – An Oxymoron?' (2012) 40 *Collaborative Research Centre* (*SFB*) *- Governance Working Paper Series* 3; Askary and Hosseinnejad (n 16); International Legal Assistance Consortium, 'ILAC Rule of Law Assessment Report: Syria 2017' (Web Page, 2017) <http://www.ilacnet.org/wp-content/uploads/2017/04/Syria2017.pdf>; Amnesty International, 'Torture was My Punishment: Abductions, Torture and Summary Killings under Armed Group Rule in Aleppo and Idleb' (Web Page, 2016) <https://www.amnestyusa.org/wp-content/uploads/2017/04/embargoed_5_july-_torture_was_my_punishment-final_version.pdf>; Hyeran Jo, *Compliant Rebels: Rebel Groups and International Law in World Politics* (CUP 2015) 124.

of the rule.[66] This normative view is premised on the position that fostering NSAG compliance with judicial guarantees is more important than insisting on unachievable standards. As Sandesh Sivakumaran puts it, 'Rules that are inherently beyond the reach of armed groups and which they have no hope of meeting serve little useful purpose'.[67]

It is no secret that most NSAGs will have significantly fewer resources than states. For many NSAGs, the executive branch (if there is one) will not be so clearly distinguishable from those tasked with performing judicial functions. Moreover, NSAGs with limited or no territorial control may be nomadic, have minimal access to persons with technical legal training, or be unable to locate or compel persons to appear. In such situations, justice may still need to be done. Indeed, trial by a NSAG may be the only practical alternative to summary justice or execution – the very rationale for the codification of the right to indispensable judicial guarantees in common article 3 and *AP II*.

It is equally clear that modifying standards of judicial guarantees for NSAGs to the point where they are no longer recognisable also defeats the purpose of the rule and contradicts the notion that such guarantees are 'indispensable'. Sivakumaran acknowledges the need to maintain this balance, stating that, 'At some point, rights cease to be modified and start to be breached'.[68] Nehal Bhuta similarly cautions that 'by relativizing further the standards of a fair trial to not only an armed conflict but also to the concrete situation of an armed group, we risk embarking upon a slippery slope that could erode the protection promised by the guarantees to vanishing point'.[69]

---

66 Sandesh Sivakumaran, 'Courts of Armed Opposition Groups: Fair Trials or Summary Justice?' (2009) 7(3) *Journal of International Criminal Justice* 489, 505–7; Provost (n 58) 303–53; Nehal Bhuta, 'Joint Series on International Law and Armed Conflict: Fair Trial Guarantees in Armed Conflict', *EJIL: Talk! Blog of the European Journal of International Law* (Blog Post, 22 September 2016) 596 <https://www.ejiltalk.org/joint-series-on-international-law-and-armed-conflict-fair-trial-guarantees-in-armed-conflict/>; cf Hannes Jöbstl, 'Bridging the Accountability Gap: Armed Non-state Actors and the Investigation and Prosecution of War Crimes' (2020) 18(3) *Journal of International Criminal Justice* 567.

67 Sivakumaran (n 66) 501.

68 Ibid 506.

69 Bhuta (n 66) ('A further dimension of relativity in the interpretation of the guarantees seems demanded by the circumstances, lest the exhortation to conduct fair trials appear nothing but a poisoned chalice to the armed group – simply another way in

Ultimately, while there may be strong normative reasons for modifying the mode of compliance with judicial guarantees in a way that accommodates the specific circumstances of the NSAG in question, the 'indispensable' nature of such guarantees means that their core content cannot be lawfully undermined. As stated by the ICRC, while the question of whether NSAGs respect judicial guarantees is a 'question of fact and needs to be determined on a case-by-case basis […] [n]o trial should be held, whether by State authorities or by non-State armed groups, if these guarantees cannot be provided'.[70]

7.4.2 *Legal Authority for Accepting Differentiated Responsibilities of NSAGs*

While there is no explicit authority for accepting differentiated responsibilities of NSAGs under IHL, at least two proposals in the scholarship provide some legal basis for this concept: Marco Sassòli's 'sliding-scale' obligations of NSAG; and Yuval Shany's application of the concept of 'common but differentiated responsibilities' to the obligations of NSAGs.[71] Neither Sassòli nor Shany discusses their proposals in relation to judicial guarantees specifically. However, Sandesh Sivakumaran and René Provost apply similar language and concepts when advocating for the acceptance of a modified implementation of judicial guarantees when applied to the courts of NSAGs.[72] Consideration of the merits of each position reveals that they provide further weight to the normative reasons for accepting differentiated responsibilities of NSAGs noted above.

7.4.2.1 Sassòli's Sliding Scale of Obligations

Writing specifically about the inferior capacity of NSAGs, Sassòli suggests that IHL may accommodate the modification or non-observance of some rules (including those without an in-built margin of appreciation)[73] under

which it will be condemned for falling short of international legal standards with which it cannot possibly comply.').

70 International Committee of the Red Cross, *Commentary on Geneva Convention III Relative to the Treatment of Prisoners of War, Second Edition* (n 37) 730.

71 Marco Sassòli and Yuval Shany, 'Should the Obligations of States and Armed groups under International Humanitarian Law Really be Equal?' (2011) 93(882) *International Review of the Red Cross* 425.

72 Sivakumaran (n 66) 505–7; Provost (n 58) 303–53.

73 Several IHL provisions contain an in-built margin of appreciation that is subject to the capacity of the party to the conflict to whom it is applied. For example, the law of

the principle that 'international law can never be construed as requiring what is materially impossible'.[74] In support, Sassòli cites the customary rule of *force majeure* (according to which a state shall not be responsible for an internationally wrongful act where unforeseen circumstances make the performance of the obligation materially impossible)[75] and the right to terminate, withdraw or suspend treaties, where performance of the treaty is materially impossible.[76] Given the considerable variance in the organisational structure of NSAGs, Sassòli proposes a 'sliding scale' of obligations that can be adjusted to the capacity of the NSAG in question.[77] This is 'not revolutionary', he argues, as *AP II*, as a matter of treaty law,[78] already restricts its obligations to those NSAGs which control territory and are capable of launching sustained military campaigns.

7.4.2.2 Shany's Application of 'Common but Differentiated Responsibilities'

Without disagreeing with the normative position that the fulfilment of IHL obligations may vary due to the capacity of the NSAG in question, Shany cautions against relativising this process to the point where the core of the obligation is sacrificed to achieve compliance.

> [S]trongly linking the scope of IHL obligations to organizational capacities and military rationales, as proposed by Sassòli, represents a dangerous concession to practical contingencies, which may decrease the

---

proportionality in article 57 of *AP I* requires the parties to the conflict to take 'all feasible precautions' to minimise civilian harm when launching an attack, the responsibility of commanders under article 86(2) of *AP I* for failing to take 'all feasible measures' to prevent or repress breaches of IHL, and the obligation under article 5(2) of *AP II* to respect certain (albeit non-fundamental) rights of persons in detention 'within the limits of their capabilities'.

74 Marco Sassòli, 'International Humanitarian Law Applicable to Non-International Armed Conflicts: The Importance of Taking Armed Groups into Account' (Online Publication, 2019) 10 <https://www.unisabana.edu.co/fileadmin/Archivos_de_usuario/Imagenes/Imagenes_Programas/Imagenes_Pregrado/Derecho/anuario_DIH/SASSOLI_FINAL_.pdf>.

75 International Law Commission, *Articles on the Responsibility of States for Internationally Wrongful Acts* (ILC, 2001) vol II, art 23.

76 Sassòli (n 74) 9.

77 Sassòli and Shany (n 71) 427–31.

78 Noting that its provisions that are now regarded as customary apply in all armed conflicts.

> incentive for compliance and put in question the applicability of IHL to changing battlefield conditions.[79]

Under a formalised scheme, Shany argues, 'parties would have a strong disincentive to invest in capacity-building (such as establishing prison camps or acquiring more discriminating weapons)', as it would divert resources from the fight while simultaneously subjecting them to increased legal regulation.[80] While it is possible to counterargue that many NSAGs have myriad reasons for wanting to engage in effective governance and military capabilities that enable them to obtain the requisite capacity (at least theoretically) to comply with IHL – indeed, in many instances, their survival may depend on such capacity – the point still stands that a formalised sliding-scale may be liable to abuse by NSAGs.

Shany's solution is to adopt the concept of 'common but differentiated responsibilities' – a term primarily employed in international environmental law and international trade law. Gabriella Blum initially advocated for this approach under the law of IAC as a means of imposing greater obligations on states with more sophisticated weaponry than the base level of what is demanded of all states during armed conflict. Blum argues that, if correlating obligation with capabilities is accepted in the context of international trade and environmental law 'at least as a normative aspiration', there is no reason why it should not apply in war.[81] When applied to NSAGs under the law of NIAC, Shany argues, the concept of 'common but differentiated responsibilities' gives effect to the principle of the equal application of the law: 'substantive equality requires us to treat differently placed legal subjects in a differentiated manner'.[82]

The principle of common but differentiated responsibilities certainly appears to be a suitable fit for NSAGs which are equally bound by the same law regulating states in NIAC but whose capacity to fulfil those obligations will not, except in the most exceptional circumstances, be equal to that of the state. It is arguably not much different from Sassòli's sliding scale in practice, but the language focuses more on differentiated means of fulfilling an obligation that remains common to both parties under the principle of equal

79 Sassòli and Shany (n 71) 433.

80 Ibid.

81 Gabriella Blum, 'On a Differential Law of War' (2011) 52(1) *Harvard International Law Journal* 163, 164–5.

82 Sassòli and Shany (n 71) 435.

application of the law. The language of common but differentiated responsibilities is therefore preferred, without discounting the merits of Sassòli's sliding-scale conception.

7.4.2.3 Applying 'Common but Differentiated Responsibilities' in Fulfilling the Obligation to Afford Judicial Guarantees

In advocating for the acceptance of differentiated responsibilities of NSAGS in the implementation of judicial guarantees, Sivakumaran draws some analogies with state practice. He argues that modifying judicial guarantees to accommodate the nature of the conflict while respecting their substance 'should not be cause for concern for there is a history of their differential interpretation based on the exigencies of the situation'.[83] In support, Sivakumaran refers to the decision of US Supreme Court Justice Stevens in *Hamdan*, which states that 'the procedures adopted to try Hamdan deviate[d] from those governing courts-martial in ways not justified by any "evident practical need"',[84] which suggests that 'practical need may allow for a variation of procedure'.[85] Sivakumaran also refers to the *gacaca* courts in Rwanda following the 1994 genocide, in which judicial guarantees were adapted to account for the large number of persons implicated in the crime and other realities of the situation.[86] Finally, Sivakumaran notes that the obligation to provide 'adequate time and facilities for the preparation of a defence' (which is the human rights equivalent of the obligation under IHL to provide the 'necessary rights and means of a defence') has been interpreted by the Human Rights Committee as requiring 'an assessment of the individual circumstances of each case'.[87] Note, however, that this is an example of an obligation with an in-built margin of appreciation, and is therefore perhaps less persuasive in justifying a general ability to modify compliance with IHL rules.

Provost's field research on the administration of justice by NSAG courts provides useful illustrations of how the differentiated responsibilities of NSAGS might operate in practice, while still satisfying the core content of

83 Sivakumaran (n 66) 505.

84 *Hamdan v Rumsfeld* 548 U.S. 557, 71 per Stevens J (United States Supreme Court, 2006) ('*Hamdan v Rumsfeld* ').

85 Sivakumaran (n 66) 505.

86 Ibid 505–6. See also: William Schabas, 'Genocide Trials and Gacaca Courts' (2005) 3 *Journal of International Criminal Justice* 879; Jacques Fierens, 'Gacaca Courts: Between Fantasy and Reality' (2005) 3(4) *Journal of International Criminal Justice* 896.

87 Sivakumaran (n 66) 506.

the judicial guarantee in question. For example, when considering the guarantee that no one shall be held guilty of any criminal offence 'which did not constitute a criminal offence, under the law, at the time it was committed' (i.e., the principle of legality), Provost notes that some NSAGs, like the FARC in Colombia had 'basically no legislation and tended to rely on community-based standards', whereas the Taliban or Islamic State 'claimed to apply "pure" Sharīʿa standards'.[88]

> The answer is not to require the formalisation or codification of rebel law, but rather to enquire whether a person in a conflict zone under the effective authority of a rebel group could reasonably appraise what conduct was prohibited. [...] Common crimes punished by insurgent courts, such as theft or sexual assault, would undoubtedly have been known to be prohibited acts by everyone concerned.[89]

In another example, Provost examines the judicial guarantee that accused persons have the right to legal counsel. As noted in a document issued by the *Farabundo Martí National Liberation Front* (FMLN) in El Salvador,

> The particular mechanism necessary for defence must be adjusted to the real possibilities of the zone where the trial is held. One cannot insist, for example, that the defence counsel be a licensed attorney when in the region no one exists with this specialization.[90]

Moreover, Provost notes, providing counsel with technical legal training under the relevant state's domestic law may be counterproductive before the courts of the Islamic State or the Taliban, as such groups 'have objected to lawyers for ideological reasons, and thus exclude them from judicial proceedings even if they may be available'.[91]

Provost also argues that the right to legal counsel is already considered as prioritising substance over form, noting that the Spanish text of the *American Convention on Human Rights* was changed to accommodate the 'reality that, in many Latin American countries, individuals who are not licensed

---

88 Provost (n 58) 315.

89 Ibid.

90 FMLN, *Principios, Normativos y Medidas Dispuestas por el* FMLN *en el Transcurso de la Guerra* (1991).

91 Provost (n 58) 326.

attorneys provide legal assistance'.[92] Similarly, he notes, the African Commission on Human and Peoples' Rights has held that 'the right to be defended by counsel' must be interpreted to accommodate legal assistance by paralegals due to the low number of qualified lawyers.[93] Provost concludes by arguing that substantive compliance with the right to legal counsel must always reflect what is fair and useful in the circumstances. For NSAGs, this may mean something different than it would for states.

> Ultimately, counsel must be able to provide meaningful advice, and what that is will mirror the nature of the court itself. A state court applying formal law may well normally call for a licenced attorney with a university legal education, but a popular assembly applying community norms will require someone with local knowledge, while a religious court applying Sharī'a will require someone with religious training.[94]

In conclusion, there is no explicit rule under IHL stipulating that the content of IHL rules may be modified due to the capacity of the group. However, there appears to be acceptance in legal scholarship that the implementation of IHL rules by NSAG will almost invariably differ in its completeness when compared to states. Indeed, it could be argued that states accepted this fact when signing reciprocal treaties governing their relationship with NSAGs. Where NSAGs are unable to comply with the core content of judicial guarantees, they are prohibited from holding trials. Suggested alternatives to criminal trials include internment where the individual poses a security risk, receiving legal training and support from third parties, or third-party transfer of accused persons.[95] Naturally, each of these alternatives comes with its own challenges.[96]

---

92 Ibid.

93 Ibid.

94 Ibid 127.

95 Jöbstl (n 66) 580–7; International Committee of the Red Cross, *Commentary on Geneva Convention III Relative to the Treatment of Prisoners of War, Second Edition* (n 37) para 730.

96 Jöbstl (n 66) 591 (noting an example in which a judicial monitoring system of the LTTE courts in Sri Lanka had to be cancelled 'for fear of legitimising the armed group', and the fact that the government of the Democratic Republic of Congo prevented defence attorneys organised by the local United Nations Mission (MONUC) to assist the *Mouvement de Libération du Congo* (MLC) from boarding the plane).

In 2024, Trial Chamber X in *Al Hassan* lent judicial weight to the notion of common but differentiated responsibilities of NSAGs applying IHL standards. When interpreting whether the Islamic Tribunals in Northern Mali were sufficiently independent to be considered 'regularly constituted', Trial Chamber X stated that it was 'mindful that a court established by a non-state actor may not be able to successfully comply with the same level of independence required of a State court'.[97] The Chamber took note of the Defence's argument that 'the requirement of "independence" should also consider how [non-state actors] have a more "fluid" and "integrated" structure', and concluded that 'reasonable flexibility should be applied in assessing non-state armed groups' capacity to adhere to these standards'.[98] The willingness of Trial Chamber X to consider the relative capacity of the Islamic Tribunal to adhere to the requirements of the *Rome Statute* sets an important precedent for realistically adjudicating NSAGs' compliance with IHL.

7.4.2 *Discretion as a Means of Accepting Differentiated Compliance with Judicial Guarantees*

In the absence of an explicit rule accepting differentiated responsibilities of NSAGs, another means of giving effect to relative capacities of NSAGS is by choosing not to prosecute mere irregularities in the fulfilment of judicial guarantees. The 'gravity requirement' in the *Rome Statute* amounts to a form of prosecutorial discretion. Article 53(2)(b) states that the Prosecutor shall inform the Pre-Trial Chamber of his or her decision not to prosecute where it is deemed that the case would be inadmissible under article 17. One reason for inadmissibility under article 17 is where the case 'is not of sufficient gravity to justify further action by the Court'.[99] If an investigation by the Prosecutor were to reveal that a NSAG's compliance with judicial guarantees was irregular in form but satisfactory in substance, the Prosecutor could opt not to proceed due to lack of sufficient gravity. Of course, if there were evidence of other crimes within the Court's jurisdiction that were of sufficient gravity, it could proceed with those instead.

97 *Al Hassan Trial Judgment* (n 3) [1173].

98 Ibid.

99 *Rome Statute of the International Criminal Court*, opened for signature 17 July 1998, 2187 UNTS 38544, art 17(1)(d) (entered into force 1 July 2002) ('*Rome Statute of the International Criminal Court*').

The *Elements of Crimes* explicitly includes a form of judicial discretion applicable to the war crime of denying a fair trial contrary to article 8(2)(c)(IV). This offence has been violated where 'the court that rendered judgement did not afford all other judicial guarantees generally recognized as indispensable under international law'. In a footnote to this element, it is stated that 'the Court should consider whether, in the light of all relevant circumstances, the cumulative effect of factors with respect to guarantees deprived the person or persons of a fair trial'.[100] This direction in the *Elements of Crimes* clearly enables the Court to consider whether the provision of fair trial guarantees was complied with in substance, notwithstanding certain irregularities. The references to 'all relevant circumstances' and 'the cumulative effect of factors with respect to guarantees' could be used to determine that the administration of justice by NSAGS, though irregular, did not amount to the denial of a fair trial in the circumstances of case.

It is necessary to highlight that the nature of the crime for which an individual is being prosecuted, and the punitive sentence that attaches to it, may also be significant in determining the content and applicability of judicial guarantees. The Human Rights Committee notes that, while judicial guarantees *not* recognised as indispensable under IHL are derogable, this is not the case where the denial of such guarantees interferes with a *non-derogable* human right, such as the freedom from the arbitrary deprivation of the right to life. Accordingly, where an individual is subject to the death penalty, the Human Rights Committee contends that *all* judicial guarantees must be protected, as otherwise the imposition of the death penalty would amount to an arbitrary deprivation of the right to life.[101]

Applying the Human Rights Committee's position to the obligation to 'afford all judicial guarantees recognized as indispensable under IHL', it could be argued that the death penalty can only be imposed where the accused has been afforded the full suite of guarantees recognised under human rights law. When applied to NSAGS courts specifically, this could mean that most NSAGS would be precluded from enforcing the death penalty. Given the significant risks that the exigencies of a NIAC pose to the impartial administration of justice (by both states and NSAGS), this would surely be a positive development.

100 *International Criminal Court, Elements of Crimes* (n 14) 34 nn 59.
101 UN Human Rights Committee (HRC), UN Doc CCPR/C/GC/32 (n 17) para 59.

7.5 Conclusion

Under article 8(2)(c)(IV) of the *Rome Statute*, criminal sentences in NIAC must be administered by a regularly constituted court affording all judicial guarantees recognised as indispensable. The determination of which guarantees are 'recognised as indispensable' requires the ICC to apply external sources of law. Interpretating the ordinary meaning of this term, in its context and in light of its object and purpose, leads to the conclusion that courts in NIAC must afford those guarantees that have been recognised as indispensable under customary IHL applicable in NIAC. In *Al Hassan*, Pre-Trial Chamber I took an overly broad approach by requiring all judicial guarantees recognised as indispensable under IHRL,[102] while Trial Chamber X was overly restrictive in only recognising those guarantees contained in *AP II*.[103] Subsequent ICC Chambers should take the necessary step of determining this question by reference to customary IHL.

This chapter has contributed to this process by proposing a list of judicial guarantees that can be considered indispensable in all situations of armed conflict under customary IHL. Starting with the guarantees recognised in the ICRC Customary IHL Study, it was suggested that only two such guarantees may lack the necessary general practice accepted as law (or state practice and *opinio juris*) to be considered applicable in NIAC. These were the right to be tried without undue delay and the right to an appeal. Although essential under human rights law and indispensable in certain situations of IAC, current practice suggests that states may view these rights as derogable in NIAC. Importantly, all other judicial guarantees could be recognised as indispensable in all conflicts under customary IHL by applying the 'contextually dependent hierarchy of evidence' developed in Chapter 3, such that the widespread evidence affirming such guarantees in treaties and other forms of representative practice is treated as more probative than evidence of non-compliance on the ground. If subsequent ICC Chambers were to engage in this process, it would help bring clarity to the list of judicial guarantees recognised under customary IHL.

Finally, it is essential to consider the different capacities of NSAGs when adjudicating compliance with the prohibition on unfair trials. NSAGs that control territory are required under international law to maintain law and order and in some cases prosecute serious international crimes. To

102 *Al Hassan Pre-Trial Judgment* (n 2) [383]–[386].

103 *Al Hassan Trial Judgment* (n 3) [1176]–[1178].

subsequently hold the members of such groups criminally responsible for attempting to discharge these obligations within their relative capabilities would be counterproductive and contrary to the spirit of the law. Accordingly, it is necessary for the ICC to adopt some form of the 'common but differentiated responsibilities' doctrine so that NSAG members are only prosecuted for violating the substance of fair trial guarantees, as opposed to mere procedural irregularities. Trial Chamber X in *Al Hassan* appears to have embraced this approach. Prosecutorial discretion will also have a role to play in ensuring that only serious violations of fair trial rights by NSAGs are prosecuted as war crimes.

CHAPTER 8

Conclusion

In this book, I have examined the extent to which judges of the International Criminal Court (ICC) should interpret the Court's war crimes jurisdiction consistently with customary international humanitarian law (customary IHL) in accordance with the principle of systemic integration in article 31(3)(c) of the *Vienna Convention on the Law of Treaties* (VCLT).[1] I proposed three hypotheses to explain the reluctance of ICC judges to apply the principle of systemic integration: (1) that they view the *Elements of Crimes* as obviating the need to rely on external sources of law; (2) that they see the *Elements* as legally binding due to the principle of legality and therefore treat customary international law ('CIL') as a subsidiary interpretive aid; and (3) that they view CIL as something to avoid due to the confusion surrounding its conceptual boundaries and the types of evidence necessary to prove its existence. Quantitative analysis reveals that the ICC is predominantly unwilling to rely on the principle of systemic integration in both form and substance. Qualitative analysis of select cases tends to confirm Hypotheses 1 and 2, although there is need for a greater sample size and further study. Hypothesis 3 could not be empirically tested against ICC jurisprudence, but finds support in the drafting history of the *Rome Statute*.

Several ICL scholars have advocated for the *Rome Statute* to be interpreted consistently with CIL;[2] some have explicitly argued that such consistency is required by the principle of systemic integration under article 31(3)(c) of the *VCLT*.[3] Leena Grover convincingly posits that, because the

1 *Vienna Convention on the Law of Treaties*, opened for signature 23 May 1969, 1155 UNTS 331 (entered into force 27 January 1980) ('*VCLT*').

2 Caroline Davidson, 'How to Read International Criminal Law: Strict Construction and the Rome Statute of the International Criminal Court' (2017) 91(1) *St John's Law Review* 37, 54–6; Leila Sadat and Jarrod Jolly, 'Seven Canons of ICC Treaty Interpretation: Making Sense of Article 25's Rorschach Blot' (2014) 27(3) *Leiden Journal of International Law* 755, 762–3, 770; Gudrun Hochmayr, 'Applicable Law in Practice and Theory: Interpreting Article 21 of the ICC Statute' (2014) 12(4) *Journal of International Criminal Justice* 655, 663.

3 Leena Grover, *Interpreting Crimes in the Rome Statute of the International Criminal Court* (CUP 2014) 347–9, 407–8; Robert Cryer, 'Royalism and the King: Article 21 of the Rome Statute and the Politics of Sources' (2009) 12(3) *New Criminal Law Review: An International and Interdisciplinary Journal* 390, 398; Fausto Pocar, 'International Criminal Justice and the Unifying Role of Customary Law' (2016) 21(2–3) *Uniform Law Review* 171, 175–6.

 | DOI:10.1163/9789004690042_009

crimes in the *Statute* reflect CIL, there is a presumption of interpretive consistency that is only rebutted by a legislative intent to depart from CIL.[4] Grover's conclusion reflects the approach of the International Law Commission ('ILC') in its 'Report on Fragmentation of International Law', in which it determined that any departure from an interpretation consistent with applicable international law rules must be justified by reference to the text of the treaty in question.[5] As a multilateral treaty, the *Rome Statute* is not exempt from these rules.

What has been missing from the literature is an analysis of whether, and to what extent, the ICC has applied the principle of systemic integration in practice. Similarly, there are relatively few attempts to explore the reasons for the ICC's reluctance to comply with this principle, consider what it means for the future of the Court, or to offer alternative approaches. This book contributes to the field in several meaningful ways. Through both quantitative and qualitative analysis, it demonstrates that that the ICC has tended to treat the *Rome Statute* as a self-contained regime, only relying on external sources of law where neither the *Statute* nor *Elements of Crimes* provides a definition of its own. It has further shown that the ICC tends to explain this approach by citing the principle of legality, implying that using external sources to interpret the meaning of crimes within the *Statute* would contradict the rights of the accused. To the contrary, this book has joined several academics in arguing that interpretations consistent with CIL promote consistency in judicial reasoning and the unity of international law, thereby safeguarding both the interests of the accused and the international system.

Beyond the issues of interpretive consistency and the unity of international law, this book has demonstrated that compliance with the principle of systemic integration can also help foster the necessary progressive development of the law, as well as safeguarding against unwarranted regressive developments. The three-part case study on the war crime of denying a fair trial in the context of a non-international national armed conflict (NIAC) illustrates this potential. By relying solely on the definition provided in the *Elements of Crimes*, the ICC in *Al Hassan* risks undermining important jurisprudence from the Second World War and subsequent state practice that

---

4 Grover (n 3) 407–8.

5 International Law Commission, Martti Koskenniemi, *Report on Fragmentation of International Law: Difficulties Arising from the Diversification and Expansion of International Law*, UN Doc A/CN.4/L.682 (13 April 2006) 412, 465, 480 ('*Fragmentation of International Law Study*').

prohibited political prosecutions by special courts with irregular jurisdiction. This prohibition was explicitly designed to regulate the establishment and judicial independence of courts in armed conflict from the political and ideological influences that often fuel such conflicts.[6] Had the Court employed the principle of systemic integration, it could have maintained the accepted customary meaning of this crime, while also integrating changes in state practice and legal opinion to provide judicial clarification on the current state of the law when applied to the courts of non-state armed groups (NSAGs).

In this book, I have also sought to contribute to the debate on how courts and tribunals can identify rules of CIL in the international criminal context, especially where such rules are marred by routine non-compliance. While there is no shortage of scholarly critique on the practice of international courts in identifying rules of CIL,[7] there are comparatively few attempts to devise a practical methodology for identifying the evidence necessary to prove their existence in a manner that remains loyal to CIL's theoretical underpinnings. The ILC addressed this gap to a significant degree between 2013 and 2018 through its 16 *Draft Conclusions on Identification of Customary International Law* (Draft Conclusions) with associated commentary and yearly Reports.[8] The ILC project helped to clarify several of the lingering

6 Otto Triffterer and Kai Ambos, 'Jurisdiction, Admissibility and Applicable Law' in Otto Triffterer and Kai Ambos (eds), *Rome Statute of the International Criminal Court: A Commentary* (Bloomsbury, 2016) 111, 554 para 907; Dieter Fleck and Michael Bothe, *The Handbook of International Humanitarian Law* (3rd ed, OUP 2013) para 576; Knut Dörmann, *Elements of War Crimes under the Rome Statute of the International Criminal Court: Sources and Commentary* (CUP 2003) 412; International Committee of the Red Cross, *Commentary on Convention (IV) relative to the Protection of Civilian Persons in Time of War* (ICRC, 1958) 340.

7 For example, see: Niels Petersen, 'The International Court of Justice and the Judicial Politics of Identifying Customary International Law' (2017) 17(2) *European Journal of International Law* 357; Stefan Talmon, 'Determining Customary International Law: The ICJ's Methodology between Induction, Deduction and Assertion' (2015) 26(2) *European Journal of International Law* 417; Stephen J Choi and Mitu Gulati, 'Customary International Law: How Do Courts Do It?' in Curtis A Bradley (ed), *Custom's Future: Customary International Law in a Changing World* (2016) 117; Birgit Schlütter, *Developments in Customary International Law: Theory and the Practice of the International Court of Justice and the International Ad Hoc Criminal Tribunals for Rwanda and Yugoslavia* (Martinus Nijhoff, 2010); Rudolf Geiger, 'Customary International Law in the Jurisprudence of the International Court of Justice: A Critical Appraisal' in Ulrich Fastenrath and others (eds), *From Bilateralism to Community Interest: Essays in Honour of Bruno Simma* (OUP 2011) 673.

8 Michael Wood, Special Rapporteur, *First Report on Formation and Evidence of Customary International Law*, UN Doc A/CN.4/663 (17 May 2013) ('*First Report on Formation and Evidence of Customary International Law*'); Michael Wood, Special Rapporteur, *Second Report on Identification of Customary International Law*, UN Doc A/CN.4/672 (22 May 2014)

ambiguities surrounding the conceptual boundaries of CIL, as well as providing guidance on the type and quantity of evidence that may be necessary to prove its existence in a court of law. This book is among a relatively small but growing number works to have critiqued the ILC's Draft Conclusions[9] and appears to constitute the only attempt to apply them to the ICC's institutional framework.[10] In doing so, this work synthesises the various approaches to identifying CIL in the face of contrary state practice in a manner that could promote a positive change in judicial practice.

8.1 Claims and Implications

I have identified three negative implications of the failure to apply the principle of systemic integration, which have the potential to adversely impact the long-term legitimacy of international criminal law ('ICL') and IHL. First, the lack of a consistent approach to interpretation across ICC Chambers could be described as 'methodological mayhem'[11] – it causes

('*Second Report on Identification of Customary International Law*'); Michael Wood, Special Rapporteur, *Third Report on Identification of Customary International Law*, UN Doc A/CN.4/682 (27 March 2015) ('*Third Report on Identification of Customary International Law*'); Michael Wood, Special Rapporteur, *Fourth Report on Identification of Customary International Law*, UN Doc A/CN.4/695 (8 March 2016) ('*Fourth Report on Identification of Customary International Law*'); *Report of the International Law Commission, Chapter V: Identification of Customary International Law*, UN GAOR, 73rd sess, Supp No 10, UN Doc A/73/10 (2018) ('*Report of the International Law Commission, Chapter V: Identification of Customary International Law*').

9 For an edited collection of works looking at the theory, practice, and interpretation of custom in light of the ILC's Draft Conclusions, see: Panos Merkouris, Jorg Kammerhofer, and Noora Arajärvi (eds) *The Theory, Practice, and Interpretation of Customary International Law* (CUP 2022); For a critique on the ILC's role in lawmaking, see: Wouter Werner, *The Making of Lawmaking: The ILC Draft Conclusions on the Identification of Customary Law* (OUP 2023); for a recent analysis of the ILC's project that reached similar conclusions to this book, see: Katie Johnston, 'Nature and Context of Rules and the Identification of Customary International Law' (2021) 32(4) *European Journal of International Law* 1167; and for a general critique of the ILC's project, see: Stefan Talmon, 'Determining Customary International Law: The ICJ's Methodology and the Idyllic World of the ILC' *EJIL: Talk! Blog of the European Journal of International Law* (Blog Post, 3 December 2015) <https://www.ejiltalk.org/determining-customary-international-law-the-icjs-methodology-and-the-idyllic-world-of-the-ilc/>.

10 Katie Johnston also tackles the issue of contrary state practice and prohibitive rules in light of the ILC Draft Conclusions, but without a specific focus on international criminal law. Johnston (n 9) 1175.

11 Harlen Cohen, 'Methodology and Misdirection: Custom and the ICJ' *EJIL: Talk! Blogpost of the European Journal of International Law* (Blog Post, 1 December 2015)

unpredictability in judicial reasoning, especially with respect to the interpretive weight of CIL. Second, deviations from CIL law in the interpretation of the *Rome Statute* threaten to fragment ICL or develop it in a manner that promotes impunity for war crimes.[12] Third, treating the *Rome Statute* and *Elements of Crimes* as a self-contained regime neglects opportunities for the incremental development of both ICL and IHL. By contrast, cases that comply with principle of systemic integration demonstrate its potential to unify the disparate threads of CIL in the interpretation of an indeterminate area of law and, in so doing, contribute to its necessary and legitimate development.

8.1.1 *'Methodological Mayhem' or a Single Unified Approach?*

Apart from the consistency with which ICC judges apply the *Elements of Crimes*, there is no perceptible coherence in their approach to interpreting the definition of crimes in the *Rome Statute*. Several cases between 2010 and 2016 developed a methodology that applied the general rule of interpretation in article 31 of the *VCLT* alongside the rules of strict construction in article 22(2) of the *Statute*. Although the application of the principle of systemic integration under article 31(3)(c) in these cases leaves something to be desired, the cases demonstrate the potential for customary rules governing the interpretation of treaties to operate in harmony with those rules that are unique to ensuring the rights of the accused in the interpretation of criminal statutes. Quantitative analysis reveals that this approach has become the exception rather than the rule.

Methodological inconsistency is apparent across the different chambers of the ICC. Specific to the principle of systemic integration, three Appeals Chamber decisions confirm that all war crimes under article 8(2)(b) and article 8(2)(e) 'must' be interpreted consistently with customary IHL.[13] No

---

<https://www.ejiltalk.org/methodology-and-misdirection-a-response-to-stefan-talmon-on-custom-and-the-icj/> (Cohen uses the term to describe the practice of the ICJ, but it is also apt in the present context).

12 Otto Triffterer, 'Can the "Elements of Crimes" Narrow or Broaden Responsibility for Criminal Behaviour Defined in the Rome Statute?' in Carsten Stahn and Göran Sluiter (eds), *The Emerging Practice of the International Criminal Court* (Brill Nijhoff, 2009) 381.

13 *Prosecutor v Thomas Lubanga Dyilo* (*Judgment*) (International Criminal Court, Appeals Chamber, Case No ICC-01/04-01/06 A5, 1 December 2014) [322] ('*Lubanga Appeals Judgement*'); *Prosecutor v Bosco Ntaganda* (*Judgement on the appeal of Mr Ntaganda against the "Second decision on the Defence's challenge to the jurisdiction of the Court in respect of Counts 6 and 9*) (International Criminal Court, Appeals Chamber, Case

other chamber has applied this ruling, including the Trial Chamber that was ostensibly applying one of those Appeals Chamber decisions.[14] Similarly, two Trial Chamber decisions interpret the principle of systemic integration under article 31(3)(c) as providing them with a 'right' to refer to external sources of law,[15] whereas one Pre-Trial Chamber determined that external sources of law may only be referred to in cases of ambiguity.[16] Most decisions do not refer to the principle of systemic integration at all and reference external sources only where it is convenient or where there is ambiguity or a gap in the *Statute*.

Adopting a single methodology for interpreting the definition of crimes will bring consistency in judicial reasoning. This will, in turn, foster predictability, legal certainty, and fairness to the accused – and ultimately enhance the legitimacy of the ICC. As Andrea Carcano has observed, 'Accurate and abundantly reasoned determinations of CIL, far from being judge-made law in disguise, help ensure a consistent and persuasive development of the applied law among different Chambers and across ICL'.[17] Building on Grover's foundational work,[18] the methodology proposed in the present study has the potential to achieve this goal.

8.1.2 *Fragmentation or Unity?*

Fragmentation is already evident in several ICC decisions. By relying exclusively on the *Elements of Crimes*, the ICC's interpretation of the war crime of pillage and the war crime of denial of a fair trial in NIAC are both contrary

---

No ICC-01/04-02/06 OA5, 15 June 2017) [52]–[53] (*'Appeals Chamber's Second Decision on Mr Ntaganda's Jurisdictional Appeal'*); *Prosecutor v Bosco Ntaganda (Judgment)* (International Criminal Court, Appeals Chamber, Case No ICC-01/04-02/06 A A2, 30 March 2021) [564] (*'Ntagnanda Appeals Judgment'*).

14 *Prosecutor v Bosco Ntaganda (Judgment)* (International Criminal Court, Trial Chamber, Case No ICC-01/04-02/06, 8 July 2019) (*'Ntagnada Trial Judgment'*).

15 *Prosecutor v Germain Katanga and Mathieu Ngudjolo Chui (Judgment)* (International Criminal Court, Trial Chamber II, Case No ICC-01/04-01/07, 7 March 2014) [47], [1100], [1395] nn 1394, [1625] (*'Katanga Trial Judgment'*); *Prosecutor v Jean-Pierre Bemba Gombo (Judgment)* (International Criminal Court, Trial Chamber III, Case No ICC-01/05-01/08, 21 March 2016) [78]–[79] (*'Bemba Trial Judgment'*).

16 *Prosecutor v Omar Hassan Al Bashir (Decision on the Prosecution's Application for a Warrant of Arrest against Omar Hassan Ahmad Al Bashir)* (International Criminal Court, Pre-Trial Chamber I, Case No ICC-02/05–01/09, 4 March 2009) [132]–[133] (*'Al Bashir Arrest Warrant'*).

17 Andrea Carcano, 'Of Fragmentation and Precedents in International Criminal Law' (2016) 14(4) *Journal of International Criminal Justice* 771, 789.

18 Grover (n 3).

to the definition and scope of these crimes under customary IHL. Other examples, in which the *Elements* threaten to fragment IHL and international criminal law by creating a specialised regime of 'ICC law', include the war crimes of rape, the launching of disproportionate attacks, declaring that no quarter will be given, and forced displacement.[19] Moreover, any failure to ground the interpretation of an offence in applicable CIL and rely uncritically on the *Elements of Crimes* risks fragmenting ICC law from general ICL, especially as the latter continues to develop outside the purview of the *Rome Statute*.[20]

One implication from such fragmentation concerns the ICC's subject-matter jurisdiction over non-state parties referred by the United Nations Security Council. The ICC has explicitly justified its exercise of jurisdiction in these situations as a non-violation of the principle of legality *because* the alleged crimes within its subject-matter jurisdiction reflect CIL.[21] The same justification was used for the establishment of the International Criminal Tribunal for the former Yugoslavia (ICTY).[22]

Broader implications also arise from the ICC's fragmentation of ICL and IHL, the first of which is to detract from the ICC's status as a model international court.[23] For example, states increasingly exercise universal jurisdiction over international crimes, as evidenced by recent high-profile trials in Sweden, Switzerland, Germany, and others.[24] Similarly, regional and *ad hoc* international criminal tribunals have been established for Kosovo and the

19 Triffterer (n 12).

20 Pocar (n 3); David Hunt, 'The International Criminal Court: High Hopes, Creative Ambiguity and an Unfortunate Mistrust in International Judges' (2004) 2(1) *Journal of International Criminal Justice* 56.

21 *Prosecutor v Ali Muhammad Ali Abd-Alrahman ("Ali Kushayb") (Appeal of Mr Abd-Al-Rahman against the Pre-Trial Chamber II's "Decision on the Defence 'Exception d'incompétence' (ICC-02/05-01/20-302)")* (International Criminal Court, Appeals Chamber, Case No ICC-02/05-01/20 OA8, 1 November 2021) [88]–[90] (*'Ali Kushayb Jurisdictional Appeal'*).

22 United Nations, *Report of the Secretary-General Pursuant to Paragraph 2 of Security Council Resolution 808 (1993)*, UN Doc S/25704 (3 May 1993) 9 para 34 (*'Secretary-General Report on Establishing the ICTY'*).

23 Pocar (n 3) 176 ('While a judicial decision based strictly on treaty provisions represents but a limited precedent for States that are not parties to the treaty, the application of customary international law makes this precedent significantly more valuable to all States.').

24 For an overview of states exercising universal jurisdiction over international crimes, see: Trial International, '2021 Activity Report' (Published Report, 2021) <https://trialinternational.org/latest-post/2021-activity-report/>.

Central African Republic, and the United Nations Investigative Mechanisms are gathering evidence for potential future tribunals to try alleged international crimes in Syria and Myanmar. The jurisdiction of all these courts with respect to international crimes committed by a non-national in a foreign territory is limited to CIL by the principle of legality. ICC law that deviates from CIL is therefore inapplicable as precedent, tarnishing its reputation as a model court with the 'promise of universal justice'.[25]

Alternatively, ICC law that deviates from CIL may be regarded as sufficiently influential to *change* CIL despite the 'without prejudice' clause in article 10.[26] This should be a particular cause for concern as departures from CIL in ICC jurisprudence tend to be influenced by judges' interpretation of the principle of legality with respect to the *Elements of Crimes* – whether justified or not – and therefore narrow the responsibility of the accused and increase the prospects that international crimes will be met with impunity. This point is usefully summarised by Otto Triffterer.

> With regard to Article 8, it is particularly obvious that the Elements deviate from the original wording of the relevant definitions and, by narrowing their application, contribute to impunity for criminal behaviour, which otherwise would fall within the jurisdiction of the Court.[27]

The *Elements of Crimes* should thus be interpreted consistently with CIL to the greatest possible extent to avoid unnecessary fragmentation. For some crimes, there is an irreconcilable conflict between the *Elements of Crimes* and CIL. For example, the *Elements* defines 'pillage' as appropriations 'for private or personal use', whereas the customary definition of pillage includes appropriations for public purposes not justified by military necessity. One could imagine that the Court would not be prepared to favour the customary definition where it broadens the criminal responsibility of an individual at trial, even if adherence to the *Elements of Crimes* is not

---

25 Kofi Annan, *Press Release of the United Nations Secretary General*, UN Doc SG/SM/6257 (12 June 1997) ('*Press Release of the United Nations Secretary General*').

26 *Rome Statute of the International Criminal Court*, opened for signature 17 July 1998, 2187 UNTS 38544, art 10 (entered into force 1 July 2002) ('*Rome Statute of the International Criminal Court*') (nothing in this Part shall be interpreted as limiting or prejudicing in any way existing or developing rules of international law for purposes other than this Statute).

27 Triffterer (n 12) 394.

technically required by the principle of legality.[28] In such cases, fragmentation is inevitable.

The solution to this problem is to amend the *Elements of Crimes*, which can be proposed under article 9(2) of the *Rome Statute* by any State Party, judges acting by an absolute majority, or by the Prosecutor. Such amendments must then be approved by a two-thirds majority of the Assembly of States Parties. A primary means of highlighting irreconcilable inconsistencies between the *Elements* and CIL will be through application of the principle of systemic integration, as can be seen in the decision of Trial Chamber III in *Bemba* with respect to the war crime of pillage, further emphasising the importance of this principle.[29]

8.1.3 *Freezing International Law or Contributing to Its Incremental Development?*

The ICC's failure to apply the principle of systemic integration also stifles the development of the law. Subject to amendment by the Assembly of States Parties, the *Rome Statute* and *Elements of Crimes* are frozen in time. Treating these two sources as a self-contained regime that is impervious to developments in CIL not only fragments international law, but also denies the ICC the opportunity to clarify the state of the law in situations where it is indeterminate and, in doing so, contribute to its incremental development.

To highlight the impact that compliance with the principle of systemic integration could have on fostering the incremental development of the law, it is worth reflecting on the ICC's interpretation of a 'regularly constituted court' in *Al -Hassan*.[30] There was – and is – a distinct lack of clarity with respect to how the definition of this term applies to courts established by NSAGs. The traditional definition, which requires courts to be established and organised in accordance with the pre-existing laws of the state, excludes NSAG courts altogether and cannot be accepted.[31] The definition in the

---

28 Cryer (n 3) 403.

29 *Bemba Trial Judgment* (n 15) [120].

30 *The Prosecutor v Al Hassan Ag Abdoul Aziz Ag Mohamed Ag Mahmoud* (Corrected version of *Décision relative à la Confirmation des Charges Portées contre Al Hassan Ag Abdoul Aziz Ag Mohamed Ag Mahmoud*) (International Criminal Court, Pree-Trial Chamber I, Case No ICC-01/12-01/18, 13 November 2019) [375]–[382] (English Translation) (*Al Hassan Pre-Trial Judgment*). *Prosecutor v Al Hassan* (International Criminal Court, Trial Chamber X, Case No ICC-01/12-01/18, 26 June 2024) [1169]–[1175] (*Al Hassan Trial Judgment*).

31 Jean-Marie Henckaerts and Louise Doswald-Beck, *Customary International Humanitarian Law (Rules)* (International Committee of the Red Cross/CUP 2005) vol 1, 355.

Elements of Crimes, as uncritically adopted by the ICC, removes all requirements concerning the legal basis and jurisdictional competence of both state and NSAG courts. Such a ruling ignores the precedent of the International Military Tribunals in Nuremberg and Tokyo,[32] the International Committee of the Red Cross' ('ICRC's') *Customary IHL Study*,[33] and the influential decision of the United States Supreme Court in *Hamdan*,[34] all of which confirm that the purpose of this rule is to outlaw courts with irregular jurisdiction established to prosecute a particular situation or individual.

If subsequent ICC Chambers were to apply the principle of systemic integration, they could reaffirm the customary definition of a regularly constituted court and clarify its scope of application with respect to courts established by NSAGs. Similarly, they could clarify which judicial guarantees are recognised as indispensable under customary IHL. This approach would simultaneously contribute to the development of the law by collating the various sources of CIL and using them to clarify the status of the rule. As it stands, the decisions in *Al Hassan* treat the ICC as a self-contained regime and neglect the opportunity to contribute to the clarification and development of the law.

In contrast, the Appeals Chamber in *Ntaganda* applied the principle of systemic integration (in substance), demonstrating its full potential. Prior to the *Ntaganda* Appeal, the most that can be said about IHL's regulation over intra-armed force violence is that the law was indeterminate. The ICRC's updated (2016) commentary on common article 3 states that, 'The fact that [...] the abuse [is] committed by their own Party *should not* be a ground to deny such persons the protection of common Article 3',[35] thereby indicating a soft or hortatory obligation under international law. The only other case to have considered the issue at the time was the *Sesay* judgement of the Special Court of Sierra-Leone ('SCSL') in 2009, in which the SCSL reached

('A court is regularly constituted if it has been established and organised in accordance with the laws and procedures already in force in a country.')

32 International Committee of the Red Cross (n 6) 340 ('The courts are to be "regularly constituted". This wording definitely excludes all special tribunals. It is the ordinary military courts of the Occupying Power which will be competent. Such courts will, of course, be set up in accordance with the recognized principles governing the administration of justice.').

33 Jean-Marie Henckaerts and Louise Doswald-Beck, *Customary International Humanitarian Law* (*Rules*) (n 31) 355.

34 *Hamdan v Rumsfeld* 548 U.S. 557 (United States Supreme Court, 2006) ('*Hamdan v Rumsfeld* ').

35 International Committee of the Red Cross, *Commentary on Geneva Convention III Relative to the Treatment of Prisoners of War, Second Edition* (ICRC, 2020) para 581 (emphasis added).

the opposite conclusion.[36] Accordingly, prior to the *Ntaganda* appeal, the law was in a state of flux.

The Appeals Chamber in *Ntaganda* applied the principle of systemic integration and determined that customary IHL does not impose a status requirement on the victims of sexual violence. In doing so, it clarified the status of customary IHL and, as is often achieved by well-reasoned determinations of CIL, it contributed to the development of the law. The case provides clear judicial support for the absolute prohibition on all forms of sexual violence as a rule of *jus cogens* and represents a significant moment in the international community's quest to end impunity for crimes of sexual violence in armed conflict. Had the Appeals Chamber neglected to apply the principle of systemic integration, the opportunity for this legitimate and necessary development of the law would have been lost.

8.2 Final Thoughts

Adherence to the principle of systemic integration promotes consistency in judicial reasoning, prevents unnecessary fragmentation, and contributes to the incremental development of the law. ICC Chambers should adopt a unified methodology for interpreting the definition of crimes that harmonises the general rule of interpretation in article 31 of the *VCLT* with the rules of strict construction in article 22(2) of the *Rome Statute*. Notably, such a methodology must include the principle of systemic integration in article 31(3)(c) of the *VCLT*, which in turn requires ICC judges to reengage with the important task of identifying rules of CIL in the international criminal context.

---

36 *Prosecutor v Issa Hassan Sesay and others (Judgment)* (Special Court of Sierra Leone, Appeals Chamber, Case No SCSL-04-15-A, 26 October 2009) [1451]–[1457] ('*Prosecutor v Issa Hassan Sesay and others*').

Bibliography

Books/Chapters

Armed Conflicts: Commentary on the Two 1977 Protocols Additional to the Geneva Conventions of 1949, vol 1 (2nd edn, Brill Nijhoff 2013)

Arajärvi N, *The Changing Nature of Customary International Law: Methods of Interpreting the Concept of Custom in International Criminal Tribunals* (Routledge 2014)

Arai Y, *The Law of Occupation: Continuity and Change of International Humanitarian Law, and its Interaction with International Human Rights Law* (Martinus Nijhoff 2009)

Bartels R, 'A Fine Line Between Protection and Humanisation: The Interplay Between the Scope of Application of International Humanitarian Law and Jurisdiction over Alleged War Crimes Under International Criminal Law' in TD Gill and others (eds), *Yearbook of International Humanitarian Law*, vol 20 (TMC Asser Press 2017)

Bederman DJ, *Custom as a Source of Law* (CUP 2010)

Berti B, 'Rebel justice? Rule of Law and Law Enforcement by Non-State Armed Groups' in Linda Hamid and Jan Wouters (eds), *The Rule of Law and Areas of Limited Statehood* (Edward Elgar, 2019)

Biddle F, *In Brief Authority* (Greenwood Press 1976)

Boister N and Cryer R (eds), *Documents on the Tokyo International Military Tribunal: Charter, Indictment and Judgments* (OUP 2008)

Bos A, 'From the International Law Commission to the Rome Conference (1994–1998)' in A Cassese, P Gaeta and JRWD Jones (eds), *The Rome Statute of the International Criminal Court: A Commentary* (OUP 2002)

Bothe M, Partsch KJ and Solf WA, *New Rules for Victims of Armed Conflicts: Commentary on the Two 1977 Protocols Additional to the Geneva Conventions of 1949* (Martinus Nijhoff, 1982)

Bothe M, Partsch KJ and Solf WA,: Civilians and Civilian Population' in Michael Bothe, Karl Josef Partsch and Waldemar A Solf (eds), *New Rules for Victims of Armed Conflicts: Commentary on the Two 1977 Protocols Additional to the Geneva Conventions of 1949* (Martinus Nijhoff 1982)

Bradley CA (ed), *Custom's Future: International Law in a Changing World* (CUP 2016)

Brierly JL and Clapham A, *Brierly's Law of Nations: An Introduction to the Role of International Law in International Relations* (OUP 2012)

Broomhall B, 'Article 22', *Commentary on the Rome Statute of the International Criminal Court – Observers' Notes* (2nd edn, Beck-Hart 2008)

Byers M, *Custom, Power and the Power of Rules: International Relations and Customary International Law* (CUP 1999)

Cameron L and others, 'Article 3: Conflicts Not of an International Character', *Geneva Convention III Relative to the Treatment of Prisoners of War (Commentary of 2020)* (International Committee of the Red Cross/ CUP 2020)

Cassese A, *International Criminal Law* (2nd edn, OUP 2008)

Choi SJ and Gulati M, 'Customary International Law: How Do Courts Do It?' in CA Bradley (ed), *Custom's Future: Customary International Law in a Changing World* (CUP 2016)

Clapham A, 'The Limits of Human Rights in Times of Armed Conflict and Other Situations of Armed Violence' in B Fassbender and K Traisbach (eds), *The Limits of Human Rights* (OUP 2019)

Cottier M, 'Article 8' in O Triffterer (ed), *Commentary on the Rome Statute of the International Criminal Court* (2nd edn, Beck-Hart 2008)

Crawford J, 'The Work of the International Law Commission' in Antonio Cassese et al (eds) *The Rome Statute of the International Criminal Court: A Commentary* (vol 1) (OUP 2002)

Daboné Z, *Le Droit International Public Relatif aux Groupes Armés Non Étatiques* (Schulthess 2012)

Darcy S, *Judges, Law and War: The Judicial Development of International Humanitarian Law* (CUP 2014)

Darcy S, 'The Reinvention of War Crimes by the International Criminal Tribunals' in Shane Darcy and Joseph Powderly (eds) *Judicial Creativity at the International Criminal Tribunals* (OUP 2010)

Darcy S and Powderly J, *Judicial Creativity at the International Criminal Tribunals* (OUP 2010)

DeGuzman M, 'Article 21, Applicable Law' in Otto Triffterer and Kai Ambros (eds), *The Rome Statute of the International Criminal Court: A Commentary* (3rd edn, Beck 2016)

Dörmann K, 'Article 8' in O Triffterer (ed), *Commentary on the Rome Statute of the International Criminal Court* (2nd edn, Beck-Hart 2008)

Dörmann K, *Elements of War Crimes under the Rome Statute of the International Criminal Court: Sources and Commentary* (CUP 2003)

Doswald-Beck L, 'Judicial Guarantees under Common Article 3' in A Clapham, P Gaeta and M Sassòli (eds), *The 1949 Geneva Conventions: A Commentary* (OUP 2016)

Fleck D, 'Comment – Perspectives on Courts Established by Armed Opposition Groups' in H Krieger (ed), *Inducing Compliance with International Humanitarian Law: Lessons from the African Great Lakes Region* (CUP 2015)

Fleck D and Bothe M, *The Handbook of International Humanitarian Law* (3rd edn, OUP 2013)

Gallant K, 'Legality in Criminal Law, Its Purposes, and Its Competitors' in K Gallant (ed), *The Principle of Legality in International and Comparative Criminal Law* (CUP 2008)

Gardiner R, *Treaty Interpretation* (OUP 2008)

Geiger R, 'Customary International Law in the Jurisprudence of the International Court of Justice: A Critical Appraisal' in U Fastenrath and others (eds), *From Bilateralism to Community Interest: Essays in Honour of Bruno Simma* (OUP 2011)

Gillett M, 'Eco-Struggles: Using International Criminal Law to Protect the Environment During and After Non-International Armed Conflict' in C Stahn, J Iverson and J Easterday (eds), *Environmental Protection and Transitions from Conflict to Peace: Clarifying Norms, Principles, and Practices* (OUP 2017)

Goss R, 'The Undermining of Article 6 ECHR' in G Oberleitner and others (eds), *European Yearbook on Human Rights 2019* (Intersentia 2019)

Grover L, *Interpreting Crimes in the Rome Statute of the International Criminal Court* (CUP 2014)

Guzman AT and Hsiang J, 'Reinvigorating Customary International Law' in CA Bradley (ed), *Custom's Future: International Law in a Changing World* (CUP 2016)

Hakimi M, 'Custom's Method and Process: Lessons from Humanitarian Law' in CA Bradley (ed), *Custom's Future: International Law in a Changing World* (CUP 2016)

Harwood S, *Judicial Activism: A Restrained Defense* (Austin & Winfield 1996)

Heffes E, 'Generating Respect for International Humanitarian Law: The Establishment of Courts by Organized Non-State Armed Groups in Light of the Principle of Equality of Belligerents' in TD Gill (ed), *Yearbook of International Humanitarian Law*, vol 18 (TMC Asser Press 2016)

Helfer LR and Meyer T, 'The Evolution of Codification: A Principal-Agent Theory of the International Law Commission's Influence' in CA Bradley (ed), *Custom's Future: International Law in a Changing World* (CUP 2016)

Henckaerts J-M and Doswald-Beck L, *Customary International Humanitarian Law* (*Rules*), vol 1 (International Committee of the Red Cross/ CUP 2005)

Henckaerts J-M and Doswald-Beck L, *Customary International Humanitarian Law* (*Practice*), vol 2 (International Committee of the Red Cross/ CUP 2005)

Hernández G, *The International Court of Justice and the Judicial Function* (OUP 2014)

Hiemstra H and Nohle E, 'The Role of Non-State Armed Groups in the Development and Interpretation of International Humanitarian Law' in TD Gill and others (eds), *Yearbook of International Humanitarian Law*, vol 20 (TMC Asser Press 2017)

Higgins R, 'Some Observations on the Inter-Temporal Rule in International Law' in J Makarczyk (ed), *Theory of International Law at the Threshold of the 21st Century – Essays in Honour of Krysztof Skubiszewski* (Brill 1997)

Hoffmann T, 'Freezing or Consolidating the Development of War Crimes Law? The International Criminal Court and the Role of Judicial Innovation', in Martin Faix and Ondřej Svaček (eds) *ICC Jurisprudence and the Development of International Humanitarian Law* (Springer, 2024)

Huang R, *The Wartime Origins of Democratization: Civil War, Rebel Governance, and Political Regimes* (CUP 2016)

International Committee of the Red Cross, *Commentary on the First Geneva Convention: Convention (I) for the Amelioration of the Condition of the Wounded and Sick in Armed Forces in the Field* (CUP 2016)

International Committee of the Red Cross, *Commentary on the Third Geneva Convention: Treatment of Prisoners of War* (CUP 2020)

Jackson A and Weigand F, *Rebel Rule of Law: Taliban Courts in the West and North-West of Afghanistan* (Humanitarian Policy Group 2020)

Jacobs D 'International Criminal Law' in Jörg Kammerhofer and Jean D'Aspremont (eds) *International Legal Positivism in a Post-Modern World* (CUP 2014)

Jennings R and Watts A, *Oppenheim's International Law* (9th edn, Longman Harlow 1992)

Jo H, 'Compliance with International Humanitarian Law by Non-State Armed Groups: How Can It Be Improved?' in TD Gill and others (eds), *Yearbook of International Humanitarian Law*, vol 19 (TMC Asser Press 2016)

Jo H, *Compliant Rebels: Rebel Groups and International Law in World Politics* (CUP 2015)

Kelly M, *Restoring and Maintaining Order in Complex Peace Operations*, vol 2 (Martinus Nijhoff 1999)

Kirsch P, 'Customary International Humanitarian Law, its Enforcement, and the Role of the International Criminal Court' in L Maybee and B Chakka (eds), *Custom as a Source of International Humanitarian Law* (International Committee of the Red Cross 2006)

Kontou N, *The Termination and Revision of Treaties in the Light of New CIL* (OUP 1994)

Kuijt E, 'Legal Challenges in the Provision of Humanitarian Assistance: The Case of Non-international Armed Conflicts' in TD Gill and others (eds), *Yearbook of International Humanitarian Law*, vol 17 (TMC Asser Press 2014)

Kress C, 'The International Criminal Court as a Turning Point in the History of International Criminal Justice', in A. Cassese (ed), *The Oxford Companion to International Criminal Justice* (OUP 2009)

La Haye E, 'Article 8(2)(b)(XXII)' in Roy S Lee (ed), *The International Criminal Court: Elements of Crimes and Rules of Procedure and Evidence* (Kluwer Law International 1999)

Lamb S, '*Nullum crimen, nulla poena sine lege* in International Criminal Law' in A Cassese (ed), *The Rome Statute of the International Criminal Court: A Commentary* (OUP 2002)

Lepard BD, 'Customary International Law as a Dynamic Process' in CA Bradley (ed), *Custom's Future: International Law in a Changing World* (CUP 2016)

Lepard BD, *Customary International Law: A New Theory with Practical Application* (CUP 2010)

Levie HS, *The Law of Non-International Armed Conflict: Protocol I to the 1949 Geneva Conventions* (Martinus Nijhoff 1987)

Makarczyk J (ed), *Theory of International Law at the Threshold of the 21st Century – Essays in Honour of Krysztof Skubiszewski* (Brill 1997)

Mampilly ZC, *Rebel Rulers: Insurgent Governance and Civilian Life during War* (Cornell UP 2011)

McCartan Brian and Jolliffe K, *Ethnic Armed Actors and Justice Provision in Myanmar* (Asia Foundation 2016)

Melzer N, *Interpretive Guidance on the Notion of Direct Participation in Hostilities under International Humanitarian Law* (International Committee of the Red Cross 2009)

Merkouris P, *Article 31(3)(c) VCLT and the Principle of Systemic Integration Normative Shadows in Plato's Cave* (Brill Nijhoff 2015)

Merkouris P, Kammerhofer J, and Arajärvi N (eds) *The Theory, Practice, and Interpretation of Customary International Law* (CUP 2022)

Meron T, 'Customary Humanitarian Law Today: From the Academy to the Courtroom' in A Clapham and P Gaeta (eds), *The Oxford Handbook of International Law in Armed Conflict* (OUP 2014)

Murray D, 'Engaging Armed Groups Through the Development of Human Rights Obligations: Incorporating Practice, Motivation and Ideology to Promote Compliance with International Law' in TD Gill and others (eds), *Yearbook of International Humanitarian Law*, vol 19 (TMC Asser Press 2016)

Nowak M, *UN Covenant on Civil and Political Rights: CPPR Commentary* (2nd edn, Engel 2005)

Okimoto K, 'Humanitarian Activities Carried Out Across Borders in Times of Armed Conflict in the Light of State Sovereignty and International Humanitarian Law' in TD Gill and others (eds), *Yearbook of International Humanitarian Law*, vol 17 (TMC Asser Press 2014)

Oosterveld V, 'The Elements of Genocide' in RS Lee (ed), *The International Criminal Court: Elements of Crimes and Rules of Procedure and Evidence* (Transnational 2001)

Orakhelashvili A, *The Interpretation of Acts and Rules in Public International Law* (OUP 2008)

Pauwelyn J, *Conflict of Norms in Public International Law: How WTO Law Relates to Other Rules of International Law* (CUP 2003)

Pejic J, 'The ECtHR's Al-Jedda Judgment: Implications for IHL', *Yearbook of International Humanitarian Law*, vol 14 (CUP 2011)

Pellet A, 'Applicable Law' in A Cassese, P Gaeta and JRWD Jones (eds), *The Rome Statute of the International Criminal Court: A Commentary*, vol 2 (OUP 2002)

Politi M, 'Elements of Crimes' in Cassese et al (eds) *The Rome Statute of the International Criminal Court: A Commentary* (OUP 2002)

Provost R, *Rebel Courts: The Administration of Justice by Armed Insurgents* (OUP 2021)

Provost R, "'Regularly Constituted' Courts of Non-State Armed Groups Between Rome and Geneva' in Martin Faix and Ondřej Svaček (eds) *ICC Jurisprudence and the Development of International Humanitarian Law* (Springer, 2024)

Radics O and Bruch C, 'The Law of Pillage, Conflict Resources, and Jus Post Bellum' in C Stahn, J Iverson and J Easterday (eds), *Environmental Protection and Transitions from Conflict to Peace: Clarifying Norms, Principles, and Practices* (OUP 2017)

Roca JG and Zapatero JMV, 'The Right to an Independent and Impartial Tribunal (Art. 6.1 ECHR): A Specific Minimum Standards Guarantee Rather than a Rule of Justice' in JG Roca and P Santolaya (eds), *Europe of Rights: A Compendium on the European Convention of Human Rights* (Brill-Nijhoff 2012)

Rodenhäuser T, *Organizing Rebellion: Non-State Armed Groups under International Humanitarian Law, Human Rights Law, and International Criminal Law* (OUP 2018)

Sassòli M, '*Ius ad Bellum* and *Ius in Bello* – The Separation Between the Legality of the Use of Force and Humanitarian Rules to Be Respected in Warfare: Crucial or Outdated?' in M Schmitt and J Pejic (eds), *International Law and Armed Conflict: Exploring the Faultlines – Essays in Honour of Yoram Dinstein* (Brill-Nijhoff 2007)

Sassòli M, 'L'administration d'un Territoire par un Groupe Armé, Peut-elle être Régie par le Droit?', in M. Hottelier et al (eds), *Études en l'Honneur du Professeur Thierry Tanquerel* (Schulthess, 2019),

Schabas W, 'Customary Law or "Judge-Made" Law? Judicial Creativity at the UN Criminal Tribunals', in Jose Doria et al (eds) *The Legal Regime of the International Criminal Court: Essays in Honour of Professor Igor Blishchenko* (Martinus Nijhoff, 2009) 77

Schabas W, 'Interpreting the Statutes of the Ad Hoc Tribunals' in LC Vohrah (ed), *Man's Inhumanity to Man: Essays in International Law in Honour of Antonio Cassese* (Kluwer Law International, 2003)

Schabas W, *The UN International Criminal Tribunals: The Former Yugoslavia, Rwanda and Sierra Leone* (CUP 2006)

Schachter Or, 'New Custom: Power, *Opinio Juris* and Contrary State Practice' in K Skubiszewski (ed), *Theory of International Law at the Threshold of the 21st Century* (Springer 1996)

Schlütter B, *Developments in Customary International Law: Theory and the Practice of the International Court of Justice and the International Ad Hoc Criminal Tribunals for Rwanda and Yugoslavia* (Martinus Nijhoff 2010)

Sender O and Wood M, 'Custom's Bright Future: The Continuing Importance of Customary International Law' in CA Bradley (ed), *Custom's Future: International Law in a Changing World* (CUP 2016)

Sergey V, 'The Making of International Criminal Law' in C Brölmann and Y Radi (eds), *Research Handbook on the Theory and Practice of International Lawmaking* (Edward Elgar 2016)

Shahabuddeen M, 'Policy-Oriented Law in the International Criminal Tribunal for the Former Yugoslavia' in LC Vohrah and others (eds), *Man's Inhumanity to Man: Essays in International Law in Honour of Antonio Cassese* (Brill 2003)

Shaw M, *International Law* (6th edn, CUP 2008)

Sivakumaran S, *The Law of Non-International Armed Conflict* (OUP 2012)

Solomon S and Kaye D, 'The International Law of Hamdan v Rumsfeld' in *Yearbook of International Humanitarian Law*, vol 8 (CUP 2005)

Stahn C and Sluiter G (eds), *The Emerging Practice of the International Criminal Court* (Brill Nijhoff 2009)

Stahn C and van den Herik L, 'Fragmentation', Diversification and '3D' Legal Pluralism: International Criminal Law as the Jack-in-The-Box?' in van den Herik and Stahn (eds), *The Diversification and Fragmentation of International Criminal Law* (Martinus Nijhoff, 2012)

Steiner C and Fuchs M-C, *Comentario Convención Americana Sobre Derechos Humanos* (2nd edn, Konrad Adenauer Stiftung 2019)

Stewart J, *Corporate War Crimes: Prosecuting the Pillage of Natural Resources* (Open Society Foundations 2011)

Tasioulas J, 'Customary International Law and the Quest for Global Justice' in A Perreau-Saussine and J Murphy (eds), *The Nature of Customary International Law* (CUP 2007)

Tasioulas J, Jus Cogens, and Human Rights' in CA Bradley (ed), *Custom's Future: International Law in a Changing World* (CUP 2016)

Triffterer O, 'Can The "Elements of Crimes" Narrow or Broaden Responsibility for Criminal Behaviour Defined in The Rome Statute?' in C Stahn and G Sluiter (eds), *The Emerging Practice of the International Criminal Court* (Brill Nijhoff 2009)

Triffterer O, 'Jurisdiction, Admissibility and Applicable Law' in O Triffterer and K Ambos (eds), *Rome Statute of the International Criminal Court: A Commentary* (Bloomsbury 2016)

UK Ministry of Defence, *The Manual of the Law of Armed Conflict* (OUP 2004)

van den Herik, L, 'The Decline of Customary International Law as a Source of International Criminal Law' in CA Bradley (ed), *Custom's Future: International Law in a Changing World* (CUP 2016)

Van Hoecke, Mark, *Methodologies of Legal Research: Which Kind of Method for What Kind of Discipline?* (Hart 2011)

Van Hoecke, Mark, 'Legal Doctrine: Which Method(s) for What Kind of Discipline?' in M Van Hoecke (ed), *Methodologies of Legal Research: Which Kind of Method for What Kind of Discipline?* (Bloomsbury 2013)

Villigier M, *Customary International Law and Treaties* (Martinus Nijhoff 1985)

von Hebel H and Robinson D, 'Crimes within the Jurisdiction of the Court' in RS Lee (ed), *The International Criminal Court: The Making of the Rome Statute* (Kluwer Law International 1999)

von Hebel H and Robinson D, 'Reflections on the Elements of Crimes' in RS Lee (ed), *The International Criminal Court: The Making of the Rome Statute* (Kluwer Law International 1999)

Werner W, *The Making of Lawmaking: The ILC Draft Conclusions on the Identification of Customary Law* (OUP 2023)

Willms J, 'Courts of Armed Groups – A Tool for Inducing Higher Compliance with International Humanitarian Law?' in H Krieger (ed), *Inducing Compliance with International Humanitarian Law: Lessons from the African Great Lakes Region* (CUP 2015)

Wolfke K, *Custom in Present International Law* (Martinus Nijhoff 1993)

Wouters J and Hamid L, 'Custom and Informal International Lawmaking' in CA Bradley (ed), *Custom's Future: International Law in a Changing World* (CUP 2016)

Zahar A 'Civilizing Civil War: Writing Morality as Law at the ICTY' in Bert Swart et al (eds) *The Legacy of the International Criminal Tribunal for the Former Yugoslavia* (OUP 2011)

Zahar A and Sluiter G, *International Criminal Law: A Critical Introduction* (OUP 2008)

Zegveld L, *The Accountability of Armed Opposition Groups in International Law* (CUP 2002)

Articles

Akande D, 'The Jurisdiction of the International Criminal Court over Nationals of Non-Parties: Legal Basis and Limits' (2003) 1 Journal of International Criminal Justice 618

Akande D, 'The Legal Nature of Security Council Referrals to the ICC and Its Impact on Al Bashir's Immunities' (2009) 7(2) Journal of International Criminal Justice 333

Alvarez-Jiménez A, 'Methods for the Identification for the Identification of Customary International Law in the International Court of Justice's Jurisprudence: 2000–2009' (2011) 60(3) International and Comparative Law Quarterly 681

American Society of International Law, 'International Military Tribunal (Nuremberg): Judgement and Sentences' (1947) 41(1) American Journal of International Law 172

Amoroso AM, 'Should the ICC Assess Complementarity with Respect to Non-state Armed Groups? Hidden Questions in the Second Al-Werfalli Arrest Warrant' (2018) 16(5) Journal of International Criminal Justice 1063

Arajärvi N, 'The Requisite Rigour in the Identification of Customary International Law: A Look at the Reports of the Special Rapporteur of the International Law Commission' (2017) 19 International Community Law Review 9

Ashworth A, 'Interpreting Criminal Statutes: A Crisis of Legality?' (1991) 107 Law Quarterly Review 419

Askary P and Hosseinnejad K, 'Non-State Courts: Illegal or Conditional?: The Case of Da'esh Courts' (2019) 10 Journal of International Humanitarian Legal Studies 240

Bailey S, 'Article 21(3) of the Rome Statute: A Plea for Clarity' (2014) 14 International Criminal Law Review 513

Baker R, 'Customary International Law: A Reconceptualization' (2016) 41(2) Brooklyn Journal of International Law 439

Baker R, 'Customary International Law in the 21st Century: Old Challenges and New Debates' (2010) 21(1) European Journal of International Law 173

Baker R, 'Legal Recursivity and International Law: Rethinking the Customary Element' (2016) 14(1) Dartmouth Law Journal 41

Barrera Moore C, 'Embracing Ambiguity and Adopting Propriety: Using Comparative Law to Explore Avenues for Protecting the LGBT Population Under Article 7 of the Rome Statute of the International Criminal Court' (2017) 101(2) Minnesota Law Review 1287

Baxter R, 'Multilateral Treaties as Evidence of Customary International Law' (1965) 41 British Yearbook of International Law 275

Benvenisti E, 'The Legal Battle to Define the Law on Transnational Asymmetric Warfare' (2010) (3) Duke Journal of Comparative & International Law 339

Blum G, 'On a Differential Law of War' (2011) 52(1) Harvard International Law Journal 163

Bodansky D, 'Customary (and Not So Customary) International Environmental Law' (1995) 3 Indiana Journal of Global Legal Studies 105

Bohlander M, '"Statute? What Statute?" Norm Hierarchy and Judicial Law-Making in International Criminal Law at the Example of the Special Tribunal for Lebanon' (2015) 36(2) Statute Law Review 186

Bohlander M, 'For a Judge-Led Generic Model of International Criminal Procedure and an End to "Draft-as-You-Go"' (2014) 45 Netherlands Yearbook of International Law 331

Bond JE, 'Application of the Law of War to Internal Conflicts (1973) 3 Georgia Journal of International and Comparative Law 345

Borda AZ, 'Formal Approach to Article 38 (1)(d) of the ICJ Statute from the Perspective of the International Criminal Courts and Tribunals' (2013) 24(3) European Journal of International Law 649

Bufalini A, 'The Principle of Legality and the Role of Customary International Law in the Interpretation of the ICC Statute' (2015) 14 The Law and Practice of International Courts and Tribunals 233

Canale D and Tuzet G, 'Analogical Reasoning and Extensive Interpretation' (2017) 103(1) Archives for Philosophy of Law and Social Philosophy 117

Carcano A, 'Of Fragmentation and Precedents in International Criminal Law' (2016) 14(4) Journal of International Criminal Justice 771

Casalin D, 'Taking Prisoners: Reviewing the International Humanitarian Law Grounds for Deprivation of Liberty by Armed Opposition Groups' (2011) 93 *International Review of the Red Cross* 743

Cassese A, 'The Statute of the International Criminal Court: Some Preliminary Reflections' (1999) 10 European Journal of International Law 144

Charney J, 'Universal International Law' (1993) 4 American Journal of International Law 529

Chodosh HE, 'Neither Treaty nor Custom: The Emergence of Declarative International Law' (1991) 26(1) Texas International Law Journal 87

Clapham A, 'Concluding Remarks: Three Tribes Engage on the Future of International Criminal Law' (2011) 9(3) Journal of International Criminal Justice 689

Clapham A, 'Human Rights Obligations of Non-State Actors in Conflict Situations' (2006) 88(863) International Review of the Red Cross 491

Colorio M, 'A Commander's Motivations and Geographical Remoteness under Command Responsibility: An Analysis of Controversial Issues of the Bemba Appeal Judgment' (2021) 21(3) International Criminal Law Review 445

Cryer R, 'Of Custom, Treaties, Scholars and the Gavel: The Influence of the International Criminal Tribunals on the ICRC Customary Law Study' (2006) 11(2) Journal of Conflict and Security Law 239

Cryer R, 'The Definitions of International Crimes in the Al Bashir Arrest Warrant Decision' (2009) 7(2) Journal of International Criminal Justice 283

Cryer R, 'Article 21 of the Rome Statute and the Politics of Sources' (2009) 12(3) New Criminal Law Review: An International and Interdisciplinary Journal 390

Cryer R, 'International Criminal Tribunals and the Sources of International Law: Antonio Cassese's Contribution to the Canon' (2012) 10(5) Journal of International Criminal Justice 1045

Cupido M, 'Facing Facts in International Criminal Law' (2016) 14(1) Journal of International Criminal Justice 1

Dabone Z, 'International Law: Armed Groups in a State-centric System' (2011) 93 International Review of the Red Cross 395

D'Amato A, 'Trashing Customary International Law' (1987) 81(1) American Journal of International Law 101

D'Amato A, 'International Customary Law and Codification. By HWA Thirlway' (1973) 67(2) American Journal of International Law 357

Dam-de Jong D, 'From Engines for Conflict into Engines for Sustainable Development: The Potential of International Law to Address Predatory Exploitation of Natural Resources in Situations of Internal Armed Conflict' (2013) 82(1) Nordic Journal of International Law 155

Danner AM, 'When Court Make Law: How the International Criminal Tribunals Recast the Laws of War' (2006) 59(1) Vanderbilt Law Review 1

Davidson C, 'How to Read International Criminal Law: Strict Construction and the Rome Statute of the International Criminal Court' (2017) 91(1) St John's Law Review 37

De La Rasilla I, 'The Shifting Origins of International Law' (2015) 28(3) Leiden Journal of International Law 419

DePiazza J, 'Denial of Fair Trial as an International Crime: Precedent for Pleading and Proving it under the Rome Statute' (2017) 15 Journal of International Criminal Justice 257

De Wet E, 'Referrals to the International Criminal Court Under Chapter VII of the United Nations Charter and the Immunity of Foreign State Officials' (2018) 112 American Journal of International Law Unbound 33

Dias T, 'The Retroactive Application of the Rome Statute in Cases of Security Council Referrals and Ad Hoc Declarations: An Appraisal of the Existing Solutions to an Under-discussed Problem' (2018) 16(1) Journal of International Criminal Justice 65

Dias T, 'The Nature of the Rome Statute and the Place of International Law before the International Criminal Court' (2019) 17 Journal of International Criminal Justice 507

Dinstein Y, 'Interaction between Customary International Law and Treaties' (2006) 322 Recueil des Cours de l'Académie de Droit International 243

Dörmann K, 'Contributions by the Ad Hoc Tribunals for the Former Yugoslavia and Rwanda to the Ongoing Work on Elements of Crimes in the Context of the ICC' (2000) 94 American Society of International Law Proceedings 284

Drumbl M, 'The Effects of the Lubanga Case on Understanding and Preventing Child Soldiering' (2012) 15 Yearbook of International Humanitarian Law 87

Dunbar H, 'The Myth of Customary International Law' (1983) 8 Australian Yearbook of International Law 1

Ezekiel A, 'The Application of International Criminal Law to Resource Exploitation: Ituri, Democratic Republic of The Congo' (2007) 47(1) Natural Resources Journal 225

Fabian KL, 'Proof and Consequences: An Analysis of the Tadic & Akayesu Trials' (2000) 49(4) DePaul Law Review 981

Fan M, 'Custom, General Principles and the Great Architect Cassese' (2012) 10(5) Journal of International Criminal Justice 1063

Fierens J, 'Gacaca Courts: Between Fantasy and Reality' (2005) 3(4) Journal of International Criminal Justice 896

French D, 'Treaty Interpretation and the Incorporation of Extraneous Legal Rules' (2006) 55(2) International and Comparative Law Quarterly 281

Gal T, 'Territorial Control by Armed Groups and the Regulation of Access to Humanitarian Assistance' (2017) 50(1) Israel Law Review 25

Galand A, 'The Nature of the Rome Statute of the International Criminal Court (and its Amended Jurisdictional Scheme)' (2019) 17(5) Journal of International Criminal Justice 933

Gallant K, 'Jurisdiction to Adjudicate and Jurisdiction to Prescribe in International Criminal Courts' (2003) 48 Villanova Law Review 763

Gejji P, 'Can Insurgent Courts Be Legitimate Within International Humanitarian Law?' (2013) 91 Texas Law Review 1525

Ginsburg T, 'Bounded Discretion in International Judicial Lawmaking' (2005) 45 Virginia Journal of International Law 631

Ginsburg T, 'Rebel Use of Law and Courts' (2019) 15 Annual Review of Law and Social Science 495

Goldstone R, 'Reflections on the Development of the Law of War' (2000) 46(1) McGill Law Journal 279

Grignon J, 'The Beginning of Application of International Humanitarian Law: A Discussion of a Few Challenges' (2014) 96 International Review of the Red Cross 139

Grover L, 'A Call to Arms: Fundamental Dilemmas Confronting the Interpretation of Crimes in the Rome Statute of the International Criminal Court' (2010) 21(3) European Journal of International Law 543

Gutierrez NC and Gulati M, 'Custom in our Courts: Reconciling Theory with Reality in the Debate about Erie Railroad and Customary International Law' (2017) 27(2) Duke Journal of Comparative and International Law 243

Hasluck N, 'Judicial Activism's Threat to the Rule of Law' (2016) 60(5) Quadrant 52

Henckaerts J-M, 'Customary International Humanitarian Law: Taking Stock of the ICRC Study' (2009) 78(4) Nordic Journal of International Law 435

Henckaerts J-M, 'The ICRC Study on Customary International Humanitarian Law: Characteristics, Conclusions and Practical Relevance' (2009) 6(1–2) Slovenian Law Review 225

Higgins R, 'Time and the Law: International Perspectives on an Old Problem' (1997) 46 International and Comparative Law Quarterly 501

Hochmayr G, 'Applicable Law in Practice and Theory: Interpreting Article 21 of the ICC Statute' (2014) 12(4) Journal of International Criminal Justice 655

Hunt D, 'The International Criminal Court: High Hopes, Creative Ambiguity and an Unfortunate Mistrust in International Judges' (2004) 2(1) Journal of International Criminal Justice 56

Hutchinson T and Duncan N, 'Defining and Describing What We Do: Doctrinal Legal Research' (2012) 17 Deakin Law Review 83

Institut de Droit International, 'The Intertemporal Problem in Public International Law' (1975) 56(1) Annuaire de l'Institut de Droit International 536

International Committee of the Red Cross, 'Humanitarian Aid to the Victims of Internal Conflicts. Meeting of a Commission of Experts in Geneva, 25–30 October 1962' (1963) 3(23) International Review of the Red Cross 79

Jain N, 'Judicial Lawmaking and General Principles of Law in International Criminal Law' (2016) 57(1) Harvard International Law Journal 111

Jenks C, 'Law as Shield, Law as Sword: The ICC's Lubanga Decision, Child Soldiers and the Perverse Mutualism of Direct Participation in Hostilities' (2013) 3 University of Miami National Security and Armed Conflict Law Review 106

Jessup P, 'The Palmas Island Arbitration' (1928) 22 American Journal of International Law 739

Jöbstl H, 'Bridging the Accountability Gap: Armed Non-state Actors and the Investigation and Prosecution of War Crimes' (2020) 18(3) Journal of International Criminal Justice 567

Johnston K, 'Nature and Context of Rules and the Identification of Customary International Law' (2021) 32(4) European Journal of International Law 1167

Kilcup J, 'Proportionality in Customary International Law: An Argument Against Aspirational Laws of War' (2016) 17 Chicago Journal of International Law 243

Kirgis F, 'Custom on a Sliding Scale' (1987) 81(1) American Journal of International Law 146

Klamberg M, 'On the Establishment of Courts in Non-international Armed Conflict by Non-state Actors' (2018) 16 Journal of International Criminal Justice 403

Klamberg M, 'The Legality of Rebel Courts during Non-International Armed Conflicts' (2018) 16(2) Journal of International Criminal Justice 235

Krieger H, 'International Law and Governance by Armed Groups: Caught in the Legitimacy Trap?' (2018) 12 Journal of Intervention and Statebuilding 563

Kunz J, 'Plus de Lois de la Guerre?' (1934) 41 Revue Générale de Droit International Public 22.

La Rosa A-M and Wuerzner C, 'Armed groups, Sanctions and the Implementation of International Humanitarian Law' (2008) 90 International Review of the Red Cross 327

Lefkowitz D, '(Dis)solving the Chronological Paradox in CIL: A Hartian Approach' (2008) 21 Canadian Journal of Law and Jurisprudence 129

Lietzau W, 'Checks and Balances and Elements of Proof: Structural Pillars for the International Criminal Court' (1999) 32 Cornell International Law Journal 477

Lincoln J, '*Nullum Crimen Sine Lege* in International Criminal Tribunal Jurisprudence: The Problem of the Residual Category of Crime' (2010) 7(1) Eyes on the ICC 137

Loyle C and Binningsbø H, 'Justice during Armed Conflict: A New Dataset on Government and Rebel Strategies' (2016) 62(2) Journal of Conflict Resolution 442

Lundberg M, 'The Plunder of Natural Resources During War: A War Crime(?)' (2008) 39 Georgetown Journal of International Law 495

Manley S, Tehrani P, and Rasiah R, 'Mapping interpretation by the International Criminal Court' (2023) 36(3) *Leiden Journal of International Law* 771

Marchesi D, 'The War Crimes of Denying Judicial Guarantees and the Uncertainties Surrounding their Material Elements' (2021) 54(2) Israel Law Review 174

McBride D, 'Who is a Member? Targeted Killings against Members of Organized Armed Groups' (2011) 30 Australian Yearbook of International Law 47

McCormack T and Robertson S, 'Jurisdictional Aspects of the *Rome Statute* for the New International Criminal Court' (1999) 23 Melbourne University Law Review 635

McDonald GK, 'The Eleventh Annual Waldemar A. Solf Lecture: The Changing Nature of the Laws of War' (1998) 156 Military Law Review 30

McLachlan C, 'The Principle of Systemic Integration and Article 31(3)(C) of the Vienna Convention' (2005) 54(2) International and Comparative Law Quarterly 279

Meron T, 'Application of Humanitarian Law in Non-International Armed Conflicts: Remarks by Theodor Meron' (1991) 85 American Society of International Law Proceedings 83

Meron T, 'International Criminalization of Internal Atrocities' (1995) 89 American Journal of International Law 554

Meron T, 'The Continuing Role of Custom in the Formation of International Humanitarian Law' (1996) 90(2) American Journal of International Law 238

Meron T, 'War Crimes Law Comes of Age' (1998) 92(3) American Journal of International Law 462

Meron T, 'Principles of Humanity and Dictates of Public Conscience' (2000) 94(1) American Journal of International Law 78

Meron T, 'Revival of Customary Humanitarian Law' (2005) 99(4) American Journal of International Law 817

Milanovic M, 'The End of Application of International Humanitarian Law' (2014) 96 International Review of the Red Cross 163

Muessig U and Seif N, 'The Common Legal Tradition of a Court Established by Law: Historical Foundations of Art. 6 para. 1 European Convention on Human Rights' (2005) 47(2) American Journal of Legal History 161

Mundis D, 'Elements of War Crimes under the Rome Statute of the International Criminal Court, Sources and Commentary' (2004) 2(3) *Journal of International Criminal Justice* 929

Murray D, 'How International Humanitarian Law Treaties Bind Non-State Armed Groups' (2015) 20(1) Journal of Conflict and Security Law 101

Nicholls L, 'The Humanitarian Monarchy Legislates: The International Committee of the Red Cross and its 161 Rules of Customary International Humanitarian Law' (2006) 17(1) Duke Journal of Comparative and International Law 223

Norman G and Trachtman J, 'The Customary International Law Game' (2005) 99(3) American Journal of International Law 541

Nuzban Y, '"For Private or Personal Use": The Meaning of the Special Intent Requirement in the War Crime of Pillage under the Rome Statute of the International Criminal Court' (2020) 102(915) International Review of the Red Cross 1249

Oberg M, 'The Legal Effects of Resolutions of the UN Security Council and General Assembly in the Jurisprudence of the ICJ' (2005) 16(5) European Journal of International Law 879

Orakhelashvili A, 'Gary D Solis, The Law of Armed Conflict: International Humanitarian Law in War. Yoram Dinstein, The Conduct of Hostilities under the Law of International Armed Conflict' (2011) 16(3) Journal of Conflict and Security Law 555

Palmer Olsen H and Toddington S, 'The End of an Era: Static and Dynamic Interpretation in International Courts' (2014) 14(4–5) International Criminal Law Review 920

Paust J, 'Still Unlawful: The Obama Military Commissions, Supreme Court Holdings, and Deviant Dicta in the D.C. Circuit' (2012) 45(2) Cornell International Law Journal 367

Perrin B, 'Searching for Law While Seeking Justice: The Difficulties of Enforcing International Humanitarian Law in International Criminal Trials' (2007) 39 Ottawa Law Review 367

Petersen N, 'Customary Law without Custom? Rules, Principles, and the Role of State Practice in International Norm Creation' (2007) 23(2) American University International Law Review 275

Petersen N, 'The International Court of Justice and the Judicial Politics of Identifying Customary International Law' (2017) 17(2) European Journal of International Law 357

Pocar F, 'International Criminal Justice and the Unifying Role of Customary Law' (2016) 21(2–3) Uniform Law Review 171

Popovic D, 'Prevailing of Judicial Activism Over Self-Restraint in the Jurisprudence of the European Court of Human Rights' (2009) 42 Creighton Law Review 361

Provost, 'FARC Justice: Rebel Rule of Law' (2018) 8(2) UC Irvine Law Review 227

Roberts A, 'What is a Military Occupation' (1985) 55 British Yearbook of International Law 249

Roberts A, 'Traditional and Modern Approaches to Customary International Law: A Reconciliation' (2001) 95(4) American Journal of International Law 757

Robinson D, 'The Identity Crisis of International Criminal Law' (2008) 21(4) Leiden Journal of International Criminal Law 925

Robinson D, 'The Tribunals and the Renaissance of International Criminal Law: Three Themes' (2016) 110(2) American Journal of International Law 191

Rodenhäuser T, 'The Legal Protection of Persons Living under the Control of Non-State Armed Groups' (2020) 102 *International Review of the Red Cross* 991

Ryngaert Cedric and Van de Meulebroucke A, 'Enhancing and Enforcing Compliance with International Humanitarian Law by Non-State Armed Groups: An Inquiry into Some Mechanisms' (2012) 16(3) Journal of Conflict and Security Law 443

Sadat L, 'Custom, Codification and Some Thoughts about the Relationship Between the Two: Article 10 to the ICC Statute' (2000) 49(4) DePaul Law Review 909

Sadat L, 'Seven Canons of ICC Treaty Interpretation: Making Sense of Article 25's Rorschach Blot' (2014) 27(3) Leiden Journal of International Law 755

Sands P, 'Treaty, Custom and the Cross-fertilization of International Law' (1998) 1 Yale Human Rights and Development Law Journal 85

Sartori D, 'Gap-Filling and Judicial Activism in the Case Law of the European Court of Human Rights' (2014) 29 Tulane European and Civil Law Forum 47

Sartori G, 'Concept Misformation in Comparative Politics' (1970) 64(4) American Political Science Review 1033

Sassòli M, 'Legislation and Maintenance of Public Order and Civil Life by Occupying Powers' (2005) 16 European Journal of International Law 661

Sassòli M, 'Taking Armed Groups Seriously: Ways to Improve their Compliance with International Humanitarian Law' (2010) 1 Journal of International Humanitarian Legal Studies 5

Sassòli M, 'Should the Obligations of States and Armed Groups Under International Humanitarian Law Really be Equal?' (2011) 93(882) International Review of the Red Cross 425

Satō H, 'Modes of International Criminal Justice and General Principles of Criminal Responsibility' (2012) 4(3) Goettingen Journal of International Law 765

Schabas W, 'Genocide Trials and Gacaca Courts' (2005) 3 Journal of International Criminal Justice 879

Schabas W,. Judicial Activism at the International Criminal Court' (2008) 6 Journal of International Criminal Justice 731

Schabas W, 'Synergy or Fragmentation? International Criminal Law and the European Convention on Human Rights' (2011) 9 *Journal of International Criminal Justice* 609

Schachter O, 'Recent Trends in International Law Making' (1989) 12 Australian Yearbook of International Law 1

Scharf M, 'Seizing the "Grotian Moment": Accelerated Customary International Law in Times of Fundamental Change' (2010) 43 Cornell International Law Journal 439

Scharf M, 'Accelerated Formation of Customary International Law' (2014) 20 ILSA Journal of International and Comparative Law 305

Shahabuddeen M, 'Does the Principle of Legality Stand in the Way of Progressive Development of Law?' (2004) 2(4) Journal of International Criminal Justice 1007

Sivakumaran S, 'Courts of Armed Opposition Groups: Fair Trials or Summary Justice?' (2009) 7(3) Journal of International Criminal Justice 489

Somer J, 'Jungle Justice: Passing Sentence on the Equality of Belligerents in Non-International Armed Conflict' (2007) 89 International Review of the Red Cross 655

Stahn C, 'Between Constructive Engagement, Collusion and Critical Distance: The ICRC and the Development of International Criminal Law' (2016) 15(1) Chinese Journal of International Law 139

Stoffels R, 'Legal Regulation of Humanitarian Assistance in Armed Conflict: Achievements and Gaps' (2004) 86(855) International Review of the Red Cross 515

Swart M, 'Judicial Lawmaking at the Ad Hoc Tribunals: The Creative Use of the Sources of International Law and "Adventurous Interpretation"' (2010) 70(3) Zeitschrift für ausländisches öffentliches Recht und Völkerrecht 459

Szewczyk BM, 'Customary International Law and Statutory Interpretation: An Empirical Analysis of Federal Court Decisions' (2014) 82(4) George Washington Law Review 1118

Talmon S, 'Determining Customary International Law: The ICJ's Methodology between Induction, Deduction and Assertion' (2015) 26(2) European Journal of International Law 417

Tasioulas J, '*Opinio Juris* and the Genesis of Custom: A Solution to the "Paradox"' (2007) 26 Australian Yearbook of International Law 199

Thirlway H, 'The Law and Procedure of the International Court of Justice, 1960–1989, Part Two' (1990) 61 British Yearbook of International Law 10

Thirlway H, 'Human Rights in Customary Law: An Attempt to Define Some of the Issues' (2015) 28(3) Leiden Journal of International Law 495

Todeschini V, 'The Impact of International Humanitarian Law on the Principle of Systemic Integration' (2018) 23(3) Journal of Conflict and Security Law 359

Van Schaack B, '*Crimen Sine Lege*: Judicial Lawmaking at the Intersection of Law and Morals' (2008) 97(1) Georgetown Law Journal 119

Vité S, 'Between Consolidation and Innovation: The International Criminal Court's Trial Chamber Judgment in the Lubanga Case' (2012) 15 Yearbook of International Humanitarian Law 61

Vohrah LC, 'Some Insights into the Early Years' (2004) 2(2) Journal of International Criminal Justice 388

Von Bogdandy A and Venzke I, 'On the Democratic Legitimation of International Judicial Lawmaking' (2011) 12(5) German Law Journal 1341

Wagner N, 'A Critical Assessment of Using Children to Participate Actively in Hostilities in Lubanga: Child Soldiers and Direct Participation' (2013) 24 Criminal Law Forum 181

Wald P, 'International Criminal Courts: Some Kudos and Concerns', 150(2) *Proceedings of the American Philosophical Society* (2006) 241

Watkin K, 'L'emploi de la Force en Période d'Occupation: Maintien de l'Ordre Public et Conduite des Hostilités' (2012) 94 (Séléction Francaise) Revue International du Croix-Rouge 179

Weisburd A, 'Customary International Law: The Problem of Treaties' (1988) 21 Vanderbilt Journal of International Law 1

Weisburd M, 'The International Court of Justice and the Concept of State Practice' (2009) 31 University of Pennsylvania Journal of International Law 295

Wessel J, 'Judicial Policy-Making at the International Criminal Court: An Institutional Guide to Analyzing International Adjudication' (2006) 44 Columbia Journal of Transnational Law 377

Yuvaraj J, 'When Does a Child "Participate Actively in Hostilities" under the Rome Statute? Protecting Children from Use in Hostilities after Lubanga' (2016) 32 Utrecht Journal of International Law 69

Zammit Borda A, 'A Formal Approach to Article 38(1)(d) of the ICJ Statute from the Perspective of the International Criminal Courts and Tribunals' (2013) 24(2) European Journal of International Law 649

Zarbiyev F, 'Judicial Activism in International Law—A Conceptual Framework for Analysis' (2012) 3(2) Journal of International Dispute Settlement 247

United Nations Documents

Annan K, *Press Release of the United Nations Secretary General*, UN Doc SG/SM/6257 (12 June 1997)

Basic Principles for the Protection of Civilian Populations in Armed Conflicts, GA Res 2675, GAOR, 25th sess, UN Doc A/RES/2675 (9 December 1970)

Bíró G, Special Rapporteur, *Report on Situation of Human Rights in the Sudan*, UN Doc E/CN.4/1996/62 (20 February 1996)

Declaration of Minimum Humanitarian Standards Adopted by a Meeting of Experts, Organised by the Human Rights Institute of Åbo Akademi in Turku/Åbo (Finland), UN Doc E/CN.4/Sub.2/1991/55 (2 December 1990)

Despouy L, Special Rapporteur, *Report on the Independence of Judges and Lawyers: Situations in Specific Countries Territories*, UN Doc A/HRC/11/41/Add.1 (19 May 2009)

Emmerson B, Special Rapporteur, *Report of the Special Rapporteur on the Promotion and Protection of Human Rights and Fundamental Freedoms while Countering Terrorism*, UN Doc A/HRC/29/51 (16 June 2015)

Human Rights Council, *Report of the Special Rapporteur on Extrajudicial, Summary or Arbitrary Executions on Armed Non-State Actors: The Protection of the Right to Life*, UN Doc A/HRC/38/44 (5 June 2018)

Human Rights Council, *Report of the Special Rapporteur on Extrajudicial, Summary or Arbitrary Executions on Armed Non State Actors: The Protection of the Right to Life*, UN Doc A/HRC/38/44 (7 December 2020)

International Law Commission, M Koskenniemi, *Report on Fragmentation of International Law: Difficulties Arising from the Diversification and Expansion of International Law*, UN Doc A/CN.4/L.682 (13 April 2006)

Kooijmans P, Special Rapporteur, *Report on Torture and Other Cruel, Inhuman or Degrading Treatment or Punishment*, UN Doc E/CN.4/1988/17 (12 January 1988)

Preparatory Commission for the International Criminal Court, *Colombia: Comments on the proposal submitted by Costa Rica, Hungary and Switzerland on Article 8, Paragraph 2 (c), of the Rome Statute of the International Criminal Court*, UN Doc PCNICC/1999/WGEC/DP.15 (29 July 1999)

Report of the Group of Eminent International and Regional Experts as Submitted to the United Nations High Commissioner for Human Rights, Situation of Human Rights in Yemen, Including Violations and Abuses since September 2014 – 9 August 2019, UN Doc A/HRC/42/17 (3 September 2019)

Report of the International Commission of Inquiry to Investigate All Alleged Violations of International Human Rights Law in the Libyan Arab Jamahiriya, UN Doc A/HRC/17/44 (1 June 2011)

Report of the International Law Commission, Chapter V: Identification of Customary International Law, UN GAOR, 73rd sess, Supp No 10, UN Doc A/73/10 (2018)

Report of the Preparatory Commission for the International Criminal Court: Addendum 2, UN Doc PCNICC/2000/1/Add.2, 2 November 2000 sess, UN Doc PCNICC/2000/1/Add.2 (2 November 2000)

Report of the United Nations Fact-Finding Mission on the Gaza Conflict, UN Doc A/HRC/12/48 (25 September 2009)

Respect for Human Rights in Armed Conflict, GA Res 2444, GAOR, 23rd sess, UN Doc A/RES/2444 (19 December 1968)

Security Council Resolution ('SC Res') 1479, UN Doc S/RES/1479 (13 May 2003)

SC Res 1509, UN Doc S/RES/1509 (19 September 2003)

SC Res 1933, UN Doc S/RES/1933 (30 June 2010)

SC Res 1962, UN Doc S/RES/1962 (20 December 2010)

SC Res 2041, UN Doc S/RES/2041 (22 March 2012)

SC Res 2076, UN Doc S/RES/2076 (20 November 2012)

SC Res 2139, UN Doc S/RES/2139 (22 February 2014)

United Nations, *Affirmation of the Principles of International Law Recognized by the Charter of the Nuremberg Tribunal*, GA Res 95(I), GAOR, 1st sess, UN Doc A/236 (11 December 1946)

United Nations, 'Declaration on Principles of International Law Concerning Friendly Relations and Cooperation among States in Accordance with the Charter of the United Nations', *Audiovisual Library of International Law* (24 October 1970) <http://legal.un.org/avl/ha/dpilfrcscun/dpilfrcscun.html>

United Nations, *Report of the Secretary-General Pursuant to Paragraph 2 of Security Council Resolution 808 (1993)*, UN Doc S/25704 (3 May 1993)

United Nations, *Report of the Independent International Commission of Inquiry on the Syrian Arab Republic*, UN Doc A/HRC/30/48 (13 August 2015)

United Nations, *Report of the Independent International Commission of Inquiry on the Syrian Arab Republic*, UN Doc A/HRC/33/55 (11 August 2016)

UN Human Rights Committee (HRC), *CCPR General Comment No 29: Article 4: Derogations During a State of Emergency*, UN Doc CCPR/C/21/Rev.1/Add.11 (31 August 2001)

UN Human Rights Committee (HRC), *General Comment No 32, Article 14: Right to Equality Before Courts and Tribunals and to Fair Trial*, UN Doc CCPR/C/GC/32 (23 August 2007)

United Nations Human Rights, 'UN Special Rapporteur on Independence of Judiciary Condemns Public Execution Following Illegal Trial in Afghanistan, Statement by Leandro Despouy, the Special Rapporteur on the Independence of Judges and Lawyers' (Statement, 8 June 2006) <https://www.ohchr.org/en/statements/2009/10/un-special-rapporteur-independence-judiciary-condemns-public-execution-following> accessed 3 July 2024

United Nations Assistance Mission in Afghanistan, *Afghanistan Annual Report 2017: Protection of Civilians on Armed Conflict* (UN Office of the High Commissioner for Human Rights, February 2018)

United Nations Office for the High Commissioner of Human Rights in Nepal, 'Human Rights Abuses by the CPN-M: Summary of Concerns' (September 2006)

United Nations Security Council, *Statement by the President of the Security Council*, S/PRST/2002/22 (23 July 2002)

United Nations War Crimes Commission, *Law Reports of the Trials of War Criminals. Volume V* (UNWCC, 1948)

Wood M, Special Rapporteur, *First Report on Formation and Evidence of Customary International Law*, UN Doc A/CN.4/663 (17 May 2013)

Wood M, *Second Report on Identification of Customary International Law*, UN Doc A/CN.4/672 (22 May 2014)

Wood M, *Third Report on Identification of Customary International Law*, UN Doc A/CN.4/682 (27 March 2015)

Wood M, *Fourth Report on Identification of Customary International Law*, UN Doc A/CN.4/695 (8 March 2016)

Wood M, *Fifth Report on Identification of Customary International Law*, UN Doc A/CN.4/717 (14 March 2018)

Reports

Amnesty International, *Torture was My Punishment: Abductions, Torture and Summary Killings under Armed Group Rule in Aleppo and Idleb* (Amnesty International 2016) <https://www.amnestyusa.org/wp-content/uploads/2017/04/embargoed_5_july-_torture_was_my_punishment-final_version.pdf>

Amnesty International, 'Human Rights Facts and Figures for 2016: 160 Countries' (Web Page, 23 February 2016) <https://www.amnesty.org/en/documents/pol10/3320/2016/en/>

Amnesty International, *Amnesty International Report 2020/21: The State of the World's Human Rights* (Amnesty International 2021) <https://www.amnesty.org/en/documents/pol10/3202/2021/en/>

Human Rights Council, *Report of the International Commission of Inquiry to Investigate All Alleged Violations of International Human Rights Law in the Libyan Arab Jamahiriya* (1 June 2011)

Human Rights Watch, *Mali Conflict and Aftermath. Compendium of Human Rights Watch Reporting 2012–2017* (Human Rights Watch 2017) <https://www.hrw.org/sites/default/files/supporting_resources/malicompendium0217.pdf>

Human Rights Watch, *Under Kurdish Rule: Abuses in PYD-run Enclaves in Syria* (Human Rights Watch 2014) <https://www.hrw.org/sites/default/files/reports/syria0614_kurds_ForUpload.pdf>

International Committee of the Red Cross, 'International Humanitarian Law and the Challenges of Contemporary Armed Conflict: Report' (Published Report, 22 November 2019) <https://www.icrc.org/en/document/icrc-report-ihl-and-challenges-contemporary-armed-conflicts>

International Law Association, *Final Report of the Committee on the Formation of Customary (General) International Law, Statement of Principles Applicable to the Formation of General Customary International Law* (Report of the 69th Conference 2000)

International Legal Assistance Consortium, *ILAC Rule of Law Assessment Report: Syria 2017* (ILAC 2017) <http://www.ilacnet.org/wp-content/uploads/2017/04/Syria2017.pdf>

Office of the Prosecutor of the International Criminal Court, *Situation in Mali; Article 53(1) Report* (ICC 2013) <https://www.icc-cpi.int/sites/default/files/itemsDocuments/SASMaliArticle53_1PublicReportENG16Jan2013.pdf>

Office of the Prosecutor of the International Criminal Court, 'Situation in Afghanistan: Summary of the Prosecutor's Request for Authorisation of an Investigation pursuant to Article 15' (2017) <https://www.refworld.org/docid/5a2a74314.html>

Office of the Prosecutor of the International Criminal Court, 'Report on Preliminary Examination Activities' (2019) <https://www.icc-cpi.int/itemsDocuments/191205-rep-otp-PE.pdf>

Panel Report – Action by the Dispute Settlement Body, *Korea – Measures Affecting Government Procurement*, WT/DS163/R (1 May 2000)

Report of the International Law Commission (2 May–10 June, 4 July–12 August 2016)

Trial International, '2021 Activity Report' (Published Report, 24 May 2022) https://trialinternational.org/latest-post/2021-activity-report/

Blogs and Web Pages

Akande D, 'Interview with Niels Petersen on his Article "The International Court of Justice and the Judicial Politics of Identifying Customary International Law"', *EJIL: Talk! Blog of the European Journal of International Law* (Blog Post, 7 September 2017) <https://www.ejiltalk.org/new-ejillive-interview-with-niels-petersen-on-his-article-the-international-court-of-justice-and-the-judicial-politics-of-identifying-customary-international-law/>

Bellal A, 'Humanitarian Access from an Armed Non-State Actor's Perspective', *Just Security* (Blog Post, 15 December 2016) <https://www.justsecurity.org/35555/humanitarian-access-armed-non-state-actors-perspective/>

Bhuta N, 'Joint Series on International Law and Armed Conflict: Fair Trial Guarantees in Armed Conflict', *EJIL: Talk! Blog of the European Journal of International Law* (Blog Post, 22 September 2016) <https://www.ejiltalk.org/joint-series-on-international-law-and-armed-conflict-fair-trial-guarantees-in-armed-conflict/>

Bordin F, 'Induction, Assertion and the Limits of the Existing Methodologies to Identify Customary International Law', *EJIL: Talk! Blog of the European Journal of International Law* (Blog Post, 2 December 2015) <https://www.ejiltalk.org/induction-assertion-and-the-limits-of-the-existing-methodologies-to-identify-customary-international-law/>

Chesney R, 'Joint Series on International Law and Armed Conflict: Hakimi on Fair Trial Guarantees in Armed Conflict', *Lawfare* (Blog Post, 23 September 2016) <https://www.lawfareblog.com/joint-series-international-law-and-armed-conflict-hakimi-fair-trial-guarantees-armed-conflict>

Chiorma U, 'A Law Court is Fundamentally Competent when Properly Constituted', *The Nigeria Lawyers* (Blog Post, 15 March 2016) <https://thenigerialawyer.com/a-law-court-is-fundamentally-competent-when-properly-constituted/>

Cohen H, 'Methodology and Misdirection: Custom and the ICJ', *EJIL: Talk! Blogpost of the European Journal of International Law* (Blog Post, 1 December 2015) <https://www.ejiltalk.org/methodology-and-misdirection-a-response-to-stefan-talmon-on-custom-and-the-icj/>

DePiazza J, 'The Al-Werfalli Arrest Warrant: Denial of Fair Trial as an Additional Allegation and a Hint at a Possible Defence', *EJIL: Talk! Blog of the European Journal of International Law* (Blog Post, 23 August 2017) <https://www.ejiltalk.org/the-al-werfalli-icc-arrest-warrant-denial-of-fair-trial-as-an-additional-allegation-and-a-hint-at-a-possible-defence/>

Filipek P, 'Only a Court Established by Law Can Be an Independent Court: The ECJ's Independence Test as an Incomplete Tool to Assess the Lawfulness of Domestic Court', *Verfassungsblog On Matters Constitutional* (Blog Post, 23 January 2020) <https://verfassungsblog.de/only-a-court-established-by-law-can-be-an-independent-court/>

Hakimi M, 'Fair Trial Guarantees in Armed Conflict', *Lawfare* (Blog Post, 23 September 2016) <https://www.lawfareblog.com/joint-series-international-law-and-armed-conflict-hakimi-fair-trial-guarantees-armed-conflict>

Heffes E, 'Armed Opposition Groups' Courts: Challenging the Lawfulness of Detentions in Light of the Serdar Mohammed Appeals Judgment', *Just Security* (Blog Post, 2 September 2015) <https://www.justsecurity.org/25775/armed-opposition

-groups-courts-challenging-lawfulness-detentions-light-serdar-mohammed-appeals-judgment/>

Heffes E, 'The Establishment of Courts by Armed Groups: What is the Legal Basis?', *Humanitarian Law and Policy* (Blog Post, 11 October 2016) <https://blogs.icrc.org/law-and-policy/2016/10/11/courts-armed-groups-legal-basis/>

Heffes E, 'Administration of Justice by Armed Groups: Some Legal and Practical Concerns', *Humanitarian Law and Policy* (Blog Post, 22 November 2018) <https://blogs.icrc.org/law-and-policy/2018/11/22/administration-of-justice-armed-groups-some-legal-practical-concerns/>

Heffes E, 'Can Armed Groups Legally Establish Their Own Courts?', *Humanitarian Law and Policy* (Blog Post, 9 March 2017) <https://blogs.icrc.org/law-and-policy/2016/10/11/courts-armed-groups-legal-basis/#:~:text=According%20to%20this%20view%2C%20IHL,from%20that%20of%20the%20State>

International Committee of the Red Cross, 'Practice Relating to Rule 100: Fair Trial Guarantees', *ICRC Customary International Humanitarian Law Database (Practice)* (Web Page, Updated Database) <https://ihl-databases.icrc.org/customary-ihl/eng/docs/v2_rul_rule100>

Jacobs D, 'Why the Vienna Convention should Not be Applied to the ICC Rome Statute: A Plea for Respecting the Principle of Legality', *Spreading the Jam: International Law, International Criminal Law, Human Rights and Transitional Justice* (Web Page, 24 August 2013) <https://dovjacobs.com/2013/08/24/why-the-vienna-convention-should-not-be-applied-to-the-icc-rome-statute-a-plea-for-respecting-the-principle-of-legality/>

Murray D, 'Non-State Armed Groups in NIAC: Does IHL Provide Legal Authority for the Establishment of Courts?', *EJIL: Talk! Blog of the European Journal of International Law* (Blog Post, 4 June 2014) <https://www.ejiltalk.org/non-state-armed-groups-in-niac-does-ihl-provide-legal-authority-for-the-establishment-of-courts/>

Nasry L, 'Interview with Chief Justice Sarath N. de Silva: LTTE has no Judicial Authority – CJ', *Sunday Times (Sri Lanka)* (Web Page, 14 November 2004) <https://sundaytimes.lk/021208/news/courts.html>

Provost R, 'Book Launch: Rebel Courts', *Geneva Academy: IHL Talks* (Web Video, 1 December 2021) <https://www.geneva-academy.ch/event/all-events/detail/312-book-launch-rebel-courts>

Sassòli M, 'International Humanitarian Law Applicable to Non-International Armed Conflicts: The Importance of Taking Armed Groups into Account' (Online Publication, 2019) <https://www.unisabana.edu.co/fileadmin/Archivos_de_usuario/Imagenes/Imagenes_Programas/Imagenes_Pregrado/Derecho/anuario_DIH/SASSOLI_FINAL_.pdf>

Sender O and Wood M, 'The International Court of Justice and Customary International Law: A Reply to Stefan Talmon', *EJIL: Talk! Blog of the European Journal of*

International Law (Blog Post, 30 November 2015) <https://www.ejiltalk.org/the-international-court-of-justice-and-customary-international-law-a-reply-to-stefan-talmon/>

Somer J, 'Opening the Floodgates, Controlling the Flow: Swedish Court Rules on the Legal Capacity of Armed Groups to Establish Courts', *EJIL: Talk! Blog of the European Journal of International Law* (Blog Post, 10 March 2017) <https://www.ejiltalk.org/opening-the-floodgates-controlling-the-flow-swedish-court-rules-on-the-legal-capacity-of-armed-groups-to-establish-courts/>

Talmon S, 'Determining Customary International Law: The ICJ's Methodology between Induction, Deduction and Assertion', *EJIL: Talk! Blog of the European Journal of International Law* (Blog Post, 27 November 2015) <https://www.ejiltalk.org/determining-customary-international-law-the-icjs-methodology-between-induction-deduction-and-assertion/>

Talmon S, 'Determining Customary International Law: The ICJ's Methodology and the Idyllic World of the ILC', *EJIL: Talk! Blog of the European Journal of International Law* (Blog Post, 3 December 2015) <https://www.ejiltalk.org/determining-customary-international-law-the-icjs-methodology-and-the-idyllic-world-of-the-ilc/>

The New Humanitarian, '"Sometimes You Cannot Apply the Rules" – Syrian Rebels and IHL' (Web Page, 13 May 2013) <https://www.thenewhumanitarian.org/analysis/2013/05/13/sometimes-you-cannot-apply-rules-syrian-rebels-and-ihl>

Thomsen M, 'Forcible Recruitment of Adults by Non-State Armed Groups in Non-International Armed Conflict', *Diakonia International Humanitarian Law Centre* (Legal Brief, May 2019) <https://apidiakoniase.cdn.triggerfish.cloud/uploads/sites/2/2021/05/Forcible-Recruitment-EN-May-2019.pdf>

Thomsen M, 'Legal Status of ISIS-Affiliated Foreign Nationals in Syria', *Diakonia International Humanitarian Law Centre* (Legal Brief, August 2019) <https://www.diakonia.se/ihl/publications/syria-and-the-region/the-legal-status-of-isis-affiliated-foreign-nationals-held-in-detention-in-north-east-syria/>

UK Foreign & Commonwealth Office, 'Joint Statement by the Governments of France, the United Kingdom, and the United States of America: ICC Arrest Warrant for Major Mahmoud Al-Werfalli in Libya' (Press Release, 9 August 2017) <https://www.gov.uk/government/news/icc-arrest-warrant-for-major-mahmoud-al-werfalli-in-libya-joint-statement-on-libya-by-the-governments-of-france-the-united-kingdom-and-the-united-s>

Urban N, 'Direct and Active Participation in Hostilities: The Unintended Consequences of the ICC's Decision in Lubanga', *EJIL: Talk! Blog of the European Journal of International Law* (Blog Post, 11 April 2012) https://www.ejiltalk.org/direct-and-active-participation-in-hostilities-the-unintended-consequences-of-the-iccs-decision-in-lubanga/

Cases

'N.V. De Bataafsche Petroleum Maatschappij and Others v The War Damage Commission' (1957) 51(4) *American Journal of International Law* 802

Ahmadou Sadio Diallo (Republic of Guinea v Democratic Republic of the Congo), Preliminary Objections of 24 May 2007 (Republic of Guinea v Democratic Republic of the Congo) (Preliminary Objections) [2007] ICJ Rep 582

Al-Adsani v the United Kingdom [2001] Application No 35763/97, XI Eur Court HR

Armed Activities on the Territory of the Congo (Democratic Republic of the Congo v Uganda) (Judgment) [2005] ICJ Rep 168

Arrest Warrant of 11 April 2000 (Democratic Republic of the Congo v Belgium) (Judgment) [2002] ICJ Rep 3

Asylum Case (Colombia v Peru) (Judgment) [1950] ICJ Rep 266

Bámaca-Velásquez v Guatemala (Merits) (Inter-American of Human Rights, Series C No 70, 25 November 2000)

Bankovic v Belgium and others (Admissibility) [2001] Application No 52207/99, Eur Court HR

Barcelona Traction, Light and Power Company, Limited (Belgium v Spain) (Judgment) [1970] ICJ Rep 3

Bosphorus Hava Yolları Turizm ve Ticaret Anonim Şirketi v Ireland [2005] Application No 45036/98, VI Eur Court HR

Case Concerning Oil Platforms (Islamic Republic of Iran v United States of America) (Merits) [2003] ICJ Reports 161

Case of Cantoral Benavides v Peru (Judgment) (Inter-American Court of Human Rights, Series C No. 69, 8 August 2000)

Case of Castillo Petruzzi et al. v Peru (Merits, Reparations and Costs) (Inter-American Court of Human Rights Series L/ V/ III.47, 30 May 1999)

Coard v United States (Merits) (Inter-American Commission on Human Rights, Report No 109/99, 29 September 1999)

Coëme and Others v Belgium [2000] Applications Nos 32492/96, 32547/96, 32548/96, 33209/96 and 33210/96, Eur Court HR

Construction of a Road in Costa Rica along the San Juan River (Nicaragua v Costa Rica) (Judgment) [2015] ICJ Rep 665

Continental Shelf (Libyan Arab Jamahiriya/Malta) (Judgment) [1985] ICJ Rep 13

Corfu Channel (UK v Albania) (Judgment) [1949] ICJ Rep 4

Corfu Channel (UK v Albania) (Judgment) [1949] ICJ Reports 4

CR v United Kingdom [1995] Application Nos 20190/92 and A/355-C, Eur Court of HR

Criminal Court, Appeals Chamber, Case No ICC-01/04-02/06, 21 February 2017

Cyprus v Turkey [2001] Application No 25781/94, IV Eur Court HR

Defence Motions Alleging Defects in the Confirmation Decision (International Criminal Court, Appeals Chamber, Case No ICC-02/04-01/15 OA4, 17 July 2019)

Democratic Republic of Congo v Burundi, Rwanda and Uganda (African Commission on Human and Peoples Rights, Communication 227/1999 33rd Ordinary Session, May 2003)

Document contennant les charges contre M. Al Hassan (*Version amendée et corrigée du Document contenant les charges contre M. Al Hassan Ag Abdoul Aziz Ag Mohamed Ag Mahmoud*) (International Criminal Court, Case No ICC-01/12-01/18, 2 July 2019)

Fisheries Jurisdiction (*United Kingdom v Iceland*) (*Merits*) [1974] ICJ Rep 3

Gorguiladzé v Georgia [2009] Application No 4313/04, Eur Court HR

Guðmundur Andri Ástráðsson v Iceland [2020] Application No 26374/18, Eur Court HR (Grand Chamber)

Hamdan v Rumsfeld 548 U.S. 557 (United States Supreme Court, 2006)

Hassan v the United Kingdom [2014] Application No 29750/09, Eur Court HR (Grand Chamber)

Holder Attorney General et al v Humanitarian Law Project et al (United States Supreme Court, Case No 08–1498, 21 June 2010)

Ilaşcu and Others v Moldova and Russia [2004] VII Eur Court HR 179

Ituango Massacres v Colombia (Inter-American Court of Human Rights, Series C No 148, 1 July 2006)

Jorgić v Germany [2007] Application No 74613/01, III Eur Court HR 583

Judgment of the Court of Justice of the European Union [2020] (Grand Chamber) Review of Erik Simpson and HG v Council of the European Union and European Commission Joined Cases C-542/18 RX-II and C-543/18 RX-II

Jurisdictional Immunities of the State (*Germany v Italy*) (*Judgment*) [2012] ICJ Rep 99

K.-H.W. v Germany [2001] Application Nos 34044/96, 35532/97, and 44801/98, Eur Court HR (Grand Chamber)

Las Palmeras v Colombia (*Preliminary Objections*) (Inter-American Court of Human Rights, Series C No 67, 4 February 2000)

Le Procureur c Al Hassan Ag Abdoul Aziz Ag Mohamed Ag Mahmoud (*Rectificatif à la Décision relative à la Confirmation des Charges Portées contre Al Hassan Ag Abdoul Aziz Ag Mohamed Ag Mahmoud*) (International Criminal Court, La Chambre Préliminaire I, Case No ICC-01/12-01/18, 13 November 2019)

Legal Consequences for States of the Continued Presence of South Africa in Namibia (*South West Africa*) *notwithstanding Security Council Resolution 276* (*Advisory Opinion*) [1971] ICJ Rep 16

Legal Consequences of the Construction of a Wall in the Occupied Palestinian Territory (*Advisory Opinion*) [2004] ICJ Rep 136

Legality of the Threat or Use of Nuclear Weapons (*Advisory Opinion*) [1996] ICJ Rep 226

Magyar Helsinki Bizottság v Hungary [2011] Application No 18030/11, Eur Court HR (Grand Chamber)

Mapiripán Massacre v Colombia (*Merits, Reparations, and Costs*) (Inter-American Human Rights, Series C no 134, 15 September 2005)

Maritime Delimitation in the Black Sea (*Romania v Ukraine*) (*Judgment*) [2009] ICJ Rep 61

Massacres of El Mozote and Nearby Places v El Salvador (*Merits, Reparations and Costs*) (Inter-American Court of Human Rights, Series C No 252, 25 October 2012)

Military and Paramilitary Activities in and against Nicaragua (*Nicaragua v United States of America*) (*Merits*) [1986] 14

Mitrovic v Serbia [2017] Application No 52142/12, Eur Court HR

Mohammed Abdullah Saleh Al-Asad v Djibout (Judgment, ACHPR 55th Ordinary Session, Communication 383/110, 14 October 2014)

North Sea Continental Shelf (*Federal Public of Germany v Denmark*) (*Merits*) [1969] ICJ Rep 3

Okçuoglu v Turkey [1999] Application Nos 24246/94 and 24408/94, Eur Court HR (Grand Chamber)

Pandjikidzé and Others v Georgia [2009] Application No 30323/02, Eur Court HR

Pope & Talbot Inc v Canada (Damages, NAFTA Arbitral Tribunal, 41 ILM 1347, 31 May 2002)

Prosecutor v Ahmad Al Faqi Al Mahdi (*Judgment and Sentence*) (International Criminal Court, Trial Chamber VIII, Case No ICC-01/12-01/15, 27 September 2016)

Prosecutor v Al Hassan (*Decision on the Prosecutor's Application for the Issuance of a Warrant of Arrest for Al Hassan*) (International Criminal Court, Pre-Trial Chamber I, Case No ICC-01/12-01/18, 22 May 2018)

Prosecutor v Al Hassan (International Criminal Court, ICC-01/12-01/18, Trial Judgment, 26 June 2024)

Prosecutor v Al-Werfalli (*Second Warrant of Arrest*) (International Criminal Court, Pre-Trial Chamber I, Case No ICC-01/11-01/17, 4 July 2018)

Prosecutor v Aleksovski (*Judgment*) (International Criminal Tribunal for the former-Yugoslavia, Trial Chamber, Case No IT-95-14/1-T, 25 June 1999)

Prosecutor v Ali Muhammad Ali Abd-Alrahman (*'Ali Kushayb'*) (*Appeal of Mr Abd-Al-Rahman against the Pre-Trial Chamber II's 'Decision on the Defence "Exception d'incompétence" (ICC-02/05-01/20-302)'*) (International Criminal Court, Appeals Chamber, Case No ICC-02/05-01/20 OA8, 1 November 2021)

Prosecutor v Bemba Gombo (*Amicus Curiae Observations on Superior Responsibility Submitted Pursuant to Rule 103 of the Rules of Procedure and Evidence*) (International Criminal Court, Pre-Trial Chamber II, Case No CC-01/05-01/08-406, 20 April 2009)

Prosecutor v Bemba Gombo (*Decision Pursuant to Article 61(7)(a) and (b) of the Rome Statute*) (International Criminal Court, Pre-Trial Chamber II, Case No ICC01/05-01/08, 15 June 2009)

Prosecutor v Bosco Ntaganda (*Decision Pursuant to Article 61(7)(a) and (b) of the Rome Statute on the Charges of the Prosecutor Against Bosco Ntaganda*) (International Criminal Court, Pre-Trial Chamber II, Case No ICC-01/04-02/06, 9 June 2014)

Prosecutor v Bosco Ntaganda (*Judgement on the appeal of Mr Ntaganda against the 'Second decision on the Defence's challenge to the jurisdiction of the Court in respect of Counts 6 and 9'*) (International Criminal Court, Appeals Chamber, Case No ICC-01/04-02/06 OA5, 15 June 2017)

Prosecutor v Bosco Ntaganda (*Judgment*) (International Criminal Court, Trial Chamber, Case No ICC-01/04-02/06, 8 July 2019)

Prosecutor v Bosco Ntaganda (*Judgment*) (International Criminal Court, Appeals Chamber, Case No ICC-01/04-02/06 A A2, 30 March 2021)

Prosecutor v Bosco Ntaganda (*Second decision on the Defence's challenge to the jurisdiction of the Court in respect of Counts 6 and 9*) (International Criminal Court, Trial Chamber VI, Case No ICC-01/04-02/06, 4 January 2017)

Prosecutor v Brima, Kamara and Kanu (*Trial Judgment*) (Special Court of Sierra Leone, Trial Chamber II, Case No SCSL-2004-16-PT, 29 June 2007)

Prosecutor v Delalić et al (*Judgment*) (International Criminal Tribunal for the former-Yugoslavia, Trial Chamber, Case No IT-96-21-T, 18 November 1998)

Prosecutor v Dominic Ongwen (*Judgment*) (International Criminal Court, Trial Chamber IX, Case No ICC-02/04-01/15, 4 February 2021)

Prosecutor v Ferdinand Nahimana, Jean-Bosco Barayagwiza, and Hassan Ngeze (*Appeal Judgment*) (International Criminal Tribunal for Rwanda, Appeals Chamber, Case No ICTR-99-52-A, 28 November 2007)

Prosecutor v Fofana and Kondewa (*Trial Judgment*) (Special Court for Sierra Leone, Trial Chamber I, Case No SCSL-04-14-T, 2 August 2007)

Prosecutor v Furundžija (*Appeal Judgment*) (International Criminal Tribunal for the former-Yugoslavia, Appeals Chamber, Case No IT-95-17/1-A, 21 July 2000)

Prosecutor v Furundzija (*Judgment*) (International Criminal Tribunal for the former-Yugoslavia, Trial Chamber, Case No IT-95-17/1-T, 10 December 1998)

Prosecutor v Germain Katanga and Mathieu Ngudjolo Chui (*Judgment*) (International Criminal Court, Trial Chamber II, Case No ICC-01/04-01/07, 7 March 2014)

Prosecutor v Hadzihasanovic (*Decision on Interlocutory Appeal Challenging Jurisdiction in Relation to Command Responsibility*) (International Criminal Tribunal for the former-Yugoslavia, Appeals Chamber, Case No IT-01-47-ar72, 16 July 2003)

Prosecutor v Hadžihasanović (*Judgment*) (International Criminal Tribunal for the Former Yugoslavia, Trial Chamber, Case No IT-01-47-T, 15 March 2006)

Prosecutor v Hadžihasanović et al (*Decision on Joint Challenge to Jurisdiction*) (International Criminal Tribunal for the Former Yugoslavia, Appeals Chamber, Case No IT-04-84-A, 12 November 2002)

Prosecutor v Issa Hassan Sesay and others (*Judgment*) (Special Court of Sierra Leone, Appeals Chamber, Case No SCSL-04-15-A, 26 October 2009)

Prosecutor v Jean-Paul Akayesu (*Judgment*) (International Criminal Tribunal for Rwanda, Appeals Chamber, Case No ICTR-96-4-T, 2 September 1998)

Prosecutor v Jean-Pierre Bemba Gombo (*Judgment*) (International Criminal Court, Trial Chamber III, Case No ICC-01/05-01/08, 21 March 2016)

Prosecutor v Jean-Pierre Bemba Gombo (*Judgment*) (International Criminal Court, Appeals Chamber, Case No ICC-01/05-01/08 A, 8 June 2018)

Prosecutor v Jelisić (*Judgment*) (International Criminal Tribunal for the Former Yugoslavia, Trial Chamber, Case No IT-95-10-T, 14 December 1999)

Prosecutor v Jokić (*Judgment*) (International Criminal Tribunal for the Former Yugoslavia, Trial Chamber, Case No IT-01-42/1-T, 18 March 2004)

Prosecutor v Kordic (*Judgement*) (International Criminal Tribunal for the Former Yugoslavia, Trial Chamber, Case No T-95-14/2-T, 26 February 2001)

Prosecutor v Krstić (*Judgment*) (International Criminal Tribunal for the Former Yugoslavia, Trial Chamber, Case No IT-98-33-T, 2 August 2001)

Prosecutor v Kunarac et al (*Judgment*) (International Criminal Tribunal for the Former Yugoslavia, Appeals Chamber, Case No T-96-23 & IT-96-23/1-A, 12 June 2002)

Prosecutor v Kunarac et al (*Judgment*) (International Criminal Tribunal for the Former Yugoslavia, Trial Chamber, Case No IT-96-23-T and IT-96-23/1-T, 22 February 2001)

Prosecutor v Kupreškić et al (*Judgment*) (International Criminal Tribunal for the Former Yugoslavia, Trial Chamber, Case No IT-95-16-T, 14 January 2000)

Prosecutor v Lubanga (*Judgment on the Appeal of Mr Thomas Lubanga Dyilo against the Decision on the Defence Challenge to the Jurisdiction of the Court pursuant to article 19(2)(a)*) (International Criminal Court, Appeals Chamber, Case No ICC-01/04-01/06-772, 14 December 2006)

Prosecutor v Martić (*Judgment*) (International Criminal Tribunal for the Former Yugoslavia, Trial Chamber, Case No IT-95-11-T, 10 June 2007)

Prosecutor v Mathieu Ngudjolo Chui (*Judgement*) (International Criminal Court, Trial Chamber ICJ, Case No ICC-01/04-02/12, 18 December 2012)

Prosecutor v Milutinović et al (*Decision on Dragoljub Ojdanić's Motion Challenging Jurisdiction - Joint Criminal Enterprise*) (International Criminal Tribunal for the Former Yugoslavia, Appeals Chamber, Case No IT-99-37-AR72, 21 May 2003)

Prosecutor v Norman (*Decision on Preliminary Motion Based on Lack of Jurisdiction*) (Special Court for Sierra Leone, Appeals Chamber, Case No SCSL-2004-14-AR72 (E), 31 May 2004)

Prosecutor v Omar Haisam Sakhanh (*Judgement*) (Stockholms Tingsrätt (Stockholm District Court), Case No 3787-16, 16 February 2017)

Prosecutor v Omar Hassan Ahmad Al Bashir (*Hearing before the Appeals Chamber in the Jordan Referral re Al-Bashir Appeal, Oral Observations of Professor Darryl Robinson on behalf of Professors Robert Cryer, Margaret deGuzman, Fannie Lafontaine, Valerie Oosterveld, and Carsten Stahn*) (International Criminal Court, Appeals Chamber, Case No ICC-02/05-01/09-T-5-ENG, 11 September 2018)

Prosecutor v Omar Hassan Al Bashir (*Decision on the Prosecution's Application for a Warrant of Arrest against Omar Hassan Ahmad Al Bashir*) (International Criminal Court, Pre-Trial Chamber I, Case No ICC-02/05–01/09, 4 March 2009)

Prosecutor v Omar Sakhanh Haisam Sakhanh (Svea Hovratt (Svea Appeal Court), Case No B 2259-17, 31 May 2017)

Prosecutor v Stakić (*Judgment*) (International Criminal Tribunal for the Former Yugoslavia, Appeals Chamber, Case No ICTY97–24-A, 22 March 2006)

Prosecutor v Tadić (*Decision on the Defence Motion for Interlocutory Appeal*) (International Criminal Tribunal for the Former Yugoslavia, Appeals Chamber, Case No IT-94-1, 2 October 1995)

Prosecutor v Tadić (*Judgment*) (International Criminal Tribunal for the Former Yugoslavia, Trial Chamber, Case No IT-94-1-T, 7 May 1997)

Prosecutor v Tadić (*Judgment*) (International Criminal Tribunal for the Former Yugoslavia, Appeals Chamber, Case No IT-94-1-A, 15 July 1999)

Prosecutor v Thomas Lubanga Dyilo (*Appeal of the Prosecutor against the Decision of Trial Chamber I entitled 'Decision on the Release of Thomas Lubanga Dyilo'*) (International Criminal Court, Appeals Chamber, Case No ICC-01/04-01/06 OA 12, 21 October 2008)

Prosecutor v Thomas Lubanga Dyilo (*Judgement*) (International Criminal Court, Trial Chamber I, Case No ICC-01/04-01/06, 14 March 2012)

Prosecutor v Thomas Lubanga Dyilo (*Judgment*) (International Criminal Court, Appeals Chamber, Case No ICC-01/04-01/06 A5, 1 December 2014)

Prosecutor v William Samoei Ruto (*Decision on Mr Ruto's Request for Excusal from Continuous Presence at Trial*) (International Criminal Court, Trial Chamber V(A), Case No ICC-01/09-01/11, 18 June 2013)

Prosecutor v Fofana and Kondewa (*CDF Case*) (*Judgment*) (International Criminal Tribunal for the Former Yugoslavia, Appeals Chamber, Case No SCSL-04-14-A, 28 May 2008)

Prosecutor v Stanilav Galić (*Appeal Judgment*) (International Criminal Tribunal for the Former Yugoslavia, Appeals Chamber, Case No IT-98-29-A, 30 November 2006)

Questions relating to the Obligation to Prosecute or Extradite (*Belgium v Senegal*) (*Judgment*) ICJ Rep 422

Reczkowicz v Poland [2021] Application No 43447/19, Eur Court HR

Richert v Poland [2011] Application No 54809/07, Eur Court HR *s.s. Lotus* (*France v Turkey*) [1927] PCIJ (ser A) No 10

Serrano-Cruz Sisters v El Salvador (*Preliminary Objections*) (Inter-American Court of Human Rights, Series C No 118, 23 November 2004)

Situation in the Islamic Republic of Afghanistan (*Decision Pursuant to Article 15 of the Rome Statute on the Authorisation of an Investigation into the Situation in the Islamic Republic of Afghanistan*) (International Criminal Court, Pre-Trial Chamber II, Case No Case No ICC-02/17, 12 April 2019)

Sokurenko and Strygun v Ukraine [2006] Applications Nos 29458/04 and 29465/04, Eur Court HR

Sovereignty over Pedra Blanca/Pulau Batu Puteh, Middle Rocks and South Ledge (*Malaysia/Singapore*) (*Judgment*) [2008] ICJ Rep 12

Texas v White (United States Supreme Court, No 74 US 700, 1868)

The Right to Information on Consular Assistance in the Framework of the Guarantees of the Due Process of Law (Advisory Opinion, IACtHR Series A no 16 No OC-16/99, 1 October 1999)

Trial of General Tanaka Hisakasu and Five Others, 'US Military Commission, Shanghai, 13 August – 3 September 1946' *Law Reports of Trials of War Criminals, Volume VI* (United Nations War Crimes Commission, 1948) 66

Trial of Lieutenant General Shigeru Sawada and Three Others, 'US Military Commission, Shanghai, 27 February – 15 April 1946' *Law Reports of Trials of War Criminals, Volume V* (United Nations War Crimes Commission, 1948) 1

Trial of Lieutenant Harukei Isayama and Seven Others, 'US Military Commission, Shanghai, 1–25 July 1946' *Law Reports of Trials of War Criminals, Volume V* (United Nations War Crimes Commission, 1947) 60

United States of America v Josef Altstötter and Others ('*The Justice Case*') (United States Military Tribunal Trials of War Criminals Before the Nuernberg Military Tribunals Under Control Council Law No. 10, Volume III)

Western Sahara (*Advisory Opinion*) [1975] ICJ Rep 12

Yesid Arteta Davila (Supreme Court of Colombia, Penal Chamber, Case No 23438, 2 July 2008)

Zand v Austria [1978] Application No 7360/76, Eur Court HR (Decisions and Reports)

Zeynalov v Azerbaijan [2013] Application No 31848/07, Eur Court HR

Treaties and Statutes

Charter of Fundamental Rights of the European Union, 2012/C 326/02 (entered into force 1 December 2009)

Charter of the International Military Tribunal – Annex to the Agreement for the Prosecution and Punishment of the Major War Criminals of the European Axis, opened for signature 8 August 1945

Charter of the Social Contract in Rojava (Syria) (Web Page, 2014) <https://www.kurdishinstitute.be/en/charter-of-the-social-contract/>

Convention to Suppress the Slave Trade and Slavery, opened for signature 25 September 1926, 60 LNTS 253 (entered into force 9 March 1927)

Draft Convention for the Protection of Civilian Populations against New Engines of War, opened for signature 9 January 1938, Fortieth Session of the International Law Association

Draft Rules for the Limitation of the Dangers incurred by the Civilian Population in Time of War, opened for signature 1957, XIX th International Red Cross Conference New Delhi

European Convention for the Protection of Human Rights and Fundamental Freedoms, as amended by Protocols Nos. 11 and 14, opened for signature 4 November 1950, ETS 5 (entered into force 3 September 1953)

Forced Labour Convention, opened for signature 28 June 1930, International Labour Organization, C29 (entered into force 1 May 1932)

Geneva Convention for the Amelioration of the Condition of the Wounded and Sick in Armed Forces in the Field, opened for signature 12 August 1949, 75 UNTS 31 (entered into force 21 October 1950)

Geneva Convention for the Amelioration of the Condition of the Wounded, Sick and Shipwrecked Members of Armed Forces at Sea, opened for signature 12 August 1949, 75 UNTS 85 (entered into force 21 October 1950)

Geneva Convention Relative to the Protection of Civilian Persons in Time of War, opened for signature 12 August 1949, 75 UNTS 287 (entered into force 21 October 1950)

Geneva Convention Relative to the Treatment of Prisoners of War, opened for signature 12 August 1949, 75 UNTS 135 (entered into force 21 October 1950)

Inter-American Commission on Human Rights, *American Declaration of the Rights and Duties of Man* (2 May 1948)

International Covenant on Civil and Political Rights, opened for signature 16 December 1966, 999 UNTS 171 (entered into force 23 March 1976)

Organization of American States, *American Convention on Human Rights* ('Pact of San Jose', Costa Rica, 22 November 1969)

Protocol Additional to the Geneva Conventions of 12 August 1949, and Relating to the Protection of Victims of International Armed Conflicts, opened for signature 8 June 1977, 1977, 1125 UNTS 3 (entered into force 7 December 1978)

Protocol Additional to the Geneva Conventions of 12 August 1949, and Relating to the Protection of Victims of Non-International Armed Conflicts, opened for signature 8 June 1977, 1977 1125 UNTS 609 (entered into force 7 December 1978)

Rome Statute of the International Criminal Court, opened for signature 17 July 1998, 2187 UNTS 38544 (entered into force 1 July 2002)

Statute of the International Criminal Tribunal for the Former Yugoslavia (*as amended 17 May 2002*) 1993

Supplementary Convention on the Abolition of Slavery, the Slave Trade, and Institutions and Practices Similar to Slavery, opened for signature 7 September 1956, United Nations Economic and Social Council (entered into force 30 April 1957)

The Covenant of the League of Nations (entered into force 1 February 1938)

Vienna Convention on the Law of Treaties, opened for signature 23 May 1969, 1155 UNTS 331 (entered into force 27 January 1980)

Other

FMLN Secretariat for the Promotion and Protection of Human Rights, *The Legitimacy of Our Methods of Struggle* (FMLN 1988)

FMLN *Principios, Normativos y Medidas Dispuestas por el FMLN en el Transcurso de la Guerra* (FMLN, 1991)

International Committee of the Red Cross, *Commentary on Convention (IV) relative to the Protection of Civilian Persons in Time of War* (ICRC 1958)

International Committee of the Red Cross, *Commentary on Geneva Convention III Relative to the Treatment of Prisoners of War, Second Edition* (ICRC 2020)

International Committee of the Red Cross, *Commentary on the Additional Protocols of 8 June 1977 to the Geneva Conventions of 12 August 1949* (Marinus Nijhoff 1987)

International Criminal Court, *Elements of Crimes* (ICC 2013)

International Law Commission, *Articles on the Responsibility of States for Internationally Wrongful Acts. Volume II* (ILC 2001)

Interpretation of the Agreement of 25 March 1951 between the WHO and Egypt (Advisory Opinion) [1980] ICJ Rep 73

Nuremberg International Military Tribunal, *Trial of the Major War Criminals Before the International Military Tribunal, Official Documents. Volume I* (1947)

Official Records of the Diplomatic Conference on the Reaffirmation and Development of International Humanitarian Law Applicable in Armed Conflicts: Geneva (1974–1977) (Federal Political Department Berne 1978) vol 8

Status Report by the European Communities – Addendum, *EC – Measures Affecting the Approval and Marketing of Biotech Products*, WT/DS291-293/INTERIM (7 February 2006)

Index

www.ingramcontent.com/pod-product-compliance
Lightning Source LLC
LaVergne TN
LVHW012051011026
849162LV00017B/142
* 9 7 8 9 0 0 4 6 9 0 0 3 5 *